PLANTS
AN INTRODUCTION TO
MODERN BOTANY

PLANTS

AN INTRODUCTION TO
MODERN BOTANY

VICTOR A. GREULACH and J. EDISON ADAMS
Professors of Botany, University of North Carolina

JOHN WILEY & SONS, INC., NEW YORK · LONDON

581
G86p

46,317

Jan. '64

Library of Congress Catalog Card Number: 62-8773
Printed in the United States of America

Preface

THIS BOOK has been written for one-semester or one-quarter courses in general botany. We believe that it will be suitable both for students who will specialize in botany or related sciences and for the larger number of students who take general botany as a required or elective part of a program of liberal education and will probably take no other courses in botany. We hope, however, that the book will assist the instructor in stimulating an interest in botany among at least the more capable students of the latter group, and that as a result some of them will decide on careers in the plant sciences.

Although the book is designed for a one-term course, it can be used for the first term of a year course in botany with the second term devoted to a survey of the Plant Kingdom, or for a year course in general biology in conjunction with a one-term zoology text. We have tailored the book for one-term courses principally by omitting the usual rather extensive survey of the Plant Kingdom, rather than by providing only a brief and sketchy treatment of all the topics covered by texts designed for year courses. The emphasis is on the vascular plants, but most chapters also consider the nonvascular plants. Furthermore, the chapter on the Plant Kingdom is designed to give the student some understanding of the scope and diversity of the plant life on Earth, and the chapter on sexual reproduction contains representative life cycles from various groups of plants.

The organization of this book differs from that of most other general botany texts in three principal respects. (1) A section on the structural organization of plants with only limited references to physiological processes is followed by a section devoted to physiology and physiological ecology. We believe this organization is less confusing to the student than the customary one, and that the student will profit by having some understanding of the different levels of plant structure before becoming involved with physiological processes. Perhaps this organization will help students avoid conclusions that photosynthesis and transpiration occur only in leaves, translocation only in stems, and absorption only in roots. (2) The related topics of reproduction, heredity, and evolution have been grouped into one section. (3) More than the usual emphasis has been placed on physiology, ecology, and genetics, with the inclusion of many of the important recent advances in these areas. Although some instructors may feel that certain of these topics are treated in too great detail, we believe that the material presented is not too comprehensive for an introductory college course and that it will provide for a clearer understanding than would a more skeletonized treatment, particularly in a one-term course with limited lecture and discussion time available.

In writing the book we have assumed that the student will have had an introductory course in chemistry, either in high school or college. For those students who have never taken chemistry we have included an appendix chapter outlining elementary basic chemical concepts essential for a reasonable understanding of the chemistry used in the text. This is, of course, no substitute for a course in chemistry but we believe it will enable intelligent students without a chemical background to use the text with a reasonable degree of understanding. This appendix may also be useful to students who wish to review their chemistry.

In general, our aim has been to present an interesting and up-to-date account of the more important concepts and principles of modern botany with emphasis on the dynamic aspects that are currently receiving so much attention in research laboratories. We have tried to limit extensive and detailed factual information to those items that contribute toward an understanding of important concepts and principles. The historical introductions to photosynthesis, mineral nutrition, and genetics are included to give the student some idea of the ways botanical concepts have developed through continuing research. We regret that space limitations have not permitted a similar historical treatment of more topics.

The bibliographical references are mostly to popular books and magazine articles, and the references have been cited at appropriate points in the text so that students can do further reading on topics of particular interest to them. The questions at the ends of the chapters have been designed to present problems that will stimulate thought and discussion, provide an opportunity for application of general principles to specific situations, and check on the student's understanding of general concepts.

We wish to thank the various botanists who reviewed the manuscript and made numerous valuable criticisms and suggestions, particularly Kenneth L. Jones of the University of Michigan, Aubrey W. Naylor and Terry W. Johnson of Duke University, and William J. Koch of the University of North Carolina, and John G. Haesloop of Pfeiffer College. Maurice Whittinghill of the University of North Carolina provided valuable criticisms of the chapter on genetics; E. C. Markham and J. C. Morrow of the Department of Chemistry at the University of North Carolina did the same for Chapter 3 and the chemistry appendix. The members of the editorial staff of John Wiley and Sons deserve our thanks and appreciation for their valued help, continued cooperation, and their patience with our repeated delays in completing the book.

Peggy-Ann Kessler merits recognition for her excellent drawings and for devoting more time, energy, and interest to them than could be expected. Acknowledgments accompany all illustrations provided by others, but we wish to express general appreciation to the many individuals and organizations who so generously supplied us with photographs, including many pictures that we were unable to use because of space limitations. Particular thanks are due to those individuals at the General Biological Supply House, the Carolina Biological Supply Company, the Boyce Thompson Institute for Plant Research, and the U. S. Department of Agriculture for the many photographs they supplied and also for their courtesy, interest, and hospitality during our picture-collecting visits with them.

VICTOR A. GREULACH

J. EDISON ADAMS

Chapel Hill, North Carolina
October, 1961

Captions and credits for special photographs are as follows:

Frontispiece. A clone of beach grass (*Ammophila*) that has spread by means of underground rhizomes. *Courtesy of Charles Phelps Cushing.*

Section I. Man has had an extensive influence on the vegetation in this landscape, but remnants of the native vegetation are present at the right and in the distance. *Photo by Richard B. Holt from Charles Phelps Cushing.*

Section II. Microscopic section across a four-year-old pine stem. *Courtesy of the copyright holder, General Biological Supply House, Chicago.*

Section III. Setting up an Avena coleoptile test for auxin at the California Institute of Technology. *Photo by Edmund Bert Gerard.*

Section IV. Synchronized meiosis in pollen parent cells of *Trillium*. *Courtesy of Arnold H. Sparrow, Brookhaven National Laboratory.*

Appendix. Model of a molecule of terramycin, one of the antibiotics derived from plants. *Courtesy of Chas. Pfizer and Co., Inc.*

To the Student

As you are reading this, you are probably just beginning your course in botany and perhaps wondering what it will be like and how interesting and difficult it will be. You may be planning to major in botany or some other biological science, or you may be a major in some other subject and taking botany because it meets a requirement or serves as an elective. If you belong to the latter group we suspect that you will find botany to be quite different from what you had anticipated and perhaps more interesting.

SOME STUDY SUGGESTIONS

Botany is not an easy subject and if you want to derive much benefit from the course you should plan to devote more than an average amount of time to studying this textbook and your lecture notes, reading references on topics of particular interest to you, and doing your laboratory work carefully and intelligently. Think about the meaning and implications of what you read, what your instructor presents in his lectures, and what you learn in the laboratory. What you get out of the course will be almost directly proportional to the effort you expend.

Some students attempt to study botany by rote memorization of many specific facts they really do not understand, and thus they never comprehend the general principles and concepts that the facts support and illustrate. In reading this textbook and the references, always read, and re-read if necessary, for understanding. After you have finished reading a chapter, ask yourself what it all means and try to identify the important general concepts and principles. Working on the questions at the ends of the chapters should help considerably. Once you understand a chapter, it will be much easier for you to identify the really important specific facts and to remember them than it would be if you were simply trying to memorize a mass of facts that have no meaning to you.

Do not pass a single word in your reading unless you are certain that you know what it means. Turn to your dictionary for meanings of terms you do not know. At first this may slow your reading considerably, but your reading will be much more meaningful and as time goes on you should have to refer to the dictionary less and less. You may find it helpful to make a card file of terms new to you and use it for ready reference until each term has become part of your vocabulary.

Another point to keep in mind is that just because something is in print it is not necessarily true. Although we and the various botanists who have reviewed this book have made every effort to make the text clear and accurate, some errors and obscure passages may have been included (as they have in most textbooks), and you should not be surprised if your instructor calls your attention to them. Research in botany, as in other sciences, is constantly providing new and more complete information about the subject and as a result some of the older theories must constantly be modified or discarded. This explains why some of the information presented in this book differs from that found in older books and articles, and why this book in turn is out of date as regards certain new discoveries that you will learn about from your instructor or your reading in current publications. Because of the time required to publish a book, every science textbook is somewhat out of date the moment it comes off the presses. This does not mean, however, that scientific facts are only temporarily true and subject to constant change. Any fact resulting from sound research remains true indefinitely. It is our interpretation of scientific facts and the conclusions and theories based on them that must be modified as research provides new and more complete information.

SCOPE OF THE BOOK

At times you may feel overwhelmed by the amount of information presented by this book and your instructor. You should know, however, that the book includes only a small fraction of man's accumulated scientific knowledge of plants. The thousands of books and scientific journals dealing with the plant sciences are sufficient to fill a large library, and each year hundreds of books and journal volumes are added. Entire books have been written on most of the subjects that are covered in this textbook in a chapter or perhaps even a paragraph or two. Some aspects of botany have not been included in this textbook at all because of space limitations.

This immensity of botanical knowledge should not discourage you or make you feel that what you learn in your botany course is inconsequential. Much scientific information about plants is of interest only to botanists or to scientists in related fields. Even the best educated and the best informed botanists have a comprehensive knowledge of only the limited areas of botany in which they have specialized. If you assimilate the material presented in this textbook you will have gained much of the knowledge of plants that is important as a part of general liberal education.

PLANTS IN YOUR FUTURE

Even though you engage in some occupation quite unrelated to botany, we hope that you will want to continue reading articles and books about plants throughout your life, particularly those relating to new botanical discoveries. As a future homeowner, you are likely to be concerned with garden and ornamental plants. You may wish to continue your study of plants as a hobby, as many people do. As a citizen and voter (and perhaps even as a legislator or government executive) you may be called on from time to time to help formulate and implement governmental policies concerning conservation, food production, and other matters involving plants. If nothing else, you will continue to be a consumer of food, fibers, paper, wood, and many other plant products.

Perhaps you may find botany so intriguing that you will want to make a career of botanical research or teaching or of work in some area of applied botany. If so, do not hesitate to ask your instructor for career information and help in planning a suitable program of studies.

V. A. G.
J. E. A.

General References

For Reference

1. Abercrombie, M., C. J. Hickman, and M. L. Johnson, *A Dictionary of Biology*. Baltimore: Penguin Books, 1957.
2. Gibbs, R. D., *Botany*. Philadelphia: The Blakiston Co., 1950.
3. Hill, J. B., L. O. Overholt, H. W. Popp, and A. R. Grove, Jr., *Botany*, 3rd. ed. New York: McGraw-Hill, 1960.
4. Reed, H. S., *A Short History of the Plant Sciences*. New York: Ronald Press, 1942.
5. Robbins, W. W., T. E. Weier, and C. R. Stocking, *Botany: An Introduction to Plant Science*, 2nd. ed. New York: John Wiley and Sons, 1957.
6. Simpson, G. C., C. S. Pittendrigh, and L. H. Tiffany, *Life: An Introduction to Biology*. New York: Harcourt-Brace, 1957.
7. Weisz, P. B., *The Science of Biology*. New York: McGraw-Hill, 1959.

For Reading

8. Anderson, E., *Plants, Man and Life*. London: Andrew Melrose, 1954.
9. Campbell, N., *What is Science?* New York: Dover Books, 1952.
10. Editors of the *Scientific American*, *Scientific American Reader*. New York: Simon and Schuster, 1953. *The Physics and Chemistry of Life*. New York: Simon and Schuster, 1955. *Plant Life*. New York: Simon and Schuster, 1957.
11. Gabriel, M. L. and S. Fogel, ed., *Great Experiments in Biology*. Englewood Cliffs, N. J.: Prentice-Hall, 1955.

12. Knobloch, I. W., ed., *Readings in Biological Science*. New York: Appleton-Century-Crofts, 1948.

13. Peattie, D. C., *Green Laurels: The Lives and Achievements of Great Naturalists*. New York: Garden City Publishing Company, 1938.

14. Singer, C., *A History of Biology*. New York: Harpers, 1950.

15. Steere, W. C., ed., *Fifty Years of Botany*. New York: McGraw-Hill, 1958.

For Identifying Plants

Note: The following list includes only a few of the less technical manuals for the identification of plants. Your instructor can probably refer you to other manuals, including more technical ones and those designed for your area of the country.

16. Christensen, C. M., *Common Edible Mushrooms*. Minneapolis: University of Minnesota Press, 1943.

17. Graves, A. H., *Illustrated Guide to Trees and Shrubs*. New York: Harpers, 1958.

18. Harlow, W. M., *North American Trees*. New York: Dover Publications, 1958.

19. Hylander, C. J., *The Macmillan Wild Flower Book*. New York: Macmillan Co., 1954.

20. Jacques, H. E., ed., *How to Know Series*. Dubuque, Iowa: Wm. H. Brown Co. (This series of illustrated, paper-back keys includes books on plant families, trees, spring flowers, fall flowers, grasses, mosses, fresh-water algae, seaweeds, and economic plants.)

21. Muenscher, W. C., *Weeds*. New York: Macmillan Co., 1935.

22. Muenscher, W. C., *Poisonous Plants of the United States*, Revised ed. New York: Macmillan Co., 1960.

23. Rickett, H. W., *Wild Flowers*. New York: Crown Press, 1953.

24. Smith, A. H., *The Mushroom Hunter's Handbook*. Ann Arbor: University of Michigan Press, 1958.

25. Symonds, George W. D., *The Tree Identification Book*. New York: M. Barrows and Co., 1958.

26. Vines, Robert A., *Trees, Shrubs and Woody Vines of the Southwest*. Austin: University of Texas Press, 1960.

For Reference on Gardening and Horticulture

27. Bailey, L. H., *Gardener's Handbook*. New York: Macmillan Co., 1941.

28. Bailey, L. H. and E. Z. Bailey, *Hortus Second*. New York: Macmillan Co., 1941.

29. Denisen, E. L., *Principles of Horticulture*. New York: Macmillan Co., 1958.

30. Rickett, H. W., *Botany for Gardeners*. New York: Macmillan Co., 1957.

Contents

CONTENTS

Section IV.   FROM GENERATION TO GENERATION

PLANTS

AN INTRODUCTION TO
MODERN BOTANY

Section I. MAN AND THE WORLD OF PLANTS

1. Plant Resources

To Know Our Resources

SOME KNOWLEDGE of the Earth and the living things on it is of great importance to us, for we are not the independent, free-living beings we often suppose ourselves to be. Our existence on Earth is controlled by many factors—the earth we stand on, the air we breathe, and the animals and plants that are our constant associates. These things make up our environment. The lower animals are simple creatures of their environment, whereas it is sometimes said that civilized man controls his environment. It is true that through the process of becoming civilized we have acquired a wide variety of skills that enable us to modify our environment, in a limited way, and to utilize our environment to meet our needs and desires. However, the new skills have in no fundamental way reduced our dependence on the Earth and its living beings, but, on the contrary, may be said to have increased it. The very technologies that appear to give us greater freedom actually tie us more and more closely to our environment, for they consist essentially of progressively more intensive and extensive processing of natural materials.

Early man satisfied his needs by taking nature's offerings as he found them. His food requirements were met by the animals he hunted and by the edible fruits, seeds, roots, and other plant parts gathered in forest and plain. He lived a wandering existence, constantly in search of food. Later he learned to domesticate certain useful food animals and in doing so probably came to realize even more fully the importance of the natural vegetation. Seasonal changes in the vegetation necessitated moving his flocks from place to place in search of abundant pasturage. Finally man discovered that by planting the seeds of useful plants in prepared soil he could, in season, produce sufficient food for his animals and himself for year-round use. This discovery was an important step along the road to the attainment of the civilized state (5), for once man was relieved of the uncertainty of his daily food supply and was thus enabled to reside more or less continuously in one place, he had the time necessary for the development of the arts and philosophy and, indeed, to indulge further his inventive genius. Continued observation and study of the world about him led to the discovery of new, useful products of nature and new techniques for modifying them to suit his needs. This process of learning, begun by early man, has been continuous and cumulative. New discoveries lead to still newer discoveries. And thus our present-day mode of existence is a result of continued exploration and exploitation of our environment. Whether the outcome of the study be the tapping of power sources in the atom, the development of new and better glue from sawmill waste, or the discovery of a new antibiotic drug from a fungus, the process is the same.

It seems clear, then, that the informed person should have some basic knowledge of himself and the elements of his environment which influence his daily living so strongly. In the pages to follow we shall inquire into the nature of one of these elements, plant life. Such study of plants is the field of natural science called botany.

Plants are generally taken for granted. They live nearly everywhere on earth, in many forms, from the cacti of the desert to the oaks of the forest and the seaweeds of the coastal waters, and from the microscopic bacteria to the Giant Sequoias. All together they constitute the earth's vegetation. Yet few people fully realize what an important part of our environment plants are. Their influence on man has been and will always be very direct and profound.

FOODS

Green plants are most significant in their role as original producers of food, for from them, directly or indirectly, come all of our foods (3). The proteins, carbohydrates and fats as well as important accessory nutrients such as certain vitamins and minerals are all made available to us and all other animals through green plants. Field and orchard yield such important staples as apples, grapes, cereal grains, potatoes (15), tomatoes, beans, and sugar, to name a few. The chief food staple of over half the people on earth is rice, whereas wheat and corn serve similarly for almost all the remainder. These plants are grasses. Add to them other grasses, such as rye, oats, sugar cane and the pasture grasses for animal feeding, and the importance of just one family of plants can be visualized. Valuable food oils are obtained from olives, peanuts, corn, cotton seed, and soybeans. Large quantities of cotton seed and soybean oils are converted to solid fats by hydrogenation and used in the manufacture of oleomargarine. Although not important for their nutritive values, we prize highly the beverages, tea, coffee, and chocolate (Figs. 1.1, 1.2) and such flavorings and condiments as those prepared from the fruits of pepper and vanilla, the flower-buds of cloves, the seeds of mustard, the bark of cinnamon (18), the leaves of peppermint and sage, the roots of licorice and horseradish. The food fish of the sea are nourished by microscopic marine plants (11). Even the strictly carnivorous animals are dependent on green plants, for ultimately in a series of "eater and eaten" an herbivorous member will be found.

Figure 1.1. Picking coffee berries in Costa Rica. The seed is dried in the sun and shipped as "green" coffee. (Photo courtesy of United Fruit Company.)

Figure 1.2. Gathering cacao pods in Panama. The roasted seeds when finely ground are chocolate. (Photo courtesy of United Fruit Company.)

RAW MATERIALS FOR INDUSTRY

Our utilization of plant materials for industrial purposes stands next in importance to their use as food. Wood is still our chief structural material for buildings. The Douglas fir trees of the great western forests furnish about a quarter of our sawtimber and a like amount is derived from various species of pines from the southern and western forests. Various hardwoods, such as birch, maple, gum, and walnut from our eastern forests as well as mahogany, rosewood, and others with beautiful color and markings from tropical regions furnish the solid stocks and veneers for the furniture industry. In recent years, the amount of timber converted to plywood has very greatly increased owing to the development of better gluing and bonding methods. The greater size range, superior strength, and light weight are features of plywood that make it more suitable than ordinary lumber for certain types of construction.

The mechanical and chemical conversion of wood to pulp for the manufacture of paper and certain synthetic textiles consumes enormous quantities of timber (9). Sawmill and pulping wastes may be chemically treated to yield plastics, glues, and special bonding agents. The distillation of wood yields a great variety of valuable industrial chemicals such as methanol and acetic acid. Turpentine and rosin (Fig. 1.3), linseed oil, tanning materials (9), rubber (8), and cork are just a few of the many other industrial raw materials we secure from plants.

Figure 1.3. Collecting turpentine from longleaf pine. Distillation of turpentine (shown in glass cylinder) yields oil ("spirit") of turpentine and rosin. (U.S. Department of Agriculture photograph.)

TEXTILES AND CORDAGE

Many species of plants yield natural fibers for the manufacture of fabrics and cordage. Such fibers as cotton and flax have a very long history of such uses. Despite the inroads of the modern synthetic fibers, cotton is still the most important fiber in the world. Besides its pre-eminence in the textile industry, cotton is used to make cording for automobile tires and light-duty rope. The manufacture of disposable absorbent tissues and even some of the competing rayon consume significant portions of the cotton crop. It may be mentioned, incidentally, that oil and protein extracted from the cotton seed (after removal of the fibers) are important articles of commerce, the latter especially in the compounding of animal feeds. Flax, now of minor commercial importance in textiles, is used in the production of certain high-quality special fabrics and some special items such as firehose, where its pliability, fineness, durability and tensile strength are especially valuable.

Other fibers such as hemp and jute are used for coarse fabrics like burlap and in rug manufacture. Manila hemp, derived from a species closely related to the banana, is superior for heavy duty ropes and twines and, along with sisal, constitutes the most important raw material of the cordage industry.

MEDICINES

The early history of botanical science is to a very large extent concerned with man's interest in the use of plant materials for the treatment of human ills. The records of the pre-Christian Egyptians, Greeks, and Romans discuss several thousand species of plants commonly used as medicinal agents. Modern botanical science is said to have started during the fifteenth to seventeenth centuries with the studies and writings of the herbalists, who devoted themselves to the description and illustration of thousands of plant species. Although their interest in plants was chiefly medical, the herbalists (17) were careful observers, and a surprisingly large proportion of the botanical conclusions drawn from their studies is still valid today. Modern chemistry has produced a vast array of synthetic drugs that have replaced many of the old and well-established botanicals, but others are still important items in our *materia medica* (13). Belladonna, opium, nux vomica, and cinchona, are the sources of the important alkaloids, atropine, morphine, strychnine, and quinine respectively. Tea and coffee owe their stimulant properties to their content of the alkaloid caffeine. Digitalis, containing several active principles known as glycosides, is used extensively in the treatment of certain heart disorders. Botanical

Figure 1.4. Colony of green mold, *Penicillium chrysogenum,* a source of penicillin. The beads of liquid seen on the surface of the colony contain measurable amounts of the antibiotic. (Photo courtesy of Chas. Pfizer & Co., New York.)

and medical researchers are ever on the lookout for new plant drugs, and in recent years, under the stimulation of new botanical and chemical knowledge, have become increasingly interested in reinvestigating many old fashioned plant drugs that have fallen into disuse. One of the most exciting chapters of medical discovery began in 1928 with the observation by Sir Alexander Fleming, that a green mold, *Penicillium* (Fig. 1.4), destroyed certain disease-causing bacteria. From this observation grew a whole new field of medical and botanical research which has produced a growing list of important antibiotics. Streptomycin, penicillin, terramycin, and aureomycin are well-known antibiotics important in the control of specific bacterial and rickettsial diseases (Fig. 1.5).

9

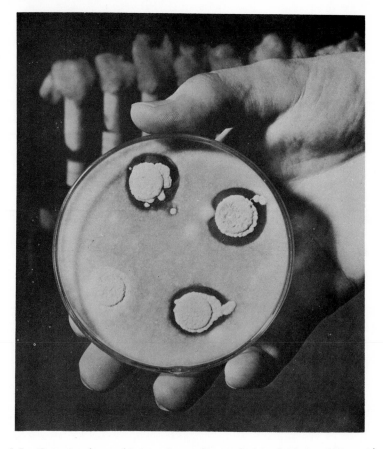

Figure 1.5. Screening for antibiotics. Paper discs soaked in fluids in which molds have grown are placed on the surface of culture plates inoculated with bacteria. The antibiotic has inhibited bacterial growth in the clear areas around the discs. (Photo courtesy Chas. Pfizer & Co., New York.)

INSECTICIDES

Man's struggle against destructive and annoying insects seems unending. Many species of plants, used in the form of extracts or powders, have been shown to possess some insecticidal value. Two of the most potent insecticides of plant origin are rotenone and pyrethrins. The former is extracted from the roots of a member of the bean family native to South America and the Far East; the latter are prepared from the unopened flower heads of certain daisy-like plants native to southeastern Europe. Both of these plants are extensively cultivated as commercial sources of insecticides. Unlike the modern synthetic insecticides such as DDT and Chlordane, and the compounds of copper and arsenic, rotenone and pyrethrins are relatively nontoxic to man and the higher animals and are thus safer for general use on certain food crops as dust or spray applications to combat the Mexican bean beetle, certain aphids, European corn borer, and other crop destroying insects. The housefly, mosquito, cockroach, flea, tick, and other obnoxious insects succumb to these insecticides. Tobacco dust and crude extracts of tobacco, byproducts of the tobacco industry, are effectively used as contact poisons for certain soft-bodies insect pests because of the nicotine content.

FUELS

The great stores of energy represented by the deposits of coal, petroleum, and natural gas were laid down mostly during the Carboniferous period, about 300 million years ago. These fossil fuels are our principal energy source. The remains of the luxuriant vegetation of those times became buried by sedimentary deposits and were subjected to tremendous pressure and high temperature. The loss of soluble minerals by leaching and the compression of the remaining carbon compounds yielded the seams of coal interlayered with sheets of slate. The organic remains that constitute the coal are the bodies of now extinct giant clubmosses, horsetails, tree ferns, and primitive seed plants, often so compressed and distorted as to be practically unrecognizable. The clues to the nature of the ancient coal-forming plants come from the study of well-preserved plant remains that became embedded in the associated layers of sedimentary rock.

Petroleum is commonly believed to be largely of marine origin and to represent principally the accumulation of oil that occurs as tiny droplets in the bodies of microscopic one-celled plants called diatoms. During the long period of underground storage, the oil has undergone considerable chemical change. The study of microscopic fossils in the rocks of petroleum-yielding regions often give clues as to where oil wells may profitably be drilled.

Natural gas occurs in coal beds, but the most important commercial supplies are found in petroleum wells. It is a by-product of the peculiar chemical and physical reactions involved in the production of the coal and petroleum. The formation of these important fuels is believed to have been effected under conditions of limited availability of oxygen and hence incomplete decay.

In many forested regions of the world, wood is still the principal fuel because of its cheapness.

VALUABLE ACTIVITIES OF NONGREEN PLANTS

Many nongreen plant species have been found useful for their very special properties (6). Many species of fungi and bacteria are responsible for the familiar process of decay whereby organic wastes and the dead bodies of plants and animals are reconverted to simple substances. These organisms, incapable of making their own primary food as do green plants, consume organic matter as food. The simple products of decay are thus returned to the environment from whence they may enter the metabolic cycles of still other organisms, principally green plants.

Some of our common foodstuffs, such as cheeses and sauerkraut, owe their distinctive flavors to the presence of metabolic end products of certain species of bacteria and molds. The alcoholic beverage industry is dependent on yeast, a fungus, which produces ethyl alcohol as a by-product from using simple sugars as food. Yeast is used in the leavening of bread dough, by virtue of its production of carbon dioxide gas in respiration. Other fungi and bacteria similarly produce a wide variety of organic acids, alcohols, and other important substances including the antibiotics already mentioned. Some free-living soil bacteria and others in the roots of certain species of the bean family are the agents for the fixation of free atmospheric nitrogen in such form that this important element becomes available to growing green plants. This is the basis for the common practice of enriching the soil by growing crops of legumes, such as clover or lespedeza, in whose roots the nitrogen-fixing bacteria live. Other bacterial species take part in converting unusable nitrogen compounds resulting from decay to usable nitrogen compounds. The natural or artificial addition of partially decayed plant remains, that is, humus, to productive soils improves or helps maintain fertility. Gardeners commonly improve the structure of soil by adding humus in the form of peat moss or leaf compost. In nature, the same effect is produced by fallen leaves and twigs.

AESTHETIC VALUES

Plants also affect our lives in ways less material than those cited. The recreational value of the great forested areas of our country is well recognized. Each year millions of vacationers visit the national parks such as Great Smoky Mountains, Yellowstone, and Yosemite. These parks and the national forests offer facilities for relaxation and education and superb scenery to satisfy our aesthetic sense. The aesthetic and recreational values of the home flower garden to the suburban dweller, and the shady park or even the window box to the city dweller are not to be underrated. Our environment is made more pleasing through the professional efforts of florists, landscape gardeners, and nurserymen.

HARMFUL EFFECTS

It must be added, finally, that although most plants are beneficial to man, some are harmful. The rank growth of certain vines and weeds chokes pastures, overruns cultivated fields and gardens, and thus constitutes an important economic problem. The cost of weed control measures plus the reduction in productivity of crop plants due to weed

Figure 1.6. Loose smut of barley, a disease caused by a fungus, *Ustilago*. (Photo courtesy of Carolina Biological Supply Company.)

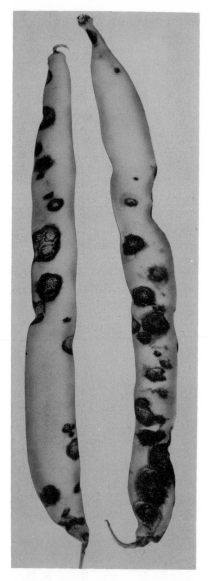

Figure 1.7. Anthracnose of bean, a disease caused by a fungus, *Colletotrichum*. (U.S. Department of Agriculture photograph.)

competition is reliably estimated to be at least 3.5 billion dollars a year. Certain bacterial species are responsible for the wilt disease of tomato and cucumber, cotton root rot, and many others, whereas apple scab, wheat rust, and potato blight result from the action of fungi upon the host crop (10). The United States Department of Agriculture has estimated that in a normal year, the loss in yield of barley, wheat, corn, and oats due to common diseases aggregates over $2\frac{1}{3}$ billion bushels

(Fig. 1.6). Similarly, disease accounts for the annual loss of 65 million bushels of potatoes, 12 million bushels of apples, 81 million pounds of tobacco, and nearly 16 thousand tons of grapes. In decreased production alone, without accounting for the cost of control measures, the annual bill for crop diseases comes to 2.8 billion dollars (Fig. 1.7). Add an annual 2 billion dollar loss attributable to insect damage to the losses caused by weeds and diseases, and the total is truly staggering. To express this food loss in another way, it has been estimated that produce equivalent to the normal yield from 120 million acres never reaches the consumer.

Fungi also cause serious diseases of many of our desirable trees [(4), Figs. 1.8, 1.9] as well as extensive decay of lumber (Fig. 1.10).

Some species of plants affect man adversely in a direct and personal way. Contact with the familiar poison ivy, poison oak, or poison sumac causes serious skin irritation. Many people are allergic to the pollen of flowering plants such as oak and ragweed, and suffer acutely from hay fever and other reactions during the season when such plants are in flower (13, 14). Many of the common vegetable foods cause allergic reactions in some individuals. Mushroom fanciers who collect their own

Figure 1.8. Blight-killed American chestnut trees in mountains of North Carolina. Causative organism is a fungus, *Endothia*. (U.S. Department of Agriculture photograph.)

15

Figure 1.9. Three stages in progress of Dutch elm disease caused by a fungus, *Ceratostomella*. (U.S. Department of Agriculture photograph.)

supply must learn to avoid certain extremely poisonous species. Some medicinally valuable plants may be fatally toxic when used in immoderate doses. Serious diseases of man, such as typhoid, tuberculosis, cholera, streptococcus infection, and tetanus are caused by bacterial species. Domesticated animals are similarly afflicted by various bacterial diseases. Species of fungus are responsible for the common skin diseases, athlete's foot, and ringworm in man, and for a variety of serious pulmonary infections (14).

To Conserve Our Resources

The foregoing section, by means of a few examples, suggests the magnitude of our dependence on plants and the products of plants. As our study progresses, other important relationships between plants and man will suggest themselves. Our tremendous consumption of and dependence on the products of forest, field, and grassland make these assemblages of plants our greatest natural resource. The dire predic-

Figure 1.10. Decay fungus, *Lenzites,* in cells of Southern yellow pine lumber. (U.S. Department of Agriculture Forest Product Laboratory photomicrograph by Dr. Carl Hartley.)

tions of some authors that we shall be faced with critical shortage of food and raw materials as population increases could come true, unless we learn to use our resources intelligently and practice conservation in its broadest sense (1).

Many people erroneously think of conservation as a kind of large scale hoarding. Conservation is an attempt at a wise, effective use of a resource for the greatest ultimate good. It aims to provide the largest amount of return from a resource for the longest possible time through avoiding waste and depletion and through restoration and improvement.

The problems of conservation are often very complex, involving many different kinds of activity and the use of principles and methods from several fields of science. Genetic research may develop new disease-resistant or more productive varieties of crop plants. Chemical and physiological research may create more effective fertilizers, weed killers, insecticides, and fungicides. These, along with the more popularly known conservation activities, such as soil erosion control and forest fire prevention, are all parts of the total conservation program.

THE SOIL RESOURCE

Most of our plant resources flourish on the thin mantle of fertile soil on the earth's crust, from which they obtain the necessary water and minerals and in which they are stably situated. The relationship of

Figure 1.11. The exposed roots of sagebrush show that 6 in. of topsoil has been removed since this area was accidentally burned. Picture taken 1 year after the burning. (U.S. Forest Service photograph.)

Figure 1.12. Burned drainage area 2 years after fire. More serious gullying will occur before effective cover can be reestablished. Roots of some shrubs survived the fire and are sprouting from root crowns. (U.S. Forest Service photograph.)

plant to soil is an intimate one, and the quality and quantity of plant product reflects the degree of soil fertility. It follows, therefore, that maintenance and improvement of productive soil make up a significant part of our conservation efforts.

The loss of fertile soil by the physical action of wind (Fig. 1.11) and water is one of the great problems arising from man's exploitation of his environment (16). The production of field crops, the timbering of forests, and even the grazing of the grasslands may entail serious disturbance or destruction of the protective vegetational cover and thus expose the soil to possible erosion (Fig. 1.12, 1.13). Well-forested areas and undisturbed grasslands are subject to practically no erosion by wind, and erosion by water is significantly reduced.

The vegetation acts as a protective cover in several ways. The spreading leafy branches of the plants reduce the force of rain falling upon the soil. The water falls gently upon the surface, with a minimum of dislodgement of soil particles. The mat of accumulated forest

Figure 1.13. Erosion following destruction of forest cover by fire. Many years will pass before this site again supports a forest. (U.S. Forest Service photograph.)

litter derived from fallen leaves and branches acts similarly and, in addition, retards the lateral flow of water, thus reducing the movement of soil by violent runoff. The widely spreading roots of plants increase the porosity and absorptive capacity of the soil and thus also reduce the surface flow. Destructive floods often result from the choking of the natural drainage channels with water-borne soil. Washed-down soil from eroding water sheds may fill reservoirs, interfere with the generation of electric power, and in some instances, render rivers unnavigable. The fish population suffers also from the silting of streams and lakes. The eroded land, of course, is unfit for agricultural use, since the fertile topsoil has been lost. Under severe conditions the land may, depending on the structure of the subsoil, become deeply gullied.

THE WATER RESOURCE

The vegetational cover is of equal importance in its influence on water resources. By reducing the rate of run-off and increasing absorption by the soil during periods of high rainfall or rapid melting of snow, the vegetational cover tends to equalize the flow of streams through the seasons. Absorbed water may ultimately find its way to greater depths, thus replenishing or maintaining the underground reserves. The rapid depletion of ground water reserves has become a critical problem in some sections of the country where deep well irrigation is practiced. Such depletion imposes a limitation on future agricultural and industrial development.

THE FOREST RESOURCE

The Forest Service of the United States Department of Agriculture estimates that by the year 2000 we shall require almost twice our present wood production to meet the needs of a population of 275 million. To assure the continued benefits of our forest resource and provide for the future demand, we must maintain, improve, and increase our productive forests by intelligent management (2). Various federal and state governmental agencies and foresighted commercial producers, through the best forestry practices in the national and state

Figure 1.14. Natural reseeding from seed trees left at logging 4 years earlier. (U.S. Forest Service photograph.)

forests and on private lands, have clearly demonstrated the value of enlightened exploitation of the forests. However, the more than 4 million small-tract owners who control and exploit one-half of our forest lands do not generally engage in the best practices. Since the public-owned forests and those of the larger commercial concerns cannot meet the future demand, it is the small owner who must be educated to the importance of proper forest management, that he may make up the future deficiency.

Various methods are employed in timber management to insure the greatest productivity. In some types of producing forests, only the mature trees are selected for harvesting. Young growing timber is left for further growth and future cutting. Natural reseeding from the remaining trees makes such stands of timber self-perpetuating (Fig. 1.14). Other types of forest yield greater returns under a method known as strip or block cutting. In this method all trees are removed from relatively small sections of the forest and the bare ground is either naturally reseeded from the older surrounding trees, or young trees are planted (Fig. 1.15). The strip or block cutting method is necessary where the more valuable timber species are intolerant of shade. Proper thinning of timber stands to reduce competition and stimulate growth, and the removal of diseased trees and undesirable competing species are additional practices of importance in profitable forest management (Fig. 1.16).

Figure 1.15. Block cutting in Montana forest. When young trees are well established in cleared blocks, other blocks will be cut. (U.S. Forest Service photograph.)

Figure 1.16. Proper thinning for improved growth of Western yellow pine. (U.S. Forest Service photograph.)

Extensive reforestation projects must also be undertaken in an effort to meet the future demand for timber. It is estimated by the Forest Service that about 52 million acres of potentially productive forest land need to be restocked. This addition to the present forest reserve would, under proper management, meet the projected need for the year 2000. An additional 5 million acres could profitably be planted for erosion control, watershed protection, and improvement of wildlife habitat.

Through the destructive effects of disease, insects, and fire, the annual loss in productivity of the forests amounts to nearly 36 billion board feet. This amount closely approaches the net timber growth. Thus almost half of the total timber producing potential of the forests is lost through the action of destructive agents. As a result of intensive effort in prevention and control, fire has become, in recent years, the third in importance among the three destructive agents, and accounts for a loss of 7.5 billion board feet. Disease leads the list, causing a loss of nearly 20 billion board feet, and insect damage accounts for an additional loss of over 8.5 billion board feet.

THE FIELD RESOURCE

Evaluating land for agricultural use is an important first step in a comprehensive conservation program. General fertility, slope, and drainage features are factors to be considered. Steeply sloping land or land of low fertility are better left with the natural vegetational cover. Eroded land on steep slopes should be planted to grass or trees. Erosion may thus be checked and further damage prevented. Special planting practices such as contour planting, strip cropping, and terracing permit the production of crops on gentler slopes with minimal danger of erosion. In contour planting of row crops, the furrows are laid off on a level across the face of the slope. Water is caught by the furrows at various levels and seeps slowly into the soil where it becomes available to the growing crop and contributes to the underground water reserve. In strip cropping, broad bands or strips of a ground-covering crop such as grass, clover, or alfalfa alternate with strips of clean-cultivated row crops. The close cover of alfalfa or clover prevents water from coursing down the slope and eroding gullies. The strips are laid out on contours, and a regular rotation of crops is followed. Terracing, effective on rolling land, consists of throwing up on contours a series of broad ridges with shallow channels above to trap the water and prevent its rapid runoff down slope.

Serious reduction of fertility is a certain result of long continued removal of the annual crops without restorative treatment (12). Every pound of crop removed from the land, whether it be cabbages or cattle, reduces the fertility of the soil. The successful producer realizes this fact and follows a definite plan of soil restoration designed to meet the needs of his main crop. Different crops make different demands on the soil. Sometimes a crop rotation plan involving the growing of legumes such as clover or alfalfa at certain intervals, is employed to replenish the nitrogen supply in the soil. The addition of other elements, notably phosphorus and potassium, are also periodically made to maintain adequate stocks of these nutrients. The best practice is to have frequent recourse to soil analyses and to use fertilizers of the kind and amount required for the intended crop.

THE GRASSLAND RESOURCE

About 40% of the land area of continental United States is natural grassland devoted to grazing. Carefully planned and controlled grazing assures a continuous supply of forage for cattle and sheep (Fig. 1.17). Placing too many animal units upon a grazing area, or grazing too early in the season, weakens or kills the grass, bares the soil, and exposes it to erosion by wind or water. The destructive dust storms of the west-

Figure 1.17. Fence line separates overgrazed and depleted range (right and foreground) from lightly grazed range. (U.S. Department of Agriculture photograph.)

ern plains during years of severe drought are traceable to mismanagement of grazing lands or the cultivation of land better left in natural grass (16).

Restoration and improvement of the grasslands are a major part of the conservation programs of the federal and state departments of agriculture. Experiments to develop methods of reseeding with adapted grasses are under way, improved grazing practices are being devised, and new methods of reducing wind erosion on cultivated lands are being studied.

Finally, a moment's reflection on the matters set forth in this chapter will make clear that there are social as well as economic implications. Malpractice in the exploitation of our resources may lead to lower productivity or exhaustion, and consequently to lower standards of living for the people. Economic disaster, starvation, and death often attend the failure of the sole food crop produced under a "one-crop" economy. Interruption or reduction of output or interference with the normal distribution of raw materials in world trade may mean ruin for a people. It is no wonder, then, that modern nations aspire to self-sufficiency in these things.

Broader education of the consuming public in these vital matters and intensive popular support for broad, coordinated programs of resource conservation are an urgent need.

► # Questions

1. Suppose you are to be exiled to an island that has essentially the same soil, climate, and natural vegetation as the area where you live, but no cultivated plants. You are permitted to take with you the seeds (or other means of propagating) of only 10 cultivated plants. Which 10 species would you select and why? How would your selection differ if you were exiled to a tropical island?

2. Suppose that before being exiled you are given the additional choice of taking with you the 10 plants you selected or 10 domesticated animals of your choice, but not both. Would you choose the plants or animals, and why? If you were offered a third choice of 5 animals and 5 plants would you substitute them for your previous choice?

3. To what general degree do modern civilizations depend on plants for each of the following: food, clothing, shelter, energy (used in homes, industry, and transportation), and oxygen of the air? How likely is it that during the next several hundred years man may become quite independent of plants for each of these?

4. If you owned a 500-acre farm, what factors should you consider in deciding which parts (or all) of it should be planted in cultivated crops, in grass for pasture, or in forest trees? Would your decisions, based on good conservation practices, be different from those based on how much money you could make from the farm? Explain your answer.

5. The conservation of our natural resources is concerned with forests, grasslands, wildlife, fresh water fish, ocean animals, soil, water, and mineral resources. Which of these involve plants and in what ways? Are plants involved in any way in the conservation of human resources?

► # References

For Reference

1. Callison, C. H., ed, *America's Natural Resources*. New York: Ronald Press, 1957.

2. Forest Service, U.S.D.A., *Timber Resources for America's Future*. Forest Service Report 14, Washington: Government Printing Office, 1958.

3. Schery, R. W., *Plants for Man*. Englewood Cliffs, N. J.: Prentice-Hall, 1952.

For Reading

4. Avery, George S., Jr., The dying oaks. *Scientific American* 196(5):112, May 1957.
5. Braidwood, R. J., The agricultural revolution. *Scientific American* 203(3):130–148, September 1960.
6. Christensen, C. M., *The Molds and Man*. Minneapolis: University of Minnesota Press, 1951.
7. Fairchild, David, *The World Was My Garden*, New York: Scribners, 1954.
8. Fisher, Harry L., Rubber. *Scientific American* 195(5):75–88, November 1956.
9. Fulling, E. H., Botanical aspects of the paper pulp and tanning industries in the United States. *American Journal of Botany* 43:621–634, 1956.
10. Horsfall, J. G., The fight with the fungi. *American Journal of Botany* 43:532–536, 1956.
11. Milner, H. W., Algae as food. *Scientific American* 189(4):31–35, October 1953.
12. Lowdermilk, W. C., The reclamation of a man-made desert. *Scientific American* 202(3):54–63, March 1960.
13. Youngken, H. W., Botany and medicine. *American Journal of Botany* 43:862–869, 1956.
14. Penfound, Wm. T., The relation of plants to public health. *Economic Botany* 7:182–187, 1953.
15. Salamon, R. N., The influence of the potato. *Scientific American* 187(6):50–56, December 1952.
16. Sears, Paul B., *Deserts on the March*. Norman: University of Oklahoma Press, 1935.
17. Unsigned. The roots of healing—ancient herbals. *Natural History* 68:578–591, 1959.
18. Wood, Alice L., Cinnamon—spice that changed history. *Natural History* 65:532–536, 1956.

Note: The journal *Economic Botany* contains many articles dealing with the uses of plants by man.

2. The Plant Kingdom

FROM CHAPTER 1 we gained some idea of the importance of plants to man. We shall consider now what kinds of plants there are and how they can be studied and made to serve us.

The number of kinds or species of plants is estimated to be about 350,000. This assemblage of plants displays a wide range of size and great diversity of form. When the species are studied carefully it is evident that they can be grouped or classified in such a way as to bring together large numbers of plants that have certain features in common. By thus classifying we facilitate our study of the Plant Kingdom, for a group embracing many similar plants may be considered as a single unit. To a certain extent, what is characteristic of one member would be characteristic of other members of a group. Of course, classifications are manmade and may be designed to suit man's convenience or reflect his primary interest in plants. Thus, a classification of plants could be based on such features as size, food value, harmfulness, medicinal properties, or habitat. However useful such groupings may be, botanists believe that the most comprehensive understanding of the Plant Kingdom may be had by devising a classification based on *relationships* among plants and reflecting, to the best of our knowledge, the course of evolutionary development. Several such classifications have been proposed in the past, each succeeding one based on new knowledge of plants or on new interpretations of data (13). The perfect system of classification has not yet, of course, been devised, for our knowledge of plants is still far from complete.

The studies by many workers over a long period of time have yielded the data on which a modern classification of plants may be based. One such scheme for classification is outlined in Table 2.1. The Plant Kingdom is conceived to consist of fifteen rather distinct groups called **phyla**. Each plant species is assigned, on the basis of its characteristics, to a phylum. A phylum is an assemblage of plant species ordinarily thought to have had a common origin in some ancestral form and showing characteristics interpreted as a distinct and major evolutionary trend or line of evolutionary development. Several of the phyla are commonly subdivided into smaller groups called **classes**. The interrelationships among the phyla may be unknown or very remote and difficult to evaluate. However, it is sometimes desirable to distribute the phyla among three larger groups to reflect their attained general levels of evolution as measured by the kind and degree of differentiation of the plant body.

The following pages summarize briefly the features of the major plant groups, leaving for discussion later in other context many detailed and important aspects of them.

TABLE 2.1. THE PLANT KINGDOM

Phyla:
- Cyanophyta—blue-green algae.
- Euglenophyta—euglenoids.
- Chlorophyta—green algae.
- Chrysophyta—yellow-green algae, diatoms. } ALGAE
- Phaeophyta—brown algae.
- Pyrrophyta—golden-brown algae, dinoflagellates.
- Rhodophyta—red algae. } THALLOPHYTES

- Schizomycophyta—bacteria.
- Myxomycophyta—slime molds. } FUNGI
- Eumycophyta—true fungi.

- Bryophyta—mosses and liverworts. } BRYOPHYTES

- Psilophyta—primitive vascular plants, mostly fossil forms.
- Lycophyta—clubmosses.
- Sphenophyta—horsetails.
- Pterophyta—ferns and seed bearing plants.

Classes:
- Filicinae—ferns. } TRACHEOPHYTES
- Gymnospermae—conifers and cycads.
- Angiospermae—true flowering plants.

Subclasses:
- Monocotyledoneae—orchids, lilies, palms, grasses, etc.
- Dicotyledoneae—broad-leaved seed plants.

Thallophytes

The thallophytes, embracing the first ten phyla, are structurally relatively simple. They lack the differentiation into roots, stems, and leaves that we recognize in the familiar flowering plants. In size, however, they range from microscopic bacteria to seaweeds many yards long. They possess no specialized absorbing organs and generally no conductive tissues. Water and other substances pass directly into the plants through all surfaces. In reproduction, these simple plants display a variety of methods. In some, whose bodies are a single cell, reproduction may be accomplished by a simple **fission,** or division into two cells. In some multicellular and some unicellular thallophytes, one or more of the cells may, by division, produce a number of **spores,** each of which may develop into a new plant. Many kinds reproduce sexually, that is, through the formation of fusing sex cells, or **gametes.** Botanists regard the thallophytes as primitive plants because of the simplicity of their structure, or lack of great differentiation. Presumably, these plants have been derived with little change in appearance and structure from their ancestral types.

The first seven phyla of thallophytes are usually collectively called **algae** (singular, **alga**). The phyla of algae are quite diverse and are thought to have had independent origins, or, rather, their interrelationships are obscure. Algae have in common the green pigment **chlorophyll,** which enables them to manufacture their food by a process called **photosynthesis.** Essentially all plants of the remaining three phyla of thallophytes lack chlorophyll or other photosynthetic pigments, and with a very few exceptions are unable to produce their own food. Plants that can make their food are said to be **autotrophic;** those which cannot, **heterotrophic.** The nongreen thallophytes are commonly classed together under the name **fungi** (singular, **fungus**). The relationships among the three phyla of fungi are uncertain and perhaps remote. About 110,000 species of thallophytes are known at the present time and doubtless thousands are yet to be discovered.

Algae

The algae are chiefly aquatic, occurring in freshwater lakes and streams, in stagnant swamps, and in the sea (4). Some algae occur in moist situations on land such as wet soil and moist surfaces of trees and rocks. Some live in symbiotic association with other organisms, as in the **lichens,** where the alga provides the food and the fungus assists in the absorption of water.

As a group the algae are of great economic value. Of chief importance is the fact that they are the basic source of food for fish and other aquatic animals. The world's most productive fishing grounds are in cool seas where algae flourish the most abundantly. Free swimming and free floating algae constitute, along with small animal species, the **plankton** of seas and lakes; the algal species growing attached to the bottom in shallow water constitute the **benthon**. Algae are also important to fish because they remove carbon dioxide from the water and restore the oxygen supply in the process of photosynthesis. Somewhat over 18,000 species of algae are known.

In some parts of the world, particularly the Orient, the larger seaweeds are consumed directly as food by man. Some marine species are rich sources of iodine, and from various brown and red algae a number of commercially important substances such as **algin** are extracted and used in the manufacture of adhesives and as stabilizers and emulsifiers in the baking, pharmaceutical and cosmetic industries. **Agar,** a jelly-like extract from species of red algae, serves as a base for culture media in bacteriological and mycological laboratories, and like algin, as a stabilizer and emulsifying agent.

CYANOPHYTA

The blue-green algae usually appear as a bluish green smear on moist surfaces of rocks and bark of trees, on and below the surface of damp soil. Some species occur in fresh or salt water, and some live on the rocks in hot springs. About 1500 species are known.

The body of a cyanophyte is a small cell which may occur singly or in variously shaped clusters or in filaments. Groups of cells or filaments are commonly embedded in a gelatinous sheath (Fig. 2.1, 15.2*b*, *f*). The predominant bluish green color is due to the presence of the pigments chlorophyll *a* and **phycocyanin.** Other pigments, such as **carotenoids** (yellow, orange, or brown) and **phycoerythrin** may also be present. When the latter is present in large amounts, the plants appear reddish. The pigments occur in a diffuse condition in the cell.

Some species of blue-green algae are able to fix atmospheric nitrogen, and thus contribute to soil fertility. Excessive growth of some species in reservoirs imparts a disagreeable odor and an unpleasant, "fishy" taste to the water.

EUGLENOPHYTA

The euglenoids can be found in fresh water in which decaying organic matter is present.

Most species are single, swimming cells with one to three whip-like **flagella** (Fig. 2.2). The cell is usually without a rigid cell wall. The

31

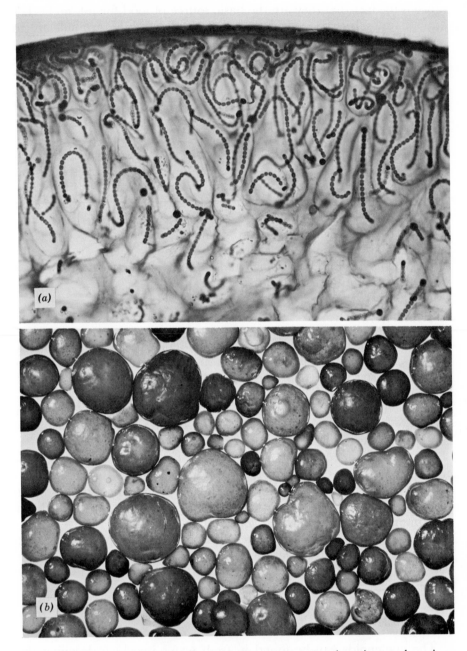

Figure 2.1. *Nostoc,* a blue-green alga. (*a*) Microscopic section through part of a colony, showing each filament embedded in a gelatinous matrix. (*b*) Colonies as they occur in quiet, shallow pools. (Copyright, General Biological Supply House, Inc., Chicago.)

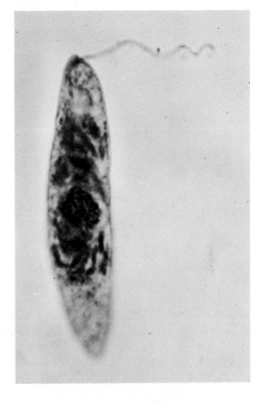

Figure 2.2. *Euglena,* a eugleno-phyte. Movement of the anterior flagellum propels the organism. Dark bodies surrounding the central nucleus are chlorophyll-bearing plastids. (Copyright, General Biological Supply House, Inc., Chicago.)

pigments, chlorophyll *a* and *b* and some carotenoids, give the plants a grassy green color, and are contained in organized protoplasmic bodies, or **plastids**. Unlike the blue-green algae, an organized nucleus is present in the cell. In the genus *Euglena* the flagella arise from a "gullet" at the anterior end of the cell. A light-sensitive red spot is present near the "gullet". Some euglenoids actually take in solid food through the gullet, and thus resemble some simple animals. It has been suggested by some biologists that the euglenoids may be plant-like animals that have evolved chlorophyll and so become autotrophic. There are about 300 species in Euglenophyta.

The euglenoids are important members of the plankton in lakes and streams and thus constitute a part of the food of fish and other aquatic animals.

CHLOROPHYTA

The green algae are found abundantly in fresh water and on moist soil, rock surfaces and tree trunks. Many are found in the salt water of the seas.

33

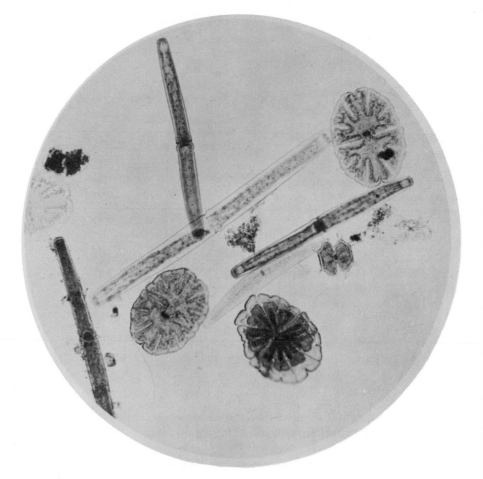

Figure 2.3. Four species of desmids. Note that each cell has a median constriction dividing it into two "semicells," the nucleus situated in the connecting isthmus. (Copyright, General Biological Supply House, Inc., Chicago.)

Many species are unicellular, the cells occurring singly, or variously associated in colonies (Figs. 2.3, 2.4, 16.1), whereas in others the cells are arranged in filaments which may be attached to the bottom of shallow pools, or may be free floating (Figs. 2.5, 16.2). In some species the plant body is a leaf-like sheet of cells from one to several cell layers in thickness. The plants are mostly grassy green, the pigments in the chloroplasts being chlorophyll *a* and *b*, along with carotenoids. The chloroplasts are of a variety of shapes, bearing, in many species, protein bodies, the **pyrenoids**, related to starch formation. The cellulose cell wall and nucleus of the cell are similar to those of the higher plants. Nearly 6000 species of green algae are known.

The economic importance of chlorophytes relates to their abundance in the plankton. They are the primary source of food for fish and contribute to the purification of the water through the absorption of carbon dioxide and production of oxygen during the photosynthetic process. Extensive experimentation is under way to test the feasibility of large-scale artificial culture of certain species as a means of producing food for direct human consumption.

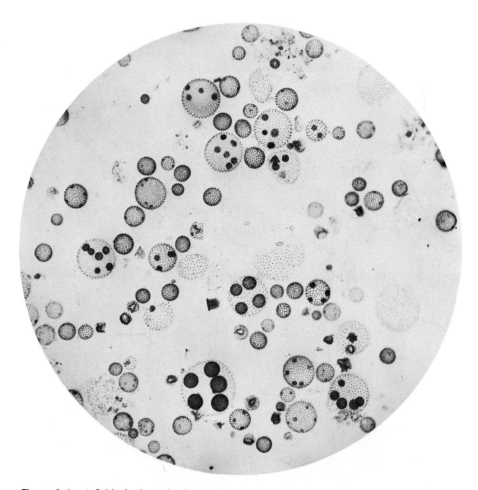

Figure 2.4. A field of spherical colonies of *Volvox*, a motile green alga. The larger colonies may consist of thousands of biflagellate cells resembling *Chlamydomonas* (Fig. 16.1) held together in a one-layered hollow sphere by a gelatinous secretion. Young colonies are present inside several of the older ones. (Copyright, General Biological Supply House, Inc., Chicago.)

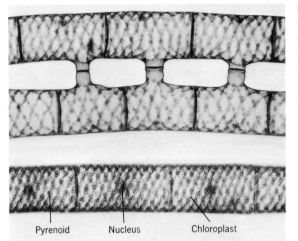

Figure 2.5. *Spirogyra*, a free-floating filamentous chlorophyte. Below, a very small portion of a vegetative filament. Note the helical ribbon-like chloroplasts with pyrenoids and the central nucleus in each cell. Above, an early stage in sexual reproduction by "conjugation" of cells of different filaments. (Carolina Biological Supply Co.)

Pyrenoid   Nucleus   Chloroplast

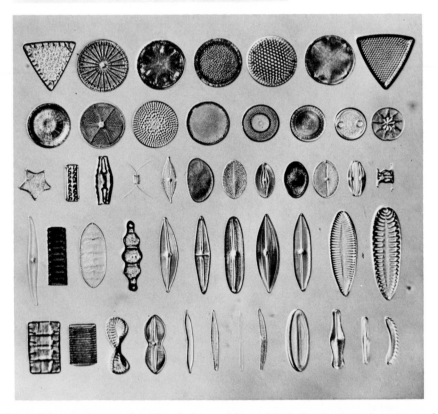

Figure 2.6. A selection of species of diatoms (chrysophytes) showing intricate patterns of their siliceous walls. (Copyright, General Biological Supply House, Inc., Chicago.)

CHRYSOPHYTA

The yellow-green algae and diatoms are predominantly fresh-water plants although some occur in marine waters and on moist soil.

Most species of chrysophytes are unicellular, sometimes motile, or the cells may form variously shaped colonies. Filamentous species are either multicellular or the plant body is a continuous tubular structure with many nuclei and without cross walls (**coenocytic**). The cell walls of some species are impregnated with silica. The organisms are yellowish green or golden brown in color. The pigments are contained in plastids and consist of chlorophyll *a* and sometimes also chlorophyll *c* along with a high proportion of yellow or brown carotenoids. There are approximately 6000 species of chrysophytes.

The siliceous-walled diatoms (7) are important members of the marine plankton and thus are a food source for marine organisms (Fig. 2.6). In several parts of the world extensive deposits of **diatomaceous earth** have resulted from the accumulation of the siliceous walls of marine diatoms. Such areas were at one time covered by the sea and later raised by geologic action. Diatomaceous earth is quarried for commercial use in the manufacture of abrasives and polishes, insulation for high temperature apparatus, as filtering agents in oil and sugar refining, and as an absorbent in industrial explosives.

PYRROPHYTA

The pyrrophytes are chiefly motile unicellular marine organisms, although a few species inhabit fresh water.

The cells have yellowish green to brownish plastids containing chlorophyll and carotenoids. Cell walls may be absent, or present and cellulosic. About 1000 species of pyrrophytes are known.

The dinoflagellates (9), a section of Pyrrophyta, are said to be the second (after diatoms) most important elements in marine plankton, and are thus valuable as a source of food for marine animals.

PHAEOPHYTA

The brown algae are almost entirely marine, growing attached to rocks along the shores of the cooler seas. Most of them grow in relatively shallow water, but some species occur in depths of almost 300 feet. A few species are free floating and occur in the open ocean. The famous Sargasso Sea of the South Atlantic Ocean is an extensive area inhabited by a free-floating species of *Sargassum*. Along the northern

37

Figure 2.7. *Fucus* or rockweed, a brown alga, growing on rocks in the intertidal zone. Note the floating bladders which keep the branches afloat at high tide. (Courtesy of Louise Keppler.)

Figure 2.8. *Nereocystis*, a brown alga, floating in laboratory tank. Note floating bladder and holdfast at base of stipe. (Copyright, General Biological Supply House, Inc., Chicago.)

coasts, the leathery brown kelp *Fucus* is common, growing on rocks exposed at low tide (Fig. 2.7).

The species of brown algae range in size from microscopic delicate filamentous plants to very large leathery frond-like or blade-like forms, often attaining 200 feet in length (11). Most of these are anchored to the rocks or ocean floor by means of a branched **holdfast**, the broad blades being kept afloat by air-filled **bladders** (Fig. 2.8). Some cellular differentiation occurs in the larger species. The mucilaginous **algin** occurs in the cell walls along with cellulose. The characteristic brown color of the plants is produced by the presence in the plastids of a brown pigment **fucoxanthin** and other carotenoids along with chlorophylls *a* and *c*. About 900 species of brown algae are known.

RHODOPHYTA

The red algae are predominantly marine plants, usually growing attached to the ocean bottom, at depths as great as 600 feet. Certain species whose bodies become calcified contribute to the formation of coral reefs.

Most red algae are multicellular. The plants are either flat sheets, ribbons, delicate cylinders, or they are finely divided and feather-like

Figure 2.9. *Polysiphonia,* a red alga. (Carolina Biological Supply Co.)

Figure 2.10. *Grinellia,* a red alga. (Carolina Biological Supply Co.)

(Figs. 2.9, 2.10). The plants are relatively small, rarely exceeding a few inches in length. The cells are commonly multinucleate and contain plastids bearing chlorophylls *a* and *d* and carotenoids along with a red pigment **phycoerythin**, and sometimes a blue one, **phycocyanin**. In most species the red pigment is present in an amount sufficient to mask the other pigments, thus imparting to the plants the characteristic red color. The walls of the cells are composed of cellulose and mucilaginous substances. The phylum Rhodophyta contains about 2500 species.

Fungi

The fungi (5), with a few exceptions, are heterotrophic plants, and thus, unlike the algae, are incapable of manufacturing their own foods. They are limited to substrates yielding organic foods. Some of them, called **parasites**, secure their food from the living bodies of other plants or animals, whereas others, called **saprophytes**, consume as food the dead tissues of other organisms or the organic products of other living plants or animals. Many species are found in waters and in moist soils rich in organic matter. Autotrophic members of this group, chiefly among the bacteria, for the most part obtain energy for the manufacture of organic compounds from the oxidation of inorganic substances, such as ferrous compounds, hydrogen sulfide, and ammonia. Such organisms are termed **chemosynthetic.** A few bacterial species utilize light as the energy source for organic construction, and are thus photosynthetic. Estimates of species number run as high as 90,000.

The fungi exert a profound influence upon man, directly and indirectly. The special activities of many of these organisms are put to good use in the processing of many food items, such as tea, coffee, cheese, and vinegar, and in the production of important industrial chemicals, such as acetone, citric acid, and alcohols. Vitamin B_2 and many antibiotics are derived from fungi. The decomposition of organic matter through putrefaction and decay and the maintenance of soil fertility through nitrogen transformation are other beneficial actions. The details of some of these activities are discussed in later chapters. A few species of the so-called higher fungi, the mushrooms, are esteemed as foods, although they are not highly nutritious.

SCHIZOMYCOPHYTA

Bacteria (3) are unicellular, occurring in rod-like (**bacillus**), spiral (**spirillum**), or spherical (**coccus**), forms, singly or in characteristic aggregations. The rod-like and spiral-shaped cells may possess numerous slender protoplasmic projections called **flagella,** whose wavelike or beating motion propels them through liquid medium (Fig. 2.11). Motility is attained by some bacilli that lack flagella by a twisting motion of the cell.

The cells, rarely exceeding 3/25,000 of an inch in length, possess a definite wall consisting, at least in part, of chitin, a substance found in the bodies of insects. The cells are often encapsulated, singly or in groups, by a slimy gelatinous substance. Organized plastids and a nucleus characteristic of most plants are commonly absent, although nuclear material is present in a dispersed condition. In some species the nuclear material appears to be clumped in the center of the cell, so as to resemble a simple, and possibly primitive, kind of nucleus.

The extremely small size of bacteria coupled with a narrow range of form differences makes it difficult to distinguish among many species on the basis of morphological characters. However, nutritional requirements and the nature of metabolic end products often differ widely among morphologically similar species, and thus the bacteriologist makes extensive use of such metabolic characteristics in identification. Some species, in general the common saprophytic ones responsible for decay, are quite catholic in their tastes, whereas others often of a parasitic and pathogenic nature are highly specific, utilizing only certain

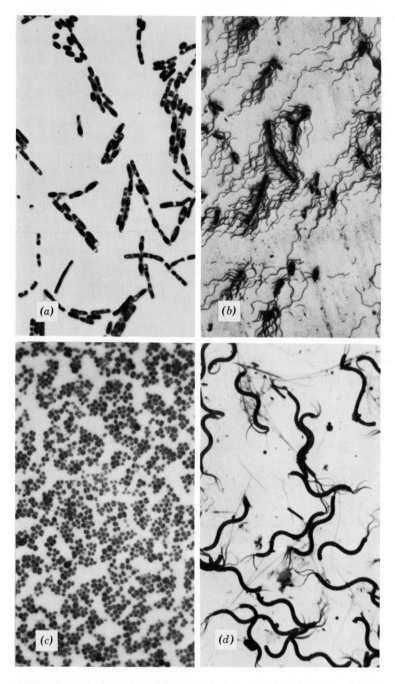

Figure 2.11. Forms of bacteria. (a) *Bacillus subtilis,* the hay bacillus. (b) *Salmonella typhosa,* a rod-like bacillus with flagella, which causes typhoid fever in man. (c) *Staphylococcus aureus,* a coccus form which causes boils. (d) *Spirillum volutans,* a spiral form found in marsh water. (Copyright, General Biological Supply House, Inc., Chicago.)

42

organic compounds, parasitizing only certain host species or even certain specific tissues of the host.

The great economic importance of bacteria in the spheres of health, industry, and agriculture have already been referred to in Chapter 1.

MYXOMYCOPHYTA

The slime molds are predominantly saprophytic, occurring on fallen decaying leaves, old tree stumps, and rotting tree trunks, in moist and shady situations, and on moist soil containing organic matter.

The vegetative plant body, termed a **plasmodium**, consists of a slimy film or delicate net of naked protoplasm containing many free nuclei. The plasmodium may be colorless, yellow, red, or purplish and may have an area of several square inches. By a creeping and flowing motion the plasmodium moves about upon the surface of the substrate, engulfing solid food particles. After a period of vegetative activity, reproductive structures, **sporangia**, of distinctive form and frequently brightly colored, are produced (Figs. 2.12, 12.19, 12.20).

A few parasitic species of slime molds are of economic importance, causing such diseases of crop plants as club-root of cabbage and powdery scab of potato.

EUMYCOPHYTA

The true fungi are heterotrophic, saprophytic, or parasitic, occurring on moist substrates yielding organic food. Like bacteria, some species have a high specificity toward food sources.

The plant body of most species consists of single or variously massed filaments termed **hyphae**. A hypha may be a single elongated multinucleate cell or a multicellular filament. The mass of hyphae constituting the body of a fungus is called the **mycelium**.

One class of eumycophytes called **Phycomycetes**, or alga-like fungi, includes plants ranging from small unicellular forms to species whose bodies consist of much branched hyphae without cross walls. These occur commonly as cottony tufts on the bodies of insects and fish, on foodstuffs, and on damp soil. Such common species as the blackmold, growing on bread and overripe fruit, and white water mold, growing on fish in aquaria, are representative (Figs. 15.1e, 15.2g).

A second class, the **Ascomycetes**, or sac fungi, are structurally very diverse. The plant body may consist of a single cell, as in yeast (Fig. 2.13) or extensive loose masses of multicellular hyphae, as in *Penicillium* (Fig. 2.14) and other molds. In sexual reproduction they give rise to a sac-like **sporangium** called an **ascus** containing four or eight ascospores. Some of them reproduce asexually by vegetative **budding** or by the

Figure 2.12. Fruiting bodies of slime molds growing on rotting wood. Above, *Stemonitis;* below *Arcyria.* (Copyright, General Biological Supply House, Inc., Chicago.)

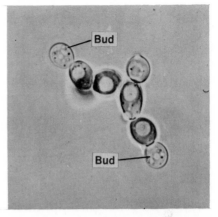

Figure 2.13. A group of yeast cells, *Saccharomyces,* an ascomycete. Two of the cells have produced young yeast cells by "budding." (Fleischmann Yeast Co.)

Figure 2.14. Photograph of glass model of *Penicillium notatum,* an ascomycete. The plant body or mycelium is a loose mat of septate hyphae. Conidia, borne in chains at tips of certain hyphae become detached and germinate under favorable conditions, giving rise to new mycelia. (Chicago Natural History Museum.)

formation of clusters of terminal spores called **conidia** at the tips of hyphae. Some species of yeast (12) are of great economic importance, as in the leavening of bread dough and in the manufacture of alcohol and other important organic chemicals, whereas others are serious pathogens to man and certain crop plants. The parasitic organisms responsible for the chestnut blight and Dutch elm disease are ascomycetes, as are the saprophytic blue and green molds found growing on citrus fruits, bread, other foodstuffs, and leather. Species of *Penicillium* are important in the culture of certain types of blue cheese and in the production of the antibiotic, penicillin (Figs. 2.14, 1.4). Some species, such as the cup fungus (Fig. 2.15) and the edible morels (Fig. 2.16) and truffles form fairly large and complex fruiting bodies.

A third class, the **Basidiomycetes**, are characterized by their manner of spore production. Usually two or four spores are formed on a swollen, club-shaped hyphal tip, the **basidium** (Fig. 14.13c). The mycelium usually consists of an irregular mass of hyphae that penetrate the sub-

Figure 2.15. Cup fungus, *Peziza*, an ascomycete. The asci with ascospores arise on the inner surface of the cup. (Carolina Biological Supply Co.)

Figure 2.16. The morel, *Morchella,* an edible ascomycete. (Copyright, General Biological Supply House, Inc., Chicago.)

strate, either living host tissues or lifeless organic matter, becoming conspicuous at the time of spore production. In the parasitic smuts (Fig. 1.6) and rusts (Figs. 14.11–13) responsible for enormous losses in grains and other crops such as pine, cherries, and beans, masses of spores burst out of the host tissues. The saprophytic mushrooms or toadstools produce a fruiting body or **sporophore** consisting of compact hyphae (Fig. 2.17). The spore-bearing basidia are borne on delicate plate-like gills or on the walls of tiny pores on the underside of the fleshy cap (Fig. 2.18). In the familiar puffballs the basidia are produced inside a closed globe-shaped sporophore, the spores escaping through a rupture or pore (Fig. 2.19).

A fourth group of fungi, called the **Imperfect Fungi,** consists of a large number of species whose life histories are incompletely known. Although assignment to one of the three main groups of fungi is uncertain, most of them are believed to be ascomycetes. Many forms are destructive parasites on certain crop plants, whereas others are responsible for

47

Figure 2.17. *Amanita verna,* a poisonous mushroom. Basidia with basidiospores are borne on the delicate gills of the cap. The mushroom arises from a subterranean mycelium. (W. C. Coker.)

Figure 2.18. A pore fungus growing on tree bark. The tough and woody sporophores arise from a mycelium growing in the bark. Basidia with basidiospores are borne on the lining of tiny tubes on the underside of the cap. (Courtesy of Louise Keppler.)

Figure 2.19. Earthstars, *Astraeus,* a puffball. Basidiospores are liberated through the pore at top of the sporophore. (Carolina Biological Supply Co.)

serious diseases of man, such as ringworm, athlete's foot, and some pulmonary infections.

LICHENS

Lichens (10) constitute a special group of thallophytes, for they are composite plants consisting of an association of an alga and a fungus (Fig. 14.14). The algal member is usually a blue-green or green alga, and the associated fungus is most commonly an ascomycete. The plants are common on the trunks of trees, on rocks, and occasionally on moist soil. Lichens occur as dry crusty patches, leaf-like scales, or as erect, much branched tufts (Figs. 2.20, 2.21). They may be gray-green, yellow-orange, white, black, or brown.

The hyphae of the fungus surround the algal cells and receive nourishment from them. It has been found that the fungus will not complete its life cycle when grown independently from its usual algal associate, although the alga is capable of independent existence. There are about 15,000 species of lichens.

Lichens are of limited direct economic value. Certain species yield blue, yellow, or brown dyestuffs. Litmus, an indicator dye employed in chemical work to determine relative acidity and alkalinity is extracted

Figure 2.20. A foliose or leafy lichen growing on bark of tree. Left, a close-up. (Copyright, General Biological Supply House, Inc., Chicago.)

Figure 2.21. *Cladonia rangiferina,* the reindeer moss, a fruticose or shrubby lichen, growing on forest soil. (Carolina Biological Supply Co.)

from lichens. On the arctic tundra lichens are a valuable food for caribou and reindeer. In some regions lichens are used in limited amounts as food for man.

Bryophytes

The Phylum Bryophta is represented by the familiar mosses that grow in green cushion-like patches on shady stream banks and in moist

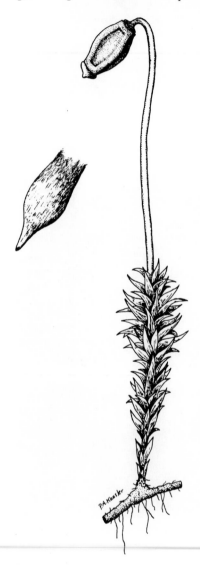

Figure 2.22. A single "fruiting" moss plant from a cushion-like colony.

Figure 2.23. *Marchantia*, a liverwort. Above, female plant; below, male plant. (Carolina Biological Supply Co.)

woods. The less familiar liverworts also belong in this phylum. **Mosses** are usually rather small, seldom exceeding a few inches in height. They seem more like familiar plants than most of the thallophytes, for the plants have an erect stem-like axis bearing many small, delicate, green leaf-like structures and are anchored in the soil by a branched root-like system of **rhizoids** (Fig. 2.22). Mosses are generally found only in moist places, or where they may be wetted frequently. They have no true absorbing roots and no special conducting tissue in their small "stems" and "leaves." Absorption of water can take place through all the plant's surfaces. Thus, although the mosses externally tend to resemble the more familiar higher plants, they are much simpler in construction. The vegetative body in the **liverworts,** another class of bryophytes, is commonly a somewhat fleshy leaf-like **thallus** growing prostrate on the moist soil (Fig. 2.23). Some liverworts with slender elongated axes and delicate leaf-like appendages resemble prostrate mosses. As in the mosses, no vascular tissue is present. Mosses and liverworts reproduce chiefly sexually. The reproductive organs are more complex than those of the thallophytes, and following fertilization a multicellular embryo is produced which is nourished for a time by the parent plant (Chapter 16).

The bryophytes are a small group, compared with the thallophytes and tracheophytes, containing a little over 20,000 species. The bryophytes are of little direct economic importance. They are early colonizers on bare rocky surfaces. By mechanical action and the deposit of organic matter they build up a fertile soil layer that may support other plants. Peat deposits are to a considerable extent the accumulated partially decomposed remains of mosses. Their biological importance is considerable, however, for they demonstrate important points concerning the evolution of the Plant Kingdom. The bryophytes are believed to have evolved from filamentous algae and are thought to be the modern representatives of an ancient group of plants that left the aquatic habitat of their algal ancestors and became terrestrial. Their lack of vascular tissues and certain features of their reproductive cycle appear, however, to have prevented their taking fullest advantage of the terrestrial habitat.

Tracheophytes

The tracheophytes are the true land plants, for they are well differentiated into specialized organs which enable most of them to occupy dry land effectively. The **roots** not only fix the plant firmly in the soil, but also serve as effective absorbing structures capable of deep penetration into the soil whence the supply of water and minerals comes. The **stems** and **leaves**, as well as the roots, have well developed vascular tissues through which substances are transported from one part of the plant to another. The specialized nature of the cells of the vascular tissues and their arrangement within the stem enable the stem to stand erect (particularly in woody plants) and, as in trees, to support tremendous weight and attain large size. The leaves are the principal site of food manufacture. The plant is protected against excessive loss of water, and in some instances against mechanical injury, by the presence of specialized protective tissues on outer surfaces. Tracheophytes reproduce sexually and also by vegetative means (Chapters 15 and 16). The reproductive structures are generally borne upon the ends of stems and branches or upon leaves in a position favorable to the dispersal of spores or seeds. Altogether the tracheophytes number somewhat more than 220,000 species.

Figure 2.24. Species of *Lycopodium*, clubmosses. Left to right, *L. obscurum*, *L. lucidulum*, *L. alopecuroides*, *L. complanatum*. (Carolina Biological Supply Co.)

PSILOPHYTA

The psilophytes are represented in the modern flora by only two genera and a few species, mainly tropical in distribution, although several fossil genera are known from Devonian or Silurian sedimentary rocks over 300 million years old (Chapter 18). The plant body consists of a branched, erect vascular stem with very small leaves arising from a **rhizome** or underground stem, but without roots. In the extinct species, sporangia were borne at the tips of branches; in the modern genus *Psilotum* they arise at the tips of very short lateral shoots. Although of no economic value, the extant psilophytes are of interest for they are widely regarded as the modern representatives of the earliest and most primitive tracheophytes (Fig. 18.4).

LYCOPHYTA

The lycophytes are represented in the modern flora by about 900 species, mainly *Lycopodium* and *Selaginella* (Figs. 2.24, 2.25) known gen-

Figure 2.25. *Selaginella apus,* a small clubmoss. (Carolina Biological Supply Co.)

Figure 2.26. Fertile, left, and vegetative, right, shoots of *Equisetum,* a horsetail. (Copyright, General Biological Supply House, Inc., Chicago.)

erally as the clubmosses. They are an ancient group with a fossil history running back to Devonian and Silurian times. Whereas the modern lycophytes are small plants rarely more than a few inches high, many members of the extinct members of the group flourishing in the great period of coal formation were tree-size and constituted the dominant forest vegetation (Chapter 18). The plants are vascular, have true roots, and usually have small leaves. Sporangia are usually borne in terminal aggregations or cones at the tips of branches. Most of the modern species are inhabitants of moderately wet situations as in moist forests, although some species are adapted to extreme seasonal dryness, as the "resurrection plant," a species of *Selaginella* that rolls up into a tight ball in times of drought. Lycophytes are of little economic importance but of considerable botanical interest because some of them produce two kinds of spores, sexually differentiated, and many of the

57

extinct arborescent lycophytes produced true seeds. This indicates, of course, that the so-called "seed habit" is very ancient and appears to have arisen independently in different phyla.

SPHENOPHYTA

The sphenophytes, represented only by about 25 species of *Equisetum*, were once an extensive group of vascular plants, some quite tree-like in habit and forming a conspicuous element in the ancient coal-forming flora. The modern *Equisetum*, or horsetails, are rarely more than a foot or two high. A distinctive feature is the conspicuously jointed and ridged stems bearing whorls of small nongreen leaves at the nodes. The walls of the outer cells of most species have deposits of silica and are usually coarse and rough to the touch. Compressed into pads, the silica-laden stems are sometimes used for scouring kitchen utensils, and for this reason the plants are sometimes called scouring rushes. The erect stems rise from a perennial rhizome. The spores are borne in sporangia on distinctive sporangiophores arranged in terminal cones [(6), Fig. 2.26]. *Equisetum* commonly occurs in moist situations, as in swamp margins, but a few are adapted to dry habitats.

PTEROPHYTA

The last phylum, Pterophyta, is the largest and economically the most directly important, yielding most of the useful products of field, forest and grassland. The phylum comprises three classes, (1) **Filicinae** or ferns [(8), Figs. 2.27, 16.6], (2) **Gymnospermae** represented by the pines (Figs. 2.30, 16.2) and other conifers such as fir and spruce, the cycads (Fig. 2.28), *Ginkgo* (Fig. 2.29) and others, and (3) **Angiospermae** or flowering plants (Figs. 2.30–32).

There are somewhat more than 6000 species of modern ferns. Although a few species attain the stature of small trees, most of the familiar ones have short and usually horizontal subterranean stems. Typically the leaves (the familiar fronds) are quite large and extensively veined. Spores are borne in sporangia arranged in characteristic clusters on the underside of the leaves. Except in a few specialized species, the spores are all alike. The modern species are derived from ancestral stocks with a long history extending back to the age of coal formation (Chapter 18). Certain fern-like plants of that time produced seeds (Fig. 18.5). The modern ferns, however, do not produce seeds, but are included along with the seed plants (gymnosperms and angiosperms) in the pterophytes because of agreement among them in important anatomical features.

The cycads, *Ginkgo*, and conifers produce their seeds in an exposed

Figure 2.27. Tree ferns in Australian Eucalyptus forest. Specimen in right foreground is about 25 ft. tall. Most of our familiar ferns have short and often subterranean stems. See Fig. 16.6. (Courtesy, Australian News & Information Bureau.)

manner, usually on flat leaf-like scales organized in a **cone**. The fern-like seed plants mentioned in the foregoing paragraph are considered to be the most primitive gymnosperms since their seeds resemble those of the modern cycads. *Ginkgo biloba* is the sole modern survivor of an ancient line, and along with the cycads, possesses a number of ancient structural features. A native of China, *Ginkgo* is widely planted as an ornament in parks and along city streets where it seems quite tolerant of the noxious dirt and fumes of city traffic. Such coniferous genera as *Pinus* (pines), *Abies* (firs), *Pseudotsuga* (Douglas firs) and *Sequoia* (redwoods) represent the economically important gymnosperms, for they and others yield the great bulk of structural timber in the northern hemisphere.

The true flowering plants or angiosperms are the most numerous and the most important of all the plant groups, numbering more than

Figure 2.28. A cycad, *Cycas circinalis*, a primitive gymnosperm with male cone, growing in cultivation. (Chicago Natural History Museum.)

Figure 2.29. *Ginkgo biloba,* a primitive gymnopsermous tree widely planted as an ornamental in parks. The "fruits," really naked seeds, and most of the leaves are borne on short spur shoots. Male and female flowers are borne on separate trees. The ripe seeds are foul smelling, so usually only male trees are cultivated. (Chicago Natural History Museum.)

200,000 species. The herbs, grasses, shrubs and broad-leaf trees from which most of our foodstuffs and many industrial materials come are flowering plants. The distinctive structural feature is the flower with the seeds produced typically in a closed **ovulary,** rather than exposed as in the gymnosperms. The ovularies develop into true fruits, structures characteristic of the angiosperms. Compared with the other plant phyla, the angiosperms are generally considered from fossil evidence to be of relatively recent origin although the nature of their earliest beginnings is very uncertain.

The tracheophytes and especially the ferns, conifers and flowering plants are subjects for more complete discussion in later chapters.

Smaller Categories of Classification

Although it is important to view the plant kingdom in its largest aspects as we have done, and to summarize it in some all-embracing scheme of classification, it is true that the common plants growing around us are thought of in terms somewhat less inclusive than phy-

Figure 2.30. *Agave,* a desert angiosperm of the lily family, with pines (gymnosperm) in the background. (Photo by Chuck Abbott, Tucson, Arizona.)

Figure 2.31. Giant bamboo, an angiosperm of the grass family. (U.S. Department of Agriculture photograph.)

Figure 2.32. The Spanish moss, *Tillandsia*, an angiosperm, growing on cypress trees, a gymnosperm, in a Louisiana swamp. It is not a moss, but related to pineapple. After it is cured, it is used for upholstery stuffing. (Courtesy, Standard Oil Co., New Jersey.)

lum or class. Just as we have seen that the plant kingdom may be sub-divided into phyla, and the phyla into classes, so botanists recognize the need for progressively smaller and smaller categories. This need becomes obvious when, on an afternoon's stroll, we encounter, for example, six different kinds of oaks, three kinds of maples and three kinds of pines.

Quite naturally, we give names to the things we know and use; so we apply names to the plants around us. First, these names are likely to be chosen with reference to some quality or attribute of the plant. A descriptive name, an allusion to a use, or a fanciful reference may, and often does, suffice as a **common name.** Thus "Blood Root," to describe the red sap exuding from the plant when cut, and "Mayflower," to describe the time of flowering, are well-chosen common names for the respective plants. But the same plants may be known by different and equally good names in other localities, or indeed, the same names may be applied to altogether different plants. There are said to be eighteen different species or kinds of plants growing in the United States that pass under the name "Snakeroot". It is clear that confusion would be unending if there were not some standard system of naming. The scientific study of plants requires a precise identification of the plants. To this end, in botanical practice, one valid name is given to each plant species, and it bears that name throughout the world, wherever scientific study of plants is pursued. The names given are in Latin or are occasionally derived from Greek. Botanists, regardless of nationality, can understand precisely what plant is indicated by its **scientific name.**

The scientific name of a plant consists of two parts, the name of the **genus** followed by the name of the **species.** Thus the sugar maple is named *Acer saccharum.* To insure greater accuracy in the designation of plant species, the identity of the author of the plant's valid scientific name is appended, usually as an abbreviation: e.g., *Acer saccharum* Marsh. (for Humphrey Marshall, the botanist who first described and named this species of maple). A species is a single *kind* of plant in which all the individual members are similar in most of the details of structure and behavior, and whose distinguishing characteristics are passed on through a succession of generations. For example, besides the sugar maple there are many other maples such as the scarlet maple, *Acer rubrum* L. (for Carolus Linnaeus), and the Sierra maple, *Acer glabrum* Torr. (for John Torrey). All of these and many more species of maples constitute the genus *Acer* (maples).

Some genera are related to other genera just as some species are related to other species. Therefore the grouping of related genera gives a higher category of classification called the **family.** Related families constitute an **order.** Related orders constitute a **subclass** or **class** and

65

related classes, a **phylum.** In botanical practice the names of the various categories of classification from phylum down through family are given distinctive endings, as shown below.

The complete classification of the sugar maple, therefore, would be:

Phylum Ptero*phyta*
Class Angiosperm*ae*
Subclass Dicotyledon*eae*
Order Sapind*ales*
Family Acer*aceae*
Genus *Acer*
Species *saccharum.*

By inspection of the complete classification, we can relate this plant to all others.

In view of the large number of plant species already known and the estimated 5000 new ones described each year, an orderly system for classifying them is a necessity. Indeed, it helps to make such a diverse group of organisms comprehensible. Although no one person can know all the species of plants, he can know a great deal about them if he knows how they fit into a scheme of classification based on relationships. As new knowledge of plants is gained from researches in the several fields of botany, it becomes the basis for the possible devising of new and improved schemes of classification. Classification is not an end in itself but an attempt to present a current summary of our knowledge of plants.

► ## *Questions*

1. Suggest possible explanations for the fact that some groups of plants (e.g. the angiosperms and fungi) contain so many more species than other groups (e.g. the horsetails and clubmosses).

2. Give as many characteristics as you can that distinguish plants from animals. Are there any with no exceptions? Which characteristics best distinguish plants from animals? What characteristics best distinguish living organisms (plants and animals) from nonliving things?

3. The statement is made that there are about 350,000 species of plants on earth. Why is an approximate number always given? Would it be possible to give a precise figure? Why? Will it be possible in the future to give a precise figure? Explain your answer. Will the estimated number of plants increase in the future, and if so, why?

4. Botanists use certain distinguishing characteristics in classifying plants into related groups. What are some of the distinguishing characteristics used in classifying plants into the major groups discussed in this chapter? Would the following be desirable characteristics for use at this level of classification: color, size, habitat in which the species grows, whether woody or herbaceous, presence or absence of roots, stems or leaves, type of reproductive structures, whether of economic value? Explain each answer.

5. What is a species? The statement has been made that God created plants and animals but that man created species. Evaluate this statement.

► *References*

For Reference

1. Bold, Harold C, *The Plant Kingdom.* Englewood Cliffs, N. J.: Prentice-Hall, 1960.
2. Coulter, Merle C. and Howard J. Ditmer, *The Story of the Plant Kingdom.* Chicago: University of Chicago Press, 1959.
3. Stanier, R. Y., Michael Dondroff, and E. A. Adelberg, *The Microbial World.* Englewood Cliffs, N. J.: Prentice-Hall, 1957.
4. Tiffany, L. H., *Algae: The Grass of Many Waters.* Springfield, Ill.: Thomas, 1938.

For Reading

5. Emerson, Ralph, Molds and men. *Scientific American* 186(1):28–32, January 1952.
6. Gerald, J. H., Horsetails. *Natural History* 62:352–354, 1953.
7. Harris, J. E., Diatoms serve modern man. *Natural History* 65:64–71, 1956.
8. Hodge, Henricks, Tree ferns. *Natural History* 65:88–91, 1956.
9. Hunter, S. H. and John J. A. McLaughlin, The red tide. (About epidemics of dinoflagellates) *Scientific American* 199(2):92–98, August 1958.
10. Lamb, I. M., Lichens. *Scientific American* 201(4):144–156, October 1959.
11. Mohler, Hazel, Kelp, giant among the algae. *Nature Magazine* 52:406–408, 1959.
12. Rose, A. H., Yeasts. *Scientific American* 202(2):136–146, February 1960.
13. Whittaker, R. H., On the broad classification of organisms. *Quarterly Review of Biology* 34:210–226, 1959.

Section II. LEVELS OF PLANT ORGANIZATION

3. Molecules

THE TERM **organism** gives a clue to a most important characteristic of living things: their high degree of structural organization. The life processes of an organism occur within the framework of this structural organization, and the normal growth, development and behavior of an organism are just as dependent on a certain specific assembly of structures as is the normal operation of a machine such as an automobile or a computer. However, the structures of an organism are not only the site of its life processes, but they are also products of the life processes. There is, then, a very close interrelation between the structure and processes of organisms.

Observation of the leaves, flowers, and other organs of a plant reveals something of its structural organization, and microscopic examination of its tissues and cells further reveals a high degree of fine internal organization. A single living cell is composed of many precisely organized structures, many of the details being so minute that only an electron microscope will reveal them. It is becoming increasingly clear that many, if not all, of the biochemical processes of cells are localized in specific cell structures. In turn, these minute units of structure are composed of organized aggregates of molecules, which themselves are organized from atoms bonded together in a specific fashion. In a plant, then, we have a hierarchy of organizational levels, each basic to the ones above it: subatomic, atomic, molecular, molecular aggregate, cell structure, cell, tissue, organ, organ system, and organism. Finally, organisms are in turn organized into biological communities. Although unicellular organisms attain only the cellular level of organization, even they are remarkably highly organized entities.

In this chapter we begin our discussion of the various levels of plant organization with a consideration of the atoms and the more important kinds of molecules and molecular aggregates that constitute the basic building units of plants. Consideration of some of the biochemical reactions involving these molecules will come in later chapters. The remainder of this section of the book will be devoted to a discussion of the higher levels of plant organization.

Since this chapter, and several of the succeeding chapters, assume some knowledge of elementary chemical concepts, you may wish to study the chapter on chemistry in the appendix to this book or refer to some of the references listed at the end of this chapter (1, 4–6) before proceeding with your reading.

The Chemical Elements of Plants

Chemical analysis of plant tissues generally shows the presence of about 40 different chemical **elements**, but only fifteen elements are definitely known to be essential constituents of vascular plants. Three elements—carbon, hydrogen, and oxygen—make up about 99% of the total fresh weight of plants (Fig. 3.1). Nitrogen is the next most abundant element in plants, and potassium, phosphorus, calcium, sulfur, magnesium, and iron follow in about this order. The other essential elements are required by plants only in minute quantities and generally occur in plants only as traces. Of these **trace elements** boron, copper, manganese, molybdenum, and zinc are definitely known to be essential for vascular plants and sodium, chlorine and cobalt may be essential. Several other elements such as iodine are essential for higher animals, whereas a variety of rare elements have been reported to be essential for at least some fungi. The roles of the various elements in plants are discussed in Chapter 11.

None of the elements essential for vascular plants is rare, oxygen and hydrogen being among the most abundant of all elements and nitrogen constituting the bulk of the earth's atmosphere. The most striking difference in the proportion of elements in organisms in contrast with the nonliving world is the high percentage of carbon in organisms (Fig. 3.1). Carbon constitutes only a small fraction of 1% of the nonliving world. There is nothing unique, however, about the atoms making

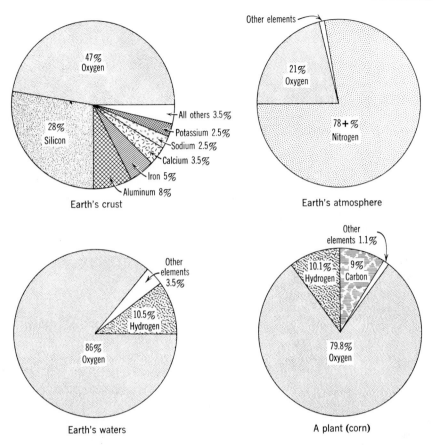

Figure 3.1. Graphic representation of the percentage (by weight) of the more abundant elements in a corn plant compared with the distribution of elements in various parts of the nonliving world.

plants and animals—indeed, they have been and will again be constituents of the air, waters, soil or rocks of the earth.

The Chemical Compounds of Plants

To find substances that are really characteristic of organisms we must turn from the atomic to the molecular level of organization. Although the **inorganic compounds** of plants—water, gases, salts, acids, and bases—are also constituents of nonliving things and are not characteristically biological, the **organic compounds** found in nature are all products of living organisms (or have been derived from these products).

All organic compounds contain carbon, and we may further limit them to compounds that also contain hydrogen. Oxygen, nitrogen, and other elements are also constituents of some organic compounds. About 95% of the dry weight of plants (what is left after the water is removed) consists of organic compounds, principally proteins, carbohydrates, fats and other lipids, and nucleic acids. Plants produce hundreds of other classes of organic compounds, many of them extremely important in the structure and processes of plants, but all of these together generally constitute only a small fraction of the total dry weight. Without organic compounds, life would not exist, but certain inorganic compounds are also essential to life. It may be noted that organisms are not only the source of all organic compounds found in nature at the present time but also of at least one inorganic substance—the oxygen of the atmosphere, a product of photosynthesis. Before there were photosynthetic plants on earth, the atmosphere probably contained no oxygen gas (Chapter 19).

Inorganic Constituents of Plants

WATER

More than 90% of the living structures of cells (**protoplasm**) consists of water, the walls of all living plant cells are impregnated with water, and a large part of the volume of many plant cells is occupied by vacuoles filled with cell sap (water with various substances dissolved in it). In vascular plants there is also considerable water in the conducting tubes of the wood on its way from the roots to the upper parts of the plant, and the spaces between cells are commonly almost, if not completely, saturated with water vapor. Water constitutes 80% or more of the total fresh weight of plants, except perhaps of large trees.

Water is just as essential to life as are the characteristic organic compounds. It not only plays an essential structural role, but also is indispensable as a solvent and a participant in many important biochemical reactions. No organism can carry on its life processes actively without an adequate quantity of water. One physical property of water of great biological importance is its high **specific heat** (the heat energy required to raise the temperature of 1 gram of a substance 1°C). The specific heat of water is 1 calorie, about twice that of oil or alcohol, four times that of air or aluminum, and nine times that of iron. The high specific heat of water is an important factor in preventing high-temperature injury to organisms exposed to direct sunlight either in the air or in the smaller bodies of water. The relations of plants to water are discussed in subsequent chapters, particularly Chapters 8 and 9.

GASES

Although gases are not really structural components of plants, various gases are always present within and between the cells of plants. The most abundant and important gases in plants are water vapor, oxygen, carbon dioxide, and nitrogen. Oxygen and carbon dioxide are both used and produced by plants, but the nitrogen of the atmosphere can be used directly only by nitrogen-fixing bacteria and algae.

SALTS

All of the essential elements except carbon, hydrogen, and oxygen generally enter plants as the **ions** of salts. Salts are primarily important in plants as the source of elements used in the synthesis of a variety of essential organic compounds, although their ions also play a number of other important roles (Chapter 11). Proteins contain nitrogen, each molecule of chlorophyll contains an atom of magnesium and four of nitrogen, many very important organic compounds contain phosphorus, and some enzymes contain iron, to give just a few examples.

Salts generally occur as ions, not only in solution but also in their crystals, and it is as ions that salts are absorbed, transported and used by plants. There are at least 10 different **cations** and 7 different **anions** in plants (Appendix, Table A.1) that can combine with one another and form 70 different salts. However, it is both more convenient and more accurate to consider the ions in both the soil solution and in plants individually rather than as the salts they can form.

Although most salts in plants are dissolved in water, plant cells may contain crystals of rather insoluble salts such as calcium oxalate and calcium sulfate. Calcium oxalate crystals are particularly abundant in

Figure 3.2. Tomato fruits are typical of plant tissues in that they consist mostly of water and organic substances. The tomato at the left weighed 150 grams. When a similar tomato was dried (center) only 8.7 grams of dry matter remained. A third fruit was dried and burned (right), and only 1 gram of inorganic compounds (ash) remained. (From *Within the Living Plant* by Erston V. Miller, McGraw-Hill, New York, 1953, through the courtesy of the author and publishers.)

the cells of *Caladium*, elephant ear, jack-in-the-pulpit and other members of the same family (Araceae) and also in the small aquatic vascular plants known as duckweeds.

When dried plant tissue is burned, only the mineral elements remain as the ash (Fig. 3.2). The burning oxidizes all organic compounds to carbon dioxide and water and the nitrogen present is also oxidized to a gas. The remaining ash is composed of oxidized mineral elements that the plants absorbed from the soil as ions.

ACIDS AND BASES

Plants contain all the ions essential for the formation of most of the common inorganic acids such as hydrochloric (HCl), sulfuric (H_2SO_4), nitric (HNO_3) and phosphoric (H_3PO_4), and most of the common inorganic bases such as sodium hydroxide ($NaOH$), potassium hydroxide (KOH), calcium hydroxide ($Ca(OH)_2$), and ammonium hydroxide (NH_4OH). However, there is no appreciable concentration of the strong acids or bases because their ions are not present in large quantities and because plant cells are highly buffered by the presence of many organic acids and other weak acids and their salts. As a result, most of the hydrogen ions (H^+, or more properly hydronium ions, H_3O^+) characteristic of acids are incorporated in the molecules of the poorly dissociated weak acids, whereas excess hydroxyl ions (OH^-) from strong bases are incorporated into water (HOH) molecules through neutralization by acids. Protoplasm is generally just on the acid side of neutrality, being buffered at a pH of about 6.8, and any very marked deviation from this pH results in a disruption of protoplasmic structure and life processes. Plant juices may, however, be quite acid, orange juice having a pH of about 3 and lemon juice a pH of about 2. Although many of the weak acids in the buffer systems of plants are organic acids synthesized by the plants, at least two of the weak acids of plant buffer systems are inorganic: phosphoric acid (H_3PO_4) and carbonic acid (H_2CO_3).

Organic Constituents of Plants

The organic compounds of plants not only constitute the great bulk of their dry weight, but are also much more numerous and varied than the inorganic constituents and are synthesized by the plants themselves. Most organic compounds have larger and more complex molecules than do inorganic compounds (6). Some organic compounds contain hundreds or even thousands of atoms. For many years chemists believed that organic compounds could be synthesized only by living cells, but in 1824 the German chemist, Wohler, synthesized urea from inorganic substances and since then chemists have synthesized many other organic compounds. However, it is still true that all naturally occurring organic compounds found on earth today were either synthesized by living organisms or derived from compounds so synthesized.

In the following pages we shall consider representatives of the classes of organic compounds that are the most abundant in plants: carbohydrates, proteins, fatty substances (lipids), and organic acids. Later on in the book we shall from time to time have occasion to refer to other organic compounds that play important roles in plants.

CARBOHYDRATES

SIMPLE SUGARS. Sugars play many important basic roles in the life of plants. They are produced by photosynthesis, used in respiration, and are the building units used in the synthesis of more complex carbohydrates such as starch and cellulose. Sugars are also used in the making of organic acids, fats, proteins and the thousands of other organic compounds of plants.

To many people "sugars" may mean cane, beet, brown, powdered, and maple sugars. Chemically, however, all these are all just one sugar —sucrose. In addition to sucrose, or ordinary table sugar, there are hundreds of other sugars differing from each other in molecular structure. All sugars, however, are sweet, white powders and are soluble in water. The simple sugars (**monosaccharides**) can not be digested (hydrolyzed) into other sugars with smaller molecules and are the basic building blocks from which all other carbohydrates are assembled. Monosaccharides usually have two hydrogen atoms and one oxygen atom for each carbon atom in their molecules ($C_nH_{2n}O_n$). Although there are monosaccharides with various numbers of carbon atoms (mostly 3 to 9), the 6-carbon sugars (**hexoses**) are the most abundant in both plants and animals.

Of the many hexoses, two deserve particular mention: **glucose** and **fructose** (Fig. 3.3). Glucose, also called dextrose and grape sugar, is the principal sugar in animal blood as well as one of the more abundant sugars in plants. Glucose assumes considerable importance in plants as the substance from which both starch and cellulose are synthesized. Fructose, also called levulose and fruit sugar, is found in plants in relatively large amounts. It plays an important role in various metabolic processes, and like glucose is used in the synthesis of more complex carbohydrates.

Since glucose and fructose, among other hexoses, have the chemical formula $C_6H_{12}O_6$, the question may arise as to how they can be differ-

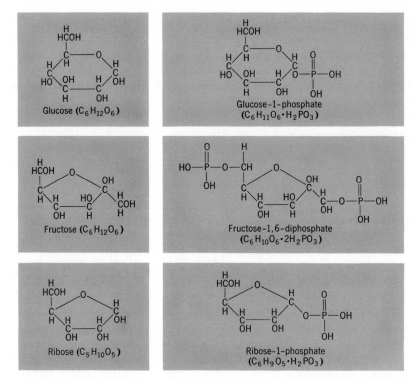

Figure 3.3. The molecular structure of three simple sugars and one phosphorylated derivative of each.

ent chemical compounds. The answer is that, although all hexoses are made of the same number and kinds of atoms, these atoms are put together in different patterns, just as many different kinds of houses can be built from a certain number of bricks, boards, and nails (Appendix A). Figure 3.3 shows how glucose and fructose differ in structure.

The 5-carbon sugars (**pentoses**) are much less abundant in plants than the hexoses, but no less important. They have the general formula $C_5H_{10}O_5$. Pentoses are used in important synthetic reactions almost as rapidly as they are formed. Several different pentoses are used in making complex carbohydrates found in cell walls and in plant gums and mucilages. **Ribose** (Fig. 3.3) is one of the most important pentoses, being a constituent of the complex nucleic acids, now considered to be the determiners of heredity traits. Another pentose, **ribulose**, is an intermediate substance in the process of photosynthesis.

Although the 3-carbon sugars (**trioses**, $C_3H_6O_3$) are not found in plants in large quantities, they play central roles in both respiration and photosynthesis as well as in various related processes (Chapter 10).

Triose sugar is now believed to be the first carbohydrate produced by photosynthesis.

The various sugars can participate in many biochemical processes only when phosphorylated. In phosphorylated sugars phosphate groups ($-H_2PO_3$) have replaced one or two of the hydrogens of the sugar molecule. The chemical formulae of several of the phosphorylated sugars are given in Fig. 3.3. For simplicity the phosphate group is sometimes written in formulae as $-$Ⓟ.

DISACCHARIDES. Two molecules of simple sugars may become joined together, forming a somewhat more complex type of sugar known as a **disaccharide**. Although disaccharides can be made from various simple sugars, the most abundant ones are all made from hexoses. **Sucrose** (ordinary table sugar) is made from one glucose and one fructose molecule. It is one of the most plentiful sugars in plants. **Maltose**, composed of two molecules of glucose, is abundant in germinating grains and other tissues in which starch is being digested. Sucrose and maltose, as well as all other hexose disaccharides, have the formula $C_{12}H_{22}O_{11}$. Disaccharides contain two less hydrogen atoms and one less oxygen atom than the two molecules of monosaccharides used in their synthesis, a net loss of H_2O. Sugars made from three or more molecules of simple sugars are also found in plants, but only in small quantities.

POLYSACCHARIDES. Dozens, hundreds, or even thousands of monosaccharide molecules may be linked together into long chains that are sometimes coiled or branched. These giant molecule carbohydrates are called **polysaccharides** (22). Most of the polysaccharides of plants are made from hexoses or pentoses. **Starch** and **cellulose** (12, 20), the two most abundant polysaccharides of plants, are both composed of glucose residues. In starch molecules the glucose linkages are under stress, resulting in the coiling of the molecule (Fig. 3.4). The somewhat different linkages in cellulose are not under stress, resulting in a straight chain structure (Fig. 3.5). Some kinds of starch molecules are branched. The differences in molecular structure of starch and cellulose are responsible for some of their differences in physical properties. The long, straight cellulose molecules are bound together into strong fibers (Fig. 3.5) that are ideal cell-wall structural materials (Fig. 4.9). The coiled and often branched starch molecules cannot be bound into fibers, but do cluster into grains (Fig. 4.7) of microscopic size that accumulate in plant cells. Many other polysaccharides besides starch and cellulose are synthesized by plants, a good many of them being cell-wall constituents. **Inulin** is a crystalline polysaccharide composed of fructose residues and is found most abundantly in certain members of the sunflower family. Most polysaccharides, unlike sugars, are neither sweet nor freely soluble in water.

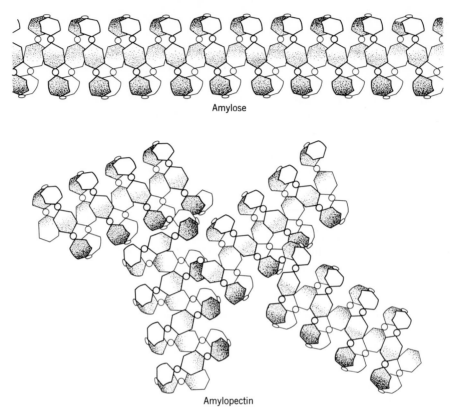

Amylose

Amylopectin

Figure 3.4. Diagram showing the helical (coiled) arrangement of the glucose residues in small portions of two different types of starch molecules. The amylose starch is an unbranched helix, whereas the amylopectin starch is highly branched. There are six glucose residues (shown as hexagons) in each turn of the helix. An entire starch molecule contains 1000 or more glucose residues. (Drawing by Evan L. Gillespie, reproduced from *Principles of Plant Physiology*, by James Bonner and A. W. Galston, 1952, through the courtesy of the authors and publisher, W. H. Freeman & Co.)

ORGANIC ACIDS

Many different organic acids occur in plants, and many of them play vital roles in the life processes of plants (24). Like inorganic acids, organic acids produce hydronium ions when in solution, the hydrogen being provided by the carboxyl (—COOH) group characteristic of organic acids. Organic acids are generally weak, since they are not highly ionized. Here we shall consider representatives of four classes of organic acids: the fatty acids, the plant acids, the amino acids, and the nucleic acids.

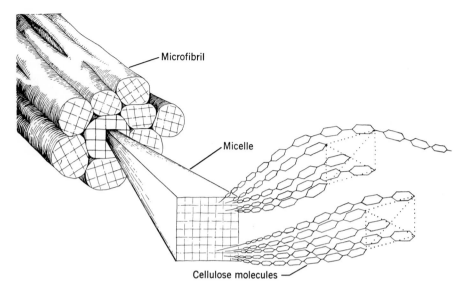

Figure 3.5. Diagram of a cellulose fiber, showing the binding of the straight chains of glucose molecules (i.e., the cellulose molecules) into basic units of five chains. These in turn are organized into crystalline micelles, a group of micelles making up a microfibril. The branched microfibrils, in turn, make up the cellulose fibers that constitute the basic framework of plant cell walls and are illustrated in Fig. 4.9. (Modified from a drawing by Evan L. Gillespie in *Principles of Plant Physiology*, by James Bonner and A. W. Galston, with the permission of the publishers, W. H. Freeman & Co.)

FATTY ACIDS. The **fatty acids** are composed of chains of carbon atoms linked together with a single —COOH group at the end of the chain. The fatty acids of plants are built up from acetic acid ($CH_3 \cdot COOH$) derivatives linked together and so all naturally occurring fatty acids have an even number of carbon atoms in them: 4, 6, 8 and on up to 20 or so. The structure of several fatty acids is given in Fig. 3.11. Fatty acids differ from one another in the number of carbons in the chain and also in the number of hydrogen atoms attached to the various carbon atoms. If all the carbon atoms of a fatty acid hold as many hydrogen atoms as possible, the fatty acid is **saturated**, as for example caproic acid: $CH_3 \cdot CH_2 \cdot CH_2 \cdot CH_2 \cdot CH_2 \cdot COOH$. If, however, some of the carbons in the chain hold only one hydrogen atom instead of two the acid is **unsaturated**: $CH_3 \cdot CH=CH \cdot CH_2 \cdot CH_2 \cdot COOH$. Unsaturated fatty acids are more common in plants than in animals. Fatty acids are generally oily liquids. They are important as constituents of fats, waxes, and other lipids.

PLANT ACIDS. The so-called "plant acids" are a rather diverse group chemically, but all have relatively small molecules with usually six or

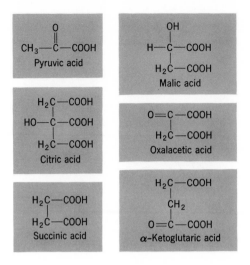

Figure 3.6. Structural formulae of a few of the important plant acids. Note the —COOH groups characteristic of the organic acids. Pyruvic, oxalacetic, and α-keto-glutaric acids contain the $>$C=O group, and thus are keto acids.

less carbon atoms in them (Fig. 3.6). They generally have from one to three —COOH groups per molecule. Among the plant acids are citric, malic, succinic, and fumaric. Acetic acid may be considered either as a fatty acid or a plant acid. Plant acids have long been known to be particularly abundant in fruits and in the leaves of succulent plants like *Sedum*, but in recent decades they have come to be recognized as important substances in respiration and other life processes of both plants and animals.

Some of the plant acids contain a carbonyl or ketone group ($>$C=O) in addition to —COOH groups and are known as **keto acids**. In addition to playing a part in respiration, the keto acids may be converted into amino acids by the substitution of an —NH_2 group from ammonia and an —H for the oxygen of the $>$C=O group.

AMINO ACIDS. The **amino acids** are important as the building units of proteins. There are many different amino acids, but only twenty or so are known to be constituents of proteins. All amino acids used in making proteins have the —NH_2 group that characterizes amino acids attached to the carbon that is adjacent to the carboxyl (—COOH) carbon. Thus, the general structure of amino acids may be represented as R·CH·COOH, the R representing the remaining atoms of the mol-
$\quad$ $\overset{|}{NH_2}$
ecule. R is different for each kind of amino acid. The simplest amino acid is glycine, and in it R is simply a hydrogen atom: CH₂·COOH.
$\qquad\qquad\qquad\qquad\qquad\qquad\qquad\qquad\qquad$ $\overset{|}{NH_2}$
The structure of several other amino acids is shown in Fig. 3.7. Several

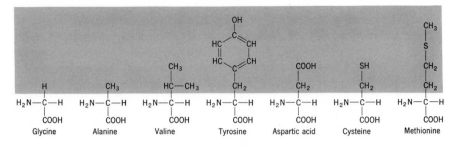

Figure 3.7. Structural formulae of several of the amino acids showing the structural units (below) characteristic of amino acids.

amino acids contain sulfur and at least a few of these sulfur-containing amino acids are found in protein molecules.

NUCLEIC ACIDS. Among the most complex and most important compounds in plants and animals are the **nucleic acids** (Figs. 3.8 and 3.9). The genes, or hereditary potentialities transmitted from one generation to another, are now considered to be essentially nucleic acids. Nucleic acids also constitute the most important part of viruses. The chromosomes in the nuclei of cells contain deoxyribonucleic acid (DNA) and it is this nucleic acid that makes up the essential part of the genes (19). DNA controls the production of another kind of nucleic acid, ribonucleic acid or RNA, that is also present in cells and plays an important role in the synthesis of proteins.

DNA molecules are presumably long double coils built up from hundreds of smaller units known as **nucleotides.** Each nucleotide is made from a molecule of deoxyribose (a 5-carbon sugar with a —H substituted for one of the —OH groups of ribose, hence the *deoxy-*), a molecule of phosphoric acid, and a molecule of one of four organic bases: adenine, guanine, cytosine or thymine (Fig. 3.10). The four kinds of nucleotides differ only in their organic bases. The phosphoric acid of one nucleotide is linked to the deoxyribose of the next, resulting in a long chain of alternating deoxyribose and phosphoric acid residues. The organic bases are attached to the deoxyribose molecules. Each DNA molecule is considered to be composed of two such chains coiled around one another (Fig. 3.9) and joined through their organic bases. Thymine can link only to adenine, and guanine only to cytosine. Since the bases can be arranged along the molecule in any sequence, they can provide a coding system that carries genetic information. This aspect of DNA is discussed in Chapter 17.

RNA differs from DNA in at least two respects: it contains ribose sugar instead of deoxyribose, and uracil in place of thymine. Whereas

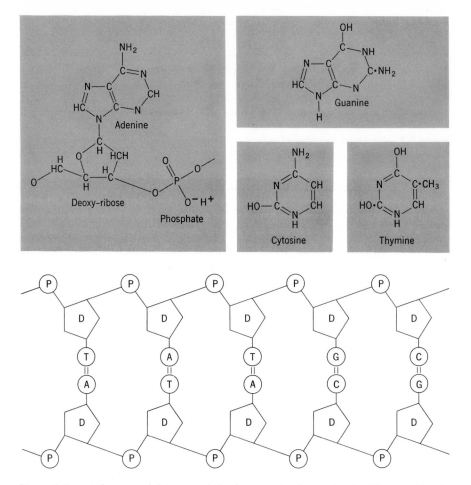

Figure 3.8. At the upper left is one of the four structural units (nucleotides) used in the synthesis of DNA. The other three are similar except that they contain guanine, cytosine, or thymine (upper right) instead of adenine attached to the deoxyribose. Below is a diagrammatic representation of a small portion of a DNA molecule showing how the nucleotides are linked lengthwise through the phosphate groups (P) and how the two chains of a DNA molecule are cross linked through the bases. Each chain is a helical coil rather than straight as shown in this simplified diagram. Since the pruines (adenine, guanine) can cross link only with the pyrimidines (cytosine, thymine), and since the upper —NH$_2$ groups can link only with the upper —OH groups, adenine (A) can cross link only with thymine (T) and guanine (G) only with cytosine (C).

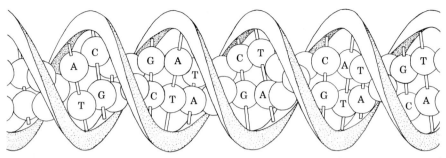

Figure 3.9. Diagram of a small portion of a DNA molecule showing the structure proposed in the Watson-Crick theory. The deoxyribose phosphate units making up each of the two helical coils are not shown individually, but the spheres represent the purine and pyrimidine units through which the two coils of the molecule are linked. One kind of DNA differs from another in the sequence of the purines and pyrimidines (A, C, G, T) in the molecule. A molecule of DNA is built up from 10,000 to 20,000 or so nucleotides. (Redrawn from *The Laboratory*, Courtesy of The Fisher Scientific Company.)

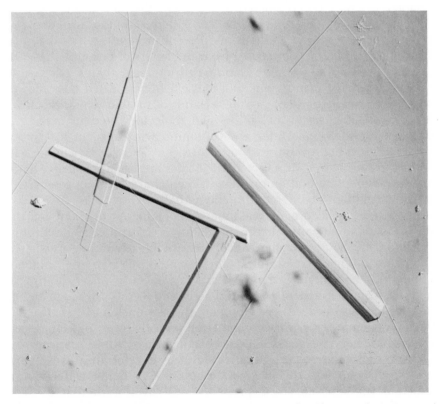

Figure 3.10. Enzymes and other proteins may occur as crystals. This is a photomicrograph (×116) of crystals of the enzyme, hexokinase. (Courtesy of M. Kunitz, Rockefeller Institute for Medical Research.)

DNA occurs only in the nuclei of cells, RNA is found both inside and outside the nuclei. Like DNA, most of the RNA is composed of hundreds of nucleotides. However, some RNA molecules are relatively small, constituting the "soluble" RNA of a cell.

PROTEINS

Proteins (7, 17) are the most abundant organic compounds of protoplasm and, along with the nucleic acids, are probably more responsible for its characteristic properties than any other class of substances. Like starch and cellulose, proteins are giant molecules. A protein molecule is composed of hundreds or thousands of amino acid residues linked together, the —COOH of one amino acid being attached to the —NH$_2$

$$\begin{matrix} H & O \\ | & \| \\ \end{matrix}$$

of the next one (—N—C—). This is known as a **peptide linkage**. The —OH and —H lost prior to the linkage process by the amino acids (Chapter 10) may be considered to represent the net production of a molecule of water. Since about twenty different amino acids may be used in protein synthesis, millions of different proteins are possible, just as many words can be constructed from the letters of our alphabet. In contrast, starch and cellulose (composed of long chains of glucose residues) would be comparable to a single letter repeated hundreds of times, for example *gggggggggg*⋯. Two kinds of protein may differ from each other in the *number* of amino acid molecules used in making a single protein molecule, in the *kinds* of amino acids used, in the *proportion* of each kind of amino acid, and in the *sequence* of the amino acid residues in the chain (17). Protein molecules are usually coiled. Since each species of plant and animal has its own characteristic proteins, we know that millions of different proteins actually exist.

Enzymes (18), the organic catalysts (Appendix A) essential for the activation of practically all the biochemical reactions of organisms, are proteins. Some enzymes have nonprotein **co-enzymes** associated with them. These co-enzymes play essential roles in the catalytic action of the enzymes. Like other catalysts, enzymes affect the rate of chemical reactions, generally greatly increasing them. Although an enzyme is not consumed in a reaction and appears unchanged at the end, it does enter into temporary combination with the reacting substances. Enzymes are very specific, each one reacting only with substances with a certain molecular configuration. Thus, an enzyme that can hydrolyze starch is unable to hydrolyze cellulose. A living cell contains numerous different enzymes, probably well over a thousand. The kinds of enzymes present in any particular organism determine the reactions that can take place in it. Although some processes that are activated by enzymes in plants, such as the breakdown of starch into glucose, can be carried on outside of organisms without enzymes, high temperatures and acids or other strong reagents are usually required.

Most enzymes act within cells, but some enzymes may be secreted by cells and act outside of them, for example the digestive enzymes of animals and fungi. Enzymes can be extracted from tissues, and some of these extracts can catalyze their characteristic reactions independently of the organism that produced them. **Diastase,** a crude extract of starch-digesting enzymes from germinating grains or molds, is sold in many drug stores as well as by chemical supply houses. **Papain,** extracted from fruits of the tropical papaya, is a protein-digesting enzyme sold by grocery stores as a meat tenderizer. Enzymes can be isolated from the crude extracts in pure crystalline form (Fig. 3.10) and over a hundred different pure enzymes have been prepared.

The **nucleoproteins** constitute another extremely important class of proteins, consisting of proteins linked with nucleic acids. Enzymes and nucleoproteins probably constitute a very substantial portion of the protoplasmic proteins. In contrast with these biologically active proteins are the apparently inert proteins that accumulate as crystals in seeds and sometimes in other parts of plants.

LIPIDS

The **lipids** are another important class of plant constituents and, like others we have discussed, are essential components of plant cells. Lipids are fatty or oily substances and include the **fats, waxes,** and **phospholipids.** These are not soluble in water, but are soluble in fat solvents such as gasoline, ether, and carbon tetrachloride. Although fats are insoluble in water, they can form **emulsions** consisting of microscopic fat globules uniformly dispersed in water, as in homogenized milk. **Emulsifying agents** such as soap, detergents, egg yolk, and gums prevent the fat globules from merging and floating to the surface as an oily layer. Fats in cells are usually present as emulsions.

FATS. The fats are compounds formed from **glycerol** (glycerine) and **fatty acids,** with three molecules of fatty acids reacting with each molecule of glycerol $[C_3H_5(OH)_3]$. The molecular structure of one fat is shown in Fig. 3.11. The many specific kinds of fats found in plants differ from each other in their constituent fatty acids. Commonly at least one of the three fatty acids is different from the others. If a fat is liquid at room temperatures it is referred to as an **oil.** Most plant fats are oils, for example corn, peanut, cottonseed, and olive oils. Oils are generally unsaturated, whereas solid fats are saturated. Drying oils used in making paints, such as linseed and tung oils, have an extra high

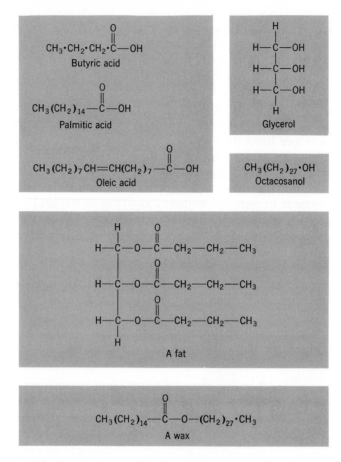

Figure 3.11. Molecular structure of three fatty acids and two alcohols (glycerol and octacosanol). Center: glycerol, combined with three molecules of fatty acids, forms a fat. Bottom: waxes are formed by the union of long chain alcohols like octacosanol with fatty acids.

degree of unsaturation. All such oils should not be confused with petroleum oils, an entirely different class of compounds (hydrocarbons).

Soaps are salts of fatty acids and are made by allowing fats to react with potassium hydroxide (KOH) or sodium hydroxide (NaOH, commonly called lye). Glycerol is also produced by the reaction.

Fat molecules contain proportionately less oxygen and more hydrogen than the molecules of carbohydrates, and as a result contain much more energy. A pound of any fat contains about twice as much energy (calories) as a pound of any carbohydrate. Consequently, fats are an excellent storage form of food.

PHOSPHOLIPIDS. Like fats, **phospholipids** are formed from glycerol and fatty acids, but a phosphoric acid molecule replaces one of the three fatty acids. Although cells contain much less phospholipid than fat, the phospholipids are probably more essential cell components. They are involved in cell membrane, chloroplast, and general protoplasmic structure and in important biochemical reactions. Much of their structural importance is probably related to the fact that whereas the bulk of the molecule is fat soluble, the phosphoric acid group is water soluble, which enables it to stabilize fat-water junctions as an emulsifier. The more complex phospholipids such as lecithin have additional compounds attached to the phosphoric acid unit.

WAXES. The **waxes** are also made from fatty acids and alcohols, but unlike the other lipids they do not contain the alcohol, glycerol. Instead, a fatty acid molecule unites with a long straight chain alcohol having 24 to 36 carbon atoms and only one —OH group at the end (Fig. 3.11). Plant waxes are primarily important as constituents of **cutin**, which covers the epidermis of leaves, stems, and fruits and of **suberin**, the waterproofing material of the walls of cork cells. Plant waxes are used in making the more expensive and better grades of polishes for shoes, floors, furniture, and automobiles.

OTHER IMPORTANT COMPOUNDS

Although the carbohydrates, proteins, lipids, and organic acids constitute the great bulk of the organic compounds synthesized by plants, many of the less abundant constituents are of great importance in the biochemical processes of plants. Among these are the hormones, vitamins, antibiotics, chlorophylls, carotenoids (8), hydrogen carriers such as DPN (diphosphopyridine nucleotide), and energy carriers such as ATP (adenosine triphosphate). These substances will be considered in later chapters. Lignin (16), a complex ring compound, is abundant in the walls of cells in wood.

Some plants also synthesize a variety of other compounds including the anthocyanins (the red, blue, violet, and pink pigments of flowers and other plant structures), alkaloids (e.g. caffeine, nicotine) (21), tannins, essential oils (10), (volatile oils such as peppermint and wintergreen), turpentine, resins, and rubber latex. Such substances, some of them produced by a limited number of plant species, are often of considerable commercial value but have generally been considered to be of little or no importance in the plants producing them. Further research may, however, reveal that they play roles of some importance.

Molecular Aggregates

The molecules of gases and of many liquids exist individually in a more or less random and unorganized fashion. The molecules of most solids and some liquids, however, cluster together in definitely organized patterns thus forming structures varying in size from those visible to the unaided eye to those too small to be detected by electron microscopes. These **molecular aggregates**, although by no means restricted to organisms, constitute an important level of organization in plants and animals which is intermediate between individual molecules and cell structures such as plastids, nuclei, and walls. Starch grains and cellulose fibers are both molecular aggregates, as are crystals and colloidal particles.

COLLOIDS. Many of the structural components of protoplasm are present as **colloids** (11). Colloidal particles are small clusters of molecules (or sometimes, as in starch or proteins, single giant molecules) dispersed through a solid, gas, or liquid. Fog, mucilage, gelatine desserts, and most clay soils are all different types of colloidal systems. In cells the medium through which colloidal particles are dispersed is usually water. The dispersed particles of a colloid range in size between $0.001\,\mu$ and $0.1\,\mu$ (μ = **micron**, $1/1000$ of a millimeter or $1/25,400$ in.). The dispersed molecules and ions of a true solution, as of a salt, are less than $0.001\,\mu$ in diameter, whereas the droplets of liquid dispersed through an emulsion and the solid particles dispersed in a suspension such as muddy water are more than $0.1\,\mu$ in diameter. The particles of a suspension and the droplets of emulsions are visible under an ordinary microscope, but both colloid particles and the molecules and ions of solutions are too small to be seen through ordinary microscopes. Colloid particles may, however, be visible by means of an electron microscope and show up as bright dots of light diffracted from a beam at right angles to the tube of a light microscope.

Dispersed colloid particles are electrically charged, each particle having numerous charges rather than a few such as carried by ions. Since all the particles of any particular colloid have the same charge—either positive or negative—they repel each other and do not clump together and settle out. Some colloidal particles are covered with a jacket of compactly arranged water molecules. This also prevents clumping of the particles. Some colloids are no more viscous than solutions whereas others, like glue, are very viscous.

Certain colloidal systems, particularly gelatin and other protein colloids, can exist in either a liquid (**sol**) or a jelly-like (**gel**) state and change from one to the other with changes in temperature and other factors.

In gelatin, and probably other gels, the semisolid consistency is a result of the aggregation of the colloid particles into a network of fibers. The protein colloids of protoplasm generally are in a state of flux between the sol and the gel forms.

Although protoplasm is a complex organization of disperse systems, solutions, emulsions, and suspensions as well as colloids, its characteristic properties are apparently more dependent on the colloids than on the others. The colloidal state facilitates chemical reactions, since the small colloid particles provide relatively immense total surface areas where the reacting substances can make contact. As a substance is divided into smaller and smaller particles, the total surface area increases and the volume remains constant. A cube of protein 1 mm. on a side has a surface area of 6 mm.^{2}, whereas the same protein in the form of colloidal particles of 0.001 μ in diameter would have a total surface area of 6,000,000 mm.^{2} Other colloid properties of biological importance are the charges on the particles, the sol-gel transformations, and the ability of colloid particles to attract and hold (adsorb) molecules and ions on their surfaces.

CRYSTALS. That substances such as salts and sugars form crystals is a matter of general knowledge, but it is not so generally recognized that many other substances including enzymes and other proteins (Fig. 3.10) and even viruses may also be crystalline (Figs. 3.12, 3.13). The molecules of a crystal are arranged in precise geometrical patterns characteristic of the substance, and as a result crystals of a compound have typical shapes that can be used in identifying the substance.

Figure 3.12. Crystals of tomato bushy stunt virus ($\times$100). (Courtesy of W. M. Stanley, University of California, Berkeley.)

Figure 3.13. Greatly enlarged crystal of tobacco necrosis virus as revealed by the electron microscope, showing the regular arrangement of the virus particles composing it. Some disruption of the crystal has occurred at the upper right ($\times 33,500$). (Courtesy of Ralph W. G. Wyckoff, National Institutes of Health.)

Although most substances in cells are either in solution or in colloidal form, salt crystals are not uncommon in cells. Most of these are crystals of calcium salts. Seeds frequently contain proteins in crystalline form.

In Perspective

Has this chapter dealt with botany or chemistry? The answer is both. Although we have been considering chemical substances, they are, after all, the basic structural units of plants, and some knowledge of them is just as essential for an understanding of plants as is some knowledge of the larger structural units fashioned from them. The molecules of cellulose, protein, lipids, and the other organic constituents of plants are, of course, just as characteristic products of plant activities as are protoplasm, cell walls, tissues, and organs. And, in the final analysis, plant activities occur at the molecular level whether these activities relate to biochemical reactions or physical energy transformations.

There is no single chemical level of plant organization, but rather a series of organizational levels of increasing complexity and particle size. From the electrons, protons, and neutrons of atoms we go up to the atomic level of organization. Atoms, in turn, are organized into molecules and molecules may be linked together to form giant molecules. Next we come to molecular aggregates such as colloidal particles, crystals, the droplets of emulsions, and starch grains. A still more complex level of structural organization is found in viruses (23), genes, and a variety of cell structures such as chromosomes, microsomes, mitochondria, and plastids, that will be discussed in Chapter 4. Each succeeding level of chemical organization is less characteristic of matter in general and more characteristic of living matter than the previous one, but it is difficult to determine the point at which organization ceases to be strictly chemical and assumes the properties of life.

Some biologists feel that no unit smaller than a cell can really be considered to be alive, whereas others feel that viruses (Figs. 3.13, 3.14) and genes should be regarded as living entities. One reason is that, unlike other chemical substances, viruses and genes appear to have the capacity for reproduction, even if they are actually just duplicated by the living cells within which they occur. Also, viruses may cause diseases of plants and animals as do bacteria and other pathogenic organisms, and may spread from one individual to another. Unlike true living organisms, however, viruses do not carry on respiration and they may be crystallized (Figs. 3.12, 3.13) without loss of activity. Whether we classify viruses as living or not, there is no doubt but that they are at the very borderline between living and nonliving substance.

As basic as the chemical level of organization is to an understanding of the structure and activities of plants, we must, of course, consider the higher levels of plant organization to have even a reasonably good picture of the nature of plants. A mixture of all the compounds making up a bean plant in just the right proportions would be a nourishing soup, but it would no more be a bean plant than a pile of the right amounts of steel, glass, gold, and jewels would be a watch. If, however, we provide a bean plant with water, oxygen, carbon dioxide, and the essential mineral elements it will fashion these simple substances into its characteristic molecules, molecular aggregates, cells, tissues, and organs,

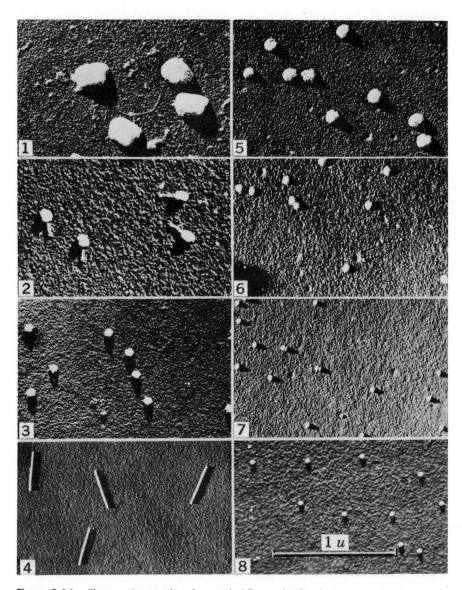

Figure 3.14. Electronmicrographs of several different kinds of virus. 1. Vaccina, 2. T$_2$ bacteriophage, 3. T$_3$ bacteriophage, 4. Tobacco mosaic, 5. Influenza, 6. Shope papilloma, 7. Tomato bushy stunt, 8. Polio. Note the 1-micron scale at the lower right. (Courtesy of C. A. Knight, University of California, Berkeley.)

a self-assembly job so characteristically limited to living things that it is ridiculous to consider a comparable accomplishment by any mechanism such as a watch. Nor could we imagine a watch reproducing itself. Like a watch, however, a bean plant must have a continuing supply of energy if it is to be an operating unit and normal operations can occur only within the framework of a properly organized structural system.

► *Questions*

1. If both a 100-year old tree and 1-year old seedlings of the same species were analyzed chemically for the compounds present in them, would you expect any difference in the percentage that any of the compounds would constitute of the total? If so, what compounds would be concerned and would each be present in the old tree in larger or smaller percentages than in the seedlings?

2. Answer the same questions with the analysis for chemical elements rather than chemical compounds.

3. Suggest a possible reason for the greater abundance of calcium oxalate crystals in some species of plants than others. Could the formation of these crystals play any important role in the life of the plant containing them?

4. What properties of carbon make it particularly suitable as the central structural element in large and complex molecules? What other elements, if any, have similar properties?

5. Indicate, for each of the following compounds (*a*) Whether it is inorganic or organic, (*b*) The general class of compounds (e.g. amino acid) to which it belongs, and (*c*) The name of the compound if it can be given on the basis of the information provided by the formula:

$C_6H_{12}O_6$; CO_2; H_2SO_4; $Ca(OH)_2$; $C_{12}H_{22}O_{11}$; CH_3CHO; $FeCl_3$; H_2CO_3; $CH_3 \cdot CH_2 \cdot CH \cdot NH_2 \cdot COOH$; $CH_3 \cdot CH_2 \cdot CO \cdot COOH$; CH_3CH_2OH; KCN; CH_4; K_2SO_4; $CH_3(CH_2)_{12}COOH$.

6. Devise a definition of life that would include viruses. Devise another definition of life that would exclude viruses as living organisms. Which definition do you prefer and why?

7. Are any of the molecules of which a living cell is constructed alive? It is possible to remove cell structures such as nuclei and chloroplasts from living cells by the use of a microdissection apparatus. Do you think these structures would still be living after their removal from the cell? Do you think it is possible to disrupt the structural organization of a cell in any way and still have a living entity? You may want to reconsider your answers after you have gotten farther along in the course.

► # *References*

For Reference

1. Brinckenhoff, Richard, et al., *The Physical World.* New York: Harcourt Brace, 1958. (Chapters 4–8 constitute an elementary introduction to chemistry. For chemical background see also items 4, 5, 6 in this bibliography, a good high school chemistry textbook, or an outline series chemistry book. Item 3 below will be useful primarily to those who have already studied chemistry.)
2. Miller, E. V., *The Chemistry of Plants.* New York: Reinhold Publishing Co., 1957.
3. Pauling, Linus, *College Chemistry.* San Francisco: W. H. Freeman Co., 1950.
4. Swenson, H. N. and J. E. Woods, *Physical Science for Liberal Arts Students,* New York: John Wiley and Sons, 1957.

For Reading

5. Asimov, Isaac and Wm. C. Boyd, *Inside the Atom.* New York: Abelard-Schuman, 1956.
6. Asimov, Isaac, *The World of Carbon.* New York: Abelard-Schuman, 1958.
7. Doty, Paul, Proteins. *Scientific American* 197(3):173, September 1957.
8. Frank, Sylvia, Carotenoids. *Scientific American* 194(1):80–86, January 1956.
9. Gamow, George, *Mr. Tompkins Explores the Atom.* Cambridge: Cambridge University Press, 1955.
10. Haagen-Smit, A. J., Essential oils. *Scientific American* 189(2):70–75, August 1953.
11. Hawley, C. G., *Small Wonder: The Story of Colloids.* New York: Knopf, 1947.
12. Haynes, Williams, *Cellulose: The Chemical that Grows.* New York: Doubleday, 1953.
13. Katz, J. J., The biology of heavy water. *Scientific American* 203(1):106–116, July 1960.
14. Meyerhof, Otto, Biochemistry. *Scientific American* 183(3):62–70, September 1950.
15. Müller, E. W., Atoms visualized. *Scientific American* 196(6):113, June 1957.
16. Nord, F. F. and W. J. Schubert, Lignin. *Scientific American* 199(4):104–113, October 1958.
17. Pauling, Linus, et al., The structure of protein molecules. *Scientific American* 191(1):51–59, July 1954.
18. Pfeiffer, John E., Enzymes. *Scientific American* 179(6):28–39, December 1948.
19. Pfeiffer, John E., DNA. *Natural History* 69(10):8–15, December 1960.
20. Preston, R. D., Cellulose. *Scientific American* 197(3):156–168, September 1957.
21. Robinson, Trevor, Alkaloids. *Scientific American* 201(1):113–121, July 1959.
22. Schmitt, F. O., Giant molecules in cells and tissues. *Scientific American* 197(3):204–216, September 1957.
23. Smith, K. M., *Beyond the Microscope.* Pelican Books edition. Baltimore: Penguin Books, 1957. (About viruses.)
24. Thomas, Meirion, Vegetable acids in higher plants. *Endeavour* 10:160–165, 1951.

4. Cells

As seen in chapter 2, the Plant Kingdom is made up of living organisms displaying such a diversity in form and range in size that by outward appearances, they seem to have little in common. But in spite of this diversity they do share important functional and structural attributes. As living organisms, large or small, they demonstrate those functional properties that are the mark of living things. That is, they maintain themselves, grow and differentiate in a controlled and orderly fashion, are responsive to varying conditions of environment, and give rise to new organisms like themselves through characteristic reproductive processes. As the chemist seeks to explain the reactions of his materials through identification and understanding of the nature of some unique unit, so the biologist comes to recognize that the seat of the multiplicity of chemical and physical interactions that manifest themselves as attributes of the living is a unique physical unit, the **cell**.

The cell as a structural unit was first observed by Robert Hooke in 1665 in thin slices of cork and other plant tissues. In Hooke's words: ". . . I could exceedingly plainly perceive it to be all perforated and porous, much like a Honeycomb . . . these pores, or cells, were not very deep, but consisted of a great many little boxes, . . . Nor is this kind of texture peculiar to Cork only; for upon examination with my micro-

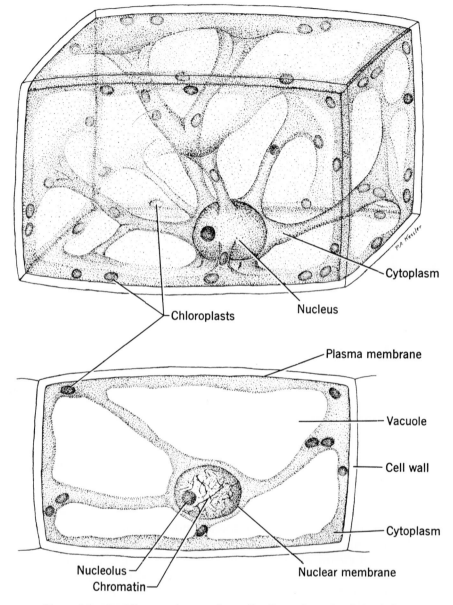

Figure 4.1. Semidiagram of green plant cell. Shown in sectional view below.

scope, I have found that the pith of an Elder, or almost any other tree, the inner pulp or pith of the Cany hollow stalks of several other Vegetables: as Fennel, Carrets, Daucus, Bur-docks, Teasels, Fearn . . . &c have much such a kind of Schematisme . . . ." As so frequently happens in the realm of scientific inquiry, the fuller significance of Hooke's discoveries came many years later. In 1839 Schleiden and Schwann formulated the Cell Theory in which, on the basis of their own studies and those of older and contemporary observers, they postulated that the bodies of all plants and animals are composed of cells and the products of cell activity. In this great generalization they focused attention on the cell as a fundamental unit of life. With the later recognition by other observers that cells come only from pre-existing cells, came the realization that the story of life in all of its manifestations is basically the story of the cell.

Plant cells, with few exceptions, are too small to be seen by the unaided eye. Yet even though microscopic, they vary widely in size. The smallest cells (0.2–$5.0\,\mu$ = $1/125000$–$1/5000$ in.) are found among the bacteria, whereas in the higher plants they generally range from 10–100 μ. Exceptional in size are some fiber cells of flax and cotton hairs that may attain a length of 5 cm. Cells also vary greatly in shape, as will be shown later in this chapter. However, with all of these variations, all living plant cells are fundamentally alike in that each consists of a minute bit of living substance, called **protoplasm**, encased, with certain exceptions, in a nonliving wall of **cellulose**. A variety of differentiations of the protoplasm may occur, and the cellulose wall may be variously modified by the presence of other substances (Fig. 4.1). Such specializations in internal organization and wall constitution, along with specialization of shape (from the simple spherical), are associated with the performance of special functions. In view of this it is not possible to identify any one cell as "typical" of all cells, but we can visualize a "composite" cell that would embrace many cellular features (3).

The Protoplast

The term **protoplast** is useful in designating the individual portion of the protoplasm of a plant contained within the limits of a single cell. Chemically, protoplasm is an organization of organic and inorganic compounds. The chief organic compounds are proteins, fats, carbohydrates, and organic acids. Proteins are the most abundant, sometimes constituting a third of the dry weight of protoplasm. The inorganic compounds are water and various salts. Water may constitute as much as 85–90% of the fresh weight of active protoplasm, inorganic salts commonly less than 1%. The high proportion of water in proto-plasm is significant. In general, the higher the water content, the higher is the rate of metabolic activity. This is shown in the phenom-enon of seed germination. So long as seeds are kept dry they remain quiescent, but when supplied with water the protoplasm becomes more active and the seed germinates. This would certainly suggest that protoplasmic activity is in part, at least, related to chemical reactions, for it is well known that many chemicals fail to react in the anhydrous condition, but do so readily when brought together in the presence of water. It must not be thought, however, that a haphazard mixture of water, inorganic salts, and organic compounds will yield living proto-plasm. On the contrary, it is a complex and highly organized chemical and physical system. The inorganic salts and most of the carbohy-drates are water soluble and present in **true solution**, whereas the pro-teins and fats are present as **colloid** and **emulsoid dispersions**.

Detailed study of the protoplast (1), sometimes by the use of special methods, reveals a number of well-defined structural differentiations. Most of them are of universal occurrence in living cells, performing basic cell functions. A few, when present, endow the cell with special capabilities.

THE CYTOPLASM AND PLASMA MEMBRANES. The preponderant bulk of the protoplast consists of the **cytoplasm**, a translucent, colorless, viscous mass. When seen with the light microscope it may appear hyaline or somewhat granular. Recent studies by electron microscopy have shown the cytoplasm to have a fine structure involving an extensive and complex system of membranes. This internal membrane complex, called the **endoplasmic reticulum**, is structurally variable. It is believed to be the site of many important metabolic reactions involving syn-theses, secretions, and conversions characteristic of the cell.

The limits of the protoplast are defined by the presence of a delicate film or membrane called the **plasma membrane**. Although it is ex-tremely thin and difficult to see with the light microscope, the plasma membrane is usually shown by the electron microscope to be two layered. Composed of proteins and lipids, the membrane is regarded as a denser expression of the colloidal system of the cytoplasm and an integral part of it. Its possible relation to the internal endoplasmic reticulum is an unresolved question. The living membrane is capable of growing as the cell enlarges and can, within limits, repair itself when mechanically damaged. Described as selectively or **differentially permeable**, it permits the passage of the molecules of some substances but not of others. Some molecules of relatively small size may be ex-cluded whereas larger ones may pass readily, and such differential permeability is not fixed, but is subject to change momentarily. Discussion of the significance of this important property of the membrane appears in later chapters.

THE NUCLEUS. The most conspicuous of the differentiated protoplasmic structures of the protoplast is the nucleus, a spherical or ellipsoid body averaging about 15 μ in diameter. It was discovered by Robert Brown in 1831 and observed to be of general occurrence in living cells. Brown named it "nucleus" (Latin, kernel) to suggest its importance. In certain lower forms of plant life, such as the cyanophytes and some bacteria, a definitely organized nucleus comparable to that of the higher plants is not discernible, although it is presumed that the requisite nuclear material is present, perhaps in a diffuse state. Some algae and fungi characteristically are multinucleate.

The nucleus is delimited by a **nuclear membrane.** Rather early in nuclear division the nuclear membrane disappears, new membranes being formed around the reconstituted daughter nuclei. The preponderant bulk of the nucleus is a gel-like mass, the **nuclear sap,** or karyolymph, through which extends a diffuse tangle of separate, fine threads of **chromatin.** The chromatin threads are colorless and not generally visible in living cells but may be rendered so by the use of appropriate dyes. In properly stained material, certain coarsely granular portions of the chromatin stain darker than the threads. These are called **chromocenters** and are thought to consist of a special type of chromatin. The chromatin is the most important constituent of the nucleus, for it is the hereditary material. In division of the nucleus the chromatin is resolved into a characteristic number of **chromosomes** that in their precise manner of distribution carry to the daughter nuclei characteristic complements of genes, the hereditary units borne within them. Chemical analysis of chromatin has revealed it to consist of a complex of proteins, ribonucleic acid (RNA), and deoxyribonucleic acid (DNA).

Finally, each nucleus also contains one or more globular bodies apparently without membrane and which are relatively homogeneous as seen with the light microscope. These are the **nucleoli.** Chemically they consist of proteins and ribonucleic acid. Little of a precise nature is known concerning the function of the nucleoli (8). During division of the nucleus the nucleoli disappear and new ones develop in each daughter nucleus.

The nucleus is the center of hereditary control over the cell. This control is apparently exerted by the DNA of the chromatin, which determines the specific kinds of RNA produced. The RNA is extruded from the nucleus into the cytoplasm as **microsomes**—minute globular structures in which enzymes and other proteins are synthesized in a pattern determined by the RNA. Thus, the nucleus apparently controls the processes of a cell by determining the kinds of enzymes and other proteins present in the cell (Chapter 10).

THE PLASTIDS. Also embedded in the cytoplasm are a variety of differentiated protoplasmic bodies that are functionally specialized and highly important in the cell economy. These conspicuous bodies, called plastids, are of various forms and some of them are distinctive for their special pigmentation. Plastids are believed to develop from smaller, less well-defined precursors, **proplastids,** which are able to increase their number by division. In division of the cell, however, the distribution of proplastids to the daughter cells is random. Whether the specific types of plastids arise from special types of proplastids or from a generalized proplastid that matures in a variety of specific patterns is unknown. Division of mature plastids has been observed in some plants.

In most of the cells of leaves and other green parts, the dominant type of plastid is the **chloroplast.** The chloroplast is green because of its content of pigments called **chlorophylls.** Several chemically different chlorophylls are known, but the chief ones, occurring in the green algae, mosses, and vascular plants, are chlorophyll *a* and chlorophyll *b* (Fig. 10.5). Associated with chlorophylls in the chloroplasts are **carotenes** and **xanthophylls,** pigments of yellow, orange, or red color. About two-thirds of the pigments of the chloroplast are chlorophylls, hence the dominant green color. In the higher plants the chloroplasts are generally discoid or saucer-shaped and numerous, whereas in some plants like the algae they may have elaborate shapes, such as the helical bands in *Spirogyra* (Fig. 2.5), a cylindrical net in *Oedogonium* (Fig. 16.3), and others. Under the light microscope the chloroplast presents a homogeneous or granular appearance and sometimes contains small starch grains. With the electron microscope the structure is seen to be highly organized (10). Each chloroplast consists of a large number of disc-shaped **grana,** each composed of a stack of thin platelets or lamellae bearing the chlorophyll on their surfaces as a very thin layer. The grana are embedded in a vacuolated, granular **stroma** or matrix with few or no lamellae (Figs. 4.2, 4.3). We depend on the chloroplast with its enormous chlorophyll-bearing surface for our energy supply, for it is the chlorophylls that absorb radiant energy from the sun. This energy is converted to chemical bond energy and eventually incorporated in the sugar produced by photosynthesis, which may later be oxidized with release of the energy.

A second type of plastid, yellow, orange, or red in color, occurs in the cells of such material as the yellow petals of sunflower, the root of carrot, or the ripe fruit of sweet pepper or tomato. These are **chromoplasts** (Fig. 4.4). They are angular, spherical, lobed, or rod-like. The

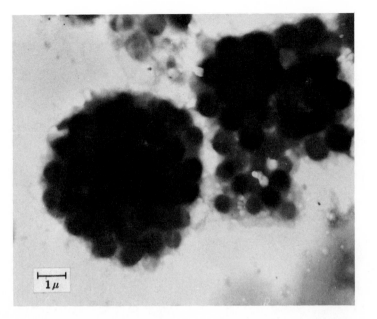

Figure 4.2. Electron micrograph of chloroplasts of spinach, showing 40 to 60 grana per chloroplast. (Courtesy of Granick & Porter.)

coloration is due to xanthophylls, carotenes, and related compounds. The color change during the ripening of certain fruits such as tomato or sweet pepper is brought about by the rapid destruction and non-replacement of chlorophylls in the chloroplasts and the simultaneous development of red xanthophyll. The change in leaf color from green to yellow in autumn results from the breakdown of chlorophyll, thus unmasking the color of the carotene and xanthophyll of the chloroplasts. In effect, therefore, the chromoplasts in such cases are degraded or altered chloroplasts. Most chromoplasts are not of this origin but apparently develop directly from proplastids. Little is known concerning the special function of chromoplasts in the plant. Animals, however, can synthesize vitamin A from the carotene they obtain from the plants they eat.

A third type of plastid is the colorless **leucoplast.** Leucoplasts are usually difficult to detect without special staining methods. They are the most common in the cells of underground parts and in tissues not exposed to light. They occur in various irregular shapes and, indeed, may change their shape from time to time. They generally present a granular appearance and often contain large starch grains. The accumulation of starch in the roots and tubers of plants is a common

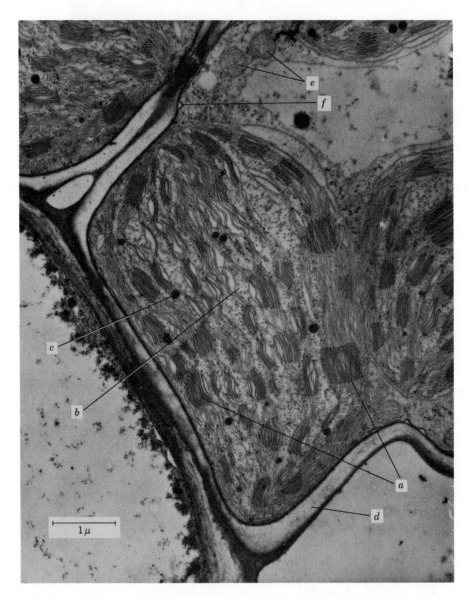

Figure 4.3. Electron micrograph of chloroplasts in cells of grass leaf showing: *a*. grana, *b*. stroma, *c*. lipoid body. Also visible are: *d*. cell wall, *e*. mitochondria, *f*. plasma membrane. (Courtesy of University of Texas, Electron Microscopy Laboratory.)

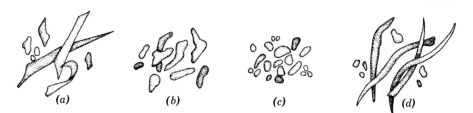

Figure 4.4. Chromoplasts. (a) From carrot root; (b) from tomato fruit; (c) from dandelion petal; (d) from rose fruit.

function of leucoplasts. Some leucoplasts are related to oil accumulation, as in the seeds of peanut, corn, and castor bean.

MITOCHONDRIA. Virtually all living cells contain in the cytoplasm large numbers of very small (0.2–3.0 μ), filamentous, rod-shaped, or globular bodies called **mitochondria** (Fig. 4.5). These structures are rendered visible by the light microscope only after special staining or by the use of special optical equipment. Electron micrographs reveal that each mitochondrion is bounded by double membranes, the outer membrane covering the surface smoothly. The inner membrane invades the body of the mitochondrion in extensive folds and convolutions, called **cristae**, thus creating an extensive surface (Fig. 4.6). Within the mito-

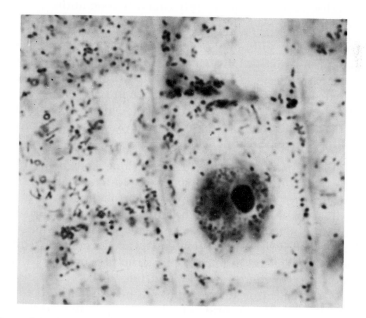

Figure 4.5. Mitochondria in cytoplasm of cells. (Courtesy of E. H. Newcomer.)

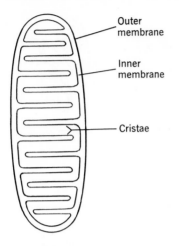

Outer membrane

Inner membrane

Cristae

Figure 4.6. Diagram of structure of a mitochondrion as shown by electron microscopy.

chondrion organic acids derived from the breakdown of complex food molecules are progressively oxidized to carbon dioxide and water through many successive steps (respiration), each controlled by a specific enzyme. The energy released in the oxidations is stored principally in adenosine triphosphate (ATP) as high-energy phosphate bonds by the phosphorylation process. ATP then passes outward to other parts of the cell where it becomes available for doing work. The mitrochondrion has been quite aptly called by one author, "the power-house of the cell." (7)

MICROSOMES. An additional protoplasmic particle of the size order of 0.1 μ has been identified by use of the electron microscope. These bodies, the **microsomes** (11), are thought to arise in the nucleus whence they are extruded into the cytoplasm. Rich in RNA, they are active in the synthesis of enzymes and other proteins. Microsomes are intimately associated with the endoplasmic reticulum, and may be considered to be one of its structural components.

THE GOLGI APPARATUS. This structure, long known in animal cells and recently shown by electron microscopy to be of general occurrence in plant cells, is a characteristic association of discrete structures. It consists of a small stack of much-flattened vesicles, called cisternae, bounded by thin membranes and associated, at their edges, with numerous spherical vesicles that apparently vary in number with changes in cell activity. Several to many Golgi structures occur in a cell. The function of these structures is at present unknown.

Figure 4.7, an electron micrograph of a meristematic root-cap cell of maize, shows clearly several of the protoplasmic differentiations discussed.

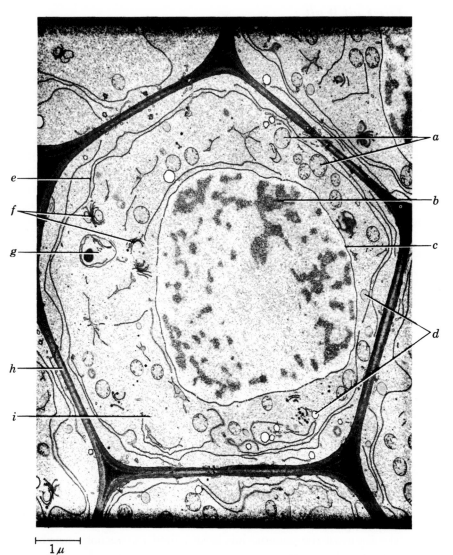

$\vdash\!\!\!\!-\!\!\!\!-\!\!\!\!\dashv$
$1\,\mu$

Figure 4.7. Electron micrograph of section through a meristematic rootcap cell of maize showing: a. mitochondria, b. chromatin, c. nuclear membrane, d. cytoplasmic inclusions, e. endoplasmic reticulum, f. Golgi apparatus, g. starch-storing leucoplast, h. cell walls, i. cytoplasm. Approximately ×5,040. (Courtesy of W. Gordon Whaley.)

The Cell Wall

The protoplasts of plants are, with few exceptions, encased by a **cell wall** composed principally of cellulose. The cell wall is secreted by the living protoplast and deposited upon its surface, that is, on the outside of the plasma membrane (Fig. 4.1). The cell wall is ordinarily continuous. However, in multicellular plants, abutting walls of adjacent protoplasts are traversed by extremely fine protoplasmic strands which thus interconnect the protoplasts. These protoplasmic connections are the **plasmodesmata** (singular, **plasmodesma**) (Fig. 4.8). The cellulose wall is a rather tough layer, and its presence imparts a certain degree of rigidity and stability of form to the cell. The importance of the cell wall on the manner and habit of growth of a plant and its general lack of motility have already been mentioned. Further discussion of the cell wall, its structure, development, and modifications appear later in this chapter.

Cell Inclusions

The active metabolism of the cell entails the construction and consumption of substances that may at various times and in varying amounts be present within the living cell. These, as substances that become included in the living protoplasm, may be called **cell inclusions.**

Most conspicuous, especially in mature plant cells, is the **vacuole** (Fig. 4.1). The vacuole consists of water and small amounts of several dissolved substances including sugars and salts. In young cells, very small individual droplets of clear fluid appear spontaneously, and as these enlarge, during growth of the cell, they coalesce and form a single drop. Commonly assuming a central position in the cell, the enlarging drop displaces the cytoplasm, so that in mature living cells the cytoplasm often appears as a thin peripheral layer. The membrane that defines the limits of the vacuole has been called the **vacuolar membrane,** although it must be remembered that it is really a part of the cytoplasm.

Other important inclusions are such substances as **starch** (Fig. 4.9). Starch grains may develop in leucoplasts and chloroplasts in cells. As a starch grain enlarges, the body of the leucoplast becomes greatly distended and envelopes the grain as a very thin inconspicuous film. The tuber of potato and the roots of many plants accumulate starch that may be used in the next season's early growth. Many kinds of seeds are rich in starch that serves, upon germination, as nourishment for the young, rapidly growing plant. Enough of such foods are usually

Figure 4.8. Plasmodesmata traversing the thick walls in the endosperm of a persimmon seed. (Copyright, General Biological Supply House, Inc., Chicago.)

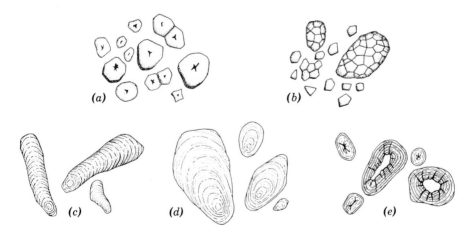

Figure 4.9. Starch grains. (*a*) From corn; (*b*) from rice; (*c*) from banana; (*d*) from potato; (*e*) from bean.

present to last until the new season's growth is well started and the plant can begin to make more.

Crystals are another kind of inclusion. These occur in various forms (Fig. 4.10). They are composed chiefly of calcium oxalate. The crystals form within the cytoplasm and become surrounded by a cytoplasmic membrane. Silica and calcium carbonate are also occasionally present as crystalline inclusions.

Figure 4.10. Types of calcium oxalate crystals.

Oil droplets and **fat globules** commonly occur in the cytoplasm, as in the cells of the endosperm and cotyledons of certain seeds.

The following scheme summarizes the relationship of the parts of a generalized plant cell:

Plant Cell
- Cell wall—chiefly cellulose, often with other substances
- The protoplast
  - cytoplasm and its membranes
  - nucleus
    - nuclear membrane
    - chromatin (chromosomes)
    - nucleolus
    - nuclear sap
  - plastids and other bodies
    - leucoplasts
    - chloroplasts
    - chromoplasts
    - mitochondria
    - microsomes
    - Golgi apparatus
- Inclusions (nonprotoplasmic)
  - vacuoles
  - crystals
  - starch
  - oil

Cells newly formed by the division of a preexisting cell generally have a dense protoplast. Small vacuoles arise spontaneously in the cytoplasm, enlarge, and ultimately coalesce. The physical enlargement or growth of the cell bears a direct relationship to the enlargement of the vacuoles. During growth of the cell, the wall stretches and the protoplast deposits additional wall substance (Chapter 12).

Finally, when the cell attains its maximal size and characteristic shape, its **primary** development is complete. Many cells subsequently continue through a **secondary** development consisting in part of wall modification. This may take the form of uniform and sometimes great thickening of the wall by the deposition of additional wall material, or the deposition of wall material in a distinctive pattern, with more or less restricted areas remaining unthickened. Such unthickened areas of small extent are called **pits**. The wall deposited by the protoplast after completion of the primary development is termed the **secondary wall;** the wall present from the beginning is the **primary wall.** These walls, originally mostly cellulose, may in secondary development become modified by the addition of other substances. **Lignin**, a complex substance that contributes strength and hardness to cell walls, may be deposited by the protoplast in either the primary or secondary wall. **Suberin**, and **cutin**, each composed of a mixture of fatty and waxy substances, may be added to cellulose in the walls of certain cells. Suberin or cutin commonly occur in certain exterior plant cells where they impart an impervious quality to the walls.

The building up of a cell wall by the deposition of successive layers of wall material upon the inner face of previously formed wall is said to be accomplished by **apposition**. Thick walls frequently present a laminated appearance because of differences in density of successive layers. In the modification of walls, as in lignification, the modifying substance is deposited within the walls, in a manner described as **intussusception.**

Studies of primary and secondary cell walls with the electron microscope show interesting differences in their microstructure. The cellulose molecule consists of a very large number of glucose units united in long lattice-like chains, the **crystal lattices.** Groups or fascicles of crystal lattices constitute the cellulose **fibrils.** In the primary wall the fibrils are loosely associated, giving the appearance of an open fabric (Fig. 4.11a). The fibrils of the secondary wall are more compact and parallel and generally follow a helical pattern about the cell (Fig. 4.11b). In successively deposited layers of fibrils in the secondary walls of cotton hairs, for example, the direction of the helix differs. Modifying substances deposited in secondary development would occupy the space between the fibrils.

The variety of shapes and wall characteristics attained by plant cells in maturation are related to their function in the plant body. This will be shown in Chapter 5 where the organization of cells into functioning tissues is discussed. It is proper at this point, however, to enumerate and describe briefly the various types of cells that may be found in a vascular plant (6).

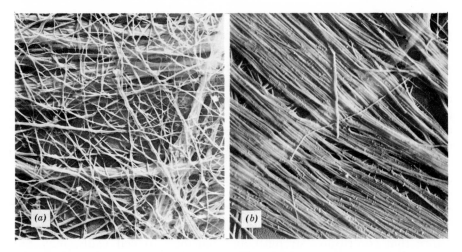

Figure 4.11. Electron micrographs of cellulose fibrils in primary wall (a) and secondary wall (b) of plant cell. (Courtesy of Ralph W. G. Wyckoff, National Institutes of Health.)

Cell Types

Structurally, the simplest type of cell is the **parenchyma cell** (Fig. 4.12a). In general, parenchyma cells are essentially isodiametric and possess a thin wall and a long-active protoplast. However, some departure from the usual form and thin wall is encountered in parenchyma cells of specialized tissues. Most of the basic metabolic and reproductive functions of the plant are performed by cells of this type. Parenchyma cells containing chloroplasts are sometimes called **chlorenchyma cells.**

Collenchyma cells are generally rectangular as seen in longitudinal section. They retain a protoplast at maturity, and the cellulose wall is unevenly thickened by the deposition of additional cellulose and pectic compounds in certain areas (Fig. 4.13). Collenchyma cells are the first-formed specialized supporting cells to develop in the young differentiating stem tip, contributing a temporary, nonrigid support.

Sclerenchyma cells are of two general shape classes, viz., isodiametric, called **sclereids** (Fig. 4.12b), and elongated, called **sclerenchyma fibers** (Fig. 4.14). These classes are not always sharply distinguishable, for sclereids are frequently moderately elongated and sometimes highly branched. Fibers, however, are generally slender, many times longer than wide and have tapering ends. Sclerenchyma cells have thick, strongly lignified secondary walls which may be pitted. At maturity these cells usually lose their protoplasts and thus play no active part in the plant metabolism. Sclerenchyma cells are commonly disposed in

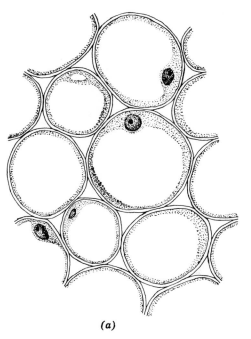

Figure 4.12. (a) Parenchyma cells; (b) sclereids.

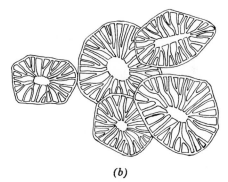

(b)

masses or in association with other cell types. Their chief function is support, and they provide resistance to compression and flexing forces. Sclereids are frequently associated in thick layers as in nut shells where they have great protective value. Familiar sclerenchyma fibers are those of flax and hemp, used for textiles and cordage.

Epidermal cells are typically tabular (Fig. 4.15a). They are associated in a continuous, usually one-layered "sheet" on the surface of leaves, young roots, and stems. The outer walls of the epidermal cells of stem and leaves are modified by the deposition of cutin. This wall modifica-

111

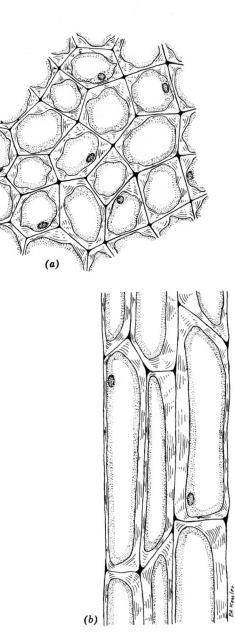

(a)

(b)

Figure 4.13. Collenchyma cells. (a) In cross section; (b) in longitudinal section.

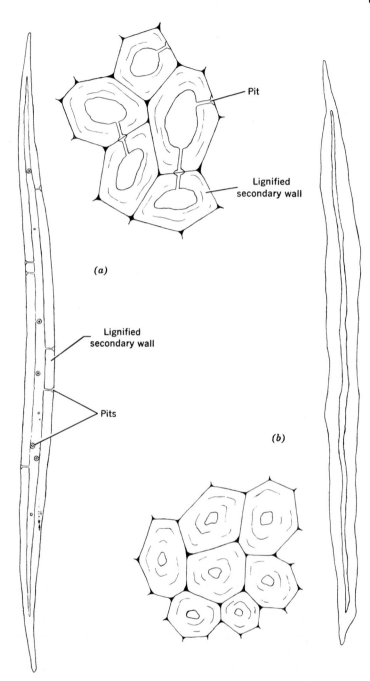

(a)

Pit

Lignified
secondary wall

Lignified
secondary wall

Pits

(b)

Figure 4.14. Fibers. (a) Wood fibers in cross and longitudinal section; (b) cortical fibers in cross and longitudinal section.

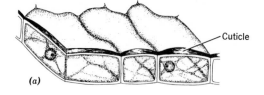

(a)

Figure 4.15. (a) Epidermal cells seen in three-dimensional view; (b) cork cells seen in cross section.

(b)

tion reduces the excessive water evaporation. The epidermal cells of young roots are not cutinized, and absorption of water from the soil takes place directly through the surface. In most seed plants, some of the epidermal cells of young roots are outwardly extended as the **root hairs** (Fig. 9.6). The absorbing surface is thus greatly increased. At maturity epidermal cells retain their active protoplasts.

Cork cells are tabular, with all walls suberized (Fig. 4.15*b*). They occur in thick layers on the outer surfaces of older stems, branches, and roots of woody plants where their spongy texture and water-proof character provide some protection against mechanical injury and drying. At maturity the protoplasts die and the cells become air filled, which accounts for the lightness and compressibility of cork. The uses of cork for bottle stoppers and as a buoyant material in life preservers, as well as for floor coverings and insulation, are related to these properties.

The cell types so far described are chiefly supportive, protective, and metabolic in function. We shall now consider a series of highly specialized cells comprising the distinctive cell types of the vascular tissues of the tracheophytes. Among these types is the **tracheid**, a long tapering cell with lignified wall thickenings (secondary wall) laid down in a variety of patterns (Fig. 4.16). The protoplast disappears at maturity.

The tracheid is a dual purpose cell, serving in both conduction and support. The cells occur in groups with much overlapping and in such a way that the pits in walls of adjacent cells are opposite each other. Water passes from cell to cell through the pits. The tracheid's supporting value is related to the wall thickness and the length and arrangement of the cells. The common gymnosperms, such as pine, depend on this cell type for conduction and support. The wood of such trees is

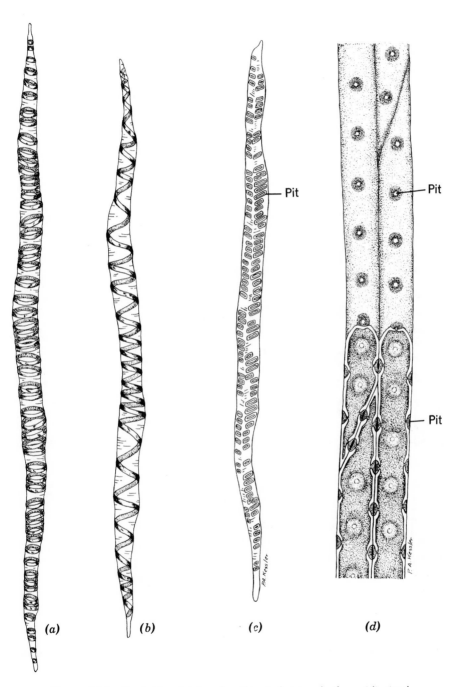

Pit

Pit

Pit

(a)   (b)   (c)   (d)

Figure 4.16. Tracheids. (a) Annular; (b) spiral; (c) scalariform; (d) pitted.

115

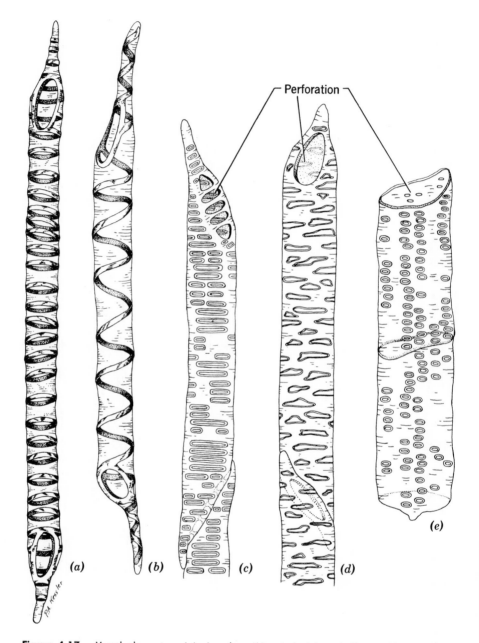

Figure 4.17. Vessel elements. (a) Annular; (b) spiral; (c) scalariform; (d) reticulate; (e) pitted.

composed almost wholly of tracheids. The development of the tracheid was very important in the evolution of terrestrial plants, for it provided the supportive and conductive facility that made possible the evolution of erect, tall stems.

During the long course of evolution, the tracheid gave rise to two other cell types that individually have assumed the tracheid's functions and have largely replaced the tracheid in the most highly evolved vascular plants. One of these, the **vessel element**, was derived through modifications involving slight shortening and widening of the cell and the loss or perforation of the end walls, which gives it an open tubular form (Fig. 4.17). The vessel element wall may be secondarily thickened in any of the patterns shown by the tracheids, and the protoplast is absent at maturity. The vessel elements are arranged end-to-end with little or no overlapping, and thus form a continuous, open pipe-like structure, called the **vessel**. A second evolutionary derivative of the tracheid is the **wood fiber** in which all of the supportive features of the tracheid have been intensified (Fig. 4.14a). The wood fiber is longer than the tracheid and more slender and tapering. It has greater overlapping, more extensive and heavier wall thickening and lignification. Pits are reduced in number and size, or are completely lost. Thus, these two derivatives of the tracheid, the vessel element, and the wood fiber, are complementary and together perform the dual functions of the original tracheid. Vessels and wood fibers together occupy, in function and position, the same place in the most highly evolved vascular plants that the tracheids do in the lower vascular plants.

Whereas the tracheid and the vessel conduct water and dissolved substances from roots to leaves, a structure of different design carries foodstuffs from leaves to roots. In angiosperms the translocation of organic substances takes place through **sieve tubes** (Fig. 4.18). A sieve tube consists of a vertical row of elongated, specialized cells, called **sieve-tube elements**. A distinctive feature is the multiperforate end walls, the **sieve plates**. The cytoplasm of adjacent sieve-tube elements appears to be connected through the pores of the sieve plates. The interconnecting cytoplasmic strands are each surrounded by a thin sleeve of a substance called **callose** where they pass through the sieve-plate pores. The nucleus of the developing sieve-tube element disintegrates as the cell becomes mature although the cytoplasm remains. The **companion cell**, an associate and sister cell of the sieve-tube element, has a dense protoplast and conspicuous nucleus. In gymnosperms, sieve-tube elements and companion cells do not occur; their places are taken by the less specialized **sieve cell** with tapering, overlapping ends and sieve areas mostly on the lateral walls.

It may be understood from the foregoing that the body of the vascular plant is composed of a considerable variety of cell types. These

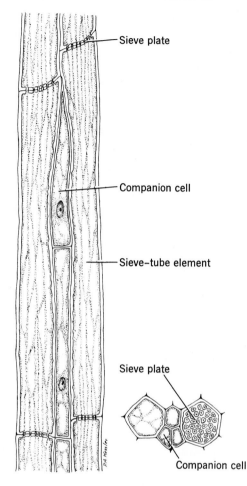

Figure 4.18. Sieve-tube elements and companion cells in longitudinal and cross section.

types are characterized by special form, wall construction, and function. All of these types are the products of cell evolution, having been derived directly or indirectly from unspecialized parenchyma-like cells. Simple plants are composed wholly or mostly of relatively unspecialized cells, whereas highly complex plants are composed of specialized cells of many kinds (4).

The Formation of New Cells

At maturity, the cells composing a stem, root, or leaf of a plant have fairly well-defined maximal sizes. Continued growth of a plant depends, therefore, on a continuous supply of new cells that in their turn become mature.

In an actively growing plant part, such as the tip of a stem or root, the supply of new cells is obtained by the *division* and duplication of existing cells. With respect to the individual cells involved, division is obviously a reproductive operation, but with respect to the plant, it is a part of the growth process. The division of a cell is a complicated two-step process (5). The first step entails the derivation of two nuclei from the original one by a process of replication. This apparent division of the nucleus is called **mitosis** (Fig. 4.19*a–g*). The second step, properly called **cytokinesis** (Fig. 4.19*h–j*), consists of dividing the cytoplasm into two parts, each containing one of the new nuclei, and the formation of a cell wall on the new surface of each new cell. The two new cells thus formed are each about half the size of the parent cell. By the production of new protoplasm and cell wall material and the uptake of water during an ensuing period, the cells grow to the original size. Both of these new cells may repeat the division process, or one or both of them may become specialized. The specialized cells so formed constitute an addition to the basic, permanent tissues of the plant whereas those which remain unspecialized continue to produce new cells. Continued growth of a stem would be possible, of course, only if some unspecialized cells remain. Specialized cells, for the most part, do not divide.

MITOSIS

Mitosis proceeds with great precision and is a very striking phenomenon. At the beginning of mitosis, the apparently tangled and interwoven mass of chromatin threads undergoes a gradual reorganization to give a number of slender threads which promptly shorten and thicken and become discernible as discrete bodies. These chromatin bodies, which quickly become enveloped with a matrix, are the **chromosomes** (Fig. 4.19*b*). The number formed in the nucleus of each root, stem, or leaf cell is characteristic for a given species. For example, the number of chromosomes in cells of the tobacco plant, *Nicotiana tabacum*, is 48. In onion, *Allium cepa*, it is 16. Each chromosome consists of a pair of spirally coiled or closely appressed threads of chromatin, the **chromonemata**, embedded in the chromosomal matrix. Further thickening and shortening of the chromosomes often obscure the distinctness of the chromonemata. It is believed that at this time the chromonemata straighten and lie closely side-by-side. At a point where the chromosome is somewhat constricted, the chromonemata appear to be joined. This specialized point on the chromosome is marked by the

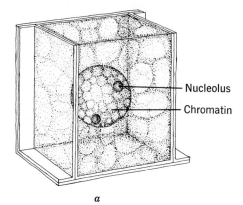

Nucleolus

Chromatin

a

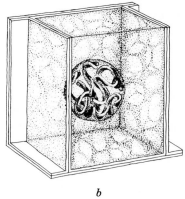

b

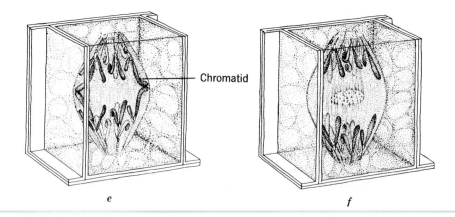

Spindle

Centromere

c

d

Chromatid

e

f

presence of a small hyaline or clear zone, called the **centromere** or **kinetochore** (Fig. 4.19*d*).

In many species of plants, the individual chromosomes of a complement may be identified by their characteristic size and form. Length of the chromosome and position of the centromere are factors in determining chromosome identity. A species may have 16 chromosomes in the cells of its root or stem, but only 8 types may be distinguished. That is, each type is represented by 2 chromosomes (a pair).

The organization of the chromosomes, as described, is accompanied by other significant changes. The first of these is the gradual disappearance of the nuclear membrane. Secondly, there appear in the cytoplasm, at opposite poles of the cell, groups of fine radiating fibers. The fibers gradually extend toward the equator of the cell, and as they do so the nucleoli gradually disappear. Eventually the fibers form a

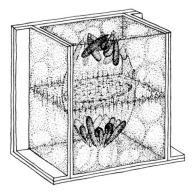

g

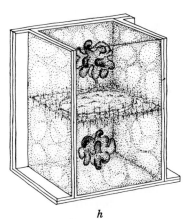

h

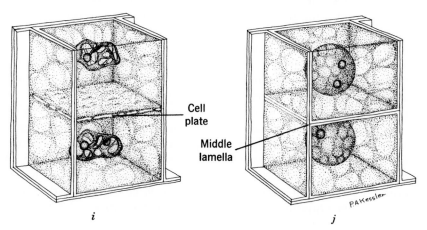

Cell plate

Middle lamella

i

j

Figure 4.19. Mitosis and cytokinesis, diagrammatic; front and top wall removed.

spindle-shaped figure appropriately called the **spindle** (Fig. 4.15c, d). The spindle fibers are believed to be composed of long-chain protein molecules. The chromosomes, now seen clearly to consist of two associated halves, **chromatids,** move to the center of the spindle in such manner that their centromeres come to lie in a horizontal plane at the equator (Fig. 4.19d). Each chromatid contains the chromatin of a single chromonema.

The fibers of the spindle are apparently of two sorts, for some of them extend from pole to pole whereas others extend only from the poles to the equator where they attach to the chromatids at the centromere. By the apparent contraction of the attached fibers, the sister chromatids derived from each chromosome become separated and move to opposite poles (Fig. 4.19e–g). Arrival at the poles is quickly followed by a reconstitution of two new nuclei by reappearance of nuclear membranes and nucleoli and the gradual return of the chromatids (daughter chromosomes) to the thin, thread-like form and tangled disposition (Fig. 4.19h–j). Mitosis is completed when the two new nuclei have been formed.

It should be emphasized that the process just described has brought about an exact duplication of the chromatin of the parent nucleus and its distribution to the new nuclei in equal portions. Each chromatid becomes a fully organized chromosome, and thus each of the two nuclei formed has the same number of chromosomes as the parent nucleus. For this reason mitosis may accurately be called an *equational* nuclear division. Special importance attaches to the precise distribution of the chromatin, for the chromosomes bear, in linear arrangement, the hereditary units or **genes.** Mitosis, therefore, endows each new cell with equal hereditary potentialities. The chromosomes evidently maintain their identities through the period between mitotic divisions, for the same chromosome set reappears in subsequent mitoses. The duplication of the chromatin thread and formation of chromonemata probably occurs during the period just prior to the onset of mitosis, and consists of the synthesis of new deoxyribonucleic acid (DNA) and proteins. Mitotic division is thus equational not only in a quantitative sense, but in a qualitative sense as well.

It is possible to recognize, during the course of mitosis, certain standard configurations. For convenience these phases have been given names. Thus, the early preparatory phase during which the chromosomes are becoming organized as discrete structures is termed the **prophase** (Figs. 4.19a–c, 4.20a). This phase is usually rather prolonged, and presents a series of stages that may be designated **early, mid-** , or **late** prophase. The equatorial position of the chromosomes is the distinctive mark of the **metaphase** (Figs. 4.19d, 4.20b). This phase is generally of relatively short duration, for the chromatids begin to separate almost at

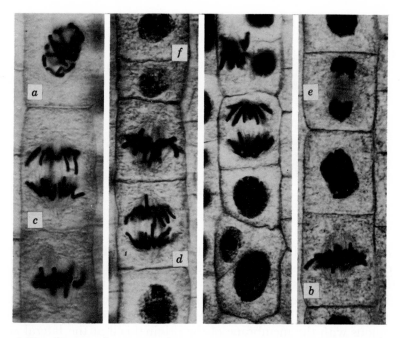

Figure 4.20. Mitosis in the root tip of onion. *a.* late prophase, *b.* metaphase, *c.* ana-phase, *d.* late anaphase, *e.* telophase, *f.* cell division complete.   (Courtesy of Carolina Biological Supply Co.)

once. The period of movement of chromatids from equator to the poles is the **anaphase** (Figs. 4.19*e, f;* 4.20*c, d*). **Early, mid-, and late** anaphases may also be recognized. The final phase of mitosis is signaled by the arrival of the chromatids at the poles of the spindle and their subse-quent change into the diffuse, tangled form of the nondividing nucleus. The changes culminating in the formation of the new nuclei constitute the **telophase** (Figs. 4.19*h, i;* 4.20*e*). Once begun, the mitotic process runs through to completion without pause, although the total time required may vary greatly from cell to cell and from species to species.

CYTOKINESIS

Cytokinesis, or the actual division of the protoplast, usually begins immediately after the completion of mitosis. The fibers of the remain-ing spindle appear to thicken and coalesce in the equatorial region while becoming fainter at their ends (Fig. 4.19*f–h*). Minute vesicles form at the equator and unite to form a thin **cell plate** within the limits of the disappearing spindle (Fig. 4.19*g, h*). As additional fibers are formed in the peripheral zone beyond the spindle, the cell plate is ex-

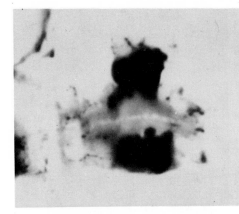

Figure 4.21. Cell plate formation in dividing cell of *Narcissus* root. (Courtesy of E. H. Newcomer.)

tended to the lateral walls (Figs. 4.19*g–i;* 4.21). The cell plate, composed of pectic substances secreted by the dividing protoplast, thus divides the protoplast into two. To what extent or in what manner the spindle fibers may be involved in formation of the cell plate is unknown. Plasma membranes form on the new surfaces thus created and become continuous with the membrane of the original cell at the lateral walls. New cellulose walls are quickly secreted on the outer surface of each new plasma membrane, flanking the pectic layer. The pectic layer, soon modified chemically, becomes an intercellular **middle lamella.** The new walls join the older lateral walls, and as the daughter cells enlarge, the lateral walls break at the edges of the middle lamella, and the daughter cells become complete and physically distinct (Figs. 4.19*j;* 4.20*f*).

The duration of cell division has been found, from studies of living cells with phase microscopy, to vary from several minutes to a few hours, depending on the organism and the kind of cell. The speed of the process is, however, markedly influenced by environmental conditions, notably temperature. At ordinary room temperature most dividing cells of the higher plants complete the process in a period of one to one and a half hours duration.

► ## *Questions*

1. What are some of the consequences of the presence of cell walls in plant cells and their absence from animal cells? Would you regard the cell walls as an essential part of plant cells? Explain your answer.

2. Protoplasm is sometimes defined as the living substance of organisms. What objections might be raised to this definition? Evaluate the following statement: "Protoplasm is a living system composed of nonliving materials." What does it mean and imply? What happens to the protoplasm of a cell when the cell dies?

3. What conclusions about cells of the pith of plants can be drawn from the following facts: (*a*) When numerous small soap bubbles are blown into a glass cylinder most of them become 14-sided. (*b*) When lead shot are placed in a cylinder and subjected to high pressure they become 14-sided. (*c*) The parenchyma cells of the pith are commonly 14-sided. (*d*) Cells of the pith can be separated from the tissue and cultured in nutrient solutions. When this is done the cells are commonly spherical.

4. How many sides would a 14-sided cell appear to have when seen in cross section? How many sides would a 6-sided cell show in cross section? Are all plant cells 6-sided or 14-sided? Would your conclusions in question 3 provide valid explanations for cell shape for all plant cells?

5. The bread mold plant (exclusive of its reproductive structures) consists of long, thread-like filaments (hyphae) containing vacuolated protoplasm with many nuclei but no cross cell walls. Some marine algae (*Valonia*) consist of a spherical structure an inch or more in diameter with a cell wall, cytoplasm, numerous nuclei, and vacuoles. Are plants such as these unicellular or non-cellular? Suppose that in the evolution of life on earth a noncellular pattern of organization had become established rather than the cellular pattern of structural organization that actually did evolve. In what ways would the plants and animals of the earth differ in external appearance from those now present on earth? Could anything comparable to higher organisms such as man or an oak tree have evolved on a noncellular structural basis? Give reasons for your answers.

► ## *References*

For Reference

1. Butler, J. A. V., *Inside the Living Cell*, New York: Basic Books, 1959.
2. Hoffman, J. G., *The Life and Death of Cells*. New York: Doubleday, 1957.
3. Swanson, Carl P., *The Cell*. Englewood Cliffs, N. J.: Prentice-Hall, 1960.

For Reading

4. Baitsell, George A., The cell as a structural unit. *American Scientist* 43:133–141, 1955.
5. Mazia, Daniel, Cell division. *Scientific American* 189(2):53–63, Aug. 1953.

  6. Smith, Cyril S., The shape of things. *Scientific American* 190(1):58–65, January 1954.
  7. Siekevitz, P., Powerhouse of the cell. *Scientific American* 197(1):131–140, July 1957. (Mitochondria)
  8. Sirlin, J. L., The nucleolus of the cell nucleus. *Endeavor* 20:146–153, July 1961.
  9. Ubell, E., New light on the living cell. *Science Digest* 46(4):36–40, October 1959.
  10. Walker, J. J., The chloroplast and photosynthesis—a structural basis for function. *American Scientist* 47:202–215, 1959.
  11. Zamecnik, P. C., The microsome. *Scientific American* 198(3):118–124, March 1958.

5. Tissues and Organs

IN THE DISCUSSION of the types of cells in Chapter 4, it was pointed out that such structural features as size, shape, wall thickness, and plastid types are related to the function of a cell. It will be found, however, upon detailed study of a seed plant body, that these specialized cells rarely serve alone, but are associated and act in conjunction with other cells of the same type. Thus vessel elements are arranged end-to-end, forming a conducting unit of some length. Similarly, fibers in groups lend support quite beyond that possible for a single fiber. Food manufacturing in the plant is performed by masses of chlorophyll-containing cells. Frequently two or more types of cells may be associated in the performance of a general function. Such working aggregations of cells, related in structure or in function, constitute the **tissues** of the plant (1). Tissues are said to be **simple** when they are composed of one type of cell, and **complex** when composed of two or more types.

The tissues occur in certain combinations and in certain spatial relationships in the several major parts or **organs** of the plant: the stems, leaves, roots, and reproductive structures. Each organ has a characteristic form and carries on a major function of the plant. The form and function of the organ are, of course, related to the type and arrangement of its component tissues and cells. It will be seen that the final disposition of all tissues and organs is the result of an orderly and progressive development that begins at the tips of the stem and root.

The continued growth and development of a stem or root depends on a continuous supply of new cells which may ultimately mature and take their places as functioning specialized cells. This supply is provided by the action of a group of perpetually youthful cells at the tips of the

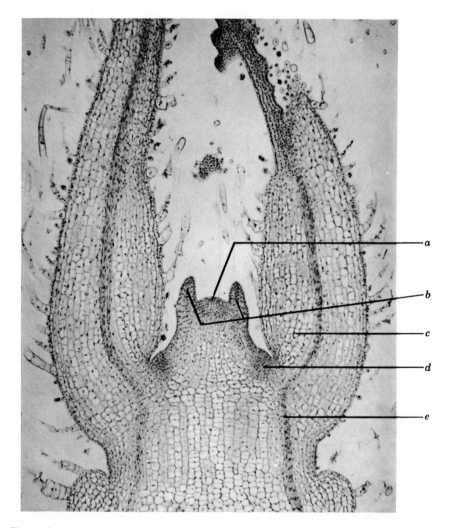

Figure 5.1. Stem tip of Coleus, median longitudinal section. *a.* Apical meristem; *b.* leaf primordia at first node; *c.* young leaf at third node; *d.* lateral bud primordium in axil of young leaf; *e.* provascular strand. (Copyright, General Biological Supply House, Inc., Chicago.)

axis. Such a group of cells constitutes a formative tissue known as a **meristem;** and the cells composing a meristem are **meristematic cells.** A meristem located at the tip of root or stem is called an **apical** meristem to distinguish it from others that occur elsewhere in the plant. The cells of the apical meristem are typically small, densely packed, thin walled, and not conspicuously vacuolate.

The Stem

The production of new cells is accomplished by the division of each meristematic cell into 2 cells, as described in Chapter 4. That the identical new cells may, however, have different fates can be seen by the examination of a median longitudinal section of the growing stem tip (Fig. 5.1). The hemispheric mass of cells at the summit is the apical meristem below which **leaf primordia** occur, the youngest and smallest primordia being at the top. The older and longer primordia typically overlap and envelop the apical meristem. The cells of the leaf primordia are meristematic for a limited time, in contrast with those of the apical meristem. Thus, although the stem tip may grow indefinitely, the leaves of the plant soon reach a maximal size. The place of origin of a leaf primordium upon the stem is called a **node,** and the portion of the stem between two successive nodes is an **internode.** The angle formed by a leaf primordium and the internode above is the **axil** of the leaf, and in this position the primordium of a **lateral bud** normally develops. The lateral, or **axillary,** bud may develop into a branch which duplicates the structure of the main stem.

Elongation of the stem occurs chiefly as the result of the enlargement of the cells of the internodes, beginning just below the first node and extending downward some distance. The "bursting" of the dormant winter buds of woody plants results from the rapid elongation of the internodes as the higher temperatures and increased water availability return in spring.

PRIMARY TISSUES OF THE STEM

The development of the mature stem from the embryonic cells just below the apical meristem proceeds in an orderly manner. One of the first indications of maturation is the differentiation of a one-cell-thick surface layer. This is accomplished by tangential divisions of the surface cells. The outer cells thus produced quickly mature as epidermal cells. Thus early in stem development a protective surface layer is provided. Often a few cell layers interior to the epidermis mature as collenchyma, which helps support the delicate stem tip. In a cross section

129

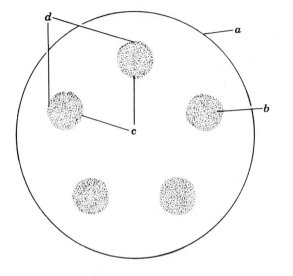

Figure 5.2. Diagram of a cross section of a young stem tip, showing position of: *a*. Epidermis; *b*. provascular strands; *c*. first-formed xylem; *d*. first-formed phloem.

cut a short distance behind the tip, several isolated groups of small cells may be seen arranged in a circle (Fig. 5.2). These groups have been formed by the continued longitudinal division of cells in those areas, and are conspicuous because of the dense cytoplasm and small cross-sectional area of the cells so formed. In a longitudinal section of the stem tip, these groups are seen to be strands of elongated cells—the **provascular strands.** These become the first vascular tissues of the stem by maturation of the cells into several specialized types.

The maturation begins by differentiation occurring first at the outer margins of the strand and somewhat later at the inner margins. Proceeding inward from the point of initiation, the cells of the outer half of the strand mature into sieve-tube elements (with companion cells) or sieve cells and specialized, small parenchyma cells. The provascular cells near the inner margin mature into annular or spiral vessel elements or tracheids, and these are followed successively outward by a sequence of scalariform, reticulate, and pitted members often associated with specialized parenchyma and a few wood fibers.

The differentiated tracheids or vessel elements and associated cells occupying the inner half of the strand constitute the **primary xylem** or **primary wood.** The sieve-tube elements and associated cells make up the **primary phloem.** Primary xylem and primary phloem together constitute the **primary vascular tissue.** With the establishment of the vascular tissue the stem section becomes clearly zoned. The epidermis is underlain by a broad zone of parenchyma cells extending inward to the vascular tissue. This is the **cortex.** Interior to the vascular tissue lies a core of parenchyma, the **pith.** The sheets of radially extended paren-

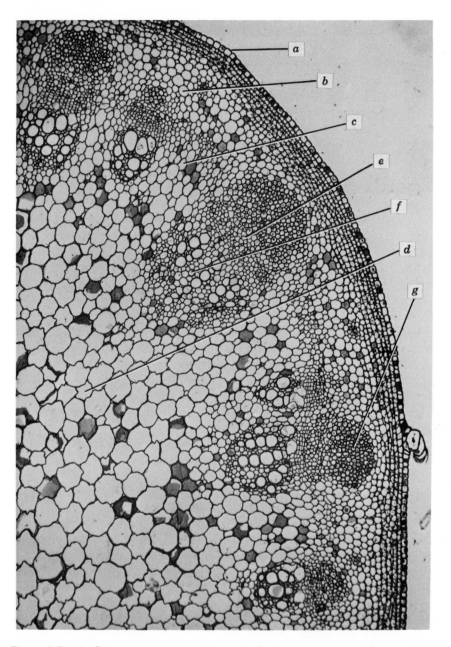

Figure 5.3. Sunflower stem, cross section. *a.* Epidermis; *b.* cortex; *c.* pith ray; *d.* pith; *e.* primary phloem; *f.* primary xylem; *g.* cortical fibers. (Copyright, General Biological Supply House, Inc., Chicago.)

chyma are the **pith rays**. Each strand of vascular tissue, consisting of xylem and phloem, is a vascular bundle (Fig. 5.3). Sometimes the originally isolated provascular strands unite laterally, producing a hollow cylinder that matures as a complete cylinder of primary vascular tissue.

At the nodal regions of the stem, where leaves and branch buds arise, the vascular tissues of the stem connect with those of the leaf and branch bud. The vascular strands leading to leaves and branches are called **leaf traces** and **branch traces**. Where a trace departs from the primary vascular tissue of the stem, it leaves a gap or opening in the vascular cylinder just above its point of departure. The gap is appropriately referred to as a **leaf gap** or **branch gap**. When the gaps are rather tall, extending over more than one internode, or when the internodes are very short, the gaps overlapping at successive nodes dissect the vascular cylinder into many separate bundles, as viewed in a cross section. In secondary growth of stems (to be described in the next section) leaf and branch gaps are closed and buried deeply by the overlay of secondary tissues.

Some species, such as the grasses, possess, in addition to the usual apical meristem, a persistent meristematic zone located at the base of each internode. These **intercalary meristems** may remain active for some time, long after the other parts of the internode have fully matured. Growth of the cells produced by such meristems contributes greatly to the rapid elongation of the stem. Eventually intercalary meristems cease to function and their cells mature into permanent tissues.

The tissues described are called **primary tissues** because they are formed first and directly from cells produced in the growing point of the stem. Many short-lived and delicate annual plants have only these primary tissues.

SECONDARY TISSUES OF THE STEM

The stems of trees and shrubs and also those of the coarser annual plants have a capacity for continued production of tissues beyond the primary ones. This **secondary growth** may be of long duration and account for the continuing increase in diameter of the trunks of trees and stems of shrubs year after year, or it may be short-lived and contribute the "woodiness" to the stem bases of coarse annuals. In perennial stems the stages in the development of the primary tissues are the same as described previously, except that the outward maturation of the primary xylem and the inward maturation of the primary phloem stop short of meeting at the center of the provascular strand. There is thus left between primary xylem and primary phloem a short arc of provascular cells. Upon completion of primary growth, usually during the

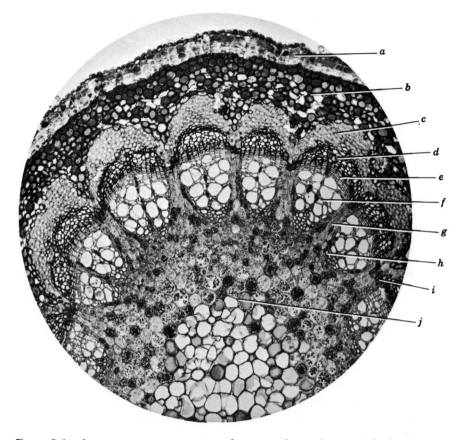

Figure 5.4. Sycamore stem, cross section, first year of growth. *a.* Cork; *b.* cortex; *c.* cortical fibers; *d.* secondary phloem and remnants of primary phloem; *e.* vascular cambium; *f.* secondary xylem; *g.* pith ray; *h.* primary xylem; *i.* interfascicular cambium; *j.* pith. (Copyright, General Biological Supply House, Inc., Chicago.)

first few weeks of a growing season, the residual provascular cells divide actively, and thus become a **secondary meristem** called the **vascular cambium** (Fig. 5.4e). It is a secondary meristem because it arises, after the primary growth is complete, from cells originally formed by the apical meristem. The new cells produced by the division of cambial cells mature as **secondary xylem** elements and as **secondary phloem** elements (Fig. 5.4d, f). Secondary xylem is laid down on the outer side of the primary xylem, and secondary phloem on the inner side of the primary phloem (Fig. 5.4d, h). Of the two cells resulting from the division of a cambial cell, only one matures; its sister cell remains meristematic.

The vessel elements or tracheids of secondary xylem are of the pitted

133

type. Occasional wood fibers and wood parenchyma cells are also produced by cambial action. Sieve-tube elements or sieve cells of the secondary phloem do not differ significantly from those of the primary and are associated with phloem fibers and phloem parenchyma. Secondary xylem elements are typically heavily lignified. They are hard and comparatively incompressible, in contrast to the thin-walled and delicate phloem elements. Spatial adjustments required as a result of the accumulation of secondary vascular tissues would, therefore, be made at the expense of primary phloem which is progressively crushed as new secondary tissues press outward. Primary phloem is thus replaced by secondary phloem (Fig. 5.4d).

As the secondary xylem continues to accumulate, the complete cambium cylinder increases circumferentially by an occasional radial division of some of its cells. Thus, in effect, the cambium moves outward as the secondary xylem increases. The radial extent of the phloem remains about constant since older secondary phloem is crushed by new secondary phloem, just as the primary phloem was crushed by the first-formed secondary phloem.

In stems where primary vascular bundles are separated by pith rays, the sections of vascular cambium within the bundles sometimes become connected by a meristematic strip developing across the ray. These new secondary meristems are **interfascicular**, that is, they lie between the vascular bundles (Fig. 5.4i). In some stems the interfascicular cambium produces more ray tissue, thus lengthening the rays as the vascular bundles increase radially. Such stems would preserve the individuality of the vascular bundles. In other stems, the interfascicular cambium produces secondary xylem and phloem. Thus separate primary vascular bundles may become united by secondary vascular tissues into a continuous cylinder.

Secondary rays, called **vascular rays,** which supplement the pith rays, are also formed by the cambium (Fig. 5.5f). These may be initiated at various points in the secondary xylem and extend outward to or through the phloem. They have limited vertical extent and are like small sheets of parenchyma inserted among the vascular elements (Figs. 5.6, 5.7). Like the pith rays, they are pathways of lateral movement of materials. Starch and crystals frequently accumulate in ray cells.

Only those tissues interior to the cambium are truly permanent, whereas those exterior to it are replaced as growth in diameter of the stem proceeds. Increase in diameter of the perennial stem, therefore, is related directly to the production of secondary xylem. In temperate regions where the seasonal cycle presents periods alternately favorable and unfavorable for growth, the secondary xylem is usually laid down in clearly marked concentric bands. Each band normally represents one year's production of wood and is called an **annual growth**

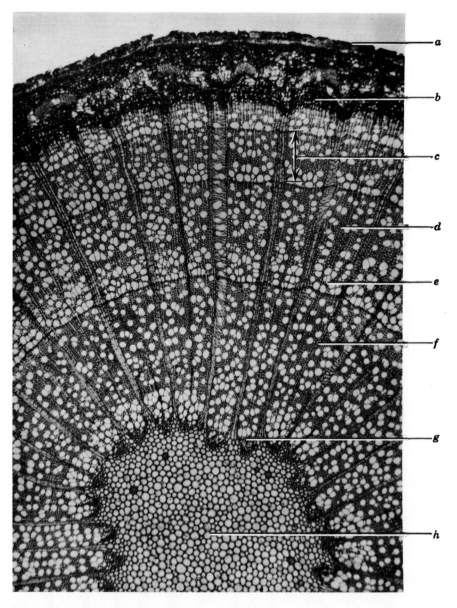

Figure 5.5. Sycamore stem, cross section, in fourth year of growth. *a.* Cork; *b.* secondary phloem; *c.* annual growth ring of third year; *d.* summer wood of second annual growth ring; *e.* spring wood of second annual growth ring; *f.* vascular ray; *g.* primary xylem; *h.* pith. (Copyright, General Biological Supply House, Inc., Chicago.)

135

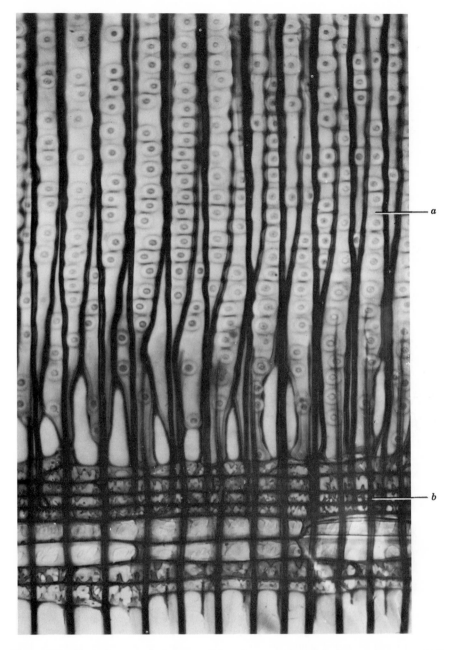

Figure 5.6. Secondary wood of pine, radial section. *a.* Tracheids; *b.* vascular ray. (U.S. Forest Products Laboratory.)

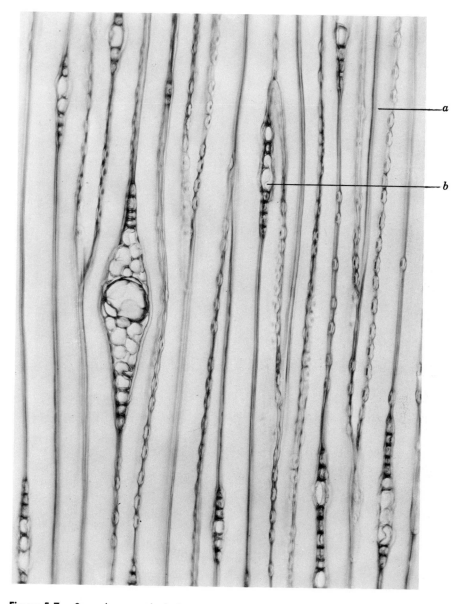

Figure 5.7. Secondary wood of pine, tangential section. *a.* Tracheids; *b.* vascular ray. (U.S. Forest Products Laboratory.)

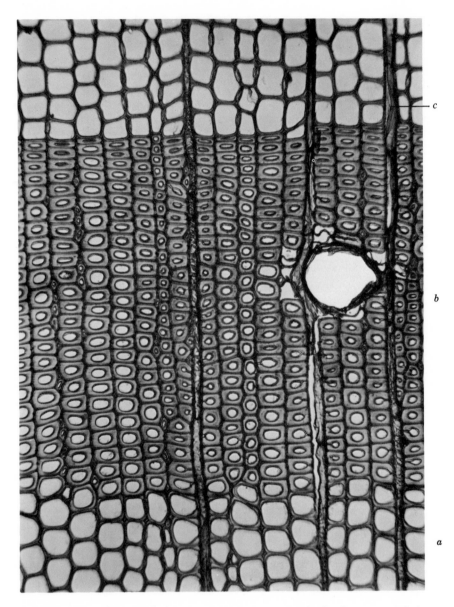

Figure 5.8. Secondary wood of pine, cross section. a. Tracheids of spring wood; b. tracheids of summer wood. c. vascular ray. (U.S. Forest Products Laboratory.)

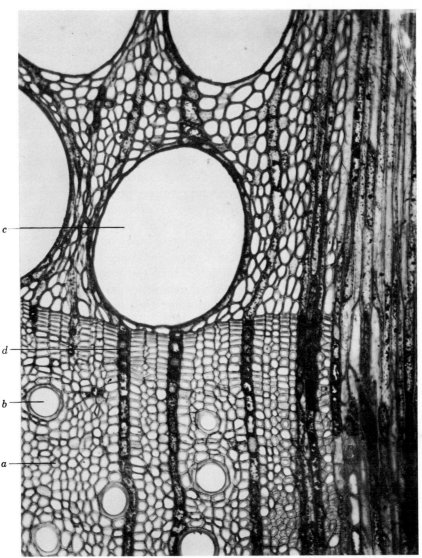

Figure 5.9. Secondary wood of oak, cross section. *a.* Fibers of summer wood; *b.* vessel of summer wood; *c.* vessel of spring wood. *d.* vascular ray. (U.S. Forest Products Laboratory.)

ring (Fig. 5.5*c*). The demarcation of one annual growth ring from another reflects the fact that cambial activity is vigorous in spring, and the prevailing more favorable conditions for cell growth result in xylem elements of larger size than in summer (Fig. 5.9). In gymnosperms, such as pine, the tracheids formed in spring are large, whereas those formed in summer are smaller (Fig. 5.8). In angiosperms, such

139

as oak, the **spring wood** may have a very high proportion of vessels, whereas the **summer wood** has a predominance of wood fibers. Thus the abrupt change in size or type of the cells marks the boundary between summer wood of one year's growth and the spring wood of the next year's. In any one annual growth ring, of course, the spring wood lies interior to the summer wood (Fig. 5.5*d, e*). Annual growth rings are generally absent or indistinct in wood formed in regions where favorable growing conditions prevail throughout the year. The radial widths of annual growth rings and the proportions of spring to summer wood are usually various, reflecting differences in environmental conditions from year to year as the rings were formed by the cambium. Conditions such as drought, low temperature, poor soil aeration, and excessive competition, which adversely affect plant growth are generally reflected in the formation of narrow rings (7, 8).

Although we call each year's production of secondary xylem a "ring," it is, in fact, an open-end cone of xylem, enclosing and extending beyond the cone of the previous year. Thus, the secondary xylem of a tree trunk may be properly visualized as a series of successively longer open-end cones stacked one over another, the longest and outermost being the last formed (Fig. 5.10). Since usually only one growth ring is formed each year, a count of the rings at the base of the trunk, where all rings are present, indicates the age of the tree. The age of a branch may be similarly determined, since, in structure, it duplicates that of the main stem.

Branches originating in the primary stem sometimes die for one reason or another after a few years' growth and break off at the surface of the trunk. The internal section of such branches, extending inward to the primary tissues will be buried ever more deeply by the continued secondary growth of the trunk. The buried, dead branch, hardened by the accumulation of resins, gums, and tannins, will be recognized as a knot in lumber sawed from the trunk.

In most species of trees, conduction of water and dissolved substances by the secondary xylem becomes limited to the outer or younger portion of that tissue as the tree grows older. Usually only a few or several annual growth rings are active in conduction at any one time. This active portion of the xylem is called the **sapwood.** In the older rings, nearer the center of the trunk, the vessels commonly become occluded by the intrusive growth of surrounding parenchyma cells through the pits in the walls of the vessels, and by deposits of gums and resins. The inactive, nonconducting wood is called the **heartwood.** As new sapwood is added each year by the cambium, the older sapwood is converted to heartwood at about the same rate. Thus the radial thickness of the cylinder of sapwood remains fairly constant through the years, and the heartwood increases (10).

140

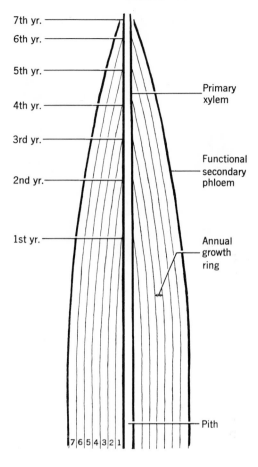

7th yr.
6th yr.
5th yr.
4th yr.
3rd yr.
2nd yr.
1st yr.

Primary xylem

Functional secondary phloem

Annual growth ring

Pith

7 6 5 4 3 2 1

Figure 5.10. Diagram showing position of successive annual growth rings and their relation to other vascular tissues in a perennial woody stem.

In most species of trees, the heartwood undergoes chemical change through the accumulation of a variety of substances, such as resins, oils, gums, and tannins. The accumulation of such materials commonly causes the heartwood to become deeply colored and harder than the sapwood. In Red Cedar, and other species, the deposit of oils and tannins also confers a resistance to decay and insect attack. Red Cedar posts are highly prized for fencing because of this. Planks and beams cut from the heartwood of timber species are stronger and more durable than those cut from the sapwood.

The woods from different species of trees differ greatly in their suitability for specific uses. Density, hardness, flexibility, shock resistance, compression strength, texture, resistance to warping, and checking, are some of the important attributes of wood that may determine its usefulness (Fig. 5.11). These qualities are related to such anatomical features as size, kinds, proportions, arrangement, and wall thickness of the cells

Figure 5.11. Relative density of two kinds of wood. Balsa, right; quebracho, left. (Chicago Natural History Museum.)

composing the secondary xylem. The distinctive grain of woods used for cabinet work and paneling is related mostly to the vertical and radial extent of the vascular rays, the length and straightness of the wood fibers, and the plane in which the log is sawed.

In most woody stems, when the secondary vascular development begins, another secondary meristem arises in the outer part of the cortex. As seen in a transverse section, a continuous or sometimes broken circle of cells of the cortex close to the epidermis or just beneath it become meristematic. Divisions of these cells occur in the tangential plane, the cells cut off on the outside usually maturing as cork cells, in regular radial rows, whereas those on the inside remain meristematic. In some divisions the inner daughter cells mature as parenchyma-like cells, the **phelloderm;** the outer cells remain meristematic. This secondary meristem is the **cork cambium** or **phellogen** (Fig. 5.12*a*, *b*). After several divisions meristematic action stops and a new phellogen arises deeper in the cortex. Cork cells are dead and have suberized walls. Because of the suberized cell walls, the cork layers prevent the passage of water and thus the living epidermis and cortical cells exterior to it dry up and eventually fall away. Ultimately all of the original cortex is lost and the successively deeper layers of cork cambium arise in the older secondary phloem. The smooth surface of compact cork cells on young stems is interrupted in small, commonly lens-shaped areas by masses of soft tissue composed of thin-walled, loosely organized cells. These patches of contrasting tissue, the **lenticels**, are produced by more intensive activity of the phellogen in those areas (Fig. 5.12*c*). The cells formed toward the outside do not mature as normal cork cells. The loose organization of the lenticel tissue is believed to permit aeration of the deeper tissues.

The surface of the cork usually becomes fissured and rough as the growth of the inner part of the stem presses outward, since it is composed of dead cells and thus cannot accommodate by growth. Its rates of production of new cork and sloughing off of old are about equal in mature trees, thus the thickness of the layer, which is fairly characteristic of mature specimens of a given species, remains about constant, ranging from a few millimeters in the beech to several decimeters in the redwoods. As a protective covering tissue, the cork is effective against mechanical impact because of the spongy and elastic qualities of its dead, air-filled cells, and against excessive loss of water from the stem because of its suberized walls. It also has insulating properties and affords some protection against the high temperatures of forest fire. The resilient, fine-textured commercial cork is obtained from the cork oak, *Quercus suber*.

All tissues exterior to the vascular cambium are collectively called the **bark**. Bark is, then, not a tissue in the usual sense, but a composite

Figure 5.12. Cork and lenticel formation. *a.* Cork; *b.* phellogen; *c.* lenticel tissue formed by active phellogen below. (Copyright, General Biological Supply House, Inc., Chicago.)

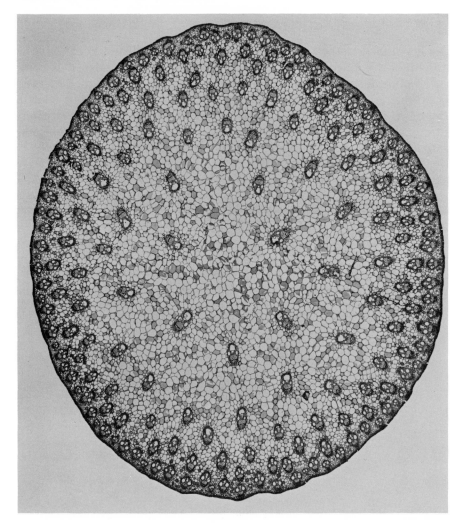

Figure 5.13. Corn stem, cross section, showing scattered vascular bundles. (Carolina Biological Supply Co.)

made up of the functioning phloem, cork cambium, cork, and the inactive remains of older phloem and cortex. The manner in which cork is formed differs in some detail from species to species. This results in the development of distinctive patterns of ridges, splits, and cracks on the outer surface of the bark. The experienced woodsman can identify many trees by the appearance of the bark surface. Even a casual observer can distinguish furrowed barks of trees such as oaks and ashes from barks of birch or cherry that split off in sheets.

HERBACEOUS AND WOODY STEMS

If vascular cambium is absent or cambial activity is limited to the first year, stems are **herbaceous** (page 129–132) rather than woody. The herbaceous stem pattern is thought, in general, to have been de-

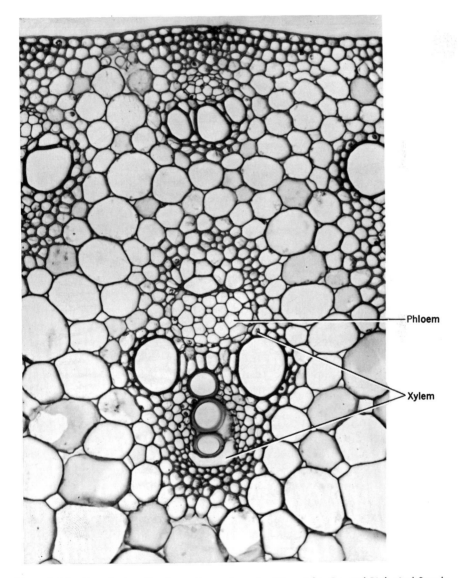

Figure 5.14. Vascular bundle of corn stem, enlarged. (Copyright, General Biological Supply House, Inc., Chicago.)

rived in evolution from the woody, through reduction of the amount of vascular tissue produced. The tissues of an herbaceous stem are similar in composition and arrangement to the primary tissues of a woody stem. All intergradations between extreme woodiness and extreme herbaceousness may be encountered among the dicotyledonous angiosperms. The gymnosperms are generally woody. Among flowering plants, the ultimate in reduction of vascular tissue is found in stems of some monocotyledons. One representative of this group, the stem of corn, shown in cross sectional view in Fig. 5.13, has scattered vascular bundles lacking cambium (Fig. 5.14). All tissues in such stems are primary. The proportion of vascular tissue to soft parenchyma is very small. Cork is absent, of course, in stems consisting wholly of primary tissues.

EXTERNAL FEATURES OF THE STEM

Externally (6) the mature stem reflects the internal development we have just discussed. The **terminal bud** at the apex of the woody stem is a condensed stem closely enveloped by scale-like leaves, the **bud scales** (Figs. 5.15, 5.16). The bud scales are often hairy, tough, or covered with gummy or resinous secretions. The overlapping bud scales effectively protect the delicate enclosed stem tip from desiccation and mechanical injury. We have already noted that in the growing stem tip, the alternation of nodes and internodes gives the stem a jointed appearance. At the nodes two lateral structures occur, namely, a **leaf** and a **lateral bud** (Fig. 5.17) in the leaf axil. The organization of the young stem within the bud was completed toward the end of the previous growing season. The opening of the terminal bud and the early growth of embryonic stem is brought about by enlargement of the cells in the internodal regions, and reflexing of the bud scales. The separation of the bud scales is the result of a rapid rate of growth on the inner faces of the scales, near the bases. Bud scales usually fall promptly after the bud opens, leaving a circle of small thin scars at the points of attachment on the stem. These circles of **bud scale scars** may remain visible on the surface for several years, or until the secondary growth of the stem obliterates them (Fig. 5.15f). Since a terminal bud is formed each year and leaves its scale scars the following spring, the age and rate of elongation of young stems and minor branches may be determined by inspection.

The lateral bud is a rudimentary stem and may develop into a full size branch which matches the main stem in structure and growth potential. Thus as the main stem grows taller, the branches elongate. The oldest, and usually therefore the longest, occur at the bottom of the crown, the youngest at the top. This accounts for the conical or spire-like shape so commonly observed in trees such as the pines, firs,

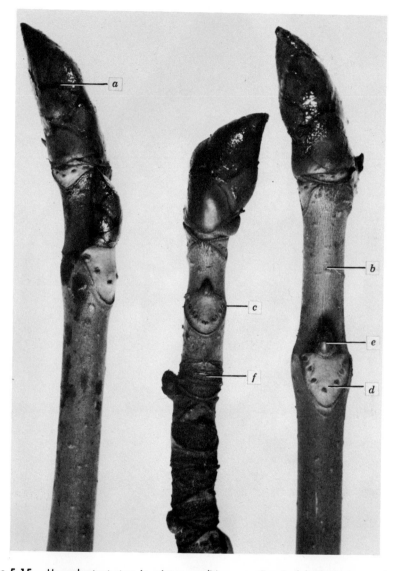

Figure 5.15. Horsechestnut stem in winter condition. *a*. Terminal bud; *b*. internode; *c*. node; *d*. leaf scar; *e*. lateral bud; *f*. bud scale scars. (Copyright, General Biological Supply House, Inc., Chicago.)

Figure 5.16. Horsechestnut, terminal mixed bud, longitudinal section, showing terminal flower cluster and later foliage branches. (Photograph by A. M. Winchester.)

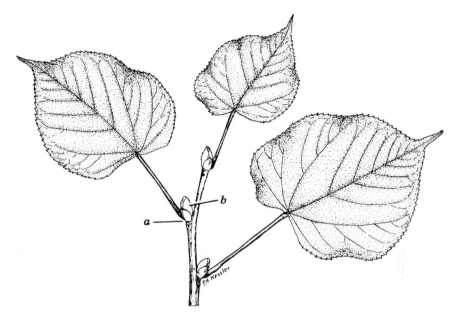

Figure 5.17. Linden stem. *a.* Node; *b.* lateral bud in axil of leaf.

and poplars. In most broad-leaved species, as the tree grows older, the rate of growth of the main stem diminishes and the branches grow more vigorously. In time the branches equal or overtake the main stem and thus produce a rounded or irregular crown (Fig. 5.18).

SPECIALIZED STEMS

The stems of many species of angiosperms are highly specialized and sometimes bear little resemblance to ordinary stems. Stems of most species of cactus, bearing reduced spine-like leaves, are expanded and green and function as the photosynthetic organs of the plant. Cactus stems store large quantities of water. The creeping stems of strawberry, **stolons,** develop new plants where the nodes rest upon the soil. The strawberry may be vegetatively propagated by setting out the small plantlets. The leaves of iris are borne at the ends of a fleshy underground stem called a **rhizome.** The **tuber** of the potato is a shortened subterranean stem whose nodes are marked by the "eyes." Each "eye" is a branch bud standing in the axil of a reduced scale-like leaf. Considerable food, mostly starch, accumulates in the tuber and is consumed by the growing sprout (branch bud) when the "seed pieces" are used for vegetative propagation. The use of stems and other plant parts in vegetative propagation is discussed in Chapter 15. The **thorns** of

149

Figure 5.18. Maple with rounded crown typical of most broad leaf species. (Photograph, courtesy of Louise Keppler.)

hawthorn are normally leafless branches situated in a leaf axil. Stems may be greatly elongated and twining and thus serve as a supporting device, as in morning glory, or support may be provided by modification into tendrils as in grape vine.

150

The Leaf

The growth of leaf primordia and small leaves at the stem tip into mature organs takes place rapidly after the opening of the terminal bud. Division, enlargement, and maturation of the leaf cells occur fairly uniformly throughout the structure, so that by the time the leaf is fully grown, all of its tissues are mature. A conspicuous vascular strand commonly occupies the central part of the leaf and constitutes the main or **mid-vein**. From the mid-vein, smaller **secondary veins** depart. As a leaf is seen in cross section, the kinds of tissues present and their arrangement suggest a strongly flattened primary stem. The mid-vein is continuous with the vascular cylinder of the stem. The vascular tissue of the leaf consists of primary xylem and primary phloem, with the phloem typically on the lower side. The vein is commonly surrounded by a mass of parenchyma, sometimes with small amounts of collenchyma or fibrous tissue above and below. The parenchyma, which contains many chloroplasts, makes up the major part of the leaf's bulk. It is called the **mesophyll** and is the chief food manufacturing tissue of the plant. Two layers of the mesophyll may commonly be distinguished. The upper layer, composed of one or more rows of vertically elongated cells, is the **palisade layer**. The lower layer of spherical or irregular, loosely associated cells is the **spongy layer** (Fig. 5.19).

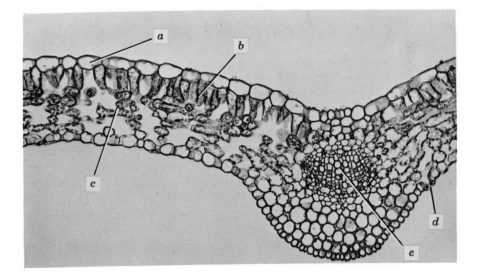

Figure 5.19. Leaf cross section showing usual mesomorphic features: *a.* Epidermis with thin cuticle; *b.* palisade layer of mesophyll; *c.* spongy layer of mesophyll; *d.* stoma flush with surface; *e.* midvein. (Copyright, General Biological Supply House, Inc., Chicago.)

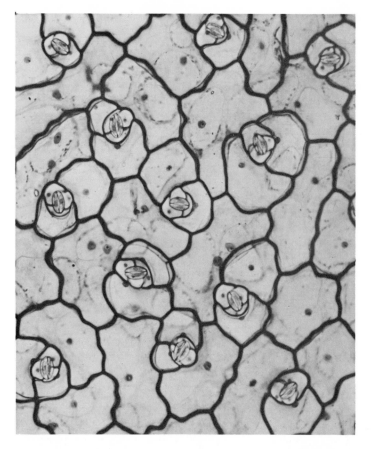

Figure 5.20. Epidermis of *Sedum* leaf, surface view, showing stomata partially closed. Note small subsidiary cells surrounding each pair of guard cells. (Copyright, General Biological Supply House, Inc., Chicago.)

Surrounding the whole leaf is the **epidermis** (4), which is continuous over all surfaces of the leaf and with the epidermis of the young stem. Epidermal cells are typically without chloroplasts. Those on the lower side of the leaf are usually smaller than those on the upper side. Dispersed among the epidermal cells are small pores called **stomata** (singular, **stoma**). Stomata are intercellular channels through which gases diffuse between the atmosphere and the interior of the leaf. The stomata communicate with large intercellular spaces among the cells of the mesophyll. If a strip of leaf epidermis is removed and examined under the microscope, each stoma is seen to be flanked by a pair of crescent shaped cells containing chloroplasts. These are the **guard cells** whose slight alteration in shape, through changes in their water

TABLE 5.1. NUMBER OF STOMATA PER SQUARE INCH OF LEAF SURFACE

Leaf	Upper Surface	Lower Surface
Scarlet oak	0	650,000
Black walnut	0	287,500
Apple	0	190,000
Oats	15,625	14,375
Kidney bean	25,000	110,000
Corn	48,000	59,000
Bluegrass	100,000	65,000
Alfalfa	109,000	89,000

content, regulate the size of the stomatal opening (Fig. 5.20). Stomata may occur on either or both surfaces of leaves, although in a given species the distribution is fairly characteristic. Table 5.1 shows the distribution and density of stomata in some common species.

The leaves of some species adapted to dry habitats commonly show a variety of **xeromorphic modifications** that tend to conserve water. In such forms the cuticle is thick, the stomata are depressed well below the general leaf surface, and the leaf is often thick and fleshy (Fig. 5.21).

In gross structure the leaf typically consists of a flat, expanded **blade** supported on a slender **petiole**, or sometimes **sessile** and attached directly to the stem (Fig. 5.24*b,c*). A system of veins, the vascular

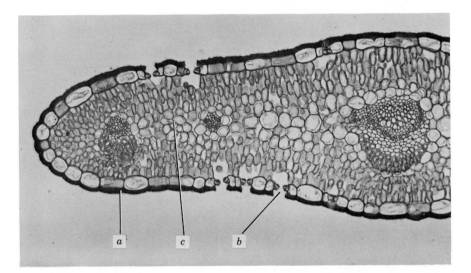

Figure 5.21. Leaf of *Dianthus*, cross section showing xeromorphic features: *a.* Heavy cuticle; *b.* sunken stomata; *c.* compact, poorly differentiated mesophyll. (Copyright, General Biological Supply House, Inc., Chicago.)

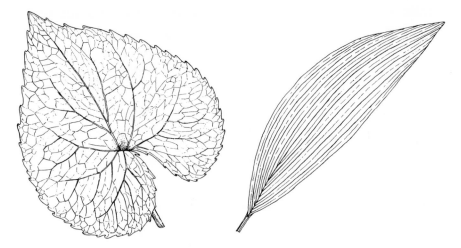

Figure 5.22. Common patterns of leaf venation: left, palmate-netted; right, parallel. See also Fig. 5.24a, pinnate.

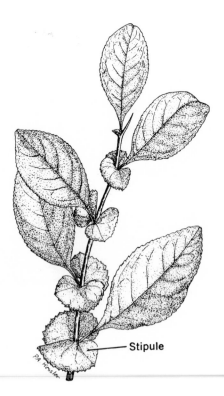

Stipule

Figure 5.23. Stipules of quince.

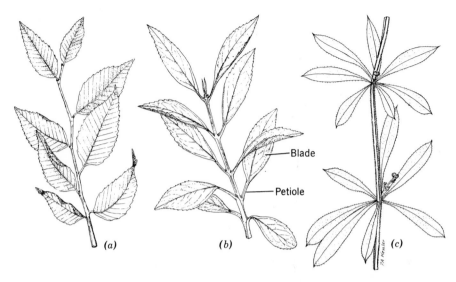

Figure 5.24. Leaf arrangements: (*a*) alternate, one leaf at a node; (*b*) opposite, two leaves at a node; (*c*) whorled, three or more leaves at a node.

supply of the leaf, traverses the blade in a variety of characteristic patterns (Figs. 5.22, 5.24*a*). Two small, leaf-like appendages, the **stipules,** may be present at the base of the leaf in some species (Fig. 5.23). One or more leaves may be borne at a node, giving arrangements called **alternate, opposite,** or **whorled** (Fig. 5.24). When the blade

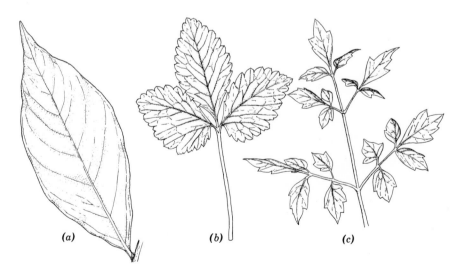

Figure 5.25. Common leaf forms: (*a*) simple; (*b*) palmately compound; (*c*) bipinnately compound.

155

is a single piece, the leaf is **simple**, when it is subdivided into free **leaflets**, it is **compound** (Fig. 5.25). Some common leaf shapes (2) and types of leaf margins are shown in the figures cited. These gross features of the leaf are generally characteristic of a species and are helpful in plant identification.

The majority of broad-leaved trees and shrubs produce a new crop of leaves each spring and lose them in the autumn. Such plants are described as **deciduous**. The profound effect of annual leaf fall upon the landscape in forested areas is one of the most striking aspects of plant behavior. Important factors in initiating leaf fall are thought to be shortening of the days and reduced water availability, resulting in a

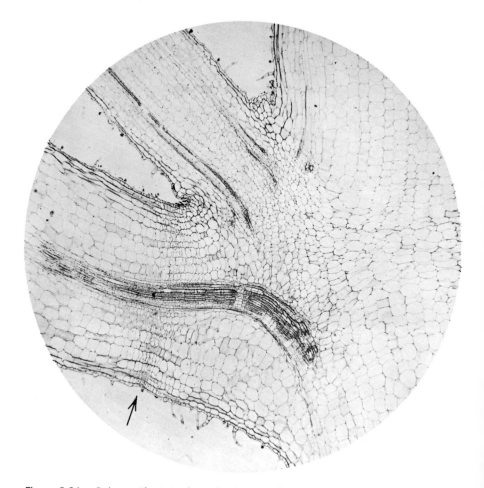

Figure 5.26. *Coleus.* Abscission layer developing in base of petiole. Note small branch in leaf axil. (Copyright, General Biological Supply House, Inc., Chicago.)

decrease in growth hormone production. Under these conditions a special layer of weak, thin-walled cells, called the **abscission layer,** develops across the petiole at its base (Fig. 5.26). This layer soon disintegrates, leaving only the vascular tissues of the petiole supporting the leaf. Air currents and the action of frost may cause the vascular tissue to break, and the leaf falls. Prior to leaf fall, however, a layer of cork develops below the abscission layer and seals the leaf scar. A few species, such as the white oak, are unusual in this respect for, although its leaves die in autumn, they remain attached to the stems, often throughout the winter. This behavior results from the absence of an abscission layer and failure of the vascular tissues to break.

The leaves of **evergreens** may persist on the plant for a few years but are eventually shed, although not all at one time. New leaves are produced each year.

Striking changes in leaf color often precede leaf abscission. It will be recalled that chloroplasts contain, in addition to the green chlorophylls, yellow and orange pigments. Chloroplasts are green because the chlorophyll predominates. In autumn new chlorophyll production ceases and as the chlorophyll decomposes, the yellow and orange pigments are revealed (9). In this manner the brilliant golden hues of the hickories, tulip trees, and some maples appear. The hard maples, sweetgums, and dogwoods turn vivid red in autumn. The red coloration is attributable to the development of **anthocyanins** in the vacuoles of the leaf cells. High sugar content of the leaves appears to be conducive to anthocyanin production. Abrupt lowering of temperature reduces the rate of sugar removal from the leaves, and thus may serve as a factor in anthocyanin formation.

SPECIALIZED LEAVES

Many peculiar and interesting structural and functional specializations of leaves may be found among the angiosperms. These specialized leaves are often quite unlike ordinary leaves, and may perform functions additional to or in place of photosynthesis. Probably the most interesting specializations are those of the leaves of the insectivorous plants. The pitcher plant, Venus' flytrap, and the sundew are examples. Although the leaves of these plants are green and photosynthetic, they supplement the usual food supply by catching, digesting, and absorbing portions of the bodies of insects. Insects crawl into the pitchers of the pitcher plant and fall to the bottom where they are drowned in water containing protein-digesting enzymes (Fig. 5.27). The leaf of the Venus' flytrap folds up quickly when sensitive hairs on the surface are touched by crawling insects (Fig. 5.28). The insect,

Figure 5.27. Pitcher plant, *Sarracenia*. (Copyright, General Biological Supply House, Inc., Chicago.)

Figure 5.28. Venus' flytrap, *Dionaea*. The trap is sprung. (Photo courtesy of Carolina Biological Supply Co.)

Figure 5.29. Sundew, *Drosera.* (Copyright, General Biological Supply House, Inc., Chicago.)

unable to escape because of the interlocking spines on the leaf margin, is digested by enzymes secreted by the leaf cells. The sundew leaf bears a large number of gland-tipped tentacles which curl over the insect and smear it with a mucilaginous digestive secretion (Fig. 5.29).

Specialized leaves frequently serve as storage organs, protective and supporting devices, and reproductive structures. Thick, fleshy leaves, as in the popular "hen-and-chickens" and *Portulaca*, store a large volume of water in their cells. Many plants of this type are well adapted to dry habitats. The fleshy bulb scales of the onion store food and water which are consumed in the development of the flowering stem in the second season (Fig. 5.30*b*). The enclosing scales of dormant buds are much reduced, tough-textured leaves providing a protective cover for the growing point of the stem. The spines of the common barberry are modified leaves whose axils bear short leaf-bearing branches (Fig. 5.30*a*). The terminal leaflets of the compound leaf of vetch and garden pea are reduced to tendrils useful for support (Fig. 5.30*c*). Many

159

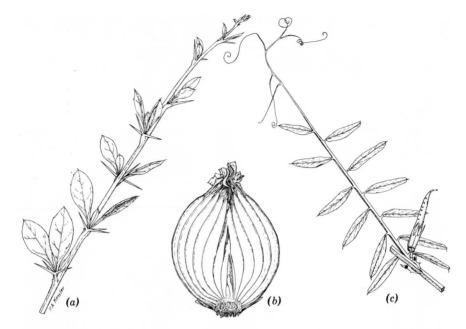

Figure 5.30. Modified leaves: (a) barberry thorns; (b) onion bulb scales; (c) tendrils of vetch.

members of the fleshy-leaved stone-crop family may be vegetatively propagated by merely placing a leaf upon the soil. Roots quickly grow from the broken leaf base and a new plant is thus started. The well-known *Kalanchoë* of the same family produces small plantlets, complete with roots, stems, and leaves, in the notches of the leaf margin (Fig. 12.15). These small plants fall to the ground and become established.

The Root

The third major vegetative organ of the seed plant is the **root**. Situated typically below ground, it commonly escapes attention, yet it is an integral part of the total plant, performing a number of important functions. Indeed, the root is the first part of the young growing plant to establish intimate contact with the environment as the seed germinates and is thus part of a critical relationship in the establishment of the new plant. Throughout the life of the plant, the root system anchors the plant in the soil and absorbs water and soluble minerals.

The apical meristem of the root, unlike that of the stem, is covered by a conical **root cap** of parenchyma cells, which provides mechanical protection to the apical meristem as the root grows forward through the soil (Fig. 5.31a, 5.32a). The outer cells of the root cap are worn away as the root grows, but are replaced by new cells formed by the apical meristem (Fig. 5.32).

New cells destined to become part of the primary tissues of the root are also produced by the apical meristem. These cells undergo a period of enlargement, chiefly elongation, and finally mature into specialized cells. Although the sequence of events is essentially the same as that described for the growing stem, it is somewhat more easily seen in the root. Roots have no nodes and internodes, and the structural complications arising in the stem from the presence of young leaves and buds and the departure of vascular traces to them are, of course, absent. Thus the growing root tip, when viewed in median longitudinal section, shows clearly the terminal region of **new cell forma-**

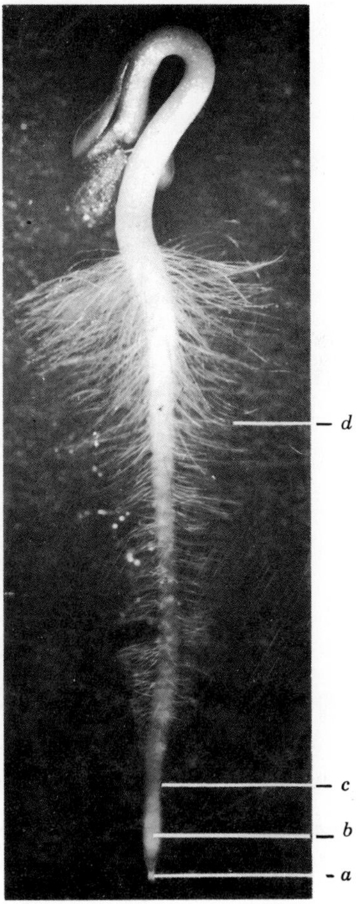

Figure 5.31. Growing root tip of radish, *Raphanus sativus.* a. Root cap; b. region of new cell formation; c. region of cell elongation; d. region of root hairs. (Robbins, Weir and Stocking, *Botany*, John Wiley & Sons, Inc.)

161

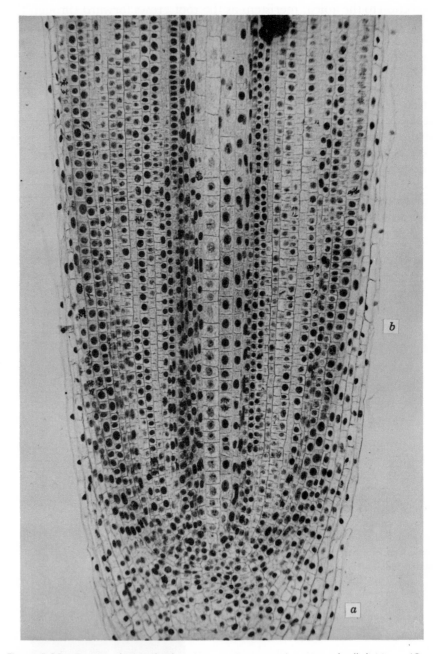

Figure 5.32. Root tip, longitudinal section. *a.* Root cap; *b.* region of cell division. (Copyright, General Biological Supply House, Inc., Chicago.)

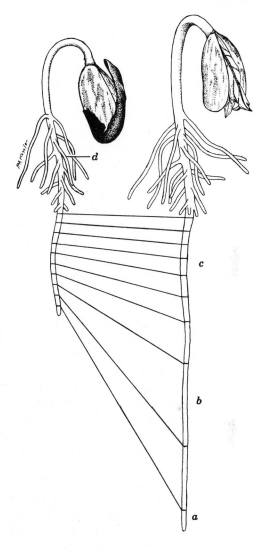

Figure 5.33. Distribution of growth in roots. *a.* Region of new cell formation; *b.* region of cell enlargement; *c.* region of cell maturation; *d.* secondary roots.

tion covered by the root cap, a second region of **cell enlargement,** and a third region of **cell maturation** (Figs. 5.32, 5.33).

The outermost cell layer of the young root is the epidermis. It must be noted, however, that the epidermal cells of the root are not cutinized as are those of the stem. The epidermis, therefore, may serve as an absorbing surface. Just behind the region of enlargement (Fig. 5.31*b*), most of the epidermal cells develop a hair-like protuberance on the outer surface, thus effecting a tremendous increase in absorbing surface (Fig. 5.31*c*). These outgrowths, called **root hairs,** are actually ex-

163

tensions of the epidermal cells, and as they grow outward the cells become highly vacuolate, the nucleus commonly occupying a terminal position in the growing hair. As the root tip grows forward, new root hairs are produced. Older root hairs collapse and die at about the same rate that new ones are produced, their period of activity usually being limited to a few days. In their outward growth the hairs penetrate the soil to a maximal distance of about one-half inch and become closely applied to the surface of soil particles. The extreme delicacy of the root hairs makes it practically impossible to remove a plant from the soil without destroying most of them, unless a large ball of soil is taken up with the plant. In the transplanting of trees and shrubs, it may not be practical to try to preserve this intimate root-soil relationship. Therefore, reliance must be placed on the ability of the plant to promptly develop absorbing surfaces by producing new root tips. In general, it is true that the less the roots are disturbed, the better the chances of survival after transplantation.

The pattern of maturation of the internal tissues of the root offers some interesting points of contrast with that of the stem. Although the same cell types and tissues are involved, certain differences of arrangement must be noted. In early maturation a circle of separate provascular strands arises. In gymnosperms and the dicotyledonous angiosperms, alternate strands become extended inwardly and laterally until they meet at the center and form a rayed or star-shaped figure, as seen in cross-sectional view. Between the points of the star are situated the other alternate set of provascular strands. The star-shaped figure represents, of course, a fluted column. Final maturation begins at the points of the star with the conversion of the provascular cells to tracheids or vessel elements, and continues inwardly, ultimately forming a solid column of primary xylem (Fig. 5.34c). At the same time maturation of the remaining provascular strands yields primary phloem (Figs. 5.34b, 5.35e). In the monocotyledonous angiosperms, the primary xylem is limited to separate radiating lines of vessels (Fig. 5.35d). It will be noted that the alternating or radial arrangement of primary xylem and primary phloem is in contrast to the so-called collateral arrangement seen in the stem (Fig. 5.3). Note also that the primary xylem begins its maturation on the outer margin of the provascular strands in the root, whereas it begins on the inner margin in the stem. Where the primary xylem development extends to the center, there is, of course, no pith.

Immediately exterior to the primary vascular tissue is a narrow zone of parenchyma cells, called the **pericycle** (Fig. 5.34d). From this layer, at positions immediately exterior to the first-formed xylem, branch roots arise by localized meristematic action. The newly developing branch roots thus arise internally and push outward through the cortex

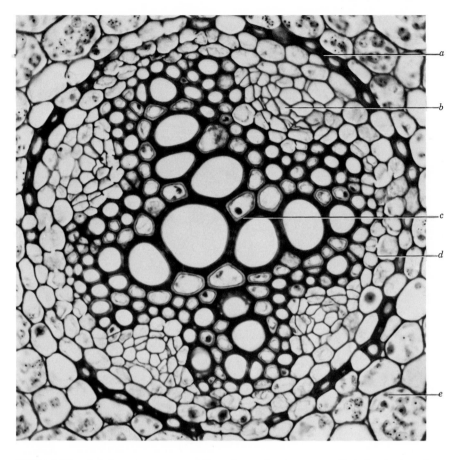

Figure 5.34. Buttercup root, cross section of vascular tissues. *a.* Endodermis; *b.* primary phloem; *c.* primary xylem; *d.* pericycle; *e.* cortex. (Photo courtesy of Carolina Biological Supply Co.)

and epidermis. The origin of branch roots should be compared with that of stem branches. The latter, it will be recalled, arise superficially and the departure of branch and leaf traces leave gaps or openings in the vascular cylinder.

The pericycle of the root is separated from the broad cortex by a single, almost complete layer of small cells, the **endodermis** (Figs. 5.34*a*, 5.35*c*). The endodermal cells have, most commonly, thickened and suberized radial walls. The endodermis is generally interpreted as the innermost layer of the cortex and is believed to function in the passage of absorbed substances from the cortex to the conducting elements of the xylem, but the manner of its action is not understood. The cortex

165

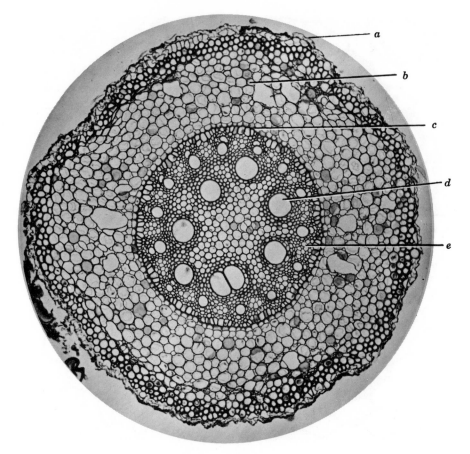

Figure 5.35. Corn root, cross section. *a.* Epidermis; *b.* cortex; *c.* endodermis; *d.* primary xylem; *e.* primary phloem. (Copyright, General Biological Supply House, Inc., Chicago.)

of the root is similar to that of the stem, except that it usually has no chloroplasts (Fig. 5.35*b*). The epidermis, as we have noted, is the outermost tissue, serving most importantly as the absorption surface (Fig. 5.35*a*).

Secondary growth in roots is effected by the action of a vascular cambium arising partly from residual provascular cells in the bays between the primary xylem arms and partly from cells of the pericycle at the ends of the arms. Production of secondary xylem begins earlier in the bays, and this action soon rounds out the cambium circle. Thereafter secondary phloem and xylem are produced as in woody stems. Continued secondary growth results in rupture and eventual loss of endodermis, cortex and epidermis.

Cork tissue is developed from a phellogen originating initially in the pericycle, and later from the older phloem. The cork fissures and sloughs off in the same manner as in the stem. Corky surfaces, of course, permit little or no absorption, therefore absorption of water and minerals occurs chiefly in the younger portions of the root tips.

The root emerges from the germinating seed as a cylindrical structure. This is the first, or **primary root**. After a period of growth, small branch roots, originating in the pericycle, may be produced from it at points above (behind) the zone of root hairs. These branch roots are called **secondary roots** (Fig. 5.33*d*), the word secondary here referring to the time of their appearance. Secondary roots may soon produce branches of their own, and so on until an elaborate root system is developed. If, in this process, the original or primary root remains dominant, the root system is described as a **tap root system**. In some species the primary root quickly loses dominance by exaggerated growth of several secondaries, all of which are of about the same size. The root system thus takes on a spreading form and is known as a **diffuse root system**. The individual roots of either the tap or diffuse systems may remain slender and become tough and woody through secondary growth, or they may become very thick and fleshy. The roots of carrot

Figure 5.36. Adventitious roots of *Pandanus*. (Chicago Natural History Museum.)

and *Dahlia* are examples of fleshy tap root and fleshy diffuse root respectively.

Roots frequently arise from plant parts other than primary roots or their branches. Such roots are called **adventitious** (Fig. 5.36). Adventitious roots may arise at higher points on the stem and, as in the English ivy, provide the means of clinging to vertical surfaces. Propagation of household plants, such as geraniums, *Coleus*, and many others, is made possible by the production of adventitious roots at the base of stem cuttings. African violets are commonly propagated by leaf cuttings from which adventitious roots and buds grow. The roots of potato plants grown from pieces of "seed" potato are also of adventitious origin, since the potato tuber is a rhizome, or modified stem. Many species of grass spread widely by the growth of slender rhizomes just beneath the soil surface, the roots arising adventitiously at the nodes of the rhizome. The Irish potato is a rhizome, whereas the sweet potato is a true root.

The Flower

So far in this chapter we have dealt with the vegetative tissues and organs of vascular plants. In most species the orderly vegetative development described culminates in the formation of characteristic reproductive organs. Reproduction by means of seeds is a complicated process involving complex and highly specialized structures. In angiosperms, seeds are produced on specialized stems or branches called **flowers.** Flowers differ in size, shape, color, arrangement, number of parts, and in many other features and yet have much in common in their basic structural plan (Fig. 5.37). The many kinds of flowers owe their variety to specialization of their parts.

The typical floral parts are attached in characteristic fashion to a short axis, the **torus** (sometimes called the **receptacle**). Typically four kinds of floral parts are borne upon the torus, always in the same order. Beginning at the base of the flower, we may find a circle or whorl of **sepals.** These are most commonly green and quite leaf-like and sometimes very small. However, they are large and white or brightly colored in some well-known plants, such as lily. All of the sepals together constitute the **calyx.**

Next above the calyx is a whorl of conspicuous **petals**, often white or colored. These make up the **corolla** and are usually the most conspicuous part of the flower. The beauty of a rose or a morning glory is due to the color and form of the corolla. In some species the corolla may be absent and the calyx may be the conspicuous member, as in the anemone. Or, the calyx, as well as the corolla, may be colored and dis-

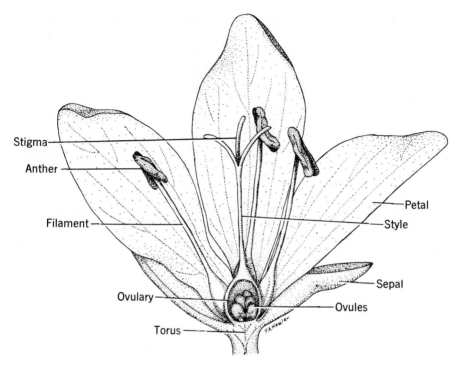

Figure 5.37. Semidiagram of generalized dicotyledonous flower in longitudinal section. Only three of the five petals, stamens, and stigma lobes are shown.

tinguishable from the corolla only by its position on the torus. The popular Christmas plant, *Poinsettia*, the flowering dogwood, and the calla lily are deceptive to the casual observer, for the conspicuous petal-like members are not parts of the flower at all, but specially modified leaves or **bracts** which surround a whole cluster of very small and inconspicuous flowers.

The filamentous or sometimes club-shaped structures occurring above the corolla are the **stamens**. Each consists of an **anther** at the tip of a slender stalk or **filament**. **Pollen** is produced in the anthers. The complement of stamens is often arranged in two whorls when the number is twice that of the petals, or in one whorl when the number is the same or less. Figure 5.38 shows an interesting condition in *Nymphaea*, a waterlily, where intergradations between typical petals and stamens exist. The separate members shown here occur along a radius of the flower.

The topmost or central position of the flower is occupied by the **pistil**, a flask-shaped structure with an enlarged basal part called the **ovulary**, above which extends a slender neck, the **style**, surmounted by a

169

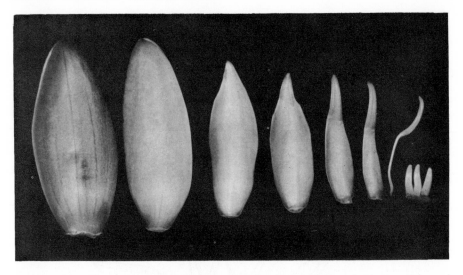

Figure 5.38. Flower parts of *Nymphaea*, showing intergradations between petals and stamens. (Copyright, General Biological Supply House, Inc., Chicago.)

somewhat enlarged tip, the **stigma**. The flowers of some species have more than one pistil (Fig. 5.42). The pistil, and more especially the ovulary, often shows external ridges or grooves which suggest that it is composed of united parts. When these parts are separated, they commonly have a form suggesting small, modified leaves that have united by their edges. The leaf-like components of the pistil are **carpels**. The pistil may consist of one carpel as in the bean or pea, when the pistil is said to be **simple**, or it may consist of more than one as in lily or mallow, when it is called **compound**. The cavity of the ovulary contains one or more **ovules** (future seeds) attached to a **placenta** (Fig. 5.39).

All flowers are essentially alike in their basic architecture. However, a wide variety of structural modification can be seen. For example, the

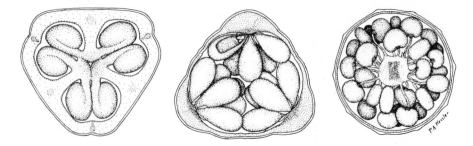

Figure 5.39. Patterns of ovule arrangement in ovularies of lily, violet, and chickweed.

Figure 5.40. Pistillate flowers of willow. Each cluster (catkin) bears many flowers each consisting only of a pistil. (Photograph, courtesy of Louise Keppler.)

Figure 5.41. Staminate flowers of willow. Each catkin bears many flowers each consisting only of two stamens. (Photograph, courtesy of Louise Keppler.)

petals are often fused, producing a saucer-like or bell shaped corolla, as in the African violet or morning glory, whereas in the pinks the sepals are fused and the petals are distinct.   In hibiscus and in legumes, the stamens are more or less fused into a tube surrounding the pistil.   Sometimes the stamens are attached to the upper surface of the petals, so they appear to arise from them, as in primrose.   In apple and pear, the pistil is partly imbedded in the torus and the fused stamens, petals, and sepals appear to originate from the top of the ovulary.   In many species certain' flower parts may be characteristically lacking, as in willow (Fig. 5.40, 41), which has neither calyx nor corolla, or *Hepatica*, which has a conspicuous, brightly colored calyx but no corolla (Fig. 5.42).   In corn and squash and many other species, the flowers are unisexual, having either stamens or pistils, but not both.   The staminate flowers of

Figure 5.42.   Flower of Hepatica.   Note many free monocarpellate pistils and many stamens.   (Photograph, courtesy of J. Arthur Herrick.)

corn are in the tassels, the pistillate flowers in the ears. In many species having unisexual flowers, such as willow, the staminate and pistillate flowers occur on separate plants (Figs. 5.40, 41). Such details, along with others, are used in the identification of flowering plants, and when considered in the light of certain established principles, make possible the arrangement of species in systems of classification expressing a possible evolutionary history of flowering plants.

The pistils and stamens of the flower are often called the **essential organs**, for they are the ones directly involved in seed production, although the corolla and the calyx may be useful in indirect ways.

Flowers are borne upon a plant in a characteristic arrangement known as the **inflorescence**. The inflorescence may consist of a solitary flower borne at the summit of an unbranched stalk, as in tulip, or of many flowers borne singly in the axils of reduced leaves along an elongated stem, as in snapdragons (Fig. 17.11) and lily of the valley. The stem may be profusely branched forming a large open cluster, as in lilac and many grasses, or extremely shortened with the flowers crowded into compact clusters of various shapes, as in clover, milkweed, and willow (Figs. 5.40, 41). The degrees and patterns of branching of the infloresence axis and the relative lengths of the individual flower stalks (pedicels) account for the great variety of inflorescence types. The tassels of corn plants are inflorescences of staminate flowers and the ears are inflorescences of pistillate flowers, each grain with its silk constituting an individual pistillate flower (Fig. 17.14). In the very compact flower heads (Fig. 17.12) of members of the sunflower family, the inflorescence often consists of two kinds of flowers. In some, like sunflowers and daisies, the center flowers have very small tubular corollas, and the marginal ones have enlarged strap-shaped corollas (rays). In other species, such as chrysanthemum and zinnia, most or all of the flowers have conspicuous rays. In still other species the heads are made up entirely of tubular flowers.

The Fruit

Although seeds are ripened ovules, **fruits** are basically the ripened ovularies that contain the seeds. However, as we shall see, certain other parts of a flower may also contribute to the structure of fruits in some species. In most species pollination is essential, not only for fertilization of the egg and the subsequent development of the embryo and seeds, but also for the development of the fruit. True fruits are limited to the angiosperms. The fruits of different species are of many different sizes, shapes, structure, and texture, and fruits are classified into a number of types on the basis of these differences. Practically all

174

fruits in the common sense of the term, such as apples, oranges, grapes, cherries, raspberries, and watermelons are fruits in the botanical sense, but many things not commonly called fruits, such as bean or pea pods, okra, tomatoes, milkweed pods, sunflower "seeds," and even the outer layers of corn or wheat grains are true fruits botanically. We shall now consider some of the more important types of fruits.

In one group of fruits, the ovulary wall is essentially dry when ripe. These may be called **dry fruits** and certain specific types may be recognized in this category. Descriptions of some of the more common dry fruits follow.

The **follicle** develops from a pistil composed of a single carpel. When the fruit is ripe it spontaneously splits open (dehisces) along one side. The ripened seeds are usually shaken out by movement of the plant stem resulting from wind action or mechanical contact. The fruits of milkweed, magnolia, and larkspur are follicles. The seeds of milkweed are equipped with a feathery tuft of hairs that facilitates their dispersal by wind (Fig. 5.43).

The **legume** is characteristic of the bean family. It is monocarpellate and typically dehisces along two sides when ripe. Because of tensions created in the ripening fruit as it dries, the dehiscence sometimes occurs with explosive force, thus throwing the seeds some distance from the plant. Peas, beans, clover, alfalfa, and lespedeza are sometimes collectively called "legumes" for their fruits are, indeed, legumes. Other examples are wistaria, locust, and peanut. The fruit of the peanut deserves special mention because it is indehiscent and ripens below ground.

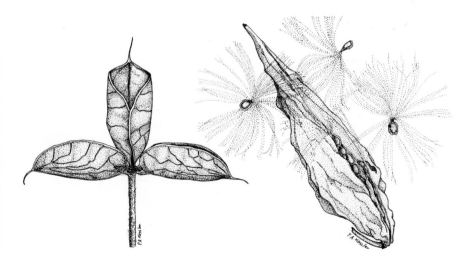

Figure 5.43. Fruits of larkspur, *left;* milkweed, *right.*

The developing fruit of the peanut is forced into the soil by the rapid growth of the pistil stalk.

The **capsule** develops from a multicarpellate pistil which at maturity frees the seeds by splitting along several lines, or by the opening of pores. Examples are the fruits of poppy, lily, and cotton. The seeds are usually shaken out by wind or mechanical contact.

The **achene** is a small indehiscent monocarpellate fruit derived wholly from the ovulary, and with a single seed attached to the fruit wall at one point. The fruits of buttercup and buckwheat are typical. The so-called "seeds" of strawberry and fig are really achenes (Fig. 5.44). The "seeds" of sunflower, beggartick, dandelion, and others of the sunflower family are also fruits. They have been called achenes, but they are bicarpellate and their walls are composed of other tissues in addition to ovulary wall (Fig. 5.45). Achenes may be widely dispersed by adhering to the fur of animals or to clothing by means of small hooks or spines. Achenes that are associated with edible structures, as in strawberry or fig, may be swallowed by animals or birds, passed through their digestive tracts without damage to the achene, and ultimately voided at some distance away from the parent plant. The ovulary wall of such fruits matures into a hard, resistant fruit coat.

The **samara** is bicarpellate and indehiscent, with a prominent wing

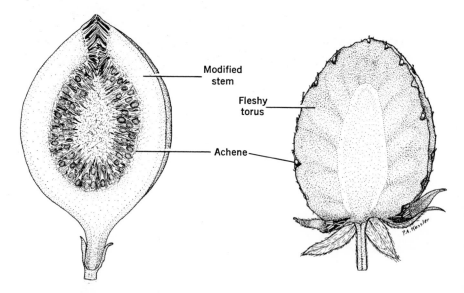

Modified
stem

Fleshy
torus

Achene

Figure 5.44. Fig, *left*, and strawberry, *right*, in longitudinal section. The true fruits are the achenes or so-called seeds; the fleshy, edible parts are modified stem or torus. Each achene of the fig is derived from a single, separate flower, whereas many achenes are produced by a single strawberry flower.

176

Figure 5.45. Fruit of *Tragopogon*, like that of dandelion, has a parachute formed from an adherent calyx. (Copyright by General Biological Supply House, Inc., Chicago.)

developed from the ovulary wall. The samaras of maple (Fig. 5.46) and ash, although fairly heavy, may be carried a considerable distance by strong wind currents.

The **nut** is one seeded and the fruit wall or part of it becomes stony or very woody at maturity. The fruit wall is composed of the ovulary wall fused with other flower parts. Examples are the fruits of oak, hickory, and walnut. The seeds of some of these species are attractive food for rodents which bury many more nuts than they eat. These large round fruits are bouyant in water and may be dispersed by streams.

The **grain** is a monocarpellate, one seeded fruit with the seed coat completely fused to the wall of the fruit. Examples are the grains of rice, wheat, corn (Fig. 5.48*b*), and other grasses.

Figure 5.46. Fruits of the sugar maple. The ovulary wall is modified into a flat wing. (Chicago Natural History Museum.)

In the second group of fruit types, one or more layers of the fruit coat become soft and **fleshy** when ripe. Many fruits of this type are attractively flavored and sweet and serve as food. This aids in seed dispersal by animals, because the seeds may be eaten along with the fruit and passed through the digestive tract unharmed.

The **berry** is the most common of the fleshy types of fruit. One or many seeds are surrounded by a fleshy fruit wall derived from the wall of a one- to several-carpellate ovulary. Grapes and tomatoes are familiar examples. In the tomato (Fig. 5.47), the placental tissues are also fleshy. Sometimes the outer layers are leathery and contain many oil glands, as in the citrus fruits. The juicy pulp of the orange consists of multicellular juice-filled sacs developed upon the inner surface of the ovulary wall. The fruits of members of Cucurbitaceae, the squash family, such as watermelon, cucumber, and pumpkin are berry-like. The leathery fruit walls consist of ovulary wall plus tissue of the torus which has grown to it. The placental tissue and inner layers of the ovulary wall remain fleshy in watermelon, whereas in squash and pumpkin they break down into a fibrous mass.

Cherry, peach, and olive are examples of the so-called stone-fruits, or **drupes**. The drupe, derived from a single carpel, is like a one-seeded berry except that the inner layer of the fruit coat is modified into a

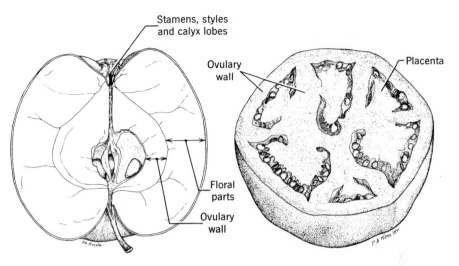

Figure 5.47. The fruits of apple, in longitudinal section, left, and tomato, in cross section, right.

hard, bony layer (the "stone" or "pit"). The "kernel" of the peach is the complete seed, with a brown, membranous seed coat.

The **pome**, represented by the apple (Fig. 5.47) and pear, is more complex than most of the foregoing types, for it consists not only of ovulary wall, but also of torus and floral tissues that have grown up around it. Pomes are composed of five or more carpels. In development, the inner layers of the ovulary wall become cartilaginous, forming the core of the fruit.

Many other specialized forms of fruit are known and the more familiar ones selected for this discussion are subject to almost infinite variation in detail of structure and in arrangement. The blackberry, for example, is a cluster of small drupes produced from numerous pistils on the enlarged torus of a single flower. The many achenes of the strawberry are also the product of a single flower, but each achene of the fig is derived from a separate flower. The pineapple and mulberry, on the other hand, are the fused fruits of many separate flowers.

The Seed

We have already noted that seeds are ripened ovules. Since the ovules of angiosperms are borne within ovularies that ripen into fruits, the seeds of angiosperms are borne within fruits. The seeds of gymnosperms, however, are borne on the upper surface of the scales of the

179

cones rather than within fruits. Since seeds contain the embryo plants of the new generation and generally considerable accumulated food, they are immensely important structures, both biologically and economically. Seeds vary greatly in size, from giant seeds such as those of the coconut to almost microscopic seeds such as those of orchids (5). For our study of seed structure we shall select three seeds of sufficient size for easy observation: bean, corn, and castorbean.

The exterior covering of the bean seed (Fig. 5.48*a*) is a tough glossy layer of high protective value. This is underlain by a thin membranous layer. When the seed is soaked in water these two layers, the **seed coats**, may be easily removed, revealing the **embryo**. Separation of the two fleshy **cotyledons** (hence, **dicotyledonous**) reveals that they are oppositely attached near the summit of a tapering axis. The part of the axis above the attachment of the cotyledons is the **epicotyl**, consisting chiefly of a pair of folded miniature leaves enclosing a growing point. This is the first bud of the embryo and is called the **plumule**. Below the cotyledons extends the **hypocotyl**, the lower tip of which is the **radicle**. The fleshy cotyledons contain reserve food, chiefly starch.

In the seeds of some other dicotyledonous species, such as the castorbean (Fig. 5.48*c*), the reserve food is present in a fleshy tissue, the **endosperm**, which envelops the embryo and lies beneath the seed coats. The cotyledons of such forms are usually membranous.

The embryo of corn (Fig. 5.48*b*) displays interesting contrasts with those described previously, although the basic plan of organization is the same. The embryonic axis consists of an epi- and a hypocotyledonary region, with the cotyledon attached laterally. There is only one cotyledon (hence, **monocotyledonous**), which is rather like a heavy shield placed between the embryonic axis and the massive endosperm. The plumule is very small and is encased by a conical sheath called the **coleoptile**. The embryonic root is similarly encased in a sheath, the **coleorhiza**. The radicle emerges first, followed shortly thereafter by emergence of the coleoptile. The cotyledon, although somewhat fleshy, does not contain the chief food reserve, but acts as a digesting and absorbing structure that transfers food from endosperm to growing embryo.

We may wonder what the cotyledons really are. It is difficult to determine this in the bean or pea because the cotyledons are specialized as food reservoirs. But in some seeds such as castorbean where the cotyledons are thin, careful dissection of the embryo and observation at germination give a clue. The cotyledons of the castorbean embryo are not food reservoirs, for the food is present in the thick enveloping endosperm. Dissection of the castorbean seed to show the surface view of the cotyledons reveals a pattern of veins very like that found in a leaf (Fig. 5.48*c*). During germination, the cotyledons at first absorb food from the endosperm. As the seedling emerges from the ground, the

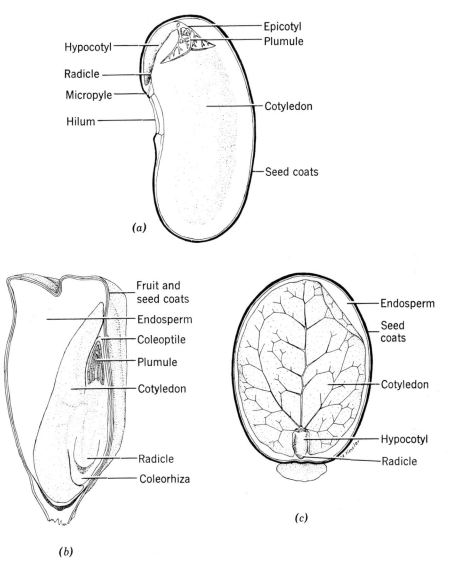

Figure 5.48. Dissections of common seeds to show detail of embryo: (a) bean, with one cotyledon removed; (b) corn grain, longitudinal section; (c) castorbean, with one cotyledon removed.

cotyledons enlarge considerably and develop chlorophyll, thus acquiring the obvious characteristics of leaves. The cotyledons remain active on the plant for several weeks, serving, along with the leaves later produced by the epicotyl, as part of the general photosynthetic equipment. Thus, cotyledons are to be regarded morphologically as leaves,

181

even though their exact nature may be obscured by specialization, as in the bean and pea. It is in recognition of this that cotyledons are sometimes called "seed leaves." Squash and cucumber seeds are, like the bean, without endosperm. In behavior at seedling stage their fleshy cotyledons are, in a way, intermediate between the bean and castorbean, for they become quite leaf-like and green and persist for some time as photosynthetic organs.

Seed coats are frequently specialized and may facilitate dispersal by wind (3) or animals. The winged seeds of some species of pine (Fig. 16.12) and *Paulownia* and the plumed seeds of milkweed (Fig. 5.43) are familiar examples of wind-dispersed types. In some the seed coat is adhesive (as in mistletoe) or becomes mucilaginous when wetted (as in mustard) and adheres to the feet of birds. Hairy seeds may cling to the bodies of animals and be transported for some distance.

The primary importance of seed coats is, however, that they protect the embryo plant against such hazards as excessive desiccation, mechanical injury, and the digestive juices of animals. The seed coats of some species are impermeable to water or oxygen or are hard and mechanically-resistant, thus bring about types of seed dormancy (Chapter 12) that may have considerable survival value. The capacity of seeds for remaining viable over considerable periods of time and through environmental conditions unfavorable for growth is one of the principal factors responsible for the dominance of seed plants in the land vegetation. This capacity results to a great extent from the presence of seed coats.

► ## Questions

1. The roots, stems, and leaves of vascular plants are commonly regarded as their principal organs. Are they really comparable with the organs of your body such as your lungs, stomach, liver, or heart? In the higher animals, organs are organized into organ systems, for example the esophagus, stomach, small intestines, and large intestines are all part of the digestive system. Does the structural organization of plants extend to the organ system level? If so, what are the organ systems of plants?

2. What factors determine whether a vascular plant will be woody or herbaceous? A tree or a shrub? An annual or a perennial?

3. What is the usual definition of a tissue? Does it leave anything to be desired? Can you suggest exceptions on the basis of what you have learned

about the tissues of plants? Try improving the definition if you think this is desirable.

4. Can you think of any plants that do not have tissues? Any that have tissues but no organs? If so, give examples of each type.

5. Just how much of a 100-year old pine tree is actually 100 years old? Suppose that the tree grew at the rate of 1 foot per year. If the trunk were sawed off at a height of $6\frac{1}{2}$ feet above the ground, how many annual rings would you find in the cross section of the trunk at that point?

6. Suppose that a nail had been driven into the trunk of the above tree at a height of 3 feet above the ground 10 years ago. How high above the ground will the nail be now? Suppose the lowest branch of the tree is 50 feet above ground level. How high above ground level was this branch when it first grew from the trunk? Were there ever any lower branches on the tree? If so, what has happened to them? What evidence for this might you expect to find within the trunk of the tree? From just observing the tree?

7. What organ or organs of each of the following plants do we commonly consume as food: potato, sweet potato, onion, beet, radish, carrot, pea, bean, celery, lettuce, cabbage, broccoli, Brussels sprouts, rhubarb, peach, eggplant, squash, pumpkin, wheat, apple, cauliflower, almond, olive, tomato, pimento, and cumcumber?

8. In several TV quiz shows contestants have been asked to name a fruit bearing its seeds on the outside. Those giving "strawberry" have been ruled correct. Was this a proper decision? Why? Do any fruits bear seeds outside rather than inside?

9. Goethe, the great German poet, was also a philosopher and scientist. Among other things he proposed a theory that flower parts are all just modified ("metamorphosed") leaves. On the basis of your present knowledge, does this seem like a plausible theory to you? Why? You may want to reconsider your answer after you have studied Chapter 16.

► ## *References*

For Reference

1. Hill, J. B., L. O. Overholts, H. W. Popp, and A. R. Grove, Jr. *Botany: A Textbook for Colleges.* New York: McGraw-Hill, 1960, Chapters 4, 6, 8.

For Reading

2. Ashby, Eric, Leaf shape. *Scientific American* 181(4):22–29, 1949.
3. Hutchins, R. E., Flight secrets of a jungle seed. *Natural History* 62:416–419, 1953.

4. Juniper, B. E., The surfaces of plants. *Endeavour* 18:20–25, 1959.

5. Moore, G., The big and small of seeds. *Science Digest* 48(5):65–67, November 1960.

6. Palmer, E. L., Winter buds and twigs. *Nature Magazine* 45:137–144, 1952.

7. Rush, J. H., Tree rings and sunspots. *Scientific American* 186(1):54–58, January 1952.

8. Schulman, Edmund, Tree rings and history in the western United States. *Economic Botany* 8:234–250, 1954.

9. Thimann, K. V., Autumn colors. *Scientific American* 183(4):40–43, October 1950.

10. Williams, Simon, Wood structure. *Scientific American* 188(1):64–68, January 1953.

6. Organisms

Ιn previous chapters we have considered plants from the levels of their constituent molecules, cells, tissues, and organs. Although the information gained there is important in the understanding of plants, it must be realized that molecules, cells, tissues, and organs are only parts of a complete, functioning **organism.** Although the organs, tissues, or even individual cells of an organism may be separated from it and kept alive in artificial culture for some time, these do not constitute an organism any more than an automobile engine removed from an old car and used to operate a rotary saw is an automobile. An organism is the free-living being that maintains itself in nature, and develops and functions according to a specific plan. It has some means of obtaining food, which it can utilize as a source of energy or as material for growth and maintenance. Each species of organism also reproduces itself. An organism is something more than the simple sum of its constituent cells, tissues, and organs. It is a coordinated functioning unit—a living thing.

An organism may exist in quite different forms as it passes through the various stages of its life. Perhaps the best known examples of this are the insects that exist successively as fertilized egg, larva, pupa, and adult winged insect, or the frog that is first a fertilized egg, then a tad-

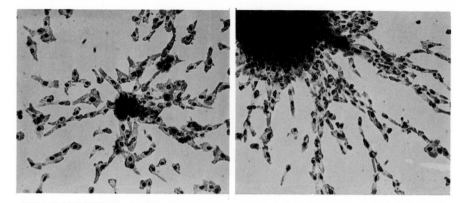

Figure 6.1. The individual amoeba-like cells of the cellular slime mold (or social amoeba) *Dictyostelium discoideum* migrating toward a central collecting point where they aggregate into a multicellular mass. In the photomicrograph at the right the process is farther advanced than in the one on the left. (Courtesy of John T. Bonner.)

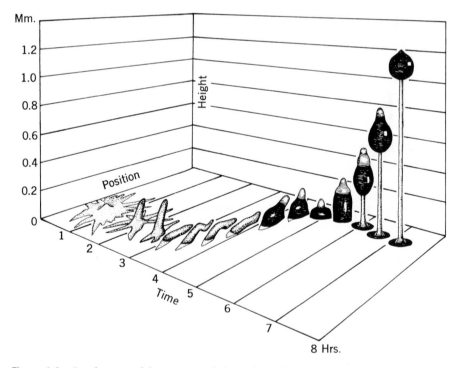

Figure 6.2. Development of the aggregated plasmodium of *Dictyostelium* (left) into a crawling "slug" and then into a stalked sporangium. The time scale is approximate. The spores released from the sporangium develop into the unicellular amoebae shown in Fig. 6.1. (Redrawn from John T. Bonner.)

pole, and finally an adult frog. Similar alterations in form occur in the plants. Ferns, for example, are successively unicellular spores, tiny heart-shaped prothalli, fertilized eggs, and finally the familiar fern plants, as they pass through the various stages of their life cycle. Slime molds (2) are successively amoeba-like single cells, multinucleate mobile masses of protoplasm, sporangia, and spores (Fig. 6.1, 2).

Unicellular and Colonial Organisms

In Chapter 2 we considered examples of the kinds of plant organisms that inhabit the earth. From this it should be evident that organisms may be of varying degrees of size and complexity. The simplest organisms—unless one wishes to consider the viruses as organisms—consist of a single cell, as in the bacteria and some algae and fungi. Such **unicellular** organisms have, of course, no tissues or organs or even any specialization of cells; all essential life processes occur within the single cell. In these unicellular organisms the tissue and organ levels of organization are absent, and the cell *is* the organism.

Among the algae and fungi are some organisms that may be considered as **colonial**, for example, the spherical green alga, *Volvox* (1), and some of the filamentous algae and fungi. Although colonial organisms may consist of a few to several hundred cells, each cell in the colony can carry on all essential life processes and will generally continue to live in nature if separated from the other cells of the colony. Streptococcus and staphlyococcus bacteria are colonial forms (Fig. 2.11).

True Multicellular Organisms

The final stage in the evolution of structural organization is the true **multicellular** type, in which some degree of cell specialization has occurred. Although cells or tissues may be removed from a multicellular organism and kept alive in culture, they lack some of the potentialities of the complete organism. Sometimes such isolated parts of an organism can regenerate the missing parts and so become a complete new organism, as in a stem cutting that forms roots (Fig. 12.10). Unless such regeneration occurs, however, the detached portion of the organism cannot survive long as a living entity in nature.

Multicellular plants are of varying degrees of structural complexity, from relatively simple algae and fungi through the mosses and liverworts to the highly organized vascular plants with their roots, stems, and leaves (6). Even more complex organization is attained in the higher animals. One essential feature of multicellular organisms is some method of coördination of the various cells, tissues, and organs into a smoothly operating entity as the organism carries on its life processes and develops from a fertilized egg into a mature individual. In animals such coördination is accomplished by both the nervous system and hormones, whereas in plants coördination is brought about largely by hormones (Chapter 12) and other chemical agents.

Some Problems Relating to the Organism Concept

It is not difficult to recognize that a man or an oak tree, an elephant or a bean plant are living organisms. However, sometimes it is more difficult to determine whether we are dealing with an organism or not. Is a virus a living organism, or is it just an immensely complex chemical entity? A lichen meets all of the usual requirements for classification as an organism, including the ability to reproduce itself, yet the lichen is a complex of a fungus and an alga (Fig. 11.14). Although the unicellular algal component of the lichen can reproduce itself by cell division, the fungus has not yet been observed to reproduce itself when isolated. Is the fungus a separate organism? Is the lichen an organism?

Cells of several higher plants, including bean and carrot, have been isolated and kept alive in culture for some time. These cells, under certain conditions, may divide into other isolated cells, thus reproducing themselves in the same way that a bacterial cell does. Are they unicellular organisms? Certainly they are not bean or carrot plants, even though they contain all the hereditary potentialities of the plants from which they came. We can say that they are not organisms because they can continue to exist only under certain cultural conditions provided by man. But if we accept this, the question then arises as to whether some of our cultivated plants deserve to be called organisms since they can survive and flourish only under man's cultural care. In the course of selecting for traits desirable to man, other traits that permitted their ancestors to survive in nature have been lost.

Some organisms can exist in two quite different forms. For example, some of the fungi that cause human infections may occur in a filamentous form while living as parasites on their host, but when cultured they become unicellular organisms.

Plants propagated by cuttings or other vegetative methods pose another problem regarding the organism concept. We may get dozens of individual coleus plants from a single plant by cutting off branches, placing them in water or moist sand until they develop roots, and then potting them. We ordinarily regard each plant produced in this way as a separate individual organism, distinct from the parent plant and each other. Yet, in another sense, they are merely portions of a single organism with identical hereditary potentialities. In contrast, coleus plants raised from seeds are products of sexual reproduction, begin life as a single cell, and commonly have assortments of hereditary potentialities different from those of either parent.

A somewhat different problem relating to the organism concept arises in connection with cultivated apple trees and other plants propagated by grafting (Fig. 15.12). Here a branch from the tree being propagated is generally grafted to a wild apple seedling. Thus, the roots and lower trunk of the resulting tree are from one orgranism and the upper trunk, leaves and branches from another. Is the tree a single organism, or is it two organisms? Certainly, each portion of the grafted tree has quite different hereditary potentialities, yet we would ordinarily consider it as a single organism.

The foregoing examples could be added to, but they may make it clear that the concept of an organism is not always as easy to define as would at first appear. In a practical sense, however, we have no difficulty in identifying the myriads of individual plants and animals as organisms, each able to carry on the processes that permit it to live for a while, and generally having the capacity for reproducing its kind before it meets the eventual fate of every organism—death.

If any single level of plant organization is more important than another it is the organism level, for only when this level of organization is attained is there a living entity that can survive and reproduce in nature and constitute a functioning unit in the biological communities of the Earth. As we study the molecules, cells, tissues and organs of plants or the life processes that occur within a cell, we may tend to lose sight of the fact that these are just isolated aspects of life and that it is the organism as a whole that is the natural living entity. This we should avoid if possible.

Another point worth considering is that only individual plant and animal organisms exist in nature—species, genera, families and other taxonomic categories are human concepts designed to provide a logical classification on the basis of apparent closeness of relationship, and to facilitate our dealing with the numerous organisms that inhabit the Earth. Species may, however, merge into one another without sharp dividing lines, and whether a certain group of plants belongs to one species or two or to one genus or two may be a matter of difference of opinion among the experts. However we may choose to classify them, the concrete entities are individual organisms, living, reproducing, and interacting with other organisms.

Organisms in Time and Space

Organisms have been described, facetiously but quite appropriately, as "four-dimensional worms," existing not only in the three dimentions of space but also in the fourth dimension, time (Fig. 6.1–5). A satisfactory general concept of any plant as an organism can be obtained only when we consider what it has been and what it will become, rather than just what it is at a particular point of time. We shall devote the remainder of this chapter to a consideration of various stages in the life cycle of a few selected plants, from their beginning as individuals through youth, maturity, and reproduction and on to eventual death, in an effort to clarify somewhat the concept of plants as four-dimensional organisms. We shall have frequent occasion to refer to material previously discussed, and to anticipate the more detailed treatments of plants as living, growing, developing, and reproducing entities in subsequent chapters.

From among the many diverse kinds of plants, we shall select two quite different representatives for consideration: *Dictyostelium discoideum*, one of the primitive and relatively simple cellular slime molds (Chapter 2), and *Phaseolus vulgaris*, the common garden bean. Comparative references to other species of the complex and highly evolved flowering plants will be made.

The spores of *Dictyostelium* (2) germinate into unicellular "amoebae" very similar to ordinary amoebae. They move and engulf food by pseudopodia and even reproduce by cell division as amoebae do. However, when their population becomes rather great and the food supply becomes exhausted the amoebae suddenly begin to move toward a central collecting point, aggregating into a multicellular mass (the **plasmodium**) (Fig. 6.1). At first the plasmodium is rather diffuse, but it soon becomes transformed into an elongated cylindrical "slug" with a pointed front end that glides along for a time before it settles down and develops into a stalked sporangium (Fig. 6.2). The spores produced in the sporangium then give rise to the next generation of amoebae. *Dictyostelium* is a good example of the diverse forms that an organism may assume in the course of its life. John T. Bonner of Princeton University and other biologists have devoted much time to the investigation of the development of this slime mold, with particular reference to the factors causing aggregation and the differentiation of specific parts of the slug into the sporangium and its stalk.

In a seed plant such as the bean a new individual arises when a sperm from a pollen grain unites with an egg inside an ovule, the resulting fertilized egg developing into the embryo plant of the seed. However, the beginnings of the plant as an *independent* individual may be considered to start with the detachment of the seed from the parent plant, or perhaps with the initiation of photosynthetic food production by the young seedling that has developed from the embryo during germination.

A viable (live) bean seed will germinate after it has imbibed sufficient water, provided that the temperature is suitable and there is an adequate supply of oxygen. The radicle or embryonic root rapidly elongates and breaks through the softened seed coats of the swollen seed, growing downward into the ground and producing root hairs. Soon secondary branch roots develop from this primary root. Firm anchorage in the soil and an extensive absorbing surface are thus established early. The upper portion of the hypocotyl arches and elongates, raising the cotyledons above the ground (Fig. 6.3). Once the hypocotyl is exposed to light its hook opens or straightens out and the small plumule between the cotyledons rapidly expands into the stem and first true leaves of the young plant. Elongation of the internodes results in the lengthening of the stem. As the food in the cotyle-

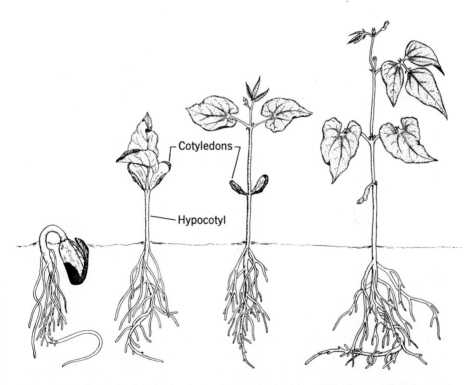

Figure 6.3. Stages in the germination and early development of the bean. The elongation and straightening of the hypocotyl brings the cotyledons into position above ground. Note the withering of the cotyledons as the food in them is consumed.

191

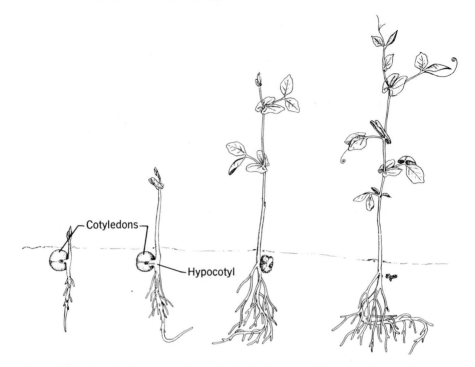

Figure 6.4. Stages in the germination and early development of the pea. Since the hypocotyl does not elongate, the cotyledons remain underground, in contrast with the bean and castor-bean.

dons is consumed in the rapid early growth, the cotyledons shrivel and fall to the ground, the food supply of the seedling now being provided by photosynthesis in the leaves and stems.

In the garden pea, a plant in the same family as the bean, the cotyledons are also fleshy and filled with food and, as in the bean, there is no endosperm in the seed. The pea cotyledons are, however, not raised above the ground during germination (Fig. 6.4), as they are in the bean, because the hypocotyl does not elongate. Otherwise, germination follows a course similar to that of the bean. The castorbean, a plant that has endosperm in its seeds, illustrates a somewhat different modification of germination (Fig. 6.5). The thin, leafy cotyledons at first absorb food from the endosperm of the germinating seed, but after they emerge above ground they expand considerably, develop chlorophyll, and for several weeks remain attached to the plant and carry on photosynthesis like the true foilage leaves. The cotyledons of the castorbean reveal more clearly than do those of the bean or pea the true nature of cotyledons as modified leaves.

In the germinating grains of corn and other grasses, both the cotyledon and endosperm remain below ground. When the first internode
above the cotyledon has elongated enough to expose the tip of the
coleoptile (Fig. 5.48) above ground, further elongation ceases, and the
rolled-up leaves of the plumule rapidly grow through the coleoptile tip,
expanding into the first true foliage leaves. In corn, adventitious roots
have meanwhile developed at the first node and these roots, rather than
the short-lived primary root developed from the radicle, contribute toward the root system of the mature plant. Except for minor differences
in detail, embryo structure and germination in other angiosperms are
similar to the examples described. It should be clear that an embryo is
really a miniature plant with all its major vegetative structures already
defined, and that germination is not a "coming to life" but rather an
acceleration of metabolic processes of the embryo resulting in a resumption of growth.

With the completion of germination, the seeding plant continues to
grow, rather slowly at first, then much more rapidly for a month or
more, and then at a somewhat reduced rate. Cell divisions in the ap-

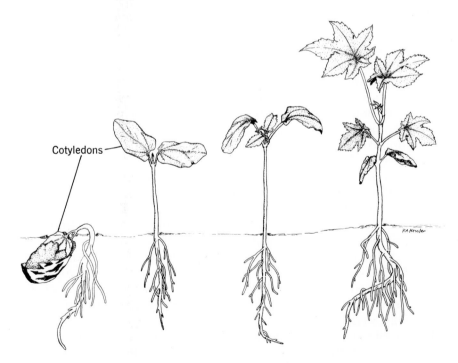

Figure 6.5. Stages in the germination and early development of the castorbean. The thin
cotyledons expand, develop chlorophyll, and carry on photosynthesis for some time before they
finally abscise.

193

ical meristems provide the new cells that enlarge and mature into the various types of cells that make up the tissues and organs of the plant. As growth continues the plant is synthesizing food by photosynthesis. Much of this food is used in growth as a source of energy or in building the new cells, tissues, and organs. Food production, however, exceeds food consumption and the excess food accumulates in the plant.

After a period of vegetative growth and development, which in the bean plant lasts for a month or so, flower buds appear and develop into flowers. Botanists have long been interested in the change from vegetative to reproductive development, and have done much research in an effort to elucidate the factors involved. In some species, initiation of flower primordia has been found to be controlled by environmental factors such as day length or temperature (Chapter 13), whereas in others such as bean, the only prerequisite seems to be the completion of a certain minimal period of vegetative development. Most trees do not bloom until they are several years old, and the well-known century plant is noted for its years of development before it blooms.

Once the flowers are open, the processes of pollination, fertilization, and seed and fruit development take place. Seed production is a complicated process involving many important structural details and specific processes that will be outlined in some detail in Chapter 16. Here we shall present only the gross features.

The mature pollen (5), freed by the opening of the pollen sacs of the anthers, is transferred to the stigma of the same or another flower of the species (pollination), commonly through the agency of wind or insects (3, 4). Some flowers, such as those of the bean and pea, are usually self-pollinated. The pollen on the stigma develops a pollen tube that grows through the tissues of the stigma, style and sometimes the ovulary and into the ovularian cavity (Fig. 5.37). When the pollen tube reaches an ovule, the tip of the tube ruptures, and one of the sperm in the tube is delivered to the egg within the ovule. The egg and sperm fuse (fertilization), and the fertilized egg develops into the embryo. As a result of other cell fusions and divisions (Chapter 16), endosperm is produced, and meanwhile the integuments of the ovule undergo modification into seed coats. Thus, a seed consisting of embryo, endosperm, and seed coats is produced. As has been noted, however, the endosperm of some plants such as bean and pea does not persist into the mature seed.

One of the first conspicuous changes in the flower following pollination is the withering and fall of the petals and stamens. This is soon followed by the rapid enlargement and modification of the ovulary (and sometimes adjacent parts) into a fruit. If pollination and fertilization do not occur, the flower usually withers and abscises. The

194

dependence of fruit development on pollination and fertilization was for many years a mystery, but it is now known that auxin and perhaps some other plant growth hormones (Chapter 12) provided by the pollen tube and the growing embryo are essential for fruit development and retention. However, in seedless fruits sufficient auxin is apparently available from other sources.

With the production of fruit containing viable seed, the life cycle of the individual plant may be said to have been completed. Species that have a short life span (annuals and biennials) generally produce only a single crop of seeds, but those with a longer life span (perennials) may produce seeds for many years before they finally die.

Despite the great differences between the slime molds and seed plants, they both illustrate characteristics common to the life cycles of most organisms: a succession in time of diverse structural organization as the individual progresses from its initiation, through youth and maturity, to reproduction and finally death. The fourth dimension—time—may be only a few hours, as in the slime molds, or thousands of years, as in the giant sequoias. Each stage in development, individually and successively, is a reflection of the coordination and control inherent in the dynamic and changing organism. No one stage of the life cycle, but rather the summation of all stages, defines the living organism.

► Questions

1. The statement is often made that the cell is the basic unit of life. At least one eminent biologist has questioned this statement, and claims that the organism is actually the basic unit of life. Which point of view would you regard as being sounder? Why?

2. Construct a definition of the word *organism*. After you have done so (but not before) compare it with definitions in an unabridged dictionary and several textbooks. Which of the following would be organisms on the basis of your and the other definitions: a virus, a lichen, a colonial alga, a culture of single cells from a carrot root, a dead oak tree, a sterile plant that has no means of reproduction?

3. At just what point do you think a plant such as the bean should be considered to begin life as an independent organism? Why?

4. Is a fertilized egg an organism? Are gametes (eggs and sperm) organisms? Are spores organisms? Explain your answers.

► ## *References*

For Reading

1. Bonner, John T., Volvox: a colony of cells. *Scientific American* 182(5):52, May 1950
2. Bonner, John T., Differentiation in the social amoeba. *Scientific American* 201(6): 152–162, December 1959.
3. Grant, Verne, The fertilization of flowers. *Scientific American* 184(6):52–57, June 1951.
4. Hodge, Henricks, A bee and a blossom. *Natural History* 64:195–199, 1955.
5. Peattie, D. C., Pollen: wonder dust of nature. *Nature Magazine* October 1946.
6. Schulman, Edmund, Bristlecone pine, oldest known living thing. *National Geographic Magazine* 113:355–371, 1958.
7. Stewart, C. D., The tree as an invention. *Atlantic Monthly* 143:433–441, April 1929.
8. Wardlaw, C. W., The study of growth and form in plants. *Endeavour* 11:97–106, 1952.

7. Communities

 At FIRST GLANCE it may appear that the complete organism represents the highest and final level of biological organization, but organization extends beyond the individual to biological communities. Like cells, tissues, organs and organisms, the communities of plants and animals that occupy most areas of the Earth have a specific and characteristic structural organization. Communities also engage in characteristic activities, and although these activities are the product of the activities of the individual members of the community, they involve a new level of interaction and interrelation beyond that of the individual organism. Communities even pass through stages of development from what might be considered birth through youth and on to maturity in a definite and predictable sequence. Some biologists have considered communities as being superorganisms, whereas others feel that community organization is hardly compact and consistent enough to warrant such a label. There is no doubt, though, that biological organization does extend beyond the individual to the community.

Certain social animals such as some bees, ants, termites, and man are organized into compact societies with a considerable specialization and division of labor among the individuals in the community. We are not concerned with such community organization here, particularly since it is limited to certain species of animals, but rather with the larger and more comprehensive types of biological communities of which practically all organisms are members. Each of these communities is composed of a considerable variety of plant and animal species tied together by interactions among them and the factors of their physical environment. Although every natural community of these broader types is composed of both plants and animals, the plants are always the basic structural members of a community and are responsible for its general character, appearance, and usually even its name. The reason for this is that photosynthetic plants always provide the basic food supply of any community and constitute the bulk of living tissue in it. We shall first consider the general nature of plant communities and then turn our attention to the major plant communities of the Earth and to their development.

Types of Plant Communities

Almost everyone is aware of the fact that the vegetation of the Earth is not uniform, but that in one place it consists of forests whereas in others there are grasslands, desert, or tundra. Still other types occur in bodies of water. These major types of vegetation generally cover large areas and are referred to as **formations** (Fig. 7.1). In the following pages the principal formations will be described and it will become evident that there are different types of forest and grassland formations.

It is not mere chance that forests, grasslands, or deserts are found at certain places. The factors of the physical environment determine what types of plants can survive in a certain region and so determine the character of the community. Availability of water is of particular importance. Only desert communities composed of plants that can thrive under conditions of low moisture (**xerophytes**) can exist in extremely dry regions. Grasslands occupy regions where water availability is somewhat greater, whereas forest formations occur in still moister regions. The plants of forest communities and some grassland plants are **mesophytes,** in contrast with the xerophytes of deserts and the drier grasslands, and the **hydrophytes** that grow partially or completely submerged in bodies of fresh water. Although temperature influences the occurrence of the plant formations we have mentioned largely through its effects on water availability, low temperature is a primary factor in determining the location of tundra formations. Temperature may, of course, determine what particular species make up a formation. Thus, trees that are not resistant to freezing cannot be a component of a temperate zone

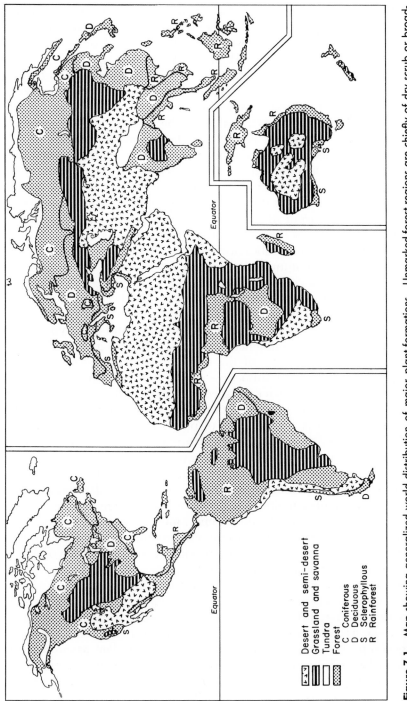

Desert and semi-desert
Grassland and savanna
Tundra
Forest
  C Coniferous
  D Deciduous
  S Sclerophyllous
  R Rainforest

Figure 7.1. Map showing generalized world distribution of major plant formations. Unmarked forest regions are chiefly of dry scrub or broad-leaf evergreen. Based on Aitoff's Equal Area Projection, condensed. (Adapted from Polunin, *Introduction to Plant Geography,* McGraw-Hill.)

199

forest formation, whereas trees that grow well only in a cool climate are not found in tropical forests. Some species require low temperatures to break dormancy of flower buds, or even leaf buds. Also, the seeds of some species require cold for breaking dormancy.

Each plant formation is composed of several different subdivisions known as **associations**. For example, in the Eastern Deciduous Forest formation there are several associations such as the swamp forest association, the oak-hickory association and the beech-maple association. Associations are commonly named for their **dominant** species, that is those larger plants that are the most abundant in the community. Local factors such as topography, differences in water availability, soil structure, fertility, and acidity, or perhaps even just the stage of successional development are important in determining which association of a formation will occur in a certain locality, even though these factors have little influence on the extent of the formation as a whole. Associations are still further subdivided into smaller, more compact and more homogeneous communities, but we shall not be concerned with these smaller units of community organization here.

Although the physical environment determines the general character of the formations and associations that occupy any particular area of the Earth, the more detailed structural organization and the dynamics of any community are also influenced to a considerable degree by the interactions among the members of the community. Thus, the trees of a forest produce shade that influences light intensity, temperature, and humidity and so they restrict the species of plants that can grow under them. The species of animals present in a community depend on the food available, that is, on the kinds of plants present, and despite their mobility, animals are just as restricted to particular formations or even associations as are plants. Once a community has reached maturity there is a remarkable stability in the proportion of individuals of each species in it year after year, unless there is a marked disturbance of the community by man or major changes in the physical environment. This balanced situation results from the checking of the great reproductive potential of any particular species by other members of the community that use it as food, parasitize it, or produce conditions unfavorable to the survival of individual members of the species.

The subdivision of biology dealing with communities, with the influence of the physical environment on the communities, and with the interactions between the members of a community is called **ecology**. A study of the distribution of plant communities over the face of the Earth is a special part of ecology sometimes referred to as **plant geography**. In Chapters 13 and 14 we shall consider some of the influences of the physical and biological environment on plants. The remainder of this chapter will be devoted to plant geography and plant succession.

Plant Formations

FORESTS

Tree species are the dominant plants in the forest formations, and these are frequently associated with one or more shade-tolerant under-stories consisting of small trees, shrubs, herbs, and, rarely, grasses. Forests occur generally in regions of relatively high water availability. A few of the several important types of forest will be described.

The **Tropical Rainforest** occurs in an area of high temperatures and abundant rainfall. The forest is dense and consists of tall, broad-leaf evergreen trees of large diameter, representing many species. In the shade on the forest floor a rank understory of shade-tolerant ferns and herbs is found, along with some moderately high shrubs and trees. In some areas, the shade of the tall trees is so dense as to exclude under-story associates. Many woody climbers ascend the tall tree trunks and display their foliage in the crowns of the trees. In reclaimed clearings and along stream banks where light is more abundant the classical tangle of the jungle prevails. The principal ranges of the rainforest are the drainage basins of the Amazon and Congo, the East Indies, the Phillipines and coastal southeastern Asia, and Central America (Fig. 7.1).

Figure 7.2. Redwood forest in Northern California. (U.S. Forest Service.)

Figure 7.3. Oak-hickory association of Eastern Deciduous Hardwood Forest. (Chicago Natural History Museum.)

The **Coniferous Forest** is indigenous chiefly to regions with cool temperate climate, as in the middle and higher latitudes of the temperate zones and higher elevations in the tropics. The trees are largely needle-leaf gymnosperms, species of spruce, fir, hemlock, pine, and larch. Locally, in the northern regions, an admixture of some birch and poplar is common, but understory associates are few except in areas having considerable rainfall (Fig. 7.2). In North America the coniferous forest characterizes a broad area in the Southeast, most of the region west of the plains except the very arid Southwest, and much of Canada. In Eurasia it extends from the Alps north to Scandinavia and eastward to the Pacific Ocean (Fig. 7.1).

The **Deciduous Hardwood Forest** occurs chiefly in temperate regions with marked seasonal cycles. Typically the trees lose their leaves in a dry or in a cold season. The forest contains many species of broad-leaf trees in relatively open stands, with many understory associates, including small trees, shrubs, annuals, and a few grasses. Oaks, hickories, tulip trees, gum, beeches, maples, and ash are common dominants (Fig. 7.3). Dogwood, sourwood, buckeye, poison ivy, huckleberry, and weedy annuals frequently compose the understory. Extensive areas in east-central United States, western Europe, and southern European Russia support typical deciduous forests, locally and regionally diversified as distinctive associations (Fig. 7.1).

The **Sclerophyll Forest** is a distinctive type made up chiefly of small trees and coarse shrubs with broad, leathery, evergreen leaves in open stands. Coarse, short grasses sparsely cover the soil between the dominants. Occurring in semiarid warm regions, the sclerophyll forest is characteristic of many regions in the lands surrounding the Mediterranean Sea, coastal southwestern United States, and areas in Chile, South Africa, and southern Australia (Fig. 7.1).

The **Savanna** is a forest type of a distinctive park-like aspect, with open or scattered stands of small broad-leaf evergreen or deciduous trees and with the space between occupied by coarse grasses. It is essentially a transitional type between forest and grassland, or forest and desert, formations. Typically it is characteristic of high-temperature, low-rainfall climates. Broad east-west zones on the northern and southern flanks of the tropical rainforests in South America, Africa, much of India, and northern Australia are covered by this type of forest (Fig. 7.1).

GRASSLANDS

Grasses are the dominant and often the only growth form in grassland. Small trees are rare and limited to the land immediately adjacent to water courses. Typically, grassland is a formation characteristic of regions of relatively low water supply. In its very dry expressions it consists chiefly of low-growing, shallow-rooted grasses in open forma-

Figure 7.4. Short-grass plains, eastern Montana. (Photograph courtesy of Northern Pacific Ry.)

Figure 7.5. East-central prairies.

tion, as in the plains grassland in western United States, Canada, and southern Asiatic Russia (Fig. 7.4). In cool areas, short-lived annuals and cactus or cactus-like plants may be present. In its moister expressions, as in the prairies of east-central United States and large areas of Asia and Africa, the grasses are taller, are sod-forming species, and are commonly associated with many annuals (Fig. 7.5).

DESERTS

Extreme aridity and commonly high day-time temperatures characterize the desert. Vegetation may be sparse, consisting of small-leaf deciduous or leafless shrubs of spiny habit, such as greasewood, or perennials with succulent stems or leaves, such as cacti or yuccas. The intervening space may be bare soil, or, in areas receiving moderate rainfall in an occasional year, short-lived annuals and sparse bunch grass may occur (Fig. 7.6). Large areas of western United States and adjacent parts of Mexico, western South America, the Sahara and Arabian deserts, and large areas of central Asia and Australia support this formation. Some extreme desert areas are, of course, destitute of vegetation (Fig. 7.1).

Figure 7.6. Arizona desert. (Photograph by Chuck Abbott.)

TUNDRA

The tundra formation (11) occurs in regions characterized by freezing temperatures during all but a few weeks of the year. During a very brief growing season the soil thaws to a depth of a few inches and the sparse vegetation, consisting of small annuals, hardy grasses, dwarf wil-

205

lows, depressed junipers, mosses, and lichens, complete their vegetative and reproductive activities. Tundra vegetation is characteristic of northern Canada, Alaska, northern Europe, and Asia, extending from the upper limits of tree growth to the region of permanent ice.

Of course, the limits of such plant assemblages are not precisely definable, for the formations blend into one another where they meet, in zones of transition, just as the environmental factors which they depend on vary gradually over a distance. As critical environmental conditions change at the margins of a formation, so will the range of the formation expand or retract.

Plant Succession

If a natural plant community, biologically balanced and so rather stable, is disturbed, either by man or by major natural changes in the physical environment, many years are usually required before a new balance is achieved (1, 9, 13). The plants that first become established in the disturbed region are replaced by other species of plants, these by still others, and so on until a stable community has developed. Each kind of plant changes the environmental conditions in such a way that they are more favorable for the survival and reproduction of other species than for themselves. Such a change in the species of plants composing the community is known as **succession**. Each group of species making up the community at any stage in the succession is known as an **association**, and the final stable association is known as the **climax association**. Such a climax association will maintain itself until it is disturbed by major changes in the environment, or by man. Whether the climax association is a certain kind of forest, grassland, or desert depends on the nature of the physical environment in the region, whereas the specific kinds of plants making up the association depend also on whether or not they are present in nearby regions and so can migrate into the disturbed region.

OLD FIELD SUCCESSION

What happens when a field is abandoned in the piedmont section of a southeastern state such as North Carolina provides a good example of a rather rapid succession following disturbance of the natural vegetation by man. The climax association in a certain region may be an oak-hickory forest, but when cultivation of the field is discontinued the vegetation does not immediately revert to an oak-hickory forest, even though there are many oak and hickory trees nearby to provide seeds. The environmental conditions in the abandoned field are not favorable to the survival of oak and hickory seedlings. However, seedlings of crabgrass flourish even though the soil is poor, and the field is hot and dry in summer and subject to early freezes in the fall. Within a year or so, seedlings of tall weedy plants such as ragweed, aster, and goldenrod become established and attain dominance within two or three years. These are gradually succeeded by a dominant stand of broomsedge over a period of three or four years.

About 6 to 8 years after abandonment of the field, conditions have become favorable for the survival of pine seedlings and they will be found growing sparsely among the broomsedge (Fig. 7.7). As the pine seedlings grow into trees they shade the low plants, which are able to carry on an adequate rate of photosynthesis only in bright light. The pines otherwise alter the environment so as to make it unfavorable for the broomsedge. The result is that these pioneer plants gradually die out. Within 25 years the pine forest is quite tall and dense, and it continues to flourish for the next 50 years or so, more or less unaltered ex-

Figure 7.7. Field succession in the southeastern Piedmont. (a) Crabgrass, *Digitaria,* pioneering in abandoned corn field; (b) tall weed stage, mostly *Aster;* (c) broomsedge stage, *Andropogon;* (d) young pine stage, *Pinus.* (Courtesy of Harold Humm.)

Figure 7.8. Young hardwood species established in a 55-year-old stand of loblolly pine. The pine timber has just been selectively cut.. (U.S. Forest Service photograph.)

cept for the increasing size of the trees. The pine seedlings cannot survive in the dense shade produced by the parent trees, and so the pine association is not able to reproduce itself. However, the shady and relatively moist forest provides favorable conditions for the growth of the seedlings of oak, hickory and other hardwood trees (Fig. 7.8). Within 75 years or so after abandonment, these young hardwood trees make up a conspicuous part of the community, and as the pine trees die, the hardwood trees take their places in the forest. The result is that about 100 years after abandonment there is a mixed pine-hardwood forest, and after 200 years or so all the pines have died and the climax oak-hickory association has taken over. Since the seedlings of these hardwood trees can survive in the forest, the association can reproduce itself and will continue to occupy the region until there is some other major natural or manmade disturbance. Although the oak-hickory association is made up of many different kinds of hardwood trees and shrubs, it is named for the two dominant kinds of trees in the association.

In some areas, the natural succession may be stopped at the stage just preceding the climax and held at that stage for long periods of time by the recurrence of major disturbances. Recurring fires often have this effect, as in the southeastern coastal plain where some forests of relatively fire-resistant pines are maintained as a **subclimax** by the constant destruction of the young hardwoods (6).

BARE ROCK SUCCESSION

Most natural successions require several thousand years instead of several hundred years to reach a climax. One such succession in the Eastern deciduous forest formation begins on bare rock, on which little else but lichens can survive. These are followed by mosses, which continue the process of rock disintergration begun by the lichens, and by herbs that can grow in the cracks in the rocks. As the rocks weather into soil, other kinds of herbs and shrubs can become established, and these are succeeded by pines and finally by an oak-hickory forest. In some places this may be the climax association, whereas in others it is succeeded by a climax beech-maple forest association.

POND SUCCESSION

Another type of natural succession begins with a pond or small lake in which aquatic plants are growing. As eroded soil and remains of dead plants accumulate on the lake bottom and make it shallower, plants such as cattails and rushes become established and these further promote the filling-in process until there remains only a swamp occupied by a sedge association. The filling-in process continues until conditions become favorable for trees such as willows and alders, and these in turn are succeeded by an elm-ash-soft maple association. Eventually, as the soil becomes more abundant, swampy conditions entirely disappear and so the environment has become favorable for the establishment of the climax beech-maple forest association.

CLIMATIC CHANGES AND SUCCESSION

Major climatic changes usually start successions that result in the replacement of one major plant formation, such as a forest, grassland, desert, or tundra, by another major plant formation. In prehistoric times, dense forests covered much of the region now occupied by our Southwestern desert. About 3,000 years ago, the region including Ohio, Indiana, and Illinois became much drier than it had been, and prairie grasslands from farther west replaced the deciduous forests. Later the climate again became moister and forests once more replaced the grasslands, except in small, isolated patches where local conditions made it impossible for the trees to become established. Fossil palm trees have been found in arctic regions, indicating that in one of the inter-glacial periods the climate there was warm enough for these tropical trees. At the present time we are apparently still recovering from the last glacial period, and within the memory of living men the northern evergreen forest has made definite advances into the regions formerly occupied only by tundra vegetation.

▶ *Questions*
_____

1. Suggest possible reasons for the fact that relaively dry regions are occupied by grassland communities rather than forest communities, that is, why grasses and the associated herbaceous plants can thrive with less available water than trees.

2. Plants dispersed by spores (such as fungi) generally have a wider geographical distribution than plants dispersed by seeds. Suggest possible explanations.

3. There are many species of plants in the North Carolina mountains that occur in lowlands much farther north. Explain.

4. Two species of *Torreya* (a genus of gymnosperm trees) are native in China, one in California, and one in the southeastern states. This genus is not found elsewhere. How could such a distribution be explained and what does it indicate about the past history of the genus?

5. Farmers in the piedmont region of the southeast would like to keep their woodlands in pines rather than hardwoods, since pines can be sold for considerably more than hardwood trees. Why are the pines more valuable economically? Suggest practices the farmers might employ to prevent succession from proceeding from the pine community to the hardwood community.

► # *References*

For Reference

1. Oosting, H. J., *The Study of Plant Communities.* San Francisco: W. H. Freeman & Co., 1956.
2. Watts, M. T., *Reading the Landscape: An Adventure in Ecology.* New York: The Macmillan Co., 1957.

For Reading

3. Amos, W. H., The life of a sand dune. *Scientific American* 201(1):91–99, July 1959.
4. Bates, Marston, *The Forest and the Sea.* New York: Random House, 1960.
5. Carson, Rachel L., *The Sea Around Us.* New York: Oxford, 1951.
6. Cooper, C. F., The ecology of fire. *Scientific American* 204(4):150–160, April 1961.
7. Deevy, E. S., Jr., Bogs. *Scientific American* 199(4):114–122, October 1958.
8. Herre, Albert, Vegetable voyagers. *Nature Magazine* 39:485–488, 1946.
9. Highsmith, R. M. and John L. Bek, Tillamook Burn: the regeneration of a forest. *Scientific Monthly* 75:139–148, 1952.
10. McCormick, Jack, *The Living Forest.* New York: Harper & Brothers, 1958.
11. Platt, Rutherford, Flowers in the arctic. *Scientific American* 194(2):88–98, February 1956.
12. Storer, J. H., *The Web of Life: A First Book of Ecology.* New York: New American Library, 1956.
13. Went, F. W., The plants of Krakatoa. *Scientific American* 181(3):52–54, September 1949.

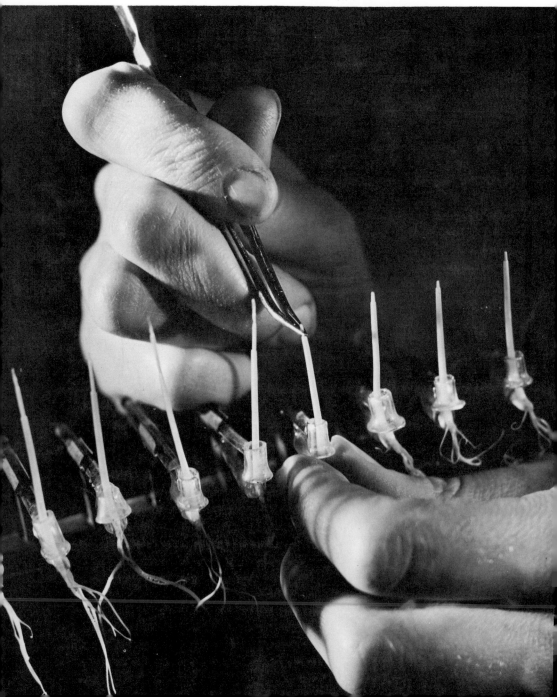

8. Molecular Traffic

LIVING PLANTS are the scene of endless activity. Numerous biochemical reactions are in progress, energy is transformed and used, substances are transported from place to place, cells divide, enlarge and become specialized, cytoplasm streams around within the cells, and the plant grows and reproduces. Essential to these activities is a considerable traffic in substances between the plant and its environment and from cell to cell within the plant. Carbon dioxide, oxygen, water, and salts enter and leave the plants, and in addition food enters those plants that cannot make their own by photosynthesis. Our concern in this chapter is with the nature of this traffic into, out of, and through plants.

Diffusion

Much, though not all, of the movement of substances into and out of plant cells is by **diffusion**, a purely physical process requiring no expenditure of energy by the plant. Diffusion is a consequence of the ceaseless movement of all molecules and other small particles such as atoms and ions.

MOLECULAR MOVEMENT

If we could see the molecules in any substance such as air or water we would note that they are swarming about in every direction, bumping into each other or into solid surfaces and rebounding off in new directions without loss of velocity, and moving in straight lines until other collisions again result in changes of direction.

An increase in temperature brings about an increase in the rate of molecular movement. The smaller and lighter a molecule, the more rapidly it moves. The molecules of gases move more rapidly and freely than those of liquids, whereas the molecules of liquids generally have a greater velocity and freedom of movement than those of solids.

INTERMOLECULAR ATTRACTIONS

Despite their constant motion, the molecules of a substance attract each other. These attractive forces become greater as the distance between molecules decreases. In gases the attractive forces are slight, but in liquids they are great enough to hold the substance together and produce a surface. The molecules of solids are still closer together and the intermolecular attractions are great enough to hold the substance together in a more or less rigid shape. The movement of molecules in a solid is generally restricted to extremely short distances by the intermolecular forces, although occasionally the molecules of some solids, such as the naphthalene of moth balls, escape and move freely through the air as gases.

Many substances can exist in solid, liquid, and gaseous states depending on the temperature and pressure. When ice (solid water) is heated, its molecules begin moving more rapidly and push one another so far apart that the water becomes a liquid. The more rapidly moving molecules in liquid water may, in turn, evaporate and so pass into the air as a gas (**water vapor**).

THE NATURE OF DIFFUSION

Diffusion is a consequence of molecular movement, but not all molecular movement results in diffusion. We may define **diffusion** as the *net* movement of molecules of a substance from a region of higher molecular activity (or **diffusion pressure**) to a region of lower molecular activity (or diffusion pressure) of that particular substance. Diffusion thus occurs only when more molecules of a substance are moving in one direction than another. The diffusion pressure of a gas is the same as its partial pressure, and may be expressed in any ordinary pressure units such as pounds per square inch or millimeters of mercury. The diffusion pressure of a liquid is generally much higher than that of a gas and is commonly measured in **atmospheres** (1 atmos. = 14.7 lb./in.^{2}).

Three principal factors determine the molecular activity or diffusion pressure of a substance: (1) The more concentrated a substance the higher the diffusion pressure, **concentration** meaning the number of molecules per unit volume. (2) The diffusion pressure of a substance increases with **temperature** because of the increased velocity of the molecules. (3) An external or **imposed pressure** on the substance will increase its diffusion pressure by the amount of the imposed pressure. Several examples should help clarify the influence of these factors.

DIFFUSION OF GASES. First let us consider the diffusion of gases between the intercellular spaces of a leaf (Fig. 5.19) carrying on photosynthesis and the outside air, assuming that the leaf is in the shade and so at essentially the same temperature as the air. Here the only one of the three factors affecting diffusion pressure will be concentration. Since the mesophyll cells of the leaf are producing oxygen by photosynthesis, the concentration of oxygen is greater in the intercellular spaces than in the outside air, and consequently oxygen will diffuse out through the stomata. Of course, molecules of oxygen will be moving through the stomata in both directions, but since there are more molecules of oxygen per unit volume inside the leaf than outside, there will be a net movement (diffusion) out.

At the same time that oxygen molecules are diffusing out through the stomata, carbon dioxide molecules are diffusing in because they are being used in photosynthesis and so are less concentrated in the intercellular spaces than in the outside air. Note that two substances may diffuse in different directions at the same time and place, each one diffusing from the region of *its own* greater diffusion pressure to the region of *its own* lesser diffusion pressure. The presence of molecules of another substance affects the *rate* of diffusion (since they increase the number of molecular collisions) but not the *direction* of diffusion.

Now, by reducing the light intensity, let us reduce the rate of photosynthesis in the leaf until it is occurring just as fast as respiration. Under these conditions, all the oxygen produced by photosynthesis will be used in respiration, and all the carbon dioxide produced by respiration will be used in photosynthesis. Soon the concentration of both gases in the intercellular spaces will be the same as their concentration in the outside air; consequently diffusion will cease. Of course, molecules of both gases are still moving through the stomata in both directions, but the number of molecules moving in during any time interval is the same as the number moving out, so there is no net movement (diffusion) in either direction. A **dynamic equilibrium** exists.

Since molecules of nitrogen gas are neither used nor produced by processes within a leaf, nitrogen does not diffuse into or out of a leaf as long as the leaf is at the same temperature as the air. Let us next turn our attention to a leaf that has just been exposed to direct sunlight, and so becomes perhaps 10°C warmer than the outside air. Despite the fact that the concentration of nitrogen in the leaf is the same as outside, nitrogen will now diffuse out of the leaf because the diffusion pressure of the nitrogen molecules in the intercellular spaces has been increased by the rise in temperature. A new dynamic equilibrium will soon be established and diffusion of nitrogen will cease when the diffusion pressure or molecular activity of nitrogen is the same inside the leaf as out. At equilibrium the nitrogen will be less concentrated in the intercellular spaces than in the air, the greater velocity of the molecules inside the leaf compensating for their lower concentration. The product of velocity times concentration yields the same *total* molecular energy as that of the nitrogen outside the leaf where the molecules are more concentrated but have lower kinetic energy (velocity). The situation is comparable with the purely mathematical one of both 6×8 and 4×12 having 48 as the product.

Although we have been using molecules as examples, other small particles including ions, atoms, and colloidial particles diffuse in the same way. The relatively large colloidial particles diffuse very slowly.

DIFFUSION OF SOLUTES. All principles of diffusion that apply to gases also apply to solute particles, although the rate of diffusion of solutes is much less rapid than that of gases because of the much greater density of the medium (the solvent) through which they are diffusing. When a few crystals of a colored substance such as potassium permanganate are placed in the bottom of a long thin glass tube filled with water (in which convection currents are reduced to a minimum) the substance diffuses through the water until a uniformly colored solution results, indicating that equilibrium has been attained. Several months are required for reaching an equilibrium in a tube a meter long.

Because of the short distances involved, diffusion provides an adequate means of movement of sugars and other solutes between adjacent cells in a plant. However, diffusion is too slow to account for the rates of solute movement through greater distances within plants, as from the leaves to the roots. As we shall see in subsequent chapters, other processes are responsible for such long-distance transport.

DIFFUSION OF WATER. Like solutes, water and other liquids diffuse much more slowly than gases. Since water vapor is a gas, it diffuses at rates comparable with those of other gases. The concentration of water is determined largely by the number of solute particles present in it, the more solute particles present the lower the concentration of the water. Only the total *number* of dispersed particles is important in affecting the concentration of the water (and thus its diffusion pressure). The kind, size, and weight of the particles is not significant. Thus, sucrose molecules have the same influence on water concentration as the same number of the smaller glucose molecules, and a potassium ion and a nitrate ion will each have the same effect as a nonionized molecule of potassium nitrate. If equal numbers of glucose and potassium nitrate molecules are added to two equal volumes of water, the solution containing the potassium nitrate will have a lower concentration of water than that containing the glucose, since the salt ionizes and the glucose does not. Pure water, of course, has a higher concentration than water containing any dispersed particles.

Suppose we have a rectangular container separated into two compartments by a removable partition and that we fill the left-hand compartment with water and the right-hand one with a water solution of sucrose. When the partition is removed water (being more concentrated on the left) will diffuse from left to right, whereas sucrose (being more concentrated on the right) will diffuse from right to left until each one reaches a dynamic equilibrium. If the demonstration were repeated with a 5% sucrose solution on the left and a 10% sucrose solution on the right, each would still diffuse in the same direction as before, but if a 10% sucrose solution were placed on both sides a dynamic equilibrium would exist from the beginning and there would be no diffusion of either water or sucrose.

If we let X atmos. equal the diffusion pressure of pure water at any stated temperature (X will, of course, increase with temperature), and if sufficient solutes are added to the water to reduce its diffusion pressure by 15 atmos. (because of the decrease in water concentration), the diffusion pressure of the water in the solution is $X - 15$ atmos. The diffusion pressure of water in the soil solution is usually around $X - 1$ atmos., whereas in root cells of many plants the diffusion pressure of water is around $X - 5$ atmos. Since water in the soil has the higher diffusion pressure, water will diffuse from the soil into the roots. In the leaf cells, the diffusion pressure of water usually ranges between $X - 8$ and $X - 30$ atmos., depending on the species of plant and other factors. The diffusion pressure of pure water (X) is about 1350 atmos. at room temperature (20°C).

So far we have considered only two of the three principal factors affecting diffusion pressure or molecular activity—concentration and temperature. The third, imposed pressure, is particularly important in regard to the diffusion pressure of water and other solvents. If we place water in a strong cylinder fitted with a watertight piston and subject the water to a pressure of 10 atmos. by means of a hydraulic press, the diffusion pressure of the water will be increased by essentially this amount, and so will be $X + 10$ atmos. If a solution containing water with a diffu-

217

sion pressure of $X - 10$ atmos. is subjected to the same imposed pressure it will now have a diffusion pressure of X atmos., the same as pure water despite its solute content. The increase in diffusion pressure resulting from the applied pressure was just enough to counteract the reduction in diffusion pressure brought about by the presence of solute particles (i.e., the reduced water concentration).

DIFFUSION THROUGH MEMBRANES. Any substance diffusing into or out of a plant cell must pass through the cell wall and the plasma membrane. If the substance enters the vacuole, it must also diffuse through the vacuolar membrane. Diffusion of particles through membranes is, then, a matter of considerable biological interest.

From the standpoint of diffusion a **membrane** may be regarded as any partition between two regions, so cell walls as well as the protoplasmic membranes could be considered as membranes. Most cell walls are **permeable,** that is, all molecules and similar particles can diffuse through them. The walls of cork cells are, however, **impermeable,** and diffusion can not occur through them. The particles of some substances can pass through the various protoplasmic membranes whereas those of others can not, so these membranes are said to be **differentially permeable.**

The protoplasmic membranes are generally very permeable to gases and water, less permeable to solutes such as salts and simple sugars, and

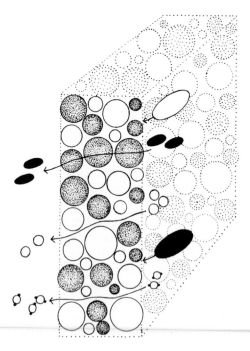

Figure 8.1. A very diagrammatic representation of the possible structural organization of a small portion of a differentially permeable cell membrane. The large stippled spheres are membrane phospholipids, the white ones are membrane proteins. Water molecules and the smaller solute particles (small white circles) diffuse through the pore spaces between the molecules making up the membrane, but larger particles (white ovals) cannot pass through the pores. Large fat-soluble molecules (black ovals) may not be able to pass through the pores, but can dissolve in the phospholipids of the membrane and thus diffuse through them. Some fat-soluble molecules (large black oval) may be too big to penetrate even this way. (Adapted from *Principles of Plant Physiology,* by Bonner & Galston, with the permission of the publishers, W. H. Freeman & Co.)

impermeable to larger solute particles and colloidal particles. Fat-soluble substances can, however, penetrate these living cell membranes with considerable ease even though their molecules are relatively large.

Much research has been done in an effort to understand this differential permeability of living membranes. The generally accepted current concept is that these membranes are composed of a mosaic of protein and phospholipid molecules with small spaces between molecules (Fig. 8.1). The smaller molecules such as water, carbon dioxide, and oxygen, as well as ions, are thought to diffuse through the intermolecular spaces of the membranes (3), but the larger particles can not get through these spaces. The fat-soluble substances, on the other hand, dissolve in the phospholipid portions of the membrane and so can diffuse through even though they are too large to pass through the pores. The permeability of living membranes to particular substances may change from time to time.

Although a membrane may decrease the rate of diffusion of a substance, it has no influence on the direction of diffusion, this being determined solely by the diffusion pressure of the substance inside and outside the membrane. If a membrane is permeable to gases or solutes they will diffuse just as they would if no membrane were present. The diffusion of water through differentially permeable membranes may, however, result in the production of pressure (**turgor pressure**) of considerable magnitude and so requires special consideration.

OSMOSIS

The diffusion of water through differentially permeable membranes is commonly called **osmosis**. This term should not be applied to the diffusion of solutes through differentially permeable membranes since, unlike water, their diffusion is not directly involved in the creation of turgor pressure. The only important reason for applying a special term to the diffusion of water through differentially permeable membranes is that it may result in turgor pressure, the diffusion process itself presumably being no different from the diffusion of water under any other conditions. Several examples should serve to clarify the process of osmosis.

OSMOSIS IN A CELL MODEL. Suppose we secure a piece of transparent plastic tubing permeable to water molecules but impermeable to sugar molecules, tie one end tightly, fill it with a sucrose solution, and then tie the other end. We now have an osmotic cell model, the tubing corresponding to both the differentially permeable protoplasmic membranes and the restraining cell wall surrounding them, and the contained solution corresponding to the cell sap of the vacuole. If the cell model is placed in a beaker of water, the water will diffuse through the membrane

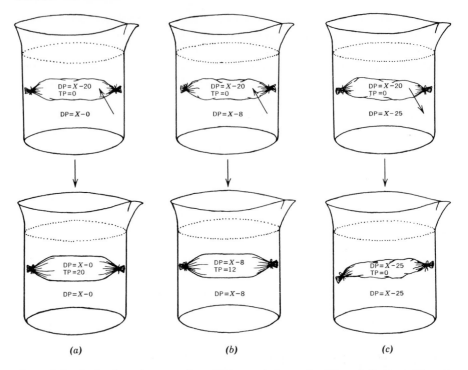

Figure 8.2. In the three demonstrations diagrammed above, the differentially permeable cell models all contained a sucrose solution in which the water had a diffusion pressure of $X - 20$ atmos. They were placed in beakers containing (a) water (DP = $X - 0$), (b) a sucrose solution in which the water had a DP of $X - 8$, and (c) a sucrose solution in which the water had a DP of $X - 25$. The upper series of beakers shows the situation at the beginning, the arrows within the beakers indicating the direction of diffusion of the water. The lower series shows the situation at dynamic equilibrium. In each series, the diffusion pressure of the water becomes the same inside as out. The relatively small changes in the diffusion pressure of the water in the external solutions resulting from the diffusion of some water molecules in or out are ignored.

into the tube (because water has a higher concentration outside than in) and the tube will become more and more swollen or **turgid** (Fig. 8.2). The pressure developed in the tube is **turgor pressure.** After several hours, the diffusion pressure of the water inside the tube will become equal to that of the outside water, diffusion will cease, and a dynamic equilibrium will exist. At equilibrium, however, the water is still more concentrated outside than inside regardless of how much has diffused in, since the sucrose molecules can not diffuse outward through the membrane. The entire system is at the same temperature, so temperature has no differential effect on the diffusion pressure of the water. This means than an imposed pressure has increased the diffusion pressure of the water in the tube just enough to counteract the decrease in diffusion pressure resulting from the lower water concentration, and so the water in the tube now has the same diffusion pressure as the pure water outside. The imposed pressure (the **wall pressure**) is the back pressure of the membrane (wall) against the contained solution, and is equal to the turgor pressure in magnitude.

The greater the initial difference in the inside and outside diffusion pressure of water, the greater will be the turgor pressure developed. If the diffusion pressure of the water in the tube were originally $X - 10$ atmos. (because of its reduced concentration) the turgor pressure would be 10 atmos., whereas if the original diffusion pressure had been $X - 15$ atmos. the turgor pressure would be 15 atmos.

Next, let us consider what will happen if we place a cell model in a solution rather than in pure water. Suppose that the water in the cell model has a diffusion pressure of $X - 15$ atmos. and that the water in the surrounding solution has a diffusion pressure of $X - 3$. Water will diffuse into the cell model until its diffusion pressure inside is the same as outside, that is, $X - 3$ (disregarding the slight decrease in the DP of the water outside as some diffuses in). The increase in diffusion pressure of the water in the cell model from $X - 15$ to $X - 3$ will have been brought about primarily through the building up of an imposed pressure. This imposed pressure and the turgor pressure giving rise to it will be 12 atmos. $[(X - 15) - (X - 3)]$, rather than 15 atmos. as when the cell model was immersed in pure water.

Turgor pressure can be built up only if there is a *differentially* permeable membrane. If the membrane of the cell model had been impermeable to both sugar and water molecules, no diffusion could have occured. If the membrane had been permeable to both substances, the sugar molecules would have been diffusing out as the water molecules were diffusing in and no turgor pressure would have existed at equilibrium.

Water will, of course, diffuse out of the cell model rather than in if its diffusion pressure is greater inside than out. In this event the turgor pressure is zero and equilibrium occurs when the concentration of the water becomes as low inside as out. For example, if the water in the cell model originally has a diffusion pressure of $X - 5$ atmos. and the outside water has a diffusion pressure of $X - 15$ atmos., water will diffuse out until its diffusion pressure in the model is $X - 15$ atmos.

OSMOSIS IN PLANT CELLS. The preceding discussion applies equally well to living plant cells. If we place a unicellular alga with enough solutes in its cell sap to reduce the diffusion pressure of the water in it to $X - 20$ atmos. in a container of pure water, then water will diffuse into the cell until its diffusion pressure is the same inside as outside $(X - 0)$. This dynamic equilibrium occurs when the turgor pressure and the counteracting imposed pressure have reached 20 atmos. If the cell had been placed in a solution in which the water had a diffusion pressure of $X - 15$ atmos., the internal diffusion pressure would have been $X - 15$ atmos. at equilibrium and the turgor pressure only 5 atmos.

There are, however, several complications in living plant cells not present in the cell models. The cell membranes are not impermeable to all solutes and so solutes are generally moving in and out of the cells. Furthermore, processes in the cell are constantly using some solutes and producing others. For example, sugar may be produced by photosynthesis or by the digestion of starch, or may be used in respiration or be converted into starch. Such changes in solute content result in changes in water concentration. The concentration of water in a cell, for example of a leaf, is reduced when water evaporates from the cell. The diffusion pressure of water in a cell is affected, not only by such changes in water concentration, but also by changes in the turgor pressure of the cell. Consequently, an equilibrium is rarely attained in living plant cells and then only for limited periods of time. The principles of diffusion still hold, however: water will diffuse into a cell whenever its diffusion pressure is greater outside than inside.

Another difference between the cell model and a cell is that in the model a single membrane served as both the differentially permeable membrane and the restraining wall. The differentially permeable protoplasmic membranes of plant cells are so elastic that if they were not restrained by the cell wall they would balloon until they burst as water continued to diffuse into the cell. The walls of plant cells, constructed as they are of several layers of cellulose fibers with the fibers oriented in different directions in the various layers, resist the high turgor pressures often developed in plant cells, or in other words, they are capable of exerting high wall pressures.

Water may diffuse into cells from adjacent cells as well as from solutions. Most of the cells of multicellular plants secure water from other cells, since only a few of the cells are in contact with the soil water or other external water supplies.

PLASMOLYSIS. If the water surrounding a plant cell has a lower diffusion pressure than the water of the cell sap then water will diffuse out of the vacuole. As the vacuole decreases in size the elastic cytoplasm contracts and pulls away from the cell wall, which shrinks only slightly (Fig. 8.3). This separation of the cytoplasm from the cell wall is known as **plasmolysis**. The lower the diffusion pressure of the external water, the greater will be the plasmolysis. In a highly plasmolyzed cell the cytoplasm may separate from the wall entirely and assume a spherical shape. If a plasmolyzed cell is placed in water soon enough it will regain turgidity and survive without apparent permanent damage, but

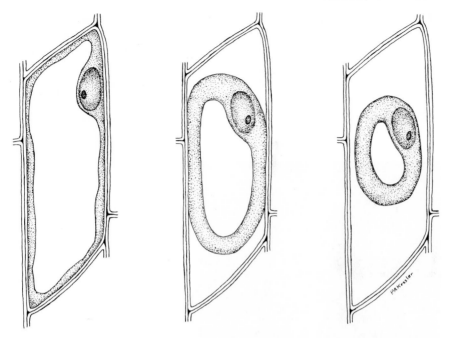

Figure 8.3. Left: a turgid cell. Center: the cell has been plasmolyzed by placing it in a solution of sucrose in which the diffusion pressure of the water is less than in the vacuole, thus causing water to diffuse out of the vacuole into the surrounding solution. The elastic cytoplasm has separated from the cell wall. Right: more extreme plasmolysis was caused by transferring the cell to another solution in which the water was still less concentrated than in the first solution, that is, the sugar was more concentrated.

continued plasmolysis results in irreversible protoplasmic changes and death of the cell.

A concentrated salt solution kills plants by plasmolyzing their cells, and the "burning" of plants by excess fertilizer is a result of plasmolysis. Most fresh-water plants are plasmolyzed when placed in ocean water. Salt marsh plants can obtain water only because the diffusion pressure of water in their cells is even lower than that of the salt water, and most kinds of plants would be plasmolyzed if planted in a salt marsh.

THE SIGNIFICANCE OF TURGOR PRESSURE. Plant cells must be turgid if the plant is to live and grow normally. Turgor pressure helps support nonwoody tissues and loss of turgor results in wilting (Fig. 8.4). Stomata close when guard cells lose turgor and so gas exchange is hampered. The folding of the leaves of oxalis, bean, mimosa, and other plants at night and when the plants lack water results from reduced turgor, whereas the rapid movements of the leaves of the Venus fly-trap

223

(Fig. 5.28) and the sensitive plant (Fig. 8.5) result from a sudden diffusion of water from certain specialized cells (2). The leaves of some grasses roll into a tube when they begin to wilt because of the rapid loss of water from longitudinal rows of specialized cells in the upper epidermis and the consequent reduction in their turgor pressures (Fig. 8.6). Since most of the stomata of these grasses are in the upper epidermis, the rolling of the leaves results in a considerable reduction in the rate of

Figure 8.4. Multiple exposure photograph (at 10-min. intervals) of a young *Smilax* plant that had wilted and was regaining turgidity after being watered. Note elevation of leaves as well as rise of the drooping stem. (Photo by Ross E. Hutchins, Mississippi State College.)

Figure 8.5. A sensitive plant (*Mimosa pudica*) with expanded leaves (left) and the same plant 3 sec. after the stems had been tapped sharply (right). The sudden folding of the leaves results from a rapid loss of turgor pressure in the pulvini of the leaves. (Courtesy of the copyright holder, General Biological Supply House, Chicago.)

water vapor diffusion out of the stomata. (The air in the tube soon becomes saturated with water vapor.) Although this may prevent excessive wilting of the leaves, the leaves do not roll up "in order to save water."

Since under natural conditions plant cells are rarely in contact with pure water, their turgor pressures are rarely at the possible maximum. Rain water, however, is relatively pure, and during rainy periods the cells of fruits such as cherries may develop unusually high turgor pressures, often resulting in stresses that burst the fruit. If rain falls directly on pollen the turgor pressure of the pollen may become so high that the wall can no longer resist the pressure and then the pollen bursts. Because of this, and also because some of the wetted pollen germinates prematurely, prolonged rains while apple trees are blooming may seriously reduce the apple crop.

OTHER SPECIAL TYPES OF DIFFUSION

IMBIBITION. The diffusion of the molecules of a liquid or a gas (usually water) in between the molecules of a solid, causing it to swell, is called

225

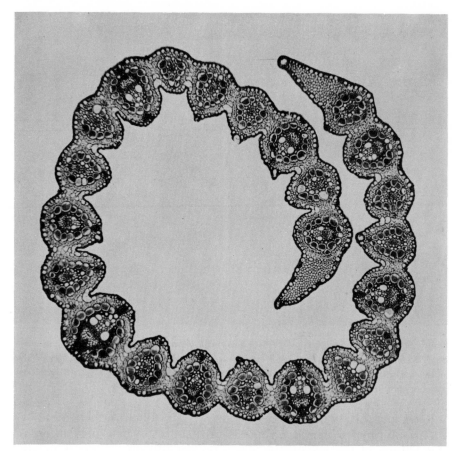

Figure 8.6. Sectional microscopic view of a rolled grass leaf (cut across the blade). The large cells in the depressions between ridges of the upper surface lose their turgor pressure when water is deficient, which causes the leaf to roll into an almost closed tube. Since grass leaves commonly have more stomata on the upper surface than the lower, the rolling may result in a decreased rate of transpiration. (Copyright, General Biological Supply House, Inc., Chicago.)

imbibition. For example, the initial absorption of water by dry seeds is largely imbibitional. A board placed on moist soil imbibes water on its under side, causing it to swell and warp. Wooden doors and windows swell in humid weather because they have imbibed water vapor from the air. The imbibitional pressures resulting from imbibition are commonly very great, often being as high as 1000 atmos.

Solids imbibe liquids or gases only when strong intermolecular attractive forces exist between them. Thus, cellulose imbibes water but not ether, and rubber imbibes ether but not water. The imbibed molecules are packed more closely together than they were in the liquid or gas and their rate of movement or kinetic energy (and thus their diffusion pressure) is greatly reduced. The lost energy is converted into heat, so a release of heat always accompanies imbibition.

EVAPORATION. The diffusion of molecules of a liquid into the air is called **evaporation**. Molecules released by evaporation exist as gases. The gaseous form of water is called **water vapor**. Water is almost constantly evaporating from the wet walls of plant cells into the air of the intercellular spaces or of the outside atmosphere. The diffusion pressure of water vapor is commonly referred to as its **vapor pressure**. The vapor pressure of the air varies greatly with the concentration of water vapor and temperature, ranging from just a few millimeters of mercury to around 40 mm. of Hg in hot, humid situations. Evaporation is slower when the vapor pressure of the air is high than when it is low.

Mineral Salt Accumulation

Although the ions of mineral salts are usually much more concentrated in plant cells than the same ions are in the surrounding soil or water, ions still continue to enter the cells and **accumulate**, principally in the vacuoles. The direction of ion movement is just the opposite of what it would be in diffusion, so it is evident that some other factor is operating in ion accumulation.

Only living cells can accumulate ions, and when a cell is killed the ions diffuse out until a concentration equilibrium is attained. Cells must expend energy in accumulating ions, in contrast with the passive role cells play in diffusion. That the energy is provided by respiration has been shown by a variety of experiments. Any decrease in the rate of respiration (brought about by reduced temperature or oxygen or application of respiratory poisons) is accompanied by a decreased rate of accumulation (Fig. 8.7). Just how energy from respiration is used in accumulation is still not well understood, but apparently carrier molecules pick up ions at the outer surface of the vacuolar membrane and transport them through the membrane to the cell sap.

It may be a bit difficult to understand how a net movement of ions can occur in a direction exactly opposite from that in which they would diffuse, but an analogy may help. A basketball will roll down hill without the application of outside force, expending the kinetic energy stored in it when it was taken up the hill. This is comparable to diffusion. The ball will not roll up hill any more than a substance can diffuse from a region of lower to higher diffusion pressure. The ball

227

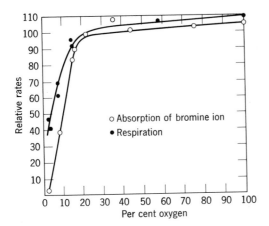

Figure 8.7. Influence of the rate of respiration of roots on the rate of absorption of bromine ions by the roots. The rate of respiration was experimentally controlled by varying the per cent of oxygen in the air bubbled through the solution in which the roots were growing. (Data of Steward, from *Plant Physiology* by B. S. Meyer and D. B. Anderson with the permission of the publisher, D. Van Nostrand & Co.)

can, however, be moved to the top of the hill by the expenditure of an outside supply of energy, just as ions can be moved from a lower to higher diffusion pressure by the expenditure of energy from respiration.

Much research has been done in an effort to determine whether cells also accumulate water and solutes other than salts against a diffusion gradient, but the results have been conflicting and the picture is not clear. Auxins (plant growth hormones) will cause increased water absorption by tissues such as slices of potato tubers, but this may only be a result of promotion of cell wall growth by the auxin. The increased cell size would bring about decreased turgor pressure and thus decreased diffusion pressure of the water in the cell. More water would then diffuse in, occupying the enlarged cell volume.

Recent studies suggest that accumulation of ions in vacuoles may be much less important in the general economy of plants than has been assumed. Ion accumulation may occur primarily at the vacuolar membrane, and the plasma membrane may be much more permeable than the vacuolar membrane, permitting relatively free diffusion in and out of the cytoplasm. However, mitochondria and perhaps other cytoplasmic structures also accumulate ions and their membranes are probably similar to the vacuolar membranes as regards permeability and accumulation.

The regions of a plant cell outside the vacuolar and mitochondrial membranes, through which ions may diffuse with considerable freedom, are referred to as **free space**. The cell walls constitute a part of the free space of a cell, but since the intercellular spaces are usually filled with air they are not considered to be a part of free space.

If the concept of free space is correct, ions and water moving through a tissue, as through the cortex of a root on their way from the soil to the xylem, probably pass through the free space rather than through the vacuole of one cell after another. Movement through free space may be by diffusion, by cytoplasmic streaming, or by mass flow through the cell walls. The ions accumulated in the vacuoles of root cells are apparently held there more or less permanently and are not transported on up to the shoot of the plant (at least not promptly). The concept of free space is still controversial and incompletely understood, and thus considerable research in this area is in progress.

Questions

1. How could you cause nitrogen (N_2) to diffuse into a leaf?

2. If you liberated some hydrogen sulfide gas (H_2S) in the neighborhood of a plant would it diffuse into the leaves? Explain your answer.

3. Natural rubber is permeable to carbon dioxide, but impermeable to oxygen, nitrogen, and water vapor. If three natural rubber balloons were inflated to the same degree with (a) carbon dioxide, (b) air, and (c) your exhaled breath respectively, what would be the relative turgidity of each after a day or two?

4. A cell model made of a membrane permeable only to water and containing a solution in which the water has a diffusion pressure of $X - 15$ atmos. is placed in pure water. Will water diffuse into or out of the cell model? What will be the diffusion pressure of the water in the cell model at equilibrium? What will the turgor pressure of the cell model be? Will the water in the cell model be at the same concentration as the surrounding water at equilibrium? Now answer all the foregoing questions for each of the following situations: (a) The foregoing cell model is placed in a solution with water having a diffusion pressure of $X - 6$ atmos.; (b) The cell model is placed in a solution with water having a diffusion pressure of $X - 19$ atmos.

5. What is happening in a wilted stalk of celery after it is placed in water to crisp it? Would it become crisp sooner if placed in ice water or in tap water? Explain. What effect would adding salt to the water have on the crisping process?

6. The water in a pollen grain has a diffusion pressure of $X - 18$ atmos. and the turgor pressure of the pollen grain is 8 atmos. If the turgor pressure became 0 atmos., what would be the diffusion pressure of the water? How much is the diffusion pressure of the water reduced by the presence of solutes (i.e., by reduced water concentration)? If the pollen is transferred to a stigma with a stigmatic fluid in which the water has a diffusion pressure of $X - 12$ atmos. what will be its turgor pressure? What will be its turgor pressure if placed in pure water?

► *References*

For Reference

1. Bonner, James and Arthur W. Galston, *Principles of Plant Physiology*. San Francisco: W. H. Freeman & Co., 1952, Chapter 4.

For Reading

2. Greulach, Victor A., Plant movements. *Scientific American* 192(2):101–106, February 1955.
3. Solomon, A. K., Pores in the cell membrane. *Scientific American* 203(6):145–156, December 1960.

9. Plants and Water

THE IMPORTANCE OF WATER in the life of plants has been discussed in Chapters 1 and 3 and mention has been made of its various roles in plants. In Chapter 8 we considered the diffusion of water into and out of cells. We now turn our attention to other aspects of the water economy of plants: the absorption of water, its transport through the xylem, and its loss from plants.

The Loss of Water

Despite the many essential roles that water plays in plants, most of the water absorbed by land plants evaporates from the cells into intercellular spaces and then diffuses through the stomata (and to a lesser degree through the cuticle and lenticels) into the outside air. The diffusion of water vapor from plants is called **transpiration** (12). Plants may also lose small quantities of liquid water.

THE LOSS OF LIQUID WATER

When soil water is abundant and the atmosphere is essentially saturated with water vapor, drops of water are frequently found on the

Figure 9.1. Guttation by a strawberry leaf. (Courtesy of J. Arthur Herrick, Kent State University.)

edges of leaves. These drops of water have been forced out of the ends of the xylem of the leaf veins under pressure. This process is known as **guttation** (Fig. 9.1). The drops of water exuded by guttation should not be confused with dew drops that are often present on the leaf surfaces at the same time. Dew is water that has condensed from moist air.

Liquid water may also exude from cut or injured stems, a process known as **bleeding.** Bleeding is the most common under conditions of high soil moisture and atmospheric humidity, particularly in deciduous plants without leaves. Grape vines may bleed especially profusely under these conditions. A limited amount of water is **secreted** by plants, as in the nectar of some kinds of flowers.

TRANSPIRATION: THE LOSS OF WATER VAPOR

Most of the water lost by plants is transpired as water vapor. The quantities of water lost by transpiration are immense. For example, in an acre of corn the plants transpire about 325,000 gallons of water during a growing season. This is equivalent to about 1300 tons of water, enough to cover an acre to a depth of 11 inches. It is estimated that the trees in an apple orchard transpire enough water during a growing season to cover the orchard to a depth of 9 inches, whereas a good stand of red maple trees may transpire enough water to cover the area under them to a depth of 23 inches.

FACTORS AFFECTING THE RATE OF TRANSPIRATION. Plants of two species growing side by side may lose quite different quantities of water by transpiration. This may result from the fact that one species has a greater total leaf area than the other. However, the rate of transpiration per unit area of leaf surface may also differ. Factors such as the diffusion pressure of water in the cells, thickness of the cuticle, size and numbers of stomata, and position of the stomata (whether flush with the epidermis or sunken below the general epidermal surface—Fig. 9.2) may influence the rate of transpiration in any particular species of plant. However, we are more concerned with the influence of environmental factors on the rate of transpiration.

Transpiration is generally very slow during the night, increases rapidly from early morning to mid-afternoon, and then decreases rapidly (Fig. 9.3). Transpiration is slower on cool, cloudy days than on warm, sunny days. Such variations in the rate of transpiration result from the interplay of two basic factors: (1) stomatal condition (whether the stomata are open or closed), and (2) the difference between the diffusion pressure of the water vapor in the intercellular spaces and in the air.

Stomata are usually closed during the night and during the late afternoon on hot, sunny days, but are generally open at other times during the day. When the stomata are closed, the rate of transpiration is very low, since little usually occurs through the cuticle. Differences in the diffusion pressure of water vapor inside and outside a leaf have little effect on the rate of transpiration when stomata are closed, but these

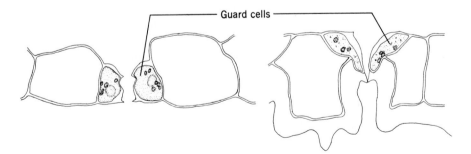

Guard cells

Figure 9.2. Sections through a surface stoma (left) and a sunken stoma (right). Both are from the lower epidermis, so the bottom sides are in contact with the outside air. Since the rate of diffusion through a tube is inversely proportional to the length of the tube, sunken stomata reduce the rate of diffusion of water vapor and other gases. (See also Figure 5.21.)

233

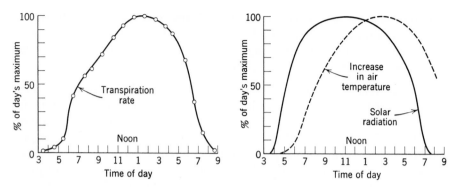

Figure 9.3. Changes in the rate of transpiration of alfalfa during an 18-hr. period, compared with changes in temperature and solar radiation. Data of Briggs and Shantz. (Modified from *Principles of Plant Physiology* by James Bonner and Arthur W. Galston, 1952, with the permission of the publishers, W. H. Freeman & Co.)

diffusion pressure differences are the important controlling factor when the stomata are open.

The diffusion pressure of water vapor inside and outside the leaf is influenced by both temperature and concentration (see Chapter 8). Since the wet cell walls provide a large evaporating surface relative to the volume of the adjacent intercellular spaces, the air inside a leaf is usually saturated (or almost saturated) with water vapor. The concentration of water vapor in the outside air is usually much lower than in the leaf, resulting in the outward diffusion of water molecules. Transpiration into the dry air of a desert is more rapid than into the moist air of a forest.

An increase in temperature results in a marked increase in the rate of transpiration, even though a leaf is in the shade and so is essentially at the same temperature as the surrounding air. The increase in transpiration results from the following: (1) The water-holding capacity of the air increases as the temperature rises. (2) As the water-holding capacity of the air in the intercellular space in a leaf increases, more water evaporates into it from the wet cell walls, increasing the concentration of water vapor in the air and saturating it to its now greater capacity. (3) Although the water-holding capacity of the outside air also increases, the concentration of water vapor increases little if at all because of the vastness of the atmosphere in proportion to the evaporating surfaces. (4) Because of the increase in water vapor concentration in the air of the intercellular spaces and the absence of any significant change in its concentration in the outside air, the difference between the internal and external diffusion pressure of water vapor becomes greater and the rate of transpiration rises (Fig. 9.4).

If a leaf is in the sun rather than in the shade it will be several degrees warmer than the surrounding air and so the rate of transpiration will be even higher. The great increase in transpiration with temperature rise, resulting in the loss of large quantities of water and so frequently in wilting, is one reason why plants of many species do not thrive at high temperatures.

DIFFUSION THROUGH STOMATA

The rate of diffusion of gases through pores the size of stomata is more nearly proportional to the perimeter of the pore than to its area. Consequently, almost as much diffusion occurs through a partially closed stoma as through one that is wide open. Only when stomata are completely, or almost completely, closed do they reduce transpiration significantly. Numerous small pores like stomata provide a very effective diffusion pathway. Although the stomatal openings generally occupy only 1 to 3% of the total leaf area, about 50 to 75% as much diffusion occurs through them as would from an open water surface with an area equal to that of the entire leaf. This high diffusive capacity of stomata

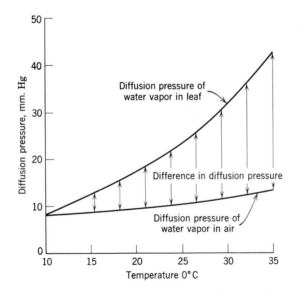

Figure 9.4. Representative changes in the vapor pressure (diffusion pressure) of water vapor in the intercellular spaces of a leaf and in the outside air as temperature increases. The leaf is in the shade and thus has essentially the same temperature as the outside air. The rapid increase in DP inside the leaf results from increased water vapor concentration as the water-holding capacity of the air increases with temperature, and the concentration of water vapor in the outside air increases little if any.

is particularly important in relation to the diffusion of oxygen and carbon dioxide while photosynthesis is in progress.

STOMATAL OPENING AND CLOSING. Stomata are open when the guard cells are turgid, and closed when the guard cells have little or no turgor pressure. At first glance this situation may seem to be just the reverse of what it should be, but guard cells of different types have a variety of structural features that provide the basis of this turgor mechanism. Many species of plants have guard cells with thickened cell walls adjacent to the stomatal opening (Fig. 9.5). As turgor pressure increases, the thinner parts of the cell wall are stretched more than the thickened parts, causing the thickened areas to cup inward and thus widen the stomatal pore.

The mid-afternoon closing of stomata on a hot, sunny day results from a water deficit in the plant and the consequent loss of turgor pressure in the guard cells. Once the stomata have closed, the reduction in transpiration may result in the guard cells regaining turgor and opening again, at least for a while.

The opening of stomata with the appearance of light and their closing in the dark, however, has a much less obvious explanation and has puzzled plant physiologists for a long time. Since about 1925 many investigators, particularly the Canadian plant physiologist, G. W. Scarth, have gradually pieced together bits of research data that have permitted the development of a reasonable theory of the effect of light on stomatal opening, at least in *Zebrina* (Wandering Jew). Although the matter is still under investigation, the sequence of events may be as follows:

1. With the appearance of light, photosynthesis begins in the guard cells as well as in the mesophyll, but the ordinary epidermal cells generally do not contain chloroplasts and so do not carry on photosynthesis.

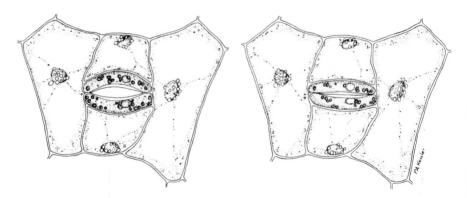

Figure 9.5. Open and closed stomata of *Zebrina* (Wandering Jew) showing the thicker walls of the guard cells adjacent to the stomatal pore.

2. As the carbon dioxide that accumulated in the guard cells during darkness is used in photosynthesis, its concentration and the concentration of carbonic acid ($H_2O + CO_2 \rightleftharpoons H_2CO_3$) in the guard cells decreases, reducing the acidity of the guard cells.

3. Since the enzyme **starch phosphorylase** catalyzes the formation of glucose phosphate from starch when acidity is relatively low (and the conversion of glucose phosphate to starch when the acidity is higher), the sugar concentration in the guard cells now increases. Sugar synthesized following photosynthesis also contributes to the increase in sugar concentration.

4. This increase in solute concentration results in a decrease in the water concentration in the guard cells, thus reducing its diffusion pressure.

5. As a result, water now diffuses into the guard cells from adjacent epidermal cells, increasing the turgor pressure of the guard cells, thus causing stomatal opening.

A series of cause and effect relations such as this illustrates the complexity of superficially simple plant responses and the dependence of an acceptable theory on the accumulation of a wide variety of research data. Contrast this *cause and effect* explanation with some of the *teleological* explanations of stomatal movement sometimes seen in print: that stomata open in the morning "so that the plant can secure carbon dioxide for photosynthesis" and that stomata close at night "in order to save water." Such teleological explanations, crediting the plant with intelligent and purposeful behavior, are easy to formulate but totally inadequate in explaining plant responses. Teleological explanations get the cart before the horse by converting a possible result into a cause. If botanists were satisfied with teleological explanations for plant behavior, research aimed at discovery of the actual course of events would cease.

WILTING

The loss of water by transpiration may at times result in the loss of turgor by cells of the plant and the consequent **wilting** of the plant. Two types of wilting can be distinguished. **Permanent wilting** occurs when all soil water the plant can absorb has been exhausted. It is really permanent only insofar as the plant will not recover from wilting unless water is added to the soil. **Temporary wilting** occurs when there is adequate soil water but when the rate of transpiration exceeds the rate of water absorption. Plants recover from temporary wilting when the rate of transpiration falls below the rate of absorption. Temporary wilting is quite common on hot, sunny days.

THE ROLE OF TRANSPIRATION

Botanists have long been interested in the question of whether or not transpiration plays an essential role in plants, particularly since most of the water absorbed by plants is lost by transpiration. Among the possible roles of transpiration that have been suggested are water and mineral salt transport through the xylem and cooling of leaves and other plant organs.

Although the rate of transpiration is the principal factor determining the rate of water flow through the xylem, both methods of water transport described in the following section could occur without transpiration. Water flow through the xylem would be much slower if transpiration were not occurring, but water would still be transported as fast as it was being *used* by the plant. Although some experimental evidence suggests that an increase in the rate of transpiration results in an increase in the rate of mineral salt absorption and transport, there is also evidence to the contrary. At any rate, it seems probable that mineral salts would be supplied to the cells of the plant rapidly enough and in adequate quantities even if there were no transpiration. The evaporation of water from wet cell walls during transpiration does have a cooling effect, like all evaporation. Calculations show, however, that even when transpiration is the most rapid, this cooling effect of evaporation is a relatively minor means of heat loss from the leaves, compared with heat loss by radiation and convection, and is probably not a critical factor in the prevention of heat injury to the cells.

On the basis of our accumulated knowledge, it seems unlikely that transpiration plays any essential role in the life of plants. Transpiration occurs simply because water vapor has a higher diffusion pressure inside a plant than outside and because there are stomata and lenticels through which water can diffuse. Plants might thrive better if there were no transpiration, since temporary wilting would never occur and permanent wilting would occur much less frequently. A plant without diffusion pathways such as stomata and lenticels would, however, be greatly handicapped, since exchanges of carbon dioxide and oxygen with the atmosphere during photosynthesis and respiration could not occur freely.

Absorption of Water

Water can enter plants through the leaves, stems, roots, or reproductive structures, but most of the water absorbed by land plants enters through the roots. Water absorption occurs primarily through the young tissues of the root tip. The root hairs, in particular, provide a

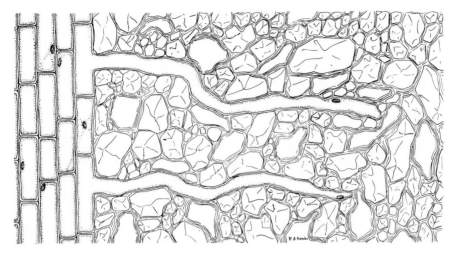

Figure 9.6. Root hairs are in close contact with soil particles and have a very large absorbing surface. Many root hairs are much longer than those shown here.

very large total absorbing surface in close contact with soil particles (Fig. 9.6). A single rye plant was found to have over 14 billion root hairs with a total surface area of about 4000 square feet, and the absorbing surface of the remainder of the root system totaled about 2500 square feet. In contrast, the total surface area of the stems and leaves was only 50 square feet. Although most land plants have abundant root hairs when growing in moist (but not flooded) soil, a good many species of trees have few or no root hairs.

THE METHOD OF WATER ABSORPTION

Since the diffusion pressure of water in moist soil is generally higher than the diffusion pressure of water in the cells of roots, it is quite possible that most of the water absorbed by roots simply diffuses in. However, plant physiologists who study absorption have much experimental evidence suggesting that absorption may not be so simple a matter. For example, if roots are deprived of oxygen (resulting in a lower rate of respiration), the rate of water absorption generally falls. Whether energy from respiration is directly concerned with absorption, or whether respiration is involved in some more indirect manner such as maintaining differential permeability of the cell membranes, is not well understood at present. It now seems possible that considerable water may flow through the free space of root tissues, and that this may play an important role in absorption (p. 228). The continuing research on water absorption will undoubtedly give us a clearer and more detailed picture of its precise nature.

SOILS. Since most land plants absorb the greater part of their water from moist soils, some basic information about the nature of soils and the ways they hold water is helpful in understanding water absorption (7, 8). Most soils are composed principally of weathered rock particles. The size of these rock particles is important in determining the nature and properties of soils, including their water-holding capacities. American soil scientists have agreed to call particles less than 0.002 mm. in diameter **clay**, particles 0.002 to 0.02 mm. in diameter **silt**, and particles 0.02 to 2.0 mm. in diameter **sand**. Although most soils contain particles of all three size ranges, soils are classified as clay, silt, or sand on the basis of the most abundant particle size range. Most soils also contain some **humus**, that is, finely divided plant and animal remains in various stages of decomposition. The gray and black colors of many soils result from their humus content. Although rock particles make up the greater part of most soils, **muck** soils contain more humus than rock particles.

The small particles in a clay soil tend to pack closely together, leaving only very small capillary spaces between them, whereas the much larger sand particles fit together more loosely, leaving larger capillary spaces and also still larger spaces filled with air. Unlike sandy soils, clay soils tend to be hard when dry and sticky when wet. These undesirable features of clay soils can be largely overcome by causing the small clay particles to cling together in irregularly shaped clusters known as **crumbs**. A clay soil with good crumb structure contains more air spaces than a packed clay soil and is much more porous. Good crumb structure may be obtained by adding lime or organic matter to the clay soil. The positively charged Ca^{++} ions from the lime become attached to the negatively charged soil particles, and since each ion can attach to two particles because of its double positive charge it binds the two particles together. Thus, a cluster of particles may be bound together into a crumb. Humus and commercial soil conditioners (11) similarly bind clay particles together into crumbs. Compacting of a clay soil, as by frequent walking over it, results in a loss of crumb structure and thus of porosity of the soil.

The pore spaces between soil particles generally constitute a considerable percentage of the soil volume, from about 30% in clay soils to 60% or so in sandy soils. The smaller pores most commonly hold water by capillary forces and the larger pores are usually filled with air, but all the pores may contain air when the soil is very dry or water when it is very wet. The presence of adequate quantities of air in the soil is as important in the growth of most kinds of plants as the availability of sufficient water (Fig. 9.7), since the rate of respiration in roots decreases

Figure 9.7. Influence of oxygen concentration on the growth of tomato roots. The plants were raised in separate solution cultures with different oxygen concentrations and assembled in one container for the photograph. The per cent of oxygen in the air above the solutions in which the roots were growing was as follows, from left to right: 1, 3, 5, 10, and 20. (Courtesy of L. C. Erickson, University of California, Riverside.)

greatly when oxygen is deficient. Decreased respiration, in turn, may result in decreased water absorption, mineral salt absorption, and growth. A relatively few species of plants, such as paddy rice, cattails, and some willows, thrive in water-logged soils. However, most species of plants grow well only in well-aerated soil. Some species of plants that grow in wet situations have large air spaces in their stems and roots through which oxygen can diffuse (Fig. 9.8), whereas others have all their roots near the soil surface. Still others can survive even though the root cells are carrying on anaerobic respiration (page 280) or a very low rate of aerobic respiration.

Because soil organisms as well as roots are constantly carrying on

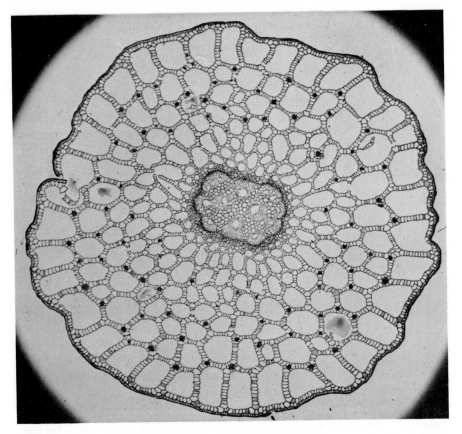

Figure 9.8. Gases can diffuse readily through the large air spaces present in the stems of some water plants such as this *Potamogeton* stem, shown in cross section through a microscope. (Courtesy of the copyright holder, General Biological Supply House.)

respiration, soil air generally has a lower concentration of oxygen and a higher concentration of carbon dioxide than the atmosphere.

SOIL WATER. The water held by soils consists of three principal fractions. First, each soil particle is covered by a film of water only a few molecules thick. This film of water is held by strong attractive forces between the molecules in the particle and the water molecules, and these forces greatly reduce the rate and freedom of movement of the water molecules. Thus, the diffusion pressure of the water in the films is so low that it is unavailable to plants. These water films are present even in air dry soil but can be removed by heating in an oven. Because clay particles are smaller and more numerous than sand particles, and so have a much greater total surface area, clay soils hold much more surface water than sandy soils. This fraction is called **hygroscopic water.**

In the smaller pores of a soil, water is held by capillary forces. These capillary forces reduce the diffusion pressure of water only slightly, and **capillary water** is readily available to plants (provided that its diffusion pressure has not been reduced too much by the presence of high concentrations of salts). In the larger pores of a soil the capillary forces are not great enough to hold water against the force of gravity. In a well-drained soil, these larger pores are only temporarily filled with water (**gravitational water**) after irrigation or a rain, becoming filled with air as the water drains out.

FIELD CAPACITY AND PERMANENT WILTING PERCENTAGE. The water content of a soil is usually expressed as its percentage of the dry weight of the soil. The percentage water content of a soil at the time plants growing in it undergo permanent wilting is the **permanent wilting percentage**. At this point, the plants have absorbed all available capillary water. The permanent wilting percentage varies with the type of soil, ranging from almost 20% in clay soils to as low as 3% in sandy soils. These differences result from the fact that there is much more total particle surface area in a clay soil than in an equal volume of silty or sandy soil, and so more unavailable water is held in the surface films. Despite the great variation in permanent wilting percentage with soil type, permanent wilting occurs in all soils when the diffusion pressure of the soil water is reduced to about $X - 15$ atmos., regardless of the species of plant used in making the determination.

The percentage water content of a soil when it holds all the capillary water it can, but no gravitational water, is known as the **field capacity** of the soil. In soils with water contents above field capacity, capillary movement of water to adjacent regions of drier soil takes places, but capillary movement essentially ceases once the water content is reduced to field capacity. Since clay soils have more numerous pores of capillary size than sandy soils, they have much higher field capacities than sandy soils. The field capacity of clay soils may be as high as 45%, whereas that of sandy soils may be as low as 5%.

Since field capacity represents the point at which maximal capillary water content is combined with adequate soil aeration, and the permanent wilting percentage represents the point at which the available soil water has been exhausted, these two levels of soil water content are important as far as plants are concerned. The difference between them may be called the **storage capacity** of a soil. Thus, a clay soil with a field capacity of 40% and a wilting percentage of 18% would have a storage capacity of 22%, whereas a sandy soil with a field capacity of 7% and a wilting percentage of 4% would have a storage capacity of only 3%.

Within 2 days or less after a rain or irrigation, movement of water through a well-drained soil brings the water content to field capacity. If more water is then supplied, the moist layer of soil will only temporarily have a water content above field capacity, because the added water is moving through the layer already at field capacity and is bringing an additional layer of soil to field capacity. The final result of a heavy rain, as compared with a light one, is to bring a thicker layer of soil to field capacity, rather than to bring the soil to a higher percentage water content. The dividing line between soil at field capacity and the dry soil below it is quite pronounced, and although the dry soil may be at the wilting percentage, water will not move into it from the adjacent soil that is at field capacity, except for the diffusion of small quantities of water vapor.

As roots absorb water, the water content of the adjacent soil is reduced, perhaps even to the wilting percentage, and there will be no capillary movement of water into this dry soil if the soil next to it is at field capacity or less. However, as the root continues to grow, it enters new soil that may still contain available water—one reason why continued root growth is important in the economy of the plant. The roots are, of course, not searching for water. They are simply growing, and

Figure 9.9. In this demonstration, a box with one glass wall was partially filled with dry soil sloping from one side to the other and then moist soil at approximately field capacity was added and corn planted in it. Root growth through the moist soil was rapid, but the roots grew only a short distance into the dry soil. Note also that there has been no capillary movement of water from the wet soil to the dry soil. (Courtesy of Richard Böhning, Ohio State University.)

the chances are that they will grow into soil with a higher water content. In dry soil, root growth is greatly restricted (Fig. 9.9).

Water Transport

The final aspect of the water economy of plants we wish to consider is that of water transport in vascular plants. We are concerned here, not with the diffusion of water from one living cell to another or with the flow of water through the "free space" of plant tissues, but with the flow of water through the tracheids or the vessels of the xylem from the roots to the stems, leaves, and reproductive structures of a plant. Botanists have known for many years that long-distance transport of water through a plant (**translocation** or **conduction**) occurs in the tracheids or vessels of the xylem, but completely satisfactory explanations of the forces responsible for the flow of water have been elusive (5). Stephen Hales (4) formulated the basic concepts of both the current explanations of water rise in plants early in the seventeenth century, but despite much subsequent research we still have only a slightly better understanding of translocation that he had.

It is obvious that some force must be applied to the water if it is to flow upward. That water flows through the xylem rather than diffusing through it is evident from the fact that water frequently moves as fast as 75 cm. per minute in the xylem, much faster than the highest rates of diffusion of liquid water. Any acceptable explanation of water flow through the xylem must account for forces great enough to raise water to the tops of the tallest trees, including redwoods and Douglas firs that are almost 400 feet high. One atmos. pressure can support a column of water 33 feet high, so about 12 atmos. pressure is required to support a 400 foot water column. About 18 atmos. additional pressure is required to overcome the resistance to the movement of water (friction) through the tissues, so a total force of about 30 atmos. is essential for lifting water to the tops of the tallest trees.

Since air pressure provides a force of only 1 atmos. and can raise water to a height of only about 33 feet, it is clearly inadequate for raising water in a tree of any great size. Furthermore, even in small plants there would have to be a vacuum at the top of the plant and the ends of the xylem in the roots would have to be exposed to the air. Although biology textbooks sometimes give capillary action as an explanation for the rise of water in plants, calculations show that in tubes the diameter of vessel elements or tracheids, the capillary rise is only a few inches to a few feet. The suggestion that water might rise much higher through the much finer capillary spaces within the cell walls was discarded because the bulk of the water flows through the cell cavities rather than through the walls.

245

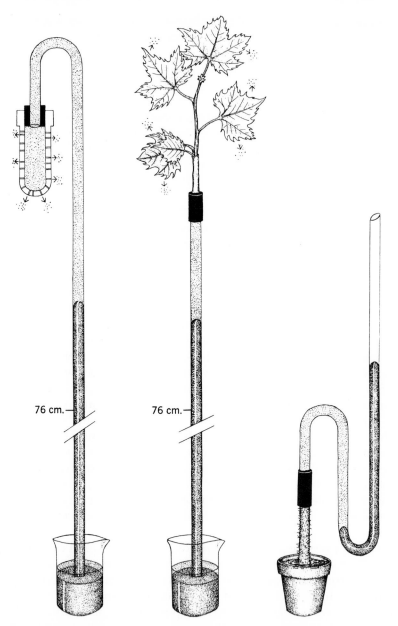

Figure 9.10. Demonstrations of root pressure (left) and the cohesion mechanism of water rise. As water evaporates from the porous clay tube or from the tree branch, the water in the glass tube is pulled up. The adhesive forces between the water and the mercury cause the mercury to be pulled up with the water. Air pressure contributes toward the rise of the mercury to a height of only 76 cm., but in demonstrations such as these, rise of the mercury to heights of around 100 cm. or more has frequently been observed. In the root-pressure demonstration,

Several botanists have proposed various theories implicating the living cells of the xylem in translocation, but since water continues to flow through the xylem even when these cells are killed, these theories have not been considered acceptable. Of the various theories of water translocation proposed, only two appear to be even partially plausible. One is **root pressure.** The other is referred to by a variety of names such as the **cohesion theory, transpiration pull,** and the **transpiration-cohesion-tension theory,** but we shall refer to it here as **shoot tension** since this latter term is analogous with the term *root pressure.*

ROOT PRESSURE

If the stem of a well-watered plant of certain species, for example tomato, is cut off, water will exude from the stump. When a piece of glass tubing is attached to the stump with a short length of rubber tubing, water may rise in the tube to a height of several feet. The force responsible for this rise of water is referred to as **root pressure.** Root pressure is a rather complicated phenomenon, and all its details are not thoroughly understood. In general, we may state that it results from the continuing movement of water from the soil, through the tissues of the root, and into the xylem, thus forcing the water already in the xylem upward. Root pressure probably involves more than the simple diffusion of water from the soil to the xylem. If roots are killed, or even just deprived of oxygen, root pressure ceases. At the time that root pressure is occurring, plants are said to be carrying on **active absorption** of water.

Despite the fact that root pressure is a real force in some plant species, most plant physiologists do not believe that it offers a satisfactory general theory of water translocation. The magnitude of root pressure may be measured by attaching a manometer to the stump of a plant (Fig. 9.10). Root pressures in excess of 2 atmos. have rarely been measured and they are frequently much less. At the most, root pressure would seem to be able to support a column of water no more than 66 ft. high on the basis of these measurements, although Philip White has reported the development of root pressures of 6 atmos. or more by single isolated tomato roots. Not only does root pressure appear to be inadequate to explain the rise of water to the top of even a moderately tall tree, but also root pressure occurs only under conditions of high soil moisture and low transpiration—not when water is flowing the most rapidly through the xylem. Furthermore, root pressure has never been demonstrated in many species of plants. Finally, the rate of water flow resulting from

the magnitude of the root pressure can be calculated from the difference in height of the mercury in the two arms of the manometer. (Redrawn from *Scientific American* through the courtesy of the editors.)

root pressure is too slow to account for the volume of water frequently flowing through the xylem. Although root pressure probably provides the motive force for the rise of water in some plants part of the time, the root pressure theory apparently is inadequate as an explanation of the rise of water in the xylem of most plants most of the time.

SHOOT TENSION

The **shoot tension** theory of water translocation is based on several facts, one of these being that water columns in enclosed tubes have a very high degree of cohesion. A pull or tension of 30 atmos. or more is required to overcome the great cohesive forces between water molecules and to break the column apart. This means that under suitable conditions a water column can be pulled up, in contrast to its being pushed up by forces such as root pressure and differential air pressure.

A second requirement of the shoot tension theory is a motive force (or forces) that can exert a pull on the cohesive water columns in the xylem. This motive force results from the loss of water from (or the use of water by) cells of the leaves and other parts of the shoot and the consequent reduction in the diffusion pressure of water in the cells. As water evaporates from cell walls during transpiration, the water content of the cellulose and other colloidal cell wall components is reduced. Since these cell wall colloids have a great affinity for water, water now diffuses into the wall from the protoplasm and vacuole or from the walls of adjacent cells, reducing its diffusion pressure in these regions. The diffusion of water from one cell to another continues until water is diffusing out of the cells adjacent to the vessels or tracheids of the xylem. Water now diffuses from the xylem, and because of the cohesiveness of the water columns they are pulled up as water leaves the xylem. Transpiration is the principal factor creating a water deficit in cells, and the rate of movement of water through the xylem is determined largely by the rate of transpiration. Any use of water by a cell (as in photosynthesis), however, creates a water deficit and so may contribute toward the diffusion of water from the xylem. The pull of water through the xylem creates a negative pressure or tension in the water columns.

We have already indicated that forces of around 30 atmos. are essential for lifting water to the tops of the tallest trees. If shoot tension is to be considered a generally acceptable theory of the rise of water in plants, water deficits of no less than 30 atmos. (i.e., diffusion pressures of $X - 30$ atmos.) must exist in the cells of the tallest trees. Measurements show that such water deficits do occur. The diffusion pressure of water in the leaf cells of herbaceous plants is often no lower than $X - 10$ atmos., but even this would be sufficient to raise water 165 feet if half the energy is used in overcoming friction. There is little doubt but that the motive forces involved in shoot tension are theoretically adequate to account for the lifting of water to the tops of even the tallest trees.

Shoot tension can be demonstrated by securing a branch of a tree to a long piece of glass tubing filled with water and having its lower end immersed in mercury (Fig. 9.10). As water is pulled up the tubing, it pulls the mercury up behind it. Since atmospheric pressure can support a column of mercury only about 76 cm. high, mercury rise beyond that height can be ascribed only to shoot tension. When the apparatus is carefully and properly set up, mercury will rise to a height of 100 cm. or more in the tube. The cohesion mechanism can also be demonstrated by a purely mechanical device, evaporation of water from a porous clay tube filled with water substituting for the loss of water from the branch (Fig. 9.10). In both demonstrations it is essential that all connections be airtight and that the dissolved gases in the water be reduced to a minimum (usually accomplished by boiling the water just before use) so that air bubbles will not form as the water is subjected to tension.

Although such demonstrations help support the shoot tension theory, perhaps the most convincing evidence that shoot tension does (as well as can) exist in plants comes from a variety of experiments showing that water in the xylem is commonly under tension. In one type of experiment, the tissues external to the xylem in the stem of a herbaceous plant such as bean are carefully removed, and a vessel element is punctured with a fine needle while it is being observed under a microscope. The water in the vessel will usually snap apart at the puncture. If the water were under pressure it would ooze or squirt out. That water in the xylem is under tension is also evident from the sinking of water into the stump when the trunk of a rapidly transpiring tree is cut down.

Shoot tension is not a new theory. Its basic outlines were proposed by E. Askenasy in Germany in 1897, and it received strong support from the work of H. H. Dixon in England from about 1914 to 1924, not to mention the fact that Stephan Hales had anticipated the theory in the early eighteenth century. Most of the work by numerous investigators has added support to the theory, and most plant physiologists consider that shoot tension is probably the mechanism reponsible for the rise of water in most plants most of the time. Perhaps the most puzzling matter is how air or other gases are prevented from getting into the water columns and accumulating in bubbles that would break the columns, particularly when a branch is cut off. Future research may provide more satisfactory answers to this and other problems relating to water transport.

While shoot tension is operating, water may be pulled, not only through the xylem, but also through the tissues of the roots from the soil. This type of absorption is referred to as **passive absorption**, and is probably the most common type of absorption. In contrast with active absorption (page 247), passive absorption does not depend on living root cells. Indeed, if a root system of a potted plant is killed by immersion in boiling water or by other means, the rate of passive absorption may increase markedly because the dead tissues offer less resistance to the movement of water through them than do living tissues. Absorption ceases, however, when the dead root tissues disintegrate.

► ## Questions

1. The rate of transpiration is sometimes measured by cutting off a branch or leaf and determining how fast it absorbs water. Are there any objections to this method of measuring transpiration? Is it really a valid way to measure transpiration? Does it have any advantages?

2. What different procedures could be used to reduce the rate of transpiration of a potted plant exposed to direct sunlight? Of a garden plant in full sunlight?

3. If half the leaves were removed from a shrub, what would be the effect on the rate of transpiration per unit leaf area of the remaining leaves? Would it matter how the leaves were removed, that is, from the lower half, the upper half, the sunny or shady side, or every other leaf all over the shrub? Would the environmental conditions such as soil water availability influence your answer?

4. How can you make a plant recover from temporary wilting?

5. A soil has a field capacity of 30%. Is it a clay, sand, or silt? The soil is dried and 1000 grams of it are placed in a container and packed down. Now 150 grams of water are carefully poured over the soil surface. What will be the percentage water content of the moist soil after capillary equilibrium is reached? How will the water be distributed in the soil? Will there be any dry soil, and if so how much?

6. If the stems of cut flowers are recut under water about 1 inch from the end just before being placed in the vase, they will recover from wilting more rapidly than similar flowers not recut under water and will also generally last considerably longer. Explain.

7. Why do recently transplanted seedlings often wilt? What procedures do gardeners use to prevent or reduce such wilting, and why are the procedures effective?

8. Could transpiration ever occur into a saturated atmosphere (100% relative humidity), and if so under what conditions? Explain your answer.

► *References*

For Reference

1. Ferry, James F. and Henry S. Ward, *Fundamentals of Plant Physiology.* New York: The Macmillan Co., 1959, Chapters 5 and 7.
2. Meyer, Bernard S., Donald B. Anderson, and Richard H. Böhning, *Introduction to Physiology.* Princeton: D. Van Nostrand Co., 1960.

For Reading

3. Bennett-Clark, T. A., Water in the architecture of plants. *Endeavour* 10:151–154, 1951.
4. Greulach, V. A., Stephan Hales—pioneer plant physiologist. *Scientific Monthly* 55:52–60, 1942.
5. Greulach, V. A., The rise of water in plants. *Scientific American* 187(4):78–82, October 1952.
6. Hudson, J. P., Plants and their water supplies. *Endeavour* 16:84–89, 1957.
7. Kellogg, Charles E., *The Soils that Support Us*, New York: Macmillan Co., 1941.
8. Kellogg, Charles E., Soils. *Scientific American* 183(1):30–39, July 1950.
9. King, Thompson, Water, miracle of nature. *Science Digest* 33(5):1–5, 1953.
10. Richards, Annette H., Water for a dying giant. *Natural History* 62:464–465, 1953.
11. Swanson, C. L. W., Soil conditioners. *Scientific American* 189(2):36–52, August 1953.
12. Syrett, P. I., Transpiration. *New Biology* 25, 1958.

10. Plants and Food

EVEN THE ANCIENT PHILOSOPHER-SCIENTISTS recognized that plants, as well as animals, can live and grow only if food is available. The nature, source, and uses of the foods of plants have, however, been a most puzzling problem, and our modern concepts have emerged only as the result of centuries of research. Aristotle and other Greek scholars considered that plants secure their food from the soil and the idea persisted through the Middle Ages. Even today many laymen hold to this discredited concept. At various times the foods of plants have been thought to be organic substances from the soil, mineral salts, water, carbon dioxide, or the carbohydrates, fats, and proteins constituting the food of animals, and even at present not all biologists agree as to the substances that should be designated as plant foods.

Van Helmont's Experiment

Although Cardinal Nicolai of Cusa suggested in 1514 that the substance of plants was derived from water rather than earth, the first experimental refutation of the Greek ideas of plant food was provided

252

in 1648 by a Flemish investigator, Jean-Baptiste Van Helmont (8). His report follows:

> That all vegetable matter immediately and materially arises from the element of water alone I learned from this experiment. I took an earthenware pot, placed in it 200 lb of earth dried in an oven, soaked this with water, and planted in it a willow shoot weighing 5 lb. After five years had passed, the tree grown therefrom weighed 169 lb and about 3 oz. But the earthenware pot was constantly wet only with rain or (when necessary) distilled water; and it was ample in size and imbedded in the ground; and, to prevent dust flying around from mixing with the earth, the rim of the pot was kept covered with an iron plate coated with tin and pierced with many holes. I did not compute the weight of the deciduous leaves of the four autumns. Finally, I again dried the earth of the pot, and it was found to be the same 200 lb minus about 2 oz. Therefore, 164 lb of wood, bark, and root had arisen from water alone.

Subsequent discoveries have shown that plants are not made from water alone, but Van Helmont's conclusion was not entirely incorrect. Water not only constitutes the bulk of the fresh weight of living plant tissues, but it is also one of the substances used in the synthesis of the food of plants. Strangely enough, **Van** Helmont did not seem to be concerned with a more fundamental **conclusion** that could be drawn from his experiment: that the willow did **not** get its food from the soil.

In 1727 Stephen Hales, the English clergyman often called the founder of plant physiology, suggested a possibility not considered by Van Helmont: that plants might be nourished in part from the atmosphere.

Development of Modern Concepts

Between 1772 and 1862, a series of important investigations revealed the existence of photosynthesis and the basic nature of this process, providing the foundation for our present-day knowledge of plant nutrition. We now know that all the organic substance of plants (except for the relatively minor mineral element content of organic compounds) is derived from the product of photosynthesis.

Current differences in opinion as to the nature of plant foods stem entirely from different definitions of *food*. A few biologists prefer to define a food as "any substance which an organism obtains from its environment and utilizes, directly or indirectly, in its metabolism." From this definition, the foods of green plants would be water, carbon dioxide, mineral salts, and even oxygen, whereas the food of animals, bacteria, and fungi would include also carbohydrates, fats, proteins, and vitamins. Most botanists and many zoologists dislike such a broad, general definition of food and prefer to consider as a food any organic substance usable by a living organism as a source of energy or as cell-building material. In other words, **foods** are substances used in respiration and assimilation. On the basis of this definition, the foods of all organisms consist of the same groups of compounds: carbohydrates, lipids, proteins, and closely related substances such as organic acids. We use the term *food* in this sense throughout the book. Excluded by the definition are carbon dioxide, water, mineral salts, and oxygen. Important as these simple inorganic substances are in the life of plants, their roles are quite different from those of foods. Excluded also are the vitamins, important in plants as well as animals, but as regulatory substances rather than as energy sources.

Sources of Plant Foods

Now that we have defined foods we can state the sources of the foods of plants. In photosynthetic plants, the food source is internal, all the food being synthesized by photosynthesis and subsequent synthetic processes. Some species of bacteria carry on photosynthesis, whereas a few other species synthesize their own food by processes similar to photosynthesis except that chemical energy rather than light energy drives the processes. Most bacteria, the vascular plants lacking chlorophyll (Fig. 10.1), and the fungi secure their foods from their environment, as do animals. The few species of insectivorous plants (Chapter 5) undoubtedly secure some food from the insects and other small animals they trap and digest, but most of their food is derived from photosynthesis.

Foods and Energy

Although both the uses of food (as cell-building materials and as energy sources) are of great fundamental biological importance, the energy aspects of food require special consideration at this point. Life may be considered as a series of controlled, interrelated, and coordinated energy transformations, and the result of their cessation is death. Because energy is important in life we should consider a few basic facts about the nature of energy.

Energy may be defined as the capacity for doing work. In the scientific sense, **work** is a force acting through a certain distance, that is, a moving force. Energy has no mass and does not occupy space, and so is not a substance, although research in nuclear physics has shown that energy may be converted into matter and matter into energy, as in nuclear reactors. Energy exists in various forms such as heat, light, and other radiation, sound, electricity, magnetism, and kinetic energy of movement (mechanical energy). Various compounds, including foods, contain considerable energy in the bonds holding the atoms of their molecules

Figure 10.1. The Indian pipe (*Monotropa uniflora*), one of the few species of vascular plants lacking chlorophyll and dependent on external food sources. The Indian pipe is often said to be saprophytic, but it is actually parasitic on (or perhaps symbiotic with) a fungus. (Courtesy of J. Arthur Herrick, Kent State University.)

together and this energy is released when the compounds are converted into other substances of lower energy content by oxidation processes such as respiration and combustion.

ENERGY TRANSFORMATIONS

One kind of energy can be converted into another, machines (as well as living organisms) being energy converters. Thus, a steam engine converts the chemical energy of coal or oil first into heat and then into mechanical energy that may be used to drive an electric generator, converting the energy into electricity. This electrical energy, in turn, may readily be converted into light, heat, sound, magnetism, mechanical energy, chemical energy, or other types of energy by appropriate devices.

OXIDATION AND REDUCTION. Energy transformations in plants will be considered later in this chapter, but it may be noted here that the energy transfers in biochemical **oxidation** and **reduction** reactions are of great biological significance. Fundamentally, oxidation is the removal of electrons from atoms or molecules while reduction is the addition of electrons, but many oxidation and reduction reactions also involve the transfer of oxygen or hydrogen. If oxygen is added to a molecule or hydrogen is removed, oxidation occurs, whereas removal of oxygen or addition of hydrogen to a molecule reduces it.

Oxidation frees energy from chemical bonds, as in the respiratory processes. Reduction incorporates energy in chemical bonds, and a supply of energy is always required for reductions. Thus, light energy is used indirectly in reducing carbon from its low energy level in carbon dioxide (CO_2) to its higher energy level in carbohydrate (CH_2O) during photosynthesis, the light energy being transformed into the chemical energy of the carbohydrate molecules. The energy used in reducing sugar to fatty acid is provided by respiration. The fatty acid contains about twice as much energy as the sugar directly used in making it, because the greater the relative proportion of hydrogen in a compound, or the lower the oxygen, the more highly reduced the compound and the greater its energy content.

QUANTITY OF ENERGY. Quantitative measurements of energy can be made, and quantity of energy can be expressed in various units. One of the most commonly used energy units in biological work is the **calorie**, the amount of heat energy required to raise the temperature of one gram of water one degree centigrade. More specifically, this unit is called a **gram-calorie** to distinguish it from the **kilogram-calorie**, or large calorie, 1000 times as great as a gram-calorie. The calories used in nutritional work, and so familiar to those on a diet, are kilogram-calories. Although calories are specifically units of heat energy, they can be used to express the quantity of any kind of energy, since one kind of energy can be converted into another. Thus, when we say that 180 grams of glucose (its gram molecular weight) contain 673 kg-cal. (or 673,000 gm-cal.) we mean that if all the energy in this glucose were converted into heat, the resulting heat would be sufficient to raise the temperature of 673,000 grams of water 1°C.

ENERGY SOURCES. Not all the energy used by plants is freed from foods by respiratory processes. Light energy is utilized in photosynthesis and also in other processes including chlorophyll synthesis, the formation of some anthocyanins, and certain reactions affecting growth. The energy released from foods in respiration is, indeed, in the final analysis derived from light energy utilized in photosynthesis and incorporated in the food produced. Molecular energy is expended, not only in diffusion, but also in other processes, such as the flow of water through the xylem, deriving their energy from diffusion. Plants, then, secure energy from three principal sources: light direct, respiration (light indirect), and the kinetic energy of molecules. In contrast, animals secure most of their energy supply from foods through respiration, with relatively little molecular energy and even less direct light energy being used.

In the final analysis, the bulk of the energy expended by living organisms can be traced back to the light energy from the sun utilized in photosynthesis (9). Molecular energy, too, can be traced to the radiant energy of the sun. Indeed, all energy on earth comes directly or indirectly from the sun (except for a negligible quantity from other suns—the stars). Even atomic energy may be considered as having a solar origin, since the materials of the Earth were probably originally derived from the sun.

Each year 13×10^{23} gm-cal. of radiant energy from the sun reach the Earth. About a third of this energy is reflected immediately, so about 9×10^{23} gm-calories are available for heating the Earth (and so making it habitable) or for photosynthesis. Only about 0.1% of this available energy is used in photosynthesis, but this amounts to the still impressive sum of about 10^{21} gm-cal. per year. It is on this supply of energy, converted into chemical energy by plants during photosynthesis, that all living things depend for their existence.

The energy in fuels such as wood, peat, coal, petroleum, and gas, like the energy in food, is chemical energy derived from the light energy of the sun during photosynthesis. The fossil fuels—coal, petroleum, and gas—that provide the bulk of the energy used in our homes, industries, and transportation (Fig. 10.2) are all partially decayed remains of ancient plants and animals, and when we burn them we are releasing energy tied up by photosynthesis millions of years ago.

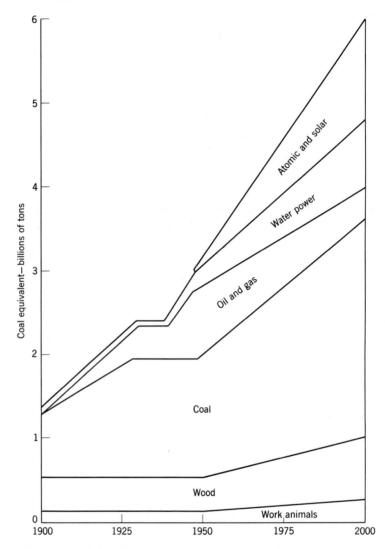

Figure 10.2. The energy used by man in home, industry, and transportation is continually increasing, with fossil fuels providing the principal source.

Photosynthesis

THE MAGNITUDE OF PHOTOSYNTHESIS

Photosynthesis is by far the greatest production process on earth. The weight of organic matter fixed each year by photosynthesis is some two-hundred times that of the combined annual products of all the farms, mines, and factories on earth. The plants of the earth are estimated to photosynthesize 470 billion tons net of organic matter a year, using 690 billion tons of carbon dioxide and 280 billion tons of water and adding 500 billion tons of oxygen to the air. Since green plants use about 80 billion tons of the food produced by photosynthesis in respiration, their true photosynthetic production is about 550 billion tons. The oxygen added to the air by photosynthesis is of great biological importance because of its use by both plants and animals in aerobic respiration. Although oxygen is continually being removed from the air by nonbiological processes such as combustion, rusting of metals, and weathering of rocks, as well as by respiration, photosynthesis is the only process that *adds* any substantial quantity of oxygen to the air. Indeed, if it were not for photosynthesis, the atmosphere would be devoid of oxygen.

Although the atmosphere contains only 0.03% carbon dioxide, there is no danger of plants exhausting the supply by using it all in photosynthesis, for the atmosphere is so vast that this small percentage represents about 2200 billion tons of carbon dioxide. The oceans of the earth contain over fifty times this quantity of carbon dioxide in the form of dissolved gas or carbonates; this vast reservoir of the gas is

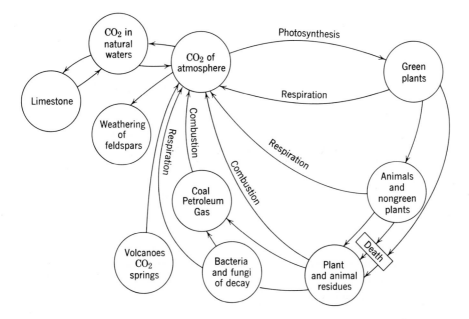

Figure 10.3. The carbon cycle. (Redrawn from *Plant Physiology* by Meyer & Anderson with the permission of the publisher, D. Van Nostrand Co.)

259

in equilibrium with the carbon dioxide of the air and holds its concentration more or less stable (18). The readily available carbon dioxide of the earth is enough to supply photosynthesis for about 250 years, even if none were added to the air. Actually, combustion, weathering of rocks, and other chemical processes, as well as respiration, add several hundred billion tons of carbon dioxide to the air each year. It is not generally realized that green plants contribute much more carbon dioxide to the air as a result of respiration than do animals, and that bacteria and fungi contribute even more than the green plants. The cycling of carbon dioxide through photosynthesis to organic compounds and the return of carbon dioxide to the air by respiration constitute the core of the carbon cycle (Fig. 10.3). During the two billion years or so that life has been present on earth, any particular carbon atom we might select for consideration has probably been through the carbon cycle millions of times and has been a constituent of innumerable and varied plants and animals.

THE PHOTOSYNTHETIC REACTIONS

Today we may speak quite glibly about photosynthesis and its important role in the biological world, but only two hundred years ago man was completely unaware that any such process existed. Since then our knowledge of photosynthesis has been pieced together slowly and painstakingly through a long series of researches. Aside from Van Helmont's conclusion that plants are derived from water and Stephen Hales' speculation that plants are nourished partly from the air, the first clue regarding photosynthesis came in 1772 when Joseph Priestley found that oxygen was evolved by plants. Seven years later the Dutch physician, Jan Ingen-Housz, found that light was required for this release of oxygen. In 1796 he discovered that carbon dioxide was absorbed by plants and concluded that it was used in their nutrition (8). In 1804 the Swiss botanist, Nicolas de Saussure, pointed out the interdependence of carbon dioxide uptake and oxygen evolution as well as the dependence of both on light. He also distinguished these gas exchanges from those of plant respiration, suggested the role of water in the process, and made the first quantitative measurements of photosynthesis. It was not until 1837, however, that the French scientist, Dutrochet, found that chlorophyll was essential. In 1845 the German biochemist, Liebig, pointed out that all the organic compounds of plants are derived from carbon dioxide, and in 1862 the German plant physiologist, Julius von Sachs, reported that starch was a product of photosynthesis. As early as 1845 the German scientist, Mayer, had recognized that in the course of the process light energy was converted into chemical energy.

By 1862, then, the main outlines of the process had been worked out, although the name *photosynthesis* was not used until 1898. In the 70 years between 1862 and 1932, the progress of research on photosynthesis was relatively slow and little was added to our understanding of the nature of the photosynthetic processes, although much information was assembled on the influence of environmental factors on the rate of photosynthesis. Perhaps the most fundamental discoveries during this period were those of the German botanist, Th. W. Engelmann, who in the 1880's used ingenious experiments (Fig. 10.4, 8) to determine the wavelengths of light most effective in photosynthesis; of F. F. Blackman, the English plant physiologist, who in 1905 found that at least one step in the photosynthetic process did not require light; and of the German chemist, R. Wilstëtter, and his associates who between 1906 and 1922 worked on the chemical structure of chlorophyll (Fig. 10.5). Beginning in 1922, the German physiologist, Otto Warburg, and his associates conducted extensive experiments on the efficiency of photosynthesis in relation to the quantity of light energy absorbed.

In 1929, C. B. van Neil summarized research data that he and others had obtained about photosynthetic and chemosynthetic bacteria and pointed out their basic similarity to green plant photosynthesis (Table 10.1). In general, the various bacterial photosynthetic processes differ from green plant photosynthesis in two principal ways: a pigment other than chlorophyll absorbs the light energy, and a substance such as hydrogen sulfide (H_2S) or hydrogen (H_2) rather than water serves as the source of hydrogen. The overall synthetic reactions of bacterial chemosynthesis are the same as those of green plant photosynthesis: carbon

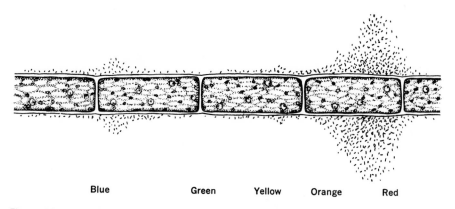

Blue   Green   Yellow   Orange   Red

Figure 10.4. Reproduction (somewhat modified) of a drawing by Th. W. Engelmann (1882) showing bacteria clustering at the parts of an algal filament exposed to the red and blue regions of a microspectrum under a microscope. Engelmann's experiment demonstrated that the red wavelengths were the most effective in photosynthesis and the blue region the next most effective, since the motile bacteria move to regions of higher oxygen concentration.

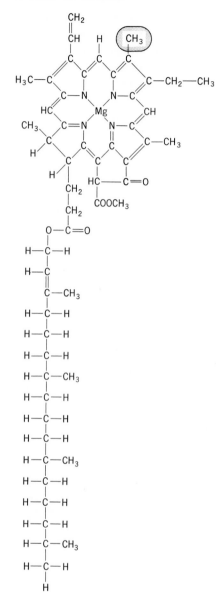

Figure 10.5. Structural formula of a chlorophyll a molecule. Chlorophyll b has the same structure except that it has a —CHO group in place of the circled —CH₃ group of chlorophyll a.

dioxide and water are used and carbohydrate, water, and oxygen are produced. The difference between the processes lies in the energy sources, with chemosynthetic bacteria securing the energy that drives the process from the oxidation of inorganic compounds rather than from light. C. B. van Neil pointed out that his data strongly suggested that

TABLE 10.1. COMPARISON OF GREEN PLANT PHOTOSYNTHESIS WITH BACTERIAL PHOTOSYNTHESIS AND CHEMOSYNTHESIS OF SEVERAL DIFFERENT TYPES

Organism	Type of Process	Substances Used	Energy Source	Substances Produced
Green plants	Photosynthesis	CO_2, H_2O	Light absorbed by chlorophyll	Sugar, H_2O, O_2
Green sulfur bacteria	Photosynthesis	CO_2, H_2S	Light absorbed by bacterial chlorophyll	Sugar, H_2O, S
Purple sulfur bacteria	Photosynthesis	CO_2, H_2S H_2O	Light absorbed by bacterio-purpurin	Sugar, H_2SO_4
Nitrifying bacteria	Chemosynthesis	CO_2, H_2O	Oxidation of ammonia to nitrites	Sugar, H_2O, O_2
Nitrifying bacteria	Chemosynthesis	CO_2, H_2O	Oxidation of nitrites to nitrates	Sugar, H_2O, O_2
Colorless sulfur bacteria	Chemosynthesis	CO_2, H_2O	Oxidation of H_2S to sulfates	Sugar, H_2O, O_2
Iron bacteria	Chemosynthesis	CO_2, H_2O	Oxidation of ferrous iron to ferric iron	Sugar, H_2O, O_2

the oxygen evolved by photosynthesis came from the water rather than from the carbon dioxide as was generally assumed, although he had no direct experimental evidence for this.

Despite such advances in our knowledge of photosynthesis, we entered the 1930's with little more knowledge of the steps in the photosynthetic process than had been available at the time of the Civil War. The most generally held theory was that formaldehyde was the principal intermediate product, although there had never been any really satisfactory evidence to support this theory. In 1938, the English biochemist, R. Hill, reported that chloroplasts removed from plant cells and exposed to light produce substantial quantities of oxygen if they are provided with hydrogen-accepting compounds such as ferric salts (8), thus providing some evidence in support of both van Neil's proposal that the oxygen evolved is derived from the water and Blackman's concept of photosynthesis as at least a two-step process, only one of the steps being directly dependent on light. The Hill reaction, as it has come to be called, is only partial photosynthesis, since carbon dioxide is not used and no carbohydrate is produced.

A more complete understanding of the processes of photosynthesis awaited some means of labeling the carbon dioxide and water used in the process so that the labeled atoms could be traced through the various intermediate substances produced during the reactions. The first attempt along this line was made in 1939 by the American biochemist, Samuel Ruben, and his associates, who used carbon dioxide containing a radioactive isotope of carbon, C^{11}. The radioactivity of this isotope, however, was exhausted so rapidly that it provided little information. In 1941, Ruben and his co-workers (8, 22), trying another approach, supplied the green alga *Chlorella* with water containing a heavy, nonradioactive isotope of oxygen, O^{18}. The carbon dioxide supplied contained the usual commonly occurring isotope of oxygen, O^{16}. They found that all of the oxygen gas evolved was O^{18}, proving beyond a doubt that the oxygen released during photosynthesis is derived from the water used and substantiating the conclusions of both van Neil and Hill.

It was now evident that light energy absorbed by the chlorophyll is used in decomposing water into hydrogen and oxygen (3). The hydrogen is not released as a gas, however, as it is in the electrolysis of water, but becomes attached to some hydrogen acceptor compound present in the chloroplasts, probably TPN (triphosphopyridine nucleotide, a coenzyme of dehydrogenase enzymes). When the TPN is reduced to $TPNH \cdot H^+$ by addition of the hydrogen from the water, some of the energy from the light is held in the new chemical bonds. The rest of the light energy absorbed by the chlorophyll is used in making ATP (adenosine triphosphate, Fig. 10.13) from ADP (adenosine diphosphate) and phosphoric acid. The net result of the light reaction of photo-synthesis is the decomposition of water with the release of oxygen and the transformation of light energy into the chemical bond energy of ATP and TPNH·H$^+$. The energy in these compounds is then used in driving the subsequent synthetic reactions that reduce carbon from its low energy state in CO_2 to a high energy state in carbohydrate.

By the use of radioactive carbon-14, which became available just after World War II, several groups of investigators (particularly Melvin Calvin and his associates at the University of California) have worked out in detail the pathway of carbon from CO_2 to carbohydrates (Fig. 10.6). Although the picture of the processes they have drawn is still

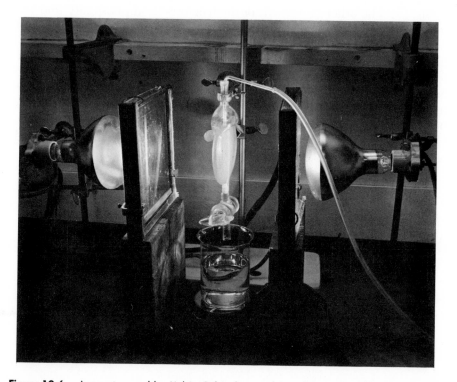

Figure 10.6. Apparatus used by Melvin Calvin for supplying algae with radioactive CO_2 for brief periods of photosynthesis. The algae are in the flat, closed flask between the two lamps and the heat filters. The radioactive CO_2 is introduced through the tube, and after a meas-ured time of a few seconds to a minute or more the algae are suddenly killed by opening the stopcock and dropping them in the beaker of organic solvent. An extract of the algae is then analyzed by paper chromatography and radioautographs to determine what compounds con-tain the radioactive carbon. Dr. Calvin and his associates have worked out intermediate steps in photosynthesis from the results of such experiments. (Courtesy of Melvin Calvin, University of California, Berkeley.)

subject to elaboration and modification, it appears to be reasonably complete and in accord with the facts.

The more critical steps in the reactions are as follows: (1) Carbon dioxide combines with a 5-carbon sugar (ribulose-1,5-diphosphate) forming two molecules of a 3-carbon organic acid (phosphoglyceric acid or PGA); (2) The phosphoglyceric acid (PGA) reacts with the ATP from the light reactions, forming diphosphoglyceric acid, a substance of higher energy content; (3) The diphosophoglyceric acid is reduced to triose phosphate (3-carbon sugar) by the addition of hydrogen from the $TPNH \cdot H^+$ produced in the light reactions; (4) Half of the triose phosphate is converted to fructose-1,6-diphosphate (a 6-carbon sugar), and a third of this is the net carbohydrate product of photosynthesis; (5) The other two-thirds of the fructose-1,6-diphosphate and the remaining half of the triose phosphate enter into a complicated series of transformations to other sugars, the eventual product being ribulose-1,5-diphosphate, which can then react with more carbon dioxide. For every 6 molecules of carbon dioxide used, 12 molecules of triose phosphate are produced, but only 2 molecules of this triose are used in making the molecule of hexose sugar that is the net product, the other 10 molecules being converted to the ribulose-1,5-diphosphate that reacts with the CO_2. The carbon balance sheet for this cyclic process may be outlined as follows:

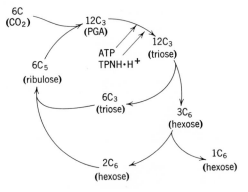

The first step (the reaction of CO_2 with the ribulose-1,5-diphosphate) is by no means unique to photosynthesis; all organisms apparently are able to combine CO_2 with suitable organic compounds with the formation of organic acid (carboxyl or —COOH) groups. What does make the reactions characteristic of photosynthesis is the incorporation of energy and hydrogen from the light reactions, first by reaction with the ATP and then with the $TPNH \cdot H^+$. Since triose phosphate is the product of these reactions between the products of the light reaction (ATP

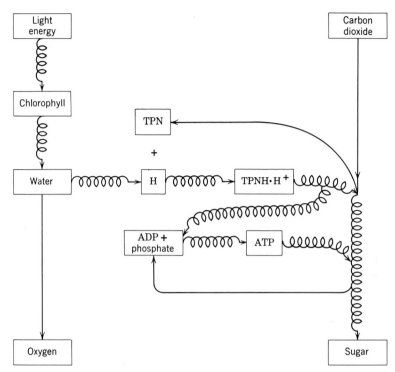

Figure 10.7. Skeletonized diagram of photosynthesis, the coiled lines representing the pathways of energy transfer. The left side represents the utilization of light energy absorbed by chlorophyll in splitting water into oxygen and hydrogen and in making ATP. The hydrogen unites with TPN, and the resulting TPNH·H$^+$ and the ATP transfer the energy to reactions that reduce carbon from the carbon dioxide to the higher energy level of sugar. Light energy is thus transformed into chemical bond energy of sugar.

and TPNH·H$^+$) and the product of CO$_2$ fixation (PGA), triose phosphate may be regarded as the initial product of photosynthesis.

By subsequent reactions not limited to photosynthetic plants, the fructose-1,6-diphosphate is converted to other carbohydrates such as fructose, sucrose, starch, and glucose, and also fats. In many plants, much of the sugar produced by photosynthesis is quickly converted to starch, and so starch tests may be used to determine whether or not photosynthesis has been taking place. However, such carbohydrates as starch, glucose, and fructose are not products of photosynthesis but rather are products of subsequent reactions.

The overall photosynthetic process is outlined in simple form in Fig. 10.7. The principal steps in the process of photosynthesis, may be summarized as follows if hexose is considered the end product:

(1) $12H_2O + 12TPN + 18ADP + 18H_3PO_4 \xrightarrow[\text{chlorophyll}]{\text{light energy}}$

$6O_2 + 18ATP + 12TPNH \cdot H^+$

(2) $6CO_2 + 18ATP + 12TPNH \cdot H^+ \longrightarrow$

$C_6H_{12}O_6 + 6H_2O + 18ADP + 18H_3PO_4 + 12TPN$

If each substance that appears on both the right and left sides of the preceding equations is cancelled out, the following standard general summary equation for photosynthesis remains:

$$6CO_2 + 6H_2O \xrightarrow[\text{chlorophyll}]{\text{light energy}} C_6H_{12}O_6 + 6O_2$$

It should be emphasized that knowledge of all details of photosynthesis, particularly of the earlier steps leading to the production of ATP and TPNH·H$^+$, is still far from complete, and that the extensive research programs now in progress are constantly providing new knowledge of the process. As a result, some of our present concepts are subject to modification as they are clarified. It may be noted that the synthetic pathways are not the same in all plants, and that foods other than sugars may be synthesized. Indeed, it is possible that photosynthesis might best be considered as a process that converts light energy into chemical bond energy of ATP and TPNH·H$^+$. The subsequent use of these substances in driving a variety of biochemical processes (of which the reduction of carbon dioxide to sugars is perhaps only the most common) might, or might not, then be considered as a component of the total photosynthetic process.

CHLOROPLASTS AND PHOTOSYNTHESIS

Daniel Arnon, of the University of California, and other investigators have evidence that the entire photosynthetic process as currently conceived, and not just the light reaction, occur within the chloroplasts (Chapter 4) of a cell. Some of the reactions following photosynthesis, including starch synthesis, may also occur within chloroplasts as well as elsewhere. Chlorophyll extracts can not participate in photosynthesis even though the chlorophyll still absorbs light energy, for the structural organization and enzyme systems of the chloroplast are essential.

Chlorophyll absorbs all wavelengths of visible light, but it absorbs red and blue best and green to a relatively small degree (Fig. 10.8). Leaves commonly absorb about 83% of the light that strikes them, reflect about 12%, and transmit about 5%. Of the 83% absorbed, only 4% is absorbed by chlorophyll. Most of the remainder is converted into heat and radiated or otherwise lost.

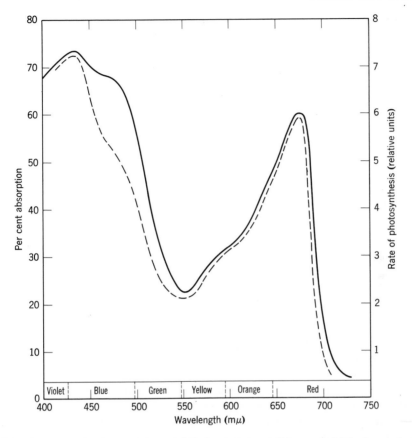

Figure 10.8. Light absorption spectrum of *Elodea* (water weed) leaves (solid line) and photosynthetic action spectrum of *Elodea* (broken line). The curves match closely in the red, orange, and yellow regions of the spectrum (550 to 700 mμ) and the violet-blue region (around 430 mμ) where most of the light absorption is by chlorophyll, but deviate in the blue and green regions (450–550 mμ) where a considerable portion of the light absorption is by the carotinoids. The absorption peaks of chlorophyll a are at about 430 and 675 mμ. Data of Max H. Hommersand and Francis T. Haxo.

THE EFFICIENCY OF PHOTOSYNTHESIS

This may suggest that plants are very inefficient converters of solar energy into chemical energy. Furthermore, only part of the light falling on an area occupied by vegetation reaches leaves and other chlorophyll-bearing organs. About 1.6% of the light reaching a corn field during the growing season is used in photosynthesis. Corn plants use about a quarter of the sugar produced by photosynthesis in respiration, so the net efficiency is only 1.2%.

269

Since the corn grains contain about a third of the net photosynthetic product, efficiency from the standpoint of food usable by man is only 0.4%, and this is reduced to less than 0.13% when adjustment is made for the fact that the growing season is about one-third of a year. The 0.13% is the fraction of the solar energy that reaches the corn field during the season and that has been converted by plants into the chemical energy of foods readily usable by man. When photosynthetic efficiency is based on the light energy absorbed by chlorophyll, however, photosynthesis is a very efficient process, because about 90% of the absorbed light energy is converted to chemical energy.

FACTORS AFFECTING THE RATE OF PHOTOSYNTHESIS

Although most of the current research on photosynthesis is directed toward a better understanding of the nature of the process, our knowledge of the influence of various factors on the rate of photosynthesis is of greater practical value at present. (Since photosynthesis is the ultimate source of food of practically all organisms, photosynthetic productivity is of general biological concern. To farmers and gardeners, whose income depends on the yield of their crops, it is a matter of monetary importance. The possibility of using algae as a source of both food and oxygen during prolonged space travel has resulted in extensive work directed toward increasing the photosynthetic productivity of algae.

Both hereditary and environmental factors affect the rate of photosynthesis. Plants of different species growing in the same environment may have quite different rates of photosyntheis. At the same time, the rate of photosynthesis in a particular plant varies greatly with the prevailing environmental conditions. Particularly important are light intensity, light quality (wavelength composition), carbon dioxide, water, temperature, and factors affecting chlorophyll content.

In any particular chloroplast and at any particular moment, only one factor limits the rate of photosynthesis, and the rate can be raised only by increasing this **limiting factor**. For example, if light intensity is limiting, an increase in light intensity will raise the rate, but supplying a higher concentration of carbon dioxide or a higher temperature would not. As light intensity is increased more and more, however, a point is reached where a further increase in light intensity is not accompanied by a rise in the rate of photosynthesis (Fig. 10.9); some other factor is now limiting. If we find that now only an increase in carbon dioxide will raise the rate of photosynthesis we know that this is the limiting factor.

Under natural conditions, deficient chlorophyll content is not commonly a limiting factor in photosynthesis unless a plant is diseased or is deficient in elements such as magnesium or nitrogen that are used in

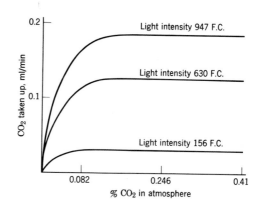

Figure 10.9. Influence of increasing concentrations of CO_2 on the rate of photosynthesis at three different light intensities. CO_2 is the limiting factor at the lower concentrations, as indicated by the increase in rate of photosynthesis with concentration of CO_2, but when light becomes limiting, the curves level off. [Data of Hoover, Johnston, and Brackett, (1933. Redrawn from *Principles of Plant Physiology*, by Bonner & Galston, 1952)], with the permission of the publisher, W. H. Freeman & Co.)

synthesizing chlorophyll molecules, or other elements such as iron, sulfur and manganese that affect chlorophyll synthesis. In most plants light is required in the final steps of chlorophyll synthesis. Thus a plant that has grown from a seed in darkness cannot begin photosynthesis as soon as it is placed in the light, but must first synthesize chlorophyll. In many seedling beds, some young plants can be found that never synthesize chlorophyll because they lack the necessary hereditary potentialities. Such plants are called **albinos** and they are, of course, unable to carry on photosynthesis.

Both light intensity and light quality may be limiting factors in photosynthesis. Light intensity is obviously the limiting factor at night, early morning, or late evening, and may also be a limiting factor on very cloudy days and in the shade. Although most plants can carry on some photosynthesis even in very dim light, a plant will survive and grow over an extended period only if the product of photosynthesis is at least equal to the amount of food used in respiration plus assimilation. Plants that naturally grow in the shade, as in a forest, carry on this basic minimal rate of photosynthesis at lower light intensities than those species found in sunny habitats. Although light quality is not a limiting factor in plants exposed to direct sunlight, the light received by the lower-growing plants in a thick forest is deficient in quality as well as intensity since wavelengths (red and blue) best absorbed by chlorophyll have largely been filtered out by the leaves of the tree canopy. Since water absorbs the longer wavelengths of light more than the shorter ones, water plants that live deep in lakes or the ocean receive light deficient in orange and red.

Carbon dioxide is very commonly a limiting factor in photosynthesis, particularly on clear summer days when plants are adequately supplied

271

with water.   Unfortunately, there is now no practical and economically feasible method of supplying field crops with more than the usual 0.03% of carbon dioxide present in the air, except perhaps by increasing the population of soil bacteria, fungi, and animals, thus increasing the total production of carbon dioxide by respiration.   Such additional carbon dioxide may promote increased photosyntheis in low-growing plants, and it is conceivable that some of the beneficial effects of manures and other organic fertilizers might be related to an increased population of soil organisms.   Carbon dioxide gas can be added to the air in greenhouses, and sometimes is.

In a wilted plant, or one that is just beginning to wilt, water is likely to be the limiting factor in photosynthesis, principally because the rate of most life processes, including photosynthesis, decreases when protoplasm has too low a water content.   When a water deficiency results in stomatal closing, photosynthesis may cease almost entirely.   Although brought about by a lack of water, this is really a situation where carbon dioxide is the limiting factor.   Under natural conditions, water may be the limiting factor in photosynthesis, not only during prolonged droughts when the plants approach permanent wilting, but also almost every afternoon during hot, summer weather when there is temporary wilting.

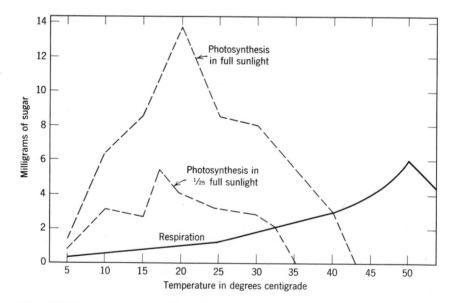

Figure 10.10. Relative rates of photosynthesis and respiration in potato leaves during 10-min. exposures to different temperatures in shade and full sunlight. (Data of Lundegardh. Redrawn from *Textbook of Botany* by Transeau, Sampson, and Tiffany with the permission of the publishers, Harper and Brothers.)

Under natural conditions, temperature is likely to be a limiting factor in photosynthesis only on very cool days. As the temperature rises, a point is reached where the rate of respiration rises more rapidly than the rate of photosynthesis (Fig. 10.10). Thus a plant may have a greater net food production at a lower temperature, even though the process of photosynthesis itself is more rapid at a higher temperature. At high temperatures, the rate of photosynthesis may start falling while that of respiration is still rising.

Respiration

As essential as photosynthesis is for the continuation of life on earth, it is no more essential than respiration, since both plants and animals depend on energy made available from food by respiration for their continued existence. Photosynthesis converts light energy into the chemical energy of sugar, but respiration makes available the chemical energy of sugar (and other foods) and permits the use of this energy in a variety of useful ways within the organism. The end products of photosynthesis (sugar, oxygen, water) are the substances used in ordinary aerobic respiration, whereas the end products of respiration (carbon dioxide and water) are the substances used in photosynthesis.

We are using the term **respiration** in its basic biological sense, referring to the series of biochemical oxidations of foods occurring in living cells, the energy contained in these foods being transferred to a substance (ATP) that serves as a readily available energy supply. Unfortunately, the term *respiration* has been used in several other ways: as a synonym for *breathing*, as a label for the diffusion of gases in and out of the lungs and gills or between the blood and tissues of animals, or even to refer to the diffusion of gases between a plant or animal and its environment. Although plants and many animals do not breathe, all living cells carry on respiration.

In animals much of the energy made available by respiration is used in muscular contraction and the generation of nerve impulses. Although plants do not use energy from respiration in these ways, they do use it (as animals do) in accumulating mineral ions (Chapter 8), in synthesizing fats, proteins, and certain other compounds, in cell division and other aspects of growth, in assimilation, in the maintenance of protoplasmic structure and differential permeability of membranes, in light production by some species (Fig. 10.11), and in other ways.

If plants used as much energy from foods in their activities as animals do in muscle contractions alone, the net food production by plants would be small and they could not serve as food suppliers to the entire living world. The extensive use of molecular energy in the transport of sub-

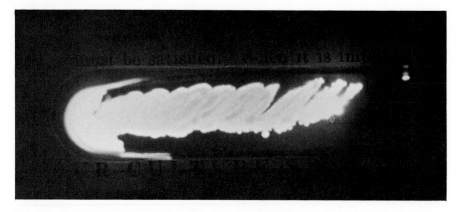

Figure 10.11. Light production by a colony of *Photobacterium fischeri*, illustrating one of the less universal transformations of energy from respiration. Some other bacteria and fungi, as well as animals such as glow worms, fireflies, and deep sea fish, convert some chemical energy into light. This photograph was made entirely with the light emitted by the bacteria, the exposure being for 6 hr. at f/4.5. (Courtesy of Carolina Biological Supply Co.)

stances through plants, in contrast with the use of energy from foods in pumping blood through the body of an animal, represents one substantial saving of food energy in plants.

AEROBIC RESPIRATION

The oxidation of foods proceeds in various ways in different species, or even in one species under different conditions, but the majority of plants and animals have very similar if not identical pathways of **aerobic respiration**, that is, respiration dependent on a supply of oxygen as well as food (11, 17). In plants, departures from this standard pattern of respiration are restricted almost entirely to some bacteria and fungi, although other plants may carry on anaerobic respiration (p. 280) for a while in the absence of oxygen. Aerobic respiration may be summarized as follows:

$$\text{sugar} + \text{oxygen} \longrightarrow \text{carbon dioxide} + \text{water} + \text{energy}$$

$$C_6H_{12}O_6 + 6O_2 \longrightarrow 6CO_2 + 6H_2O$$

This summary equation, however, provides little information about the nature of respiration. The process occurs in many steps, just as photosynthesis does, and in recent years biochemists have worked out the series of reactions in great detail. It is not necessary or desirable to give the complete details in an introductory course, but Fig. 10.12 outlines the process in a general way.

Four main stages, or series of reactions, in aerobic respiration can be identified:

(1) **Glycolysis,** a series of reactions resulting in the conversion of sugar to pyruvic acid with the release of a small amount of energy by the transfer of some H from the sugar to a hydrogen acceptor (DPN).

(2) The **citric acid cycle (Krebs cycle),** a series of reactions resulting in the decomposition of pyruvic acid into CO_2 and H, the latter being transferred to hydrogen acceptors (DPN and TPN).

(3) The **terminal oxidations,** where the H of the DPNH·H$^+$ and TPNH·H$^+$ produced in the first two stages is transferred through a series of enzymes to oxygen, resulting in the final production of water, the energy released at each transfer being used in synthesizing ATP (adenosine triphosphate) from ADP (adenosine diphosphate) and phosphate (Fig. 10.13).

(4) **Energy release,** when the ATP decomposes into ADP and phos-

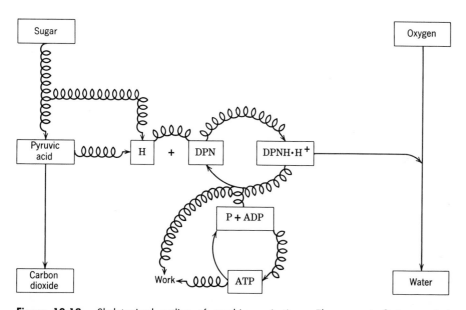

Figure 10.12. Skeletonized outline of aerobic respiration. The sugar is first converted to pyruvic acid (glycolysis), one-sixth of its hydrogen atoms being removed. Next, pyruvic is broken down in steps (citric acid cycle) to carbon dioxide and hydrogen. The hydrogen combines with hydrogen acceptors (mostly DPN), forming reduced acceptors (DPNH·H$^+$) that now contain the energy originally present in the sugar. When DPNH·H$^+$ is decomposed into DPN and hydrogen (terminal oxidations) most of the energy is used in making ATP from phosphate and ADP, the hydrogen finally uniting with oxygen and forming water. When ATP is decomposed into ADP and P, energy that may be used in useful work is released. DPNH·H$^+$ may also be used directly in doing useful work.

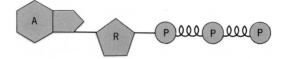

Figure 10.13. Adenosine triphosphate (ATP) is built up from adenine (A), ribose sugar (R), and three phosphate (P) groups, as shown in the diagram. The second and third phosphates are held by high-energy bonds. When the end phosphate group is detached, energy usable in useful work in organisms is released, and ATP becomes converted to ADP (adenosine diphosphate). Subsequently, energy from respiration can be used in adding a third phosphate, converting ADP back to ATP.

phate, the released energy being used in a variety of ways as outlined earlier.

We shall consider each of these four main stages in order. Although DPN plays a much more extensive role as a hydrogen acceptor in respiration than does TPN, both are involved and we shall simply use the symbol A for both of these hydrogen acceptors, and AH_2 for the reduced forms. Sometimes an even greater simplification is made, the hydrogen carried by an acceptor merely being represented thus: [H].

GLYCOLYSIS

Glucose is first phosphorylated and then .converted in a series of reactions to phosphorylated trioses, and on through phosphoglyceric acid to pyruvic acid. The series of reactions making up glycolysis may be summarized as follows:

sugar   + hydrogen acceptor ⟶   pyruvic acid   + reduced hydrogen acceptor

$$C_6H_{12}O_6 + \qquad 2A \qquad \longrightarrow 2CH_3 \cdot CO \cdot COOH + \qquad 2AH_2$$

About 96% of the energy originally present in the sugar is now in the pyruvic acid, the remainder in the reduced hydrogen acceptor. Glycolysis results, not only in the production of pyruvic acid, but also in removal of some of the hydrogen originally present in the sugar (an oxidation process).

THE CITRIC ACID CYCLE

Since 2 molecules of pyruvic acid are formed from 1 molecule of glucose, each reaction sequence described from here on occurs twice for each glucose molecule used. Pyruvic acid is now converted into a

2-carbon compound related to acetic acid by the removal of a molecule of CO_2, and the 2-carbon compounds enters the citric acid cycle by combining with the 4-carbon oxalacetic acid. The result is citric acid, a 6-carbon organic acid. By several steps the citric acid is converted to other organic acids, including α-ketoglutaric (5C), succinic (4C), fumaric (4C), malic (4C), and finally back to oxalacetic (4C). In the course of these reactions, 2 molecules of CO_2 and 4 atoms of hydrogen are split off, the net result being the complete breakdown of pyruvic acid into CO_2 and [H]. Three molecules of water enter into the reactions, providing 6 additional [H] and some of the oxygen of the CO_2:

$$\text{pyruvic acid} + \text{water} + \begin{array}{c} \text{hydrogen} \\ \text{acceptor} \end{array} \longrightarrow \begin{array}{c} \text{carbon} \\ \text{dioxide} \end{array} + \begin{array}{c} \text{reduced hydrogen} \\ \text{acceptor} \end{array}$$

$$CH_3 \cdot CO \cdot COOH + 3H_2O + \quad 5A \quad \longrightarrow \quad 3CO_2 + \quad 5AH_2$$

The citric acid cycle may be outlined in some, though not complete, detail as follows:

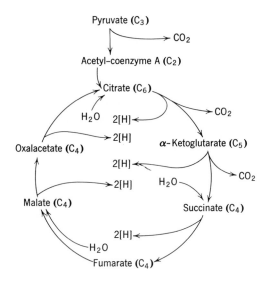

THE TERMINAL OXIDATIONS

The chemical energy originally present in 1 molecule of glucose is now divided among 12 molecules of the reduced hydrogen acceptor (2 molecules produced during glycolysis and 10 from two turns of the citric acid cycle). Up to this point there has been no use of oxygen (O_2) or any net production of water, but during the terminal oxidations, oxygen finally combines with the hydrogen held by the AH_2 and so water is produced:

277

$$\text{reduced H acceptor} + \text{oxygen} \longrightarrow \text{H acceptor} + \text{water}$$

$$12AH_2 \quad + \quad 6O_2 \quad \longrightarrow \quad 12A \quad + 12H_2O$$

The oxygen does not really react directly with the AH_2, as the foregoing summary equation might suggest. Instead, the hydrogen is first transferred to a series of respiratory enzymes, energy release occurring in steps with each transfer. Oxygen is the final hydrogen acceptor in the series. The energy thus released from the AH_2 (all the energy originally present in the sugar) consists of two fractions: (1) About 34% of the energy is converted to heat (Fig. 10.14). This energy is essentially wasted in plants and cold-blooded animals. (2) The remaining 66% of the energy is used in driving the synthesis of adenosine triphosphate (ATP, Fig. 10.13) from adenosine diphosphate (ADP) and inorganic phosphate:

$$\text{adenosine diphosphate} + \text{phosphate} \longrightarrow \text{adenosine triphosphate}$$

$$38ADP \quad + \quad 38H_3PO_4 \quad \longrightarrow \quad 38ATP$$

The energy originally present in the sugar is now largely in the high-energy chemical bonds holding the added phosphate to the remainder of the ATP molecule (5, 21). Since this bond is easily broken, ATP provides a ready energy source. As the foregoing equation indicates, about 38 molecules of ATP are formed for every molecule of glucose used in respiration.

Not all the reduced hydrogen acceptor (AH_2) produced during glycolysis and the citric acid cycle necessarily goes through the terminal oxidations with the final transfer of its [H] to oxygen. Instead, some AH_2 may be used as a hydrogen donor in reduction processes such as the

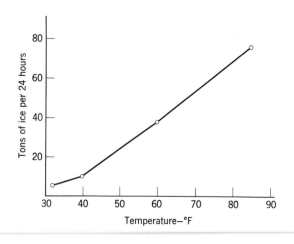

Figure 10.14. Tons of ice that would be melted during a 24-hour period by the heat produced by the respiration of a ton of apples stored at the indicated temperatures. Much of the energy used in refrigerating stored plant products is consumed in removing heat produced by respiration. The heat produced by respiration in leaves and other thin, well-ventilated plant organs is rapidly lost and does not raise their temperature appreciably. (Drawn from the data of Rose, Wright, and Whiteman.)

conversion of nitrates ($—NO_3$) to ammonia (NH_3), the synthesis of glycerol, and the synthesis of fatty acids.

ATP ENERGY RELEASE

Respiration is often considered to end with the terminal oxidations and the production of ATP. However, the actual use of the energy in useful work in a plant or animal does not occur until the ATP later breaks down into ADP and phosphate:

$$\text{adenosine triphosphate} \longrightarrow \text{adenosine diphosphate} + \text{phosphate}$$
$$\text{ATP} \qquad \qquad \searrow \qquad \qquad \text{ADP} \qquad \qquad H_3PO_4$$
$$\text{energy}$$
$$\searrow \text{useful work in the organism}$$

Since the result of respiration is the transfer of chemical energy from sugar to ATP, and particularly since some of the energy from the sugar is dissipated as heat, the long and rather complicated series of reactions making up the process of respiration might appear to be lost motion. This is not the case. Sugars are quite stable and unreactive compounds with their energy scattered through many low energy bonds and do not provide a readily available energy source. The energy derived from the sugar during respiration is partitioned among many ATP molecules, each of them with the energy contained in a high-energy bond that is readily broken, thus releasing a burst of energy usable in a variety of cellular work. We might compare the transfer of energy from sugar to ATP during respiration with the refining and concentrating of a bulk product, and the packaging of the product in smaller containers of usable size. Or, we might compare respiration with the conversion of securities into readily negotiable bank notes of convenient size. Then the ATP would represent a cell's readily available cash supply of energy.

ENZYMES AND RESPIRATION

Each of the many individual chemical reactions making up the process of respiration is activated by a specific enzyme, hence several dozen different enzymes are involved in the complete process. This is why it is impossible to give *the* respiratory enzyme in the summary equation of respiration. All the enzymes involved in the citric acid cycle and the terminal oxidations are found in the mitochondria of a cell, probably arranged in an orderly fashion (20). Thus, the mitochondria appear to be the site of the major part of respiration, just as chloroplasts are the site of photosynthesis. As more and more is learned about the structure and chemistry of cells, it is becoming evident that many, if not all, biochemical processes are localized in specific cell structures. The organized proximity of the various enzymes involved in successive steps of processes such as respiration and photosynthesis undoubtedly greatly facilitates the reactions and eliminates the diffusion of the product of one step to another place in the cell before it reacts in the next step.

ANAEROBIC RESPIRATION

The widespread type of aerobic respiration just described and other less common types of aerobic respiration can proceed to completion only when oxygen is available. However, some plants can carry on anaerobic respiration in the absence of free oxygen. The most common type of anaerobic respiration is alcoholic fermentation, a process carried on by yeasts (19), a variety of other fungi, some bacteria, and even green plants when deprived of oxygen. In summary, alcoholic fermentation proceeds as follows:

$$\text{sugar} \longrightarrow \text{ethyl alcohol} + \text{carbon dioxide}$$

$$C_6H_{12}O_6 \longrightarrow 2C_2H_5OH + 2CO_2$$

When the process is considered in greater detail, we find that the first series of reactions in alcoholic fermentation are the same glycolysis series that occurs in aerobic respiration. The pyruvic acid resulting from glycolysis is then converted in two steps to alcohol and CO_2:

(1) sugar + hydrogen acceptor $\longrightarrow$ pyruvic acid + reduced H acceptor

$$C_6H_{12}O_6 + \quad 2A \quad \longrightarrow 2CH_3 \cdot CO \cdot COOH + \quad 2AH_2$$

(2) pyruvic acid $\longrightarrow$ acetaldehyde + carbon dioxide

$$2CH_3 \cdot CO \cdot COOH \longrightarrow 2CH_3 \cdot CHO + \quad 2CO_2$$

(3) acetaldehyde + reduced H acceptor $\longrightarrow$ ethyl alcohol + H acceptor

$$2CH_3 \cdot CHO + \quad 2AH_2 \quad \longrightarrow \quad 2C_2H_5OH + \quad 2A$$

During alcoholic fermentation there is a net production of only two molecules of ATP for each molecule of sugar used. The great bulk of the energy originally present in the sugar is now in the alcohol. Anaerobic respiration is a very inefficient energy-releasing process compared with aerobic respiration, which results in the formation of some 38 molecules of ATP from one molecule of sugar. On the other hand, anaerobic respiration does have the advantage of proceeding in the absence of oxygen.

The two principal commercial uses of yeasts—baking and brewing—

are dependent on the two products of alcoholic fermentation—carbon dioxide and alcohol. When the alcohol concentration of the yeast culture medium reaches 12 to 14%, the alcohol kills the yeast cells. This is why unfortified wines and undistilled beverages never contain more than this concentration of alcohol. Yeast and some other microorganisms that carry on anaerobic respiration can also carry on ordinary aerobic respiration in the presence of an adequate supply of oxygen.

If higher plants are deprived of oxygen they may carry on alcoholic fermentation in the same way as yeast. Under natural conditions this is most likely to occur in roots when the soil is water-logged, thus reducing the available oxygen to a low level. Although the roots of some species of plants thrive in flooded soil, those of most species are seriously injured or killed after being deprived of oxygen for several days.

RESPIRATION VS. COMBUSTION

Although the summary equation for aerobic respiration (p. 274) could also be used for the complete combustion of sugar, and although both processes involve the oxidation of the sugar and the release of the same total quantity of energy from it, they are vastly different in detail and should not be confused. It is quite improper to refer to the burning of sugar within plant and animal cells. Whereas the oxidation of sugar during respiration is a step process activated by enzymes, releasing energy in small controlled quantities and transferring it from one compound to another, combustion is a rapid release of energy at high temperatures, the energy being converted into heat and light. If we compare respiratory energy release with the energy released as a person walks down a flight of stairs, combustion could be compared with the person jumping out of the window. Both methods of descent involve the loss of the same amount of potential energy, and both carry him to the same level, but there is certainly a marked difference in the methods of descent and energy expenditure, not to mention the effects on the individual.

FACTORS AFFECTING THE RATE OF RESPIRATION

Various environmental factors have a marked effect on the rate of respiration in plants and the principle of limiting factors operates just as it does in photosynthesis (and all other biological processes). The principal factors affecting the rate of respiration are temperature (Fig. 10.10), water content of the cells (Fig. 10.15), food availability, and oxygen concentration (Fig. 10.16). Adequate food supplies are usually present in a healthy plant, and oxygen is generally not a limiting factor unless its concentration is less than the 20% or so normally present in the

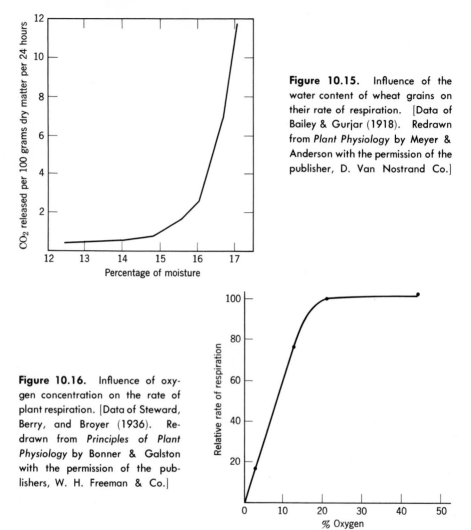

Figure 10.15. Influence of the water content of wheat grains on their rate of respiration. [Data of Bailey & Gurjar (1918). Redrawn from *Plant Physiology* by Meyer & Anderson with the permission of the publisher, D. Van Nostrand Co.]

Figure 10.16. Influence of oxygen concentration on the rate of plant respiration. [Data of Steward, Berry, and Broyer (1936). Redrawn from *Principles of Plant Physiology* by Bonner & Galston with the permission of the publishers, W. H. Freeman & Co.]

air. Low water content of the protoplasm is generally the limiting factor in dry, mature seeds, and probably also in most wilted plants. The most common limiting factor in respiration is, however, temperature, and most of the time the rate of respiration in plants will increase with temperature up to the point (about 50°C) where enzymes are inactivated.

PHOTOSYNTHETIC/RESPIRATORY RATIO

The rate of photosynthesis divided by the rate of respiration of a plant is known as the **photosynthetic/respiratory ratio** (P/R ratio). The P/R ratio may be based on a single cell, a leaf, the shoot of the plant, the entire plant, or even a community. The time period used may range from a few minutes to an entire 24-hour day or even a whole growing season. Perhaps the most useful base for the P/R ratio from the stand-point of the general economy of the plant is the entire plant for a period of at least 24 hours. On this base, a P/R ratio of 1 would mean that just as much food was used in respiration as was produced in photosynthesis, that no food would accumulate, and that any assimilation would occur at the expense of accumulated food. A P/R ratio of less than 1 would result in the use of accumulated food even in respiration, and if con-tinued over a long period of time the plant would eventually starve. Actually, under ordinary favorable growing conditions plants usually have a P/R ratio of around 5 or even more. Thus there is an abundance of food that can be used in respiration and assimilation, with a surplus that accumulates.

GAS EXCHANGES OF PLANTS

Because oxygen diffuses out of chlorophyll-bearing plants during the day and carbon dioxide diffuses into them, many people have the mis-taken idea that plants carry on a type of respiration just the reverse of animal respiration, even though they may know that during the night oxygen diffuses into plants and carbon dioxide out. The miscon-ception arises, of course, from the confusion of photosynthesis and respiration. Respiration occurs continuously in plants, both day and night, whereas photosynthesis occurs only in the presence of light. Since the rate of photosynthesis is generally much higher than the rate of respiration during the day, oxygen does diffuse out and carbon dioxide in, although respiration is still using oxygen and producing carbon dioxide. In the dark, and at all times in tissues lacking chloro-plasts, only the respiratory gas exchange occurs. In dim light, or under other conditions severely limiting the rate of photosynthesis, the rates of photosynthesis and respiration may be the same and neither gas will be diffusing into or out of the leaf.

Assimilation

Although our discussion of respiration has been quite lengthy, we have presented only a rather small fraction of the information that has been accumulated as a result of research on respiration. We cannot devote as much space to the other way organisms use food, that is, as-similation, simply because very little is really known about it. Whereas some biologists restrict the term *assimilation* to the making of living matter (protoplasm) from food and water, we shall use it in its broader sense, including the formation of all essential cell structures—cell walls as well as protoplasm.

Much is known about how plants synthesize cell wall substances like cellulose, lignin, and pectic compounds, but there is still much to be learned about how such components of cell walls are organized into the characteristic structural patterns of cell walls. Among the variety of useful bits of information that we do possess is the fact that the plant hormone, auxin, is essential in cell wall enlargement (Chapter 12), and the fact that in regions of cell wall formation there is an aggregation of rather distinct masses of actively moving protoplasm.

Even less is known about how chemical compounds are converted into protoplasm than about cell wall assimilation, although there is much information on the synthesis of the various constituents of protoplasm by cells. Assimilation itself is probably more a matter of physical organization of the various cell structures than of chemical change. The electron microscope has helped reveal the fact that organized cell structure extends to a far smaller level and a greater degree of complex and precise structural patterns than had been realized previously. Assimilation is one of the key problems of biology, and merges into the related problem of cell differentiation and the development of organisms.

Food Accumulation

Whenever a green plant makes more food by photosynthesis than it uses in respiration and assimilation, or when the food intake of a nongreen plant or animal exceeds its use of food in respiration and assimilation, the excess food **accumulates**. This is frequently referred to as food *storage*, but the term *accumulation* is more descriptive of what actually happens.

Fats constitute the great bulk of food accumulated in animals. In plants, foods such as starch, sucrose, and proteins, as well as fats, may accumulate. Foods can accumulate in almost any organ of a plant but they are usually the most abundant in seeds, fruits, fleshy roots, and tubers and other fleshy underground stems. Sugar cane plants have large quantities of sucrose in their stems, and there is considerable food in the twigs of trees and shrubs.

Surplus foods may be digested and used by plants at some later time. For example, the food in twigs is used in the initial stages of growth in the spring before the leaves provide much food from photosynthesis, and the food in seeds supports the respiration and assimilation of the seedlings before they begin carrying on photosynthesis.

Some species of plants accumulate substantial quantities of substances other than foods, including rubber latex, turpentine, resins, alkaloids, and volatile oils like peppermint oil. Unlike foods, these substances apparently cannot be digested and used in respiration or assimilation and their roles (if any) in the life of the plants are not generally known. That they are not of general importance in plants is suggested by the fact that any one of these substances is produced by only a few species of plants. Although they may not play essential roles in the plants that produce them, many of them are among man's more important items of commerce.

Food Syntheses

From the sugar produced during photosynthesis, plants synthesize all of the numerous organic compounds present, including other carbohydrates, fats, proteins, a great variety of organic acids, hormones, vitamins, pectic compounds, lignin, volatile oils, carotenoids, chlorophylls, latex, alkaloids, purines, and pyrimidines, to mention only a few groups of compounds. Many of these organic compounds contain only the carbon, hydrogen, and oxygen derived from the sugar (or, in the final analysis, from carbon dioxide and water), whereas others also contain other elements derived from salts. Some of the synthetic pathways leading from the sugar are long and involved, with many intermediate substances produced along the way; other pathways are quite short and direct. Some of the synthetic pathways are well known, others are still imperfectly understood, but we can be certain that they lead back to the product of photosynthesis. A consideration of more than a few of these synthetic processes of plants is far beyond the scope of an introductory textbook. We shall discuss here only the synthesis of four foods—starch, sucrose, fats, and proteins. These synthetic pathways are also outlined in Fig. 10.17.

SUCROSE SYNTHESIS

Sucrose, ordinary table sugar and one of the most abundant sugars synthesized by plants, is one of the **disaccharides**. Disaccharides are formed by the union of two molecules of simple sugars. The simple sugars used in the synthesis of sucrose are glucose phosphate and fructose, both of them being hexoses. We shall not consider the various reactions involved in the formation of these hexoses from the triose phosphate produced in photosynthesis, although it should be pointed out that it can be converted quite readily into all the other kinds of simple sugars such as pentoses as well as into the various hexose sugars. If glucose phosphate,

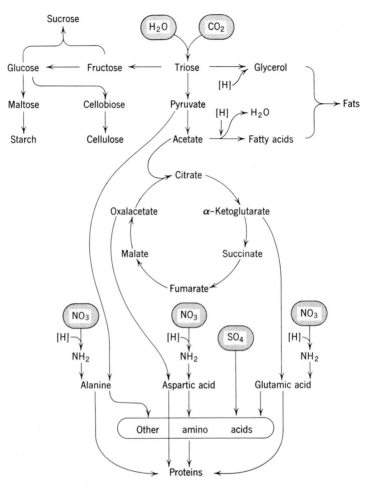

Figure 10.17. Summary outline of some food syntheses in plants. Most of the reactions also proceed in the reverse direction, although not necessarily by the same pathways. Although the reactions form an interconnecting network, triose sugars may be considered as a basic starting point. The triose comes from carbon dioxide and water by way of photosynthesis. The role of the citric acid cycle of respiration in amino acid synthesis is illustrated here. Substances entering the plant from the environment are shown in shaded ovals.

fructose, and the enzyme sucrose phosphorylase are present the synthesis of sucrose can proceed as follows:

$$\text{glucose phosphate} + \text{fructose} \xrightarrow{\underset{\text{phosphorylase}}{\text{sucrose}}} \text{sucrose} + \text{phosphoric acid}$$

$$C_6H_{11}O_6 \cdot H_2PO_3 + C_6H_{12}O_6 \longrightarrow C_{12}H_{22}O_{11} + H_3PO_4$$

The synthesis of other disaccharides proceeds in a similar manner. For example, by substituting glucose for fructose and changing the enzyme, the preceding equation would represent the synthesis of the disaccharide *maltose*.

STARCH SYNTHESIS

Plants synthesize starch by linking hundreds to a thousand or more glucose molecules together, forming long spiral starch molecules that are sometimes branched (Chapter 3). The formula for starch may be written $(C_6H_{10}O_5)_n$, where n is the number of glucose molecules used in making a molecule of starch. If in a particular starch molecule n were 1000, we could write its formula $C_{6000}H_{10000}O_{5000}$. The formula of starch suggests that at each glucose linkage a molecule of water is produced as starch is being synthesized. Actually, phosphate is produced rather than water, since glucose can participate in starch synthesis only after it has been phosphorylated.

Starch synthesis can occur in most living plant cells, although some lower plants and a few seed plants such as onion and other members of the lily family are unable to synthesize starch. The use of the iodine test for starch to determine whether photosynthesis has been occuring in a leaf might suggest that starch is the production of photosynthesis. Actually, photosynthesis is completed with the production of sugar, but in most plants the sugar is almost immediately converted into starch.

FAT SYNTHESIS

Animals are unable to synthesize either sucrose or true starch, but both plants and animals can synthesize fats (10) from sugars. Fat synthesis occurs in three principal steps: (1) The synthesis of glycerol (glycerine) from phosphorylated triose, (2) the synthesis of various fatty acids from triose by way of an acetic acid derivative, and (3) the linking of glycerol and fatty acids into molecules of fat (Fig. 10.17).

We shall not consider the first two series of reactions in detail, but it is worth noting that glycerol $[C_3H_5(OH)_3]$ molecules contain the same number of carbon and oxygen atoms as triose $(C_3H_6O_3)$ molecules, but two more hydrogen atoms. The added hydrogen comes from reduced hydrogen acceptor (AH_2). Since addition of hydrogen to a molecule results in its reduction, each glycerol molecule contains more energy than a triose molecule. The extra energy was provided by respiration.

For the synthesis of three molecules of palmitic acid $(C_{15}H_{31}COOH)$, a typical fatty acid, 16 molecules of triose are used. A little calculation will reveal that the three molecules of palmitic acid contain just the same number of C and H atoms as the 16 molecules of triose, but the palmitic acid contains only 6 oxygen atoms in comparison with 48 in the triose molecules. The fatty acid has been produced from the sugar by reduction processes and has a much higher energy content than the sugar, but here reduction has occurred by the removal of oxygen rather than by the addition of hydrogen. The oxygen does not appear as a gas (O_2), but instead combines with hydrogen from AH_2 and so forms water. Again, the energy used in the reduction comes from ATP produced in respiration.

Thus, both glycerol and fatty acids have a higher energy content per unit weight than the triose (or any other carbohydrate), and the fats formed by the union of fatty acids and glycerol also have this high energy content. A pound of fat contains about twice as many calories as a pound of sugar or starch. The final reaction in fat synthesis follows:

$$\text{glycerol} \ + \ \text{fatty acids} \ \longrightarrow \ \text{fat} \ + \text{water}$$

$$C_3H_5(OH)_3 + 3C_{15}H_{31}COOH \longrightarrow C_3H_5(C_{15}H_{31}COO)_3 + 3H_2O$$

Fats differ from one another chemically in the kinds of fatty acids used in their synthesis.

PROTEIN SYNTHESIS

All organisms can synthesize their own particular proteins by linking various amino acids together in specific and characteristic sequences (14). Although animals and some bacteria and fungi must depend on the proteins they absorb and digest for their basic supply of amino acids, green plants (and some bacteria and fungi) can synthesize their own amino acids from sugars, nitrates, and sulfates. The sugar used first passes through glycolysis to pyruvic acid and then part way through the citric acid to several of the keto acids of the cycle (Fig. 10.17). These keto acids are converted to amino acids by substitution of an $—NH_2$ (amino) group derived from ammonium salts for the oxygen of the $>C{=}O$ group of the keto acid. The amino group is the characteristic structural feature of all amino acids, along with the $—COOH$ group common to all organic acids. Although the ammonia may come from ammonium salts absorbed by the plant, it is generally formed by the reduction of nitrate ($—NO_3$) salts. The energy used in this reduction is derived from respiration through AH_2. Since the keto acids are intermediate products formed in the course of the respiratory reactions, respiration is even more intimately associated with their synthesis. Respiration may, indeed, be considered as a synthetic process as well as an energy-releasing process, since glycerol, fatty acids, and other compounds, as well as amino acids are derived from substances produced during respiration.

Only a few of the amino acids are formed directly by the basic processes just outlined; however, these amino acids can be converted into others that are generally somewhat more complicated in structure. Three of the common amino acids contain sulfur, and most proteins include a few molecules of these sulfur-containing amino acids.

The next step in protein synthesis is the linking together of amino acid molecules into the long molecules of protein. The $-NH_2$ group of one amino acid is linked to the $-COOH$ group of another (a **peptide linkage**), for example:

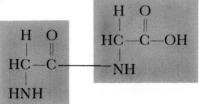

Before this linkage can occur, the amino acids must react with ATP, an amino acid replacing the two high-energy phosphate groups of the ATP and thus producing an amino acid-AMP (adenosine monophosphate or adenylic acid) complex.

Since each kind of protein is composed of certain amino acids linked in a specific sequence, and since even a single deviation from this sequence results in a different protein (Chapter 3), there must be some coding system controlling protein synthesis. It now appears that the basic code is provided by the DNA (the genes) of the chromosomes, the DNA code controlling the synthesis of the RNA and so transferring its coded information to the RNA of the microsomes. The RNA code in turn controls the order of amino acid assembly in the microsomes as proteins are synthesized. It appears that this may be accomplished by the intervention of the **soluble RNA** (or **transfer RNA**) found outside the microsomes in the cytoplasm (14). Transfer RNA molecules are much smaller than microsome RNA molecules, and each kind of transfer RNA can combine with only one kind of amino acid.

The amino acid-AMP molecules combine with the appropriate transfer RNA molecule, and all of them are held by the enzyme activating the process. There are as many kinds of these complexes as there are amino acids, and the RNA portion of each complex will fit into only one code unit of the much larger microsome RNA molecules, just as a key may fit only one of a series of locks. This assures that the amino acids will be assembled against the microsome RNA in a certain specific order determined by the sequence of code units of the microsome RNA.

Once assembled in the proper order on the RNA, the amino acids become linked to one another, are detached from the RNA, AMP, and enzyme, and now constitute a new molecule of protein. Finally, the chain of amino acid residues may be cross linked with another similar chain and folded or coiled, thus completing protein synthesis. The localization of protein synthesis in the microsomes is one more example of the restriction of certain biological processes to certain cell structures.

Digestion

We have seen that plants synthesize more complex foods from simple foods: sucrose and starch from simple sugars, fats from fatty acids and glycerol, and proteins from amino acids, for example. Plants also break down these more complex foods into the simpler foods composing them. The two sets of processes might be compared with building and subsequent wrecking of a house, or perhaps better with the assembly and disassembly of a prefabricated house. Even though plants break down the more complex foods through several different pathways, we shall restrict our discussion to the type of decomposition reactions involving the use of water in breaking the chemical bonds between the component units, a type of reaction referred to chemically as **hydrolysis** and biologically as **digestion** (19).

Green plants do not have digestive tracts as most animals do, and they do not secrete digestive enzymes into the surrounding medium as bacteria and fungi do, but the chemical reactions of digestion are essentially similar in all groups of organisms. In general, digestion in green plants occurs within cells (**intracellular digestion**), whereas in most animals and nongreen plants, the digestive enzymes are commonly secreted by

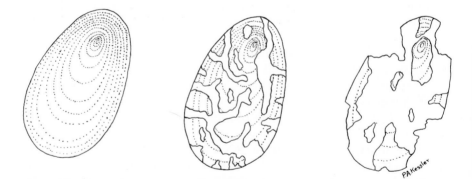

Figure 10.18. Intact starch grains and starch grains partly eroded as they were being digested through the action of amylase.

the cells producing them and the digestion reactions occur outside of cells (**extracellular digestion**), either in a digestive tract or the surrounding food medium. Considerable intracellular digestion also occurs in fungi. The biological significance of digestion is similar in all organisms. Digestion converts large, complex molecules that are frequently insoluble into smaller, soluble molecules that can diffuse through cell membranes, can be transported through the organism, and can be used in respiration. Neither a starch grain nor a single starch molecule could possibly leave the cell in which it was formed without disrupting the cell membranes. However, the glucose produced by digestion of the starch (Fig. 10.18) can diffuse through the cell membranes. Similarly, a fungus cannot absorb starch, cellulose, or proteins, though it can absorb the products of their digestion. Accumulated foods must first be digested before they can be used by the organism.

DIGESTIVE PROCESSES

Since the various processes are relatively simple and in general quite similar, we can list several of them in a single group:

(1) Sucrose digestion: sucrose $+$ water $\xrightarrow{\text{sucrase}}$ glucose $+$ fructose

$$C_{12}H_{22}O_{11} + H_2O \longrightarrow C_6H_{12}O_6 + C_6H_{12}O_6$$

(2) Starch digestion: starch $+$ water $\xrightarrow{\text{amylase}}$ maltose

$$(C_6H_{10}O_5)n + nH_2O \longrightarrow \tfrac{1}{2}nC_{12}H_{22}O_{11}$$

maltose $+$ water $\xrightarrow{\text{maltase}}$ glucose $+$ glucose

$$C_{12}H_{22}O_{11} + H_2O \longrightarrow C_6H_{12}O_6 + C_6H_{12}O_6$$

(3) Fat digestion:

a fat $+$ water $\xrightarrow{\text{lipase}}$ fatty acids $+$ glycerol

$$C_3H_5(C_{15}H_{31}COO)_3 + H_2O \longrightarrow 3C_{15}H_{31}COOH + C_3H_5(OH)_3$$

(4) Protein digestion: a protein $+$ water $\xrightarrow{\text{proteases}}$ amino acids

No energy changes of consequence occur during digestion. The products of digestion, then, are simple sugars, fatty acids, glycerol, and amino acids, all of them soluble and relatively simple substances.

DIGESTIVE ENZYMES

In writing the foregoing equations, we have departed from our usual practice of not indicating the enzymes that increase the rate of biochemical reactions. Since the digestion processes represented (except for protein digestion) are specific reactions, rather than summary equations for a series of reactions as in many previous instances, listing the enzymes involved is a simple matter. It has been done for several reasons: to emphasize the fact that enzymes catalyze practically all biochemical reactions, to point out again the specificity of enzymes, to illustrate the current method of naming enzymes, and because digestive enzymes are the ones most likely to be encountered in the laboratory work of introductory courses.

Although sucrose and maltose are both disaccharide sugars, different enzymes are involved in their digestion. The digestion of cellulose would be represented by the same chemical formulae (but by different compound names) used for starch digestion, and even though both result in the production of glucose, amylase will not catalyze the digestion of cellulose. Another enzyme, **cellulase,** is essential. Whether or not cellulose is a food for a specific organism depends on whether it produces cellulase. Thus, some fungi and bacteria, as well as the protozoa that live in the digestive tracts of termites, produce cellulase and so can digest and use cellulose, whereas most species of plants and animals do not. At present, enzymes are generally named by suffixing -**ase** to the root of the name of the substrate or a term descriptive of the reaction. **Amylase** is so named because starch is technically called **amylose.** However, enzymes named before the present system was adopted generally ended in -**in,** for example **pepsin, ptyalin,** and **papain.**

Several of the many digestive enzymes produced by plants are extracted and sold commercially. **Diastase** is a crude enzyme extract secured principally from germinating barley or from molds, and contains both amylase and maltase. It is available at many drug stores. Meat tenderizers contain a protease (papain) extracted from the fruits of the papaya or tropical pawpaw. Fresh pineapples also contain a protease and when added to gelatin desserts the gelatin (a protein) is digested and liquified instead of forming the usual semisolid gel.

Food Translocation

One other aspect of the food economy of plants remains to be considered: the problem of food transport from one part of a plant to another, for example from leaves to roots or from tubers or other sites of accumulation to meristems (Fig. 10.19). Simple, soluble foods to

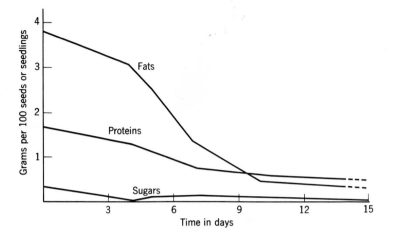

Figure 10.19. The changing content of foods in the cotyledons of a young bean plant during germination and early growth. Most of the food originally present was digested and translocated to other parts of the plant. (Data of E. C. Miller. Redrawn from *Textbook of Botany* by Transeau, Sampson, and Tiffany with the permission of the publishers, Harper and Brothers.)

which the cell membranes are permeable may move from one cell to another by simple diffusion. However, diffusion is far too slow a process to account for the observed rates of food transport through a distance of a few centimeters to many meters within a plant. Calculations show that sugars are transported to a developing pumpkin fruit at rates ranging from 500 to 1000 cm./hr., and rates of 100 cm./hr. or so are quite commonly found in many species of plants. In contrast, sugar diffusing from a 10% solution would take about two and half *years* to diffuse a distance of 100 cm. If diffusion were the only means of food transport in plants no plant more than a few centimeters in size could survive, unless its chlorenchyma tissues were distributed throughout the plant.

Food transport (**translocation**) from one part of a plant to another occurs within the sieve elements of the phloem (26). Although translocation is shown to occur through mechanisms other than simple diffusion, no completely satisfactory explanation of translocation has yet been proposed (4). There are two principal theories—**cytoplasmic streaming** and **mass flow** but despite the fact that both have substantial supporting evidence neither one is free from serious objections.

CYTOPLASMIC STREAMING

This theory holds that foods and other solutes are transported from one end of a sieve element to another by the cyclic flow of the cytoplasm.

293

This theory is supported by the fact that conditions known to retard or stop cytoplasmic streaming, such as reduced temperature or oxygen supply or death of the sieve elements, will retard or stop translocation, and by the reports that solutes may be transported simultaneously in opposite directions through sieve elements. There are, however, several serious objections to the cytoplasmic streaming theory. The observed rates of cytoplasmic streaming are too slow to account for many measured translocation rates, and besides, cytoplasmic streaming has rarely (if ever) been observed in mature sieve elements.

MASS FLOW

This theory holds that the high turgor pressure of leaf cells produces a flow of the solution of sugar and other substances through the plasmodesmata to adjacent cells and then on to and through the sieve elements into cells with lower turgor pressures, particularly those of the roots. The evidence for mass flow includes exudation from cut or injured phloem and the fact that viruses, hormones, and other substances present in leaf cells in low concentration are translocated from the leaves only when sugar is being translocated out.

Among the objections to the mass flow theory is the fact that the cytoplasm of sieve elements is rather viscous and would seem to offer very high resistance to the flow of a solution through it. Mass flow can account for translocation in only one direction at a time, and it cannot account for the fact that lowering the temperature or oxygen supply of the cells reduces the rate of translocation through them. Another objection is that the receiving cells may not always have a lower turgor pressure than the supplying cells. Like cytoplasmic streaming, mass flow appears to be too slow to explain some observed translocation rates.

Clarification of the mechanism of translocation awaits further research, and perhaps the development of entirely new theories. At present, however, it is clear that translocation occurs in the phloem and that sucrose is the principal food translocated in at least some species of plants. Recent research indicates that translocation by both mass flow and cytoplasmic streaming may occur in the same plant.

GIRDLING AND TRANSLOCATION

Since the phloem of trees is in the bark (26), removal of a ring of bark from the entire circumference of a stem (**girdling**) will stop food translocation at the girdle (Fig. 10.20). When a tree trunk is girdled, the stem and roots below the girdle receive no more food from the leaves and will starve when all previously accumulated food is exhausted, although starvation may not occur for several years. Once the roots have starved,

Figure 10.20. Effect of girdling a cherry stem, shown here two growth seasons after girdling. Cambial growth below the ring was inhibited by lack of food. (Courtesy of Carl L. Wilson. From *Botany* by Wilson & Loomis with the permission of the publisher, The Dryden Press.)

the shoot of the tree will die from lack of water. Pioneers frequently girdled trees a year or more before clearing land for cultivation. This practice led to little or no root sprouting. Orchard owners sometimes girdle branches of fruit trees to secure unusually large fruits for exhibition at fairs. Rabbits and similar herbivorous animals sometimes injure trees by eating their bark and at times girdling them. Girdling is frequently used by plant physiologists as an experimental device in the study of translocation.

► ## *Questions*

1. Greenhouse operators have found that at times addition of CO_2 to the air in greenhouses promotes photosynthesis, whereas at other times it has no effect. Explain. If too much CO_2 is added to the air photosynthesis is greatly reduced, rather than increased. Explain.

2. Why are protein foods, such as beans and bread, derived directly from plants generally much less expensive than protein foods such as meat, eggs, and milk derived from animals?

3. How would the dry weight of a piece of undecayed firewood compare with the dry weight of the same piece after it had been partially decayed by fungi? Would the total dry weight of the wood plus the fungi be the same as the dry weight of the undecayed wood? Explain. Compare the amount of heat produced by the burning of the decayed wood with the heat that would have been produced by burning the wood before it decayed.

4. What, if anything, could a farmer do to increase the rate of photosynthesis in a field of corn? Would an increased rate of photosynthesis be desirable?

5. Ripe watermelon seeds will germinate if the melon is opened, but not if it is intact. Suggest possible explanations, and design experiments that would indicate which explanation was correct.

6. A botanist found that when a leaf was supplied radioactive CO_2, the cells of the palisade layer were much more radioactive than those of the spongy layer. Give some possible explanations.

7. Presumably the contribution of the light reactions of photosynthesis to the subsequent reduction of CO_2 to sugars consists only of reduced pyridine nucleotide ($TPNH \cdot H^+$) and ATP. Respiration also produces reduced pyridine nucleotides (some $TPNH \cdot H^+$ and more $DPNH \cdot H^+$) and ATP. Why, then, can the reduction of CO_2 to sugars not occur in the dark? Suggest as many possible explanations as you can.

► ## *References*

For Reference

1. Galston, A. W., *The Life of the Green Plant*, Englewood Cliffs, N. J.: Prentice-Hall, 1961.
2. McElroy, Wm. D., *Cellular Physiology and Biochemistry*, Englewood Cliffs, N. J.: Prentice-Hall, 1960.

For Reading

3. Arnon, Daniel I., The role of light in photosynthesis. *Scientific American* 203(5):104–118, November 1960.
4. Biddulph, Susan and Orlin, The circulatory system of plants. *Scientific American* 200(2):44–49, February 1959.
5. Eisley, Loren C., The secret of Life. *Harper's Magazine* 207(1241):64–68, October 1953. (About ATP)
6. Eulach, V. A., Those improbable little green men. *Science Digest* 40(6):1–3, December 1956.

7. Frieden, Earl, The enzyme-substrate complex. *Scientific American* 201(2):119–125, August 1959.

8. Gabriel, M. L. and Seymour Fogel, *Great Experiments in Biology*. Englewood Cliffs, N. J.: Prentice-Hall, 1955. (See pp. 23–53 for classical papers on enzymes, pp. 84–104 for papers on metabolism, and pp. 152–184 for papers on photosynthesis.)

9. Gray, George W., Our bridge from the sun. *Harper's Magazine* 211(1264):62–72, September 1955. (Photosynthesis)

10. Green, David E., The metabolism of fats, *Scientific American* 190(1):32–47, January 1954. The synthesis of fat. *Scientific American* 202(2):46–51, February 1960.

11. Green, David E., Biological oxidation. *Scientific American* 199(1):56–62, July 1958.

12. Haneda, Y., Glow plants. *Natural History* 65:482–484, 1956. (Luminescent fungi)

13. Harvey, E. Newton, The luminescence of living things. *Scientific American* 178(5):46–49, May 1948.

14. Hoagland, M. B., Nucleic acids and proteins. *Scientific American* 201(6):55–61, December 1959.

15. Kamen, Martin D., Tracers. *Scientific American* 180(2):30–41, February 1949.

16. Kamen, Martin D., A universal molecule of living matter. *Scientific American* 199(2):77–82, August 1958. (The tetrapyrrole ring of chlorophyll, haemoglobin, etc.)

17. Lehniger, A. L., Energy transformations in the cell. *Scientific American* 202(5):102–114, May 1960.

18. Plass, G. N., Carbon dioxide and climate. *Scientific American* 201(1):41–47, July 1959.

19. Rose, A. H., Beer. *Scientific American* 200(6):90–100, June 1959. Yeasts. *Scientific American* 202(2):136–142, February 1960.

20. Siekevitz, Philip, Powerhouse of the cell. *Scientific American* 197(1):131–140, July 1957. (Mitochondria and respiration)

21. Stumpf, Paul K., ATP. *Scientific American* 188(4):84–93, April 1953.

22. Rabinowitch, E. I., Photosynthesis. *Scientific American* 179(2):24–35, August 1948. Progress in photosyntheis. *Scientific American* 189(5):80–85, November 1953.

23. Walker, J. J., The chloroplast and photosynthesis—a structural basis for function. *American Scientist* 47:202–215, 1959.

24. Whittingham, C. P., Photosynthesis. *Endeavour* 14:173–180, 1955.

25. Zamecnik, P. C., The microsome. *Scientific American* 198(3):118–124, March 1958. (Protein synthesis in microsomes)

26. Zimmermann, M. H., Movement of organic substances in trees. *Science* 133:73–79, 1961.

11. Plants and Minerals

$\mathbf{M}$ANY PEOPLE HAVE BEEN INTRIGUED with **hydroponics**, the cultivation of plants in solutions containing the essential mineral elements, either as a hobby or as a means of commercial crop production (3). In some hydroponic facilities the plants are supported in one way or another so that their roots are growing in the solution, some means of aerating the water usually being provided. In other types of facilities the plants are raised in some substance such as gravel, cinders, sand or vermiculite and are watered with the mineral solution, thus simplifying the problem of both support and oxygen supply to the roots. Despite the claims of some hydroponic enthusiasts, crops raised by hydroponics are not necessarily better than those raised in good fertile soil, but hydroponics has proved to be a desirable cultural technique in greenhouses and in experiments where it is necessary to control the environment of plants as precisely as possible. During and after World War II the armed forces raised vegetables by hydroponics on some of the small coral islands where there was poor and scanty soil and in Japan and other areas where the soil was contaminated with worms and other human parasites.

As a cultural practice, hydroponics developed only during the second quarter of the present century, but plant physiologists have long used similar techniques in experiments designed to determine which mineral elements are essential for plants and in what quantities. These experiments have provided the information needed for formulating hydroponic solutions containing all essential elements, and more important, they have provided information of great value to farmers and gardeners as regards the use of fertilizers in maintaining soil fertility.

Development of Concepts of Mineral Nutrition

Up to the beginning of the nineteenth century practically nothing was known about the mineral nutrition of plants. Van Helmont's conclusion, early in the seventeenth century (page 252), that plants were composed entirely of water, was for some time accepted by those who did not continue to cling to the old Greek idea that plants derived all their substance from the soil. One of the first suggestions that mineral salts might be essential for plants came from J. R. Glauber, a German chemist, in 1656. He found that potassium nitrate applied to the soil increased plant growth and concluded that this substance was the "essential principle of vegetation." In 1699 Woodward raised spearmint plants in rain water, Thames River water, conduit water, and conduit water plus garden mold, and found that growth was proportional to the quantity of dissolved material present. He concluded that van Helmont was wrong, and that an unknown earthy substance as well as water entered into the composition of plants. At about the same time Stephen Hales was conducting experiments on plant nutrition, but the real beginning of our modern knowledge of the mineral nutrition of plants was in the early nineteenth century. At the same time that increasing knowledge of photosynthesis was making it clear that the organic constituents of plants were derived from the carbon, oxygen, and hydrogen of carbon dioxide and water, our present day knowledge of the mineral nutrition of plants was beginning to be pieced together.

In 1804, Theodore de Sassure provided some of the basic concepts of the mineral nutrition of plants, as well as of photosynthesis (Chapter 10). He found that the nitrogen of plants came from the nitrogen compounds in the soil rather than directly from the air, that good plant growth could not occur without mineral elements, that plants absorb mineral substances in ratios different than those in which they occurred in the soil, and that plants absorbed substances regardless of whether they were useful, useless, or even poisonous. It was not until 1842 that other investigators began reporting on the mineral nutrition of plants. By 1861, considerable information had been secured on what elements are essential for plant growth. The technique of raising plants in wax-coated pots containing well-washed sand or pulverized quartz and supplying the plants with solutions of mineral salts lacking only one of the elements suspected of being essential gradually made it evident that the essential elements included phosphorus, potassium, nitrogen, calcium, iron, sulfur, and magnesium. These are now known as the **major elements,** since they are used by plants in relatively large quantities. Whether or not still other elements were essential in plant nutrition could not be determined by the experimental techniques then available, and it was frequently assumed that only these seven elements were essential.

The first step toward a more complete understanding of the mineral nutrition of plants was taken by the German plant physiologist, Julius von Sachs, who in 1860 introduced the method of raising the experimental plants with their roots immersed in the mineral salt solutions, thus eliminating the possibility of introducing unwanted elements as contaminants of the sand or quartz. It was not until the second quarter of the present century, however, that it became clearly evident that a number of elements—boron, copper, manganese, molybdenum, chlorine, and zinc—are essential in very small quantities. These are referred to as the **minor** or **trace elements** (6, 12). Demonstration of the essential nature of the trace elements could not be made until very pure chemical compounds were available, and extreme precautions had to be taken to make sure that the culture solutions were not contaminated by substances from the pots and glassware used or even by dust from the air. The seeds sometimes contained enough of a trace element to permit normal growth to maturity, and it was necessary to use seeds from these experimental plants in a second experiment before it could be determined that the element was essential. Although we are quite certain that all the major elements are known, additional essential trace elements will probably still be discovered. At present there is doubt as to whether or not sodium and cobalt are essential trace elements. Some fungi have been reported to require traces of various rare elements such as gallium, scandium, and vanadium, and it is at least possible that these or other elements may eventually be found to be essential to higher plants.

Associated with the development of our fundamental knowledge of the mineral nutrition of plants has been the development of much practical information about fertilizers and soil fertility that has been of incalculable value to farmers and horticulturists. Much of the research in agricultural experiment stations deals with soil fertility and the development of better fertilizers for specific soils and crops. One of the first scientists to stress the importance of soil fertility was the German chemist Justus von Liebig, who between 1840 and 1873 devoted much effort to convincing agricultural scientists and farmers of the importance of replenishing the mineral elements of the soil, and whose researches along these lines have led to his designation as the father of agricultural chemistry.

Mineral Deficiency Symptoms

Plants lacking adequate quantities of one or more of the essential elements usually develop characteristic **mineral deficiency symptoms** (Fig. 11.1) that can be used by experts to determine which element or elements are deficient (1, 5, 17). Diagnosis is frequently complicated by the fact that certain plant diseases, particularly those caused by viruses, have symptoms similar to some mineral deficiency symptoms. Toxic gases, such as those in smog, or the sulfur dioxide produced during some manufacturing processes, may also give rise to symptoms in plants

Figure 11.1. Tobacco plants showing mineral deficiency symptoms. The plant in the center received all essential elements; the others were supplied with all essential elements except the one indicated on the label. All plants are the same age and variety. Note the marked growth inhibition resulting from lack of N and K, the green but distorted leaves of the plant lacking Ca, the general chlorosis (except along the veins) of the —Mg plant, and the chlorosis in older leaves only when P was lacking. The other leaves of the —P plant are dark blue-green. The leaves of the —S plant show different degrees of chlorosis, but more commonly the younger leaves are the most chlorotic. Note also the necrosis in the —N, —P, and —K plants. (Courtesy of W. Rei Robbins, Rutgers University.)

resembling mineral deficiency symptoms. In general, the following are the most common and striking types of mineral deficiency symptoms:

(1) *Stunted Growth.* Although a deficiency of almost any essential element may stunt plant growth, growth is usually retarded the most by a deficiency of nitrogen, phosphorus, potassium, calcium, magnesium, or boron (Fig. 11.1). Plants completely deprived of nitrogen will hardly grow at all.

(2) *Chlorosis.* One of the most common mineral deficiency symptoms is chlorosis, the pale green or yellow color resulting from a reduced chlorophyll content. Chlorosis may be uniform over all the leaves, present in only the older or younger leaves, or present only along the veins or between the veins (Fig. 11.2). The pattern of chlorosis depends on which element is deficient and so provides one of the better diagnostic symptoms. Since both nitrogen and magnesium are components of the chlorophyll molecule it is obvious why deficiencies of these elements cause chlorosis. Other elements like iron, though not a part of chlorophyll, are essential in its synthesis and so chlorosis results when they are lacking. Plants lacking phosphorus do not develop chlorosis initially, but instead have an unusual dark bluish-green color.

(3) *Necrosis.* The death of parts of a plant, necrosis, is another com-

Figure 11.2. Leaf from a sunflower plant deficient in iron (left) compared with a leaf from a plant with all essential elements (center). Note the general chlorosis except along the veins. The leaf at right, showing typical iron deficiency symptoms, was from a plant supplied with iron and an excess of manganese, the latter making the iron unavailable to the plant. (Courtesy of W. Rei Robbins, Rutgers University.)

Figure 11.3. Black necrotic areas in redbeets deficient in boron (B) compared with a beet supplied with adequate boron (left). (Courtesy of R. C. Burrell, Ohio State University.)

mon mineral deficiency symptom. For example, scattered spots of dead tissue may occur in leaves if iron is deficient, leaf tips and edges may die when phosphorus is lacking, and roots and buds may die and turn black when boron is deficient (Fig. 11.3).

(4) *Anthocyanin Formation.* The formation of anthocyanin, and a consequent red color, in plant structures that usually do not produce this pigment may indicate a mineral deficiency, particularly of nitrogen or phosphorus.

(5) *Stem Symptoms.* Unusually slender, woody stems may be developed by herbaceous plants lacking nitrogen, phosphorus, potassium, or magnesium.

(6) *Poor Reproductive Development.* Mineral deficiencies, particularly of nitrogen, phosphorus, calcium, and potassium, may result in the development of unusually small and light seeds and fruits or even a complete failure to produce fruits and seeds.

CHEMICAL TESTS FOR MINERAL DEFICIENCIES

Both plants and soils may be analyzed chemically to determine how much of each essential mineral element they contain. The various state

303

agricultural experiment stations will usually make such tests, at least for nitrogen, phosphorus, and potassium, for residents of their states at little or no cost. Accurate chemical analyses can be made only by experts, but kits for making approximate analyses of the nitrogen, potassium and phosphorus content of plants and soils are available in the larger seed stores to anyone and may provide more reliable diagnostic information to the amateur than mineral deficiency symptoms.

Roles of Mineral Elements in Plants

The question now arises as to how mineral salts are used in plants, and as to how such uses are related to mineral deficiency symptoms. One important use of mineral elements is in the synthesis of various chemical compounds, many of them essential to the life of the plant. For example, nitrogen is an essential component of all amino acids, and so of proteins. Nitrogen is also a constituent of the molecules of chlorophyll, nucleic acids, and alkaloids as well as of many coenzymes, hormones, and vitamins. Calcium is a constituent of the calcium pectate of the middle lamella, and we have noted that magnesium is an essential part of the chlorophyll molecules. Proteins contain sulfur, as do vitamin B_1 and coenzyme A. Phosphorus (14) is a constituent of many important compounds such as ATP, DPN, nucleic acids, the phosphorylated sugars, and the phospholipids. Some evidence indicates that sugar must combine with boron before it can be translocated through the phloem. Many other compounds in plants contain mineral elements, although the abundant carbohydrates and fats and a variety of other compounds such as xanthophyll contain only carbon, hydrogen, and oxygen, and a relatively few compounds such as carotene and turpentine contain only carbon and hydrogen. Iron, magnesium, copper, zinc, and probably the other trace elements are components of enzyme systems.

In addition to being used in the making of enzymes and coenzymes, mineral ions may themselves act as coenzymes, enzyme activators, or in some other catalytic function. This may be considered as a second general role of mineral elements. That all trace elements have some sort of catalytic action is suggested by the very small quantities required.

Mineral salts play several other roles in plants (13). Dissolved salts contribute to the lowering of the diffusion pressure of water in cells, even though sugars and other organic solvents are probably more important in this respect. The ions formed when salts dissolve in water have many different effects on protoplasm. For example, they influence the amount of water that can be imbibed and affect the degree of permeability of cell membranes. Different ions may have opposing effects, for example sodium ions (Na^+) increase membrane permeability and calcium ions (Ca^{++}) decrease membrane permeability.

Translocation of Mineral Salts

The absorption of mineral salts is discussed in Chapter 8, but we have not considered the translocation of mineral salts through plants. Like water and foods, mineral salts are translocated through the vascular tissues, but there has been considerable doubt as to whether salts are translocated through the xylem or the phloem or both. For many years it was considered that salts were translocated upward through the xylem and downward through the phloem, but during the second and third decades of this century at least one group of plant physiologists accumulated considerable data suggesting that most mineral transport might be through the phloem. When radioactive elements became available for use as tracers (Fig. 11.4), much research was conducted on the translocation of mineral salts, and as a result it now appears clear that the bulk of the salts are translocated upward through the xylem, although some translocation in both directions may occur through the phloem. Tracer studies show that salts readily pass back and forth between the xylem and phloem. Most mineral elements can be translocated both upward and downward in plants; however, a few like calcium can be translocated only upward. Like water and foods, mineral salts are translocated much faster than they can diffuse. In both the phloem and the xylem the salts are dissolved in water and the forces involved in their transport are presumably those already described for water (Chapter 9) and food (Chapter 10).

The Nitrogen Cycle

Nitrogen (8) is a somewhat different category from the other essential elements we have been discussing. Strictly speaking it is not really a mineral element, although it is commonly considered along with the mineral salts since plants usually obtain their nitrogen through nitrogen salts absorbed with the other salts. The basic source of the true mineral elements is the disintegrated rock that constitutes the bulk of most soils, but the important basic source of nitrogen is the atmosphere, which is about 78% nitrogen (N_2). Neither animals nor most plants are able to tap this great reservoir of nitrogen directly, but a few species of bacteria and algae can synthesize nitrogen compounds from atmospheric nitrogen by processes known as **nitrogen fixation**. These nitrogen compounds may then be used by plants, and in turn plants

305

Figure 11.4. This soybean plant was supplied with radioactive iron. When the plant was placed against an X-ray film, the radiation from the iron exposed the film, showing the generally uniform distribution of the iron throughout the plant, even though the buds, roots, and lower part of the vascular tissue of the stem contained a somewhat higher concentration than the rest of the plant. (Courtesy of the U.S. Department of Agriculture.)

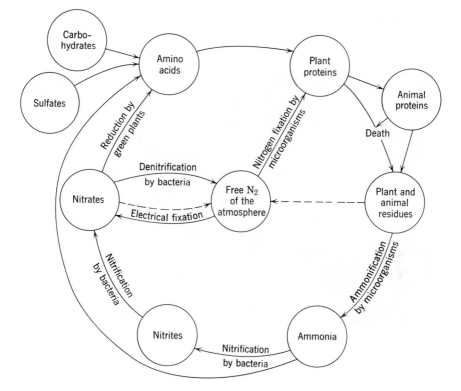

Figure 11.5. Outline of the nitrogen cycle. (Redrawn from *Plant Physiology* by Meyer & Anderson with the permission of the publisher, D. Van Nostrand Co.)

serve as the basic nitrogen source of animals. The flow of nitrogen and nitrogen compounds from one organism to another and between organisms and environment is called the **nitrogen cycle** (Fig. 11.5). Consideration of the nitrogen cycle may begin at any point, but we shall start with nitrogen fixation.

NITROGEN FIXATION

Most species of nitrogen-fixing bacteria and algae are free-living soil or water organisms (Fig. 11.6). Some of the nitrogen compounds they synthesize diffuse out and may be absorbed by plants, whereas other compounds may not be available until the nitrogen-fixing organisms die. The nitrogen-fixing organisms in an acre of typical midwestern soil fix about 15 to 25 pounds of atmospheric nitrogen in a year. A second class of nitrogen-fixing bacteria invade the roots of leguminous

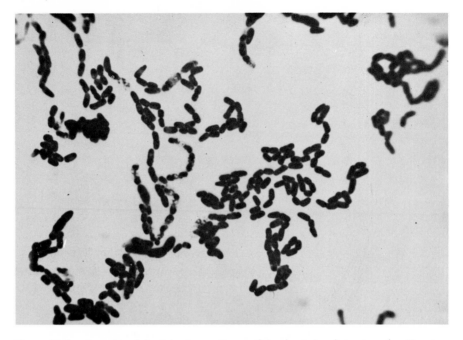

Figure 11.6. A species of *Azotobacter*, a nitrogen-fixing bacterium living in soil. (Courtesy of the copyright holder, General Biological Supply House.)

plants (such as peas, beans, clover, and alfalfa), causing the formation of **root nodules** filled with the bacteria (Figs. 11.7, 11.8). These bacteria can fix nitrogen only when in the nodules. Both the legumes and the bacteria benefit from this relationship. The legumes are provided a supply of nitrogen (Fig. 11.9), and the bacteria secure food from the roots. Such relationships between two organisms benefiting both are known as **mutualism** or **symbiosis**. About 100 pounds of nitrogen are commonly fixed in an acre of most leguminous crops per year, but as much as 250 pounds may be fixed in an acre of alfalfa. There is generally an excess of nitrogen beyond that used by the legumes, and this may supply much of the nitrogen used by nonleguminous crops (about 60 pounds per acre per year) planted in the same fields during the next season or two.

Lightning and other electrical discharges also fix atmospheric nitrogen, and the resulting nitrogen compounds are carried to the soil by rain. Electrical nitrogen fixation is a relatively minor source of nitrogen compounds compared with biological fixation, for only about 5 pounds of nitrogen are added to an acre of typical midwestern soil by electrical fixation during a year.

Figure 11.7. The root system of an *Erythrina indica* plant, a member of the legume family, that was inoculated with nitrogen-fixing bacteria, showing abundant nodule formation. (Courtesy of O. N. Allen, University of Wisconsin.)

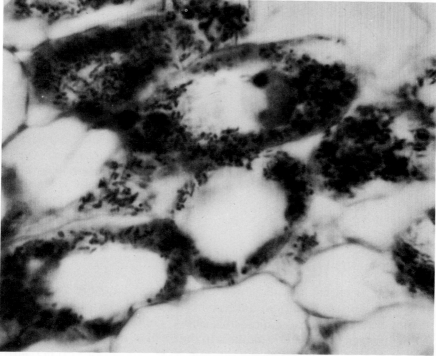

Figure 11.8. Symbiotic nitrogen-fixing bacteria (*Rhizobium*) in newly invaded host cells of a nodule of *Sesbania grandiflora*, a legume. Some cells have not yet been invaded by the bacteria. (Courtesy of O. N. Allen, University of Wisconsin.)

Figure 11.9. The effect of inoculating red clover with nitrogen-fixing bacteria. All plants have been supplied with a nutrient solution minus nitrogen and are growing in sterile white quartz sand. The seeds planted in the jar on the right were inoculated with *Rhizobium trifolium* and those planted in the jar on the left were not inoculated. (Courtesy of O. N. Allen, University of Wisconsin.)

GREEN PLANTS IN THE NITROGEN CYCLE

The nitrogen compounds absorbed by green plants are derived, not only from nitrogen fixation, but also from decomposed plant or animal tissues and animal excretions, and under cultivation from fertilizers. Most nitrogen absorbed by plants is in the form of nitrate ($-NO_3$) salts, although plants also absorb ammonium (NH_4-) salts and other nitrogen compounds. The first step in the utilization of nitrates by plants is their reduction to ammonium compounds (Chapter 10), a process that requires the expenditure of considerable energy. Although plants synthesize many different nitrogen-containing compounds, the amino acids and proteins are of particular importance in the nitrogen cycle.

ANIMALS AND NONGREEN PLANTS

The proteins synthesized by plants are the principal nitrogen source, either directly or indirectly, of all animals and of many species of fungi and bacteria. After digesting the proteins to amino acids they use the amino acids in synthesizing their own proteins. Some species of fungi and bacteria can, however, use inorganic nitrogen compounds in the synthesis of amino acids and from these they synthesize proteins.

RETURN OF NITROGEN TO THE SOIL

Animal excretions contain urea and other nitrogen compounds. These may be absorbed by plants, but they are commonly converted first into ammonium compounds and then nitrates before absorption. When plants or animals die, bacteria and fungi may cause decay of the tissues, using the proteins and amino acids in them as a source of their own proteins, and in doing so also produce considerable quantities of ammonia (NH_3) and ammonium compounds. Although plants may absorb these ammonium salts directly, they are usually converted into nitrite salts ($-NO_2$) quite rapidly by soil bacteria commonly called **nitrifying bacteria**. Next, another type of nitrifying bacteria convert the nitrites into nitrate ($-NO_3$) salts that may then be absorbed by plants. Both the conversion of ammonium compounds to nitrites and the conversion of nitrites to nitrates are oxidation processes, and both kinds of bacteria use the energy released in the chemosynthesis of carbohydrate from carbon dioxide and water.

LOSS OF SOIL NITROGEN

Nitrogen, once fixed, may continue to circulate from plants to animals to fungi and bacteria to the soil and back again to plants, but there are several ways nitrogen may be lost from the soil. In many soils there are **denitrifying bacteria** that break down nitrates and release gaseous nitrogen into the atmosphere. In contrast with the nitrifying and most kinds of nitrogen-fixing bacteria, the denitrifying bacteria thrive in situations where oxygen is deficient, and so are likely to be abundant and active in poorly drained soils. Like other salts, nitrogen salts may also be lost from the soil by leaching and erosion of the soil. Both leaching and erosion are likely to be much more severe in a cultivated field than in a natural plant habitat. An even greater loss of nitrogen from cultivated areas results from harvesting and removal of crops. Soils under cultiva-

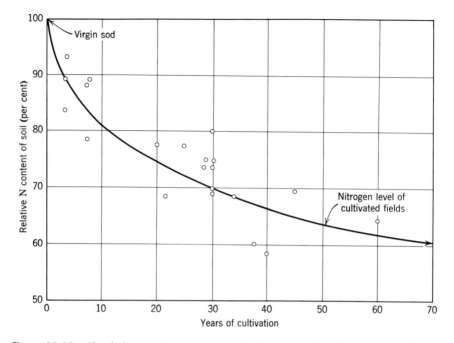

Figure 11.10. The decline in nitrogen content of midwestern soils with period of cultivation. (Redrawn from the 1938 *Yearbook* of the U.S. Department of Agriculture.)

tion show a continued decrease in nitrogen content (Fig. 11.10) unless the supply is replenished by planting leguminous crops or by using fertilizers. In most natural plant communities, soil nitrogen is maintained at a rather stable level that is frequently adequate for good plant growth. However, the nitrogen level is generally low in bogs, and it tends to be lower in dry than in humid regions and lower in hot than in cool climates. These differences result from effects of the environment on the operation of the nitrogen cycle. For example, where the temperature is frequently high, nitrogen-fixing bacteria are relatively inactive and decay is rapid.

Fertilizers and Soil Fertility

Unless a farmer or gardener adds mineral elements to his soils, the fertility level will constantly decrease and his crop yields will decline. The amount and kind of fertilizer needed depends on a variety of factors such as the original fertility of the soil, the types of crop plants, the amount of leaching and erosion, and the soil structure. Since positively-charged ions (cations) are held on the surface of soil particles where they are relatively resistent to leaching, clay soils hold much greater quantities of cations than do sandy soils because of the much greater total particle surface area in clay soils. The colloidial clay particles bear multiple negative electrical charges. Different cations are held on the particle surfaces by electrical attraction with different degrees of firmness, the order from greatest to least for several common cations being H^+, Ca^{++}, Mg^{++}, K^+, NH_4^+, and Na^+. Any ion in the series can displace an ion to the right of it from the soil particles, a process known as **cation exchange.** Ions displaced from the surface of a particle can be absorbed by plants, but they are also subject to leaching from the soil. One reason for the low fertility of acid soils is that the H^+ ions have displaced most other ions from particle surfaces and these ions have been absorbed or leached away.

TYPES OF FERTILIZERS

The term *fertilizer* may be applied to any material containing essential mineral elements that may be applied to the soil (or to bodies of water). Some fertilizers also improve soil structure. Although fertilizers supply mineral salts rather than foods (page 253), they are frequently referred to as plant foods. **Commercial fertilizers,** or **chemical fertilizers** as they are sometimes called, are made from a variety of things such as pulverized rock, bone meal, dried blood and other animal remains, cottonseed meal, and soybean meal. A so-called complete fertilizer contains the three elements that are most likely to be deficient in soils (N, P, K), the percentage of each present usually being indicated on the container. Thus, a 4-12-4 fertilizer contains 4% nitrogen, 12% phosphorus, and 4% potassium (potash). A few of the more expensive fertilizers contain all the known essential elements and so are really complete, although ordinary fertilizers may contain more than the three common elements as impurities. In recent years mixtures of essential mineral salts have become available at garden supply stores. These are sometimes referred to as instant or concentrated fertilizers, and may be used in hydroponics, or dissolved in water and applied to the soil or to the leaves of plants as **foliar sprays.** The latter practice is becoming more widely used and is particularly valuable for elements such as iron that may become converted into insoluble and unavailable forms in the soil. Calcium, however, cannot be supplied to plants in foliar sprays since it is not translocated out of the leaves.

Lime is applied to soils principally to reduce soil acidity, but since it consists of calcium carbonate or other calcium compounds it also corrects calcium deficiencies. In addition, it helps release other elements from the soil particle surfaces and improves the crumb structure of clay soils (Chapter 9).

The **organic fertilizers** include barnyard manure, green manure (legumes or other plants plowed under), compost, and sludge from sewage disposal plants. In some countries it is a common practice to leach the solutes from manures with water and water plants with the solution. In addition to supplying mineral elements, organic fertilizers generally improve soil structure, making the soil easier to cultivate and increasing its capacity for holding air, water, and mineral salts. Some substances such as peat moss, vermiculite, and synthetic soil conditioners contain few or no mineral salts and are used primarily to improve soil structure.

ORGANIC GARDENING

Some amateur gardeners and farmers are enthusiasts for the cult of organic gardening (10, 18). The promotors of organic gardening claim that only "natural" organic fertilizers, such as compost and manure, should be used, that plants can reach their maximum development only when supplied with such organic fertilizers, that plants provided with them are highly resistant to insects and diseases, and that both the plants and the animals or people who eat them are harmed by commercial fertilizers. Such ideas are based on incorrect, incomplete, and distorted information about plants and soils. Although the practice of organic gardening may be quite sound, the ideas behind it are not (15). Mineral elements from organic fertilizers are just the same as those from commercial fertilizers and either type of fertilizer can provide good soil fertility. Organic fertilizers do improve soil structure more than commercial fertilizers and are not so likely to burn plants when they are used in excess because of their lower solute content, but they also have some disadvantages. At times they may not contain adequate quantities of all the essential elements and they frequently do contain weed seeds, destructive insects, parasitic bacteria and fungi, and other pests. The burning of plants by commercial fertilizers results from plasmolysis of root cells (page 223) rather than from a toxic effect, and may readily be avoided by using smaller quantities of the fertilizer. The beautiful crops produced by hydroponics should make it evident that not only organic fertilizers but even soil itself are quite unessential for the excellent growth and development of plants.

PLANTS IN THE MINERAL NUTRITION OF ANIMALS

Man and other animals require about the same essential mineral elements as do plants, and they secure most of their supply either directly or indirectly from plants. Therefore, good mineral nutrition of our crop plants is important for man and his domestic animals as well as for the plants themselves. At times, crops in soils slightly deficient in one or more elements may grow reasonably well even though they are less nutritious for the animals or humans that eat them than might be desired. This situation is likely to be the most widespread for elements like iodine, sodium, and chlorine that are essential for animals but unessential for plants, except perhaps in trace quantities.

On the other hand, plants may absorb mineral elements that are not particularly toxic to themselves but may be quite poisonous to the animals that eat the plants. The element *selenium*, present in many soils from Alberta to Arizona, is an outstanding example of this (16). Selenium accumulates in quantity in some plants, particularly the vetch. When animals graze on these plants they develop a serious poisoning known as alkali disease or blind staggers. Fortunately, most crop plants do not accumulate enough selenium to become toxic to animals or humans. Selenium is generally toxic to these crop plants, but it is not toxic to plants like vetch that accumulate it and may even be an essential element for them. The accumulation of various kinds of radioactive ions from fallout by plants, and the possible subsequent consumption of these radioactive substances by humans and other animals is a problem that is causing much concern and may well become more serious in the future.

Plants as Indicators of Mineral Deposits

Prospectors for deposits of valuable mineral ores are making increasing use of plants in their work in at least three principal ways. First, chemical analysis of plants growing in a certain region may reveal the location of underlying ore deposits by the presence of an unusually high concentration of the desired elements in the tissues of the plants. The sensitivity of this method of analysis is increased by the fact that plants may accumulate ions even though they are not essential. Second, there are certain indicator plants whose distribution is affected by ore deposits. For example, *Merceya latifolia* is an excellent indicator of copper deposits since it thrives only in soils with an unusually high copper content. This plant is commonly called "copper moss." Finally, high concentrations of certain elements may influence the pattern of growth and development of plants. Thus, plants growing over certain iron ore deposits have stunted shoots, thickened roots, and changes in cell structure. High cobalt concentrations may result in white necrotic spots on leaves, and molybdenum may cause stunting and a yellow-orange chlorosis. Russian prospectors have reported that plants growing in soil rich in boron are two or three times their usual

315

size and have a spherical shape and exceptionally large, dark green leaves.

Toxic Effects of Mineral Elements

The ions of a number of elements are quite toxic to plants, at least in excessive amounts. These elements include aluminum, arsenic, copper, boron, lead, magnesium, manganese, molybdenum, nickel, selenium, silver, and zinc. Although some of these are essential elements, concentrations only slightly higher than the required ones may be quite toxic. Several examples of toxicity have just been given in the previous paragraph. Perhaps the most striking example of mineral toxicity is the copper basin of southeastern Tennessee, where copper discharged into the air from copper smelters killed the vegetation over an area of many square miles (7), followed by severe erosion of the hilly terrain. True toxicity involves an adverse influence of the ions on metabolic processes. Neither the burning of plants by plasmolysis when too much fertilizer is applied, or the unavailability of one element when another is present in the soil in too high a concentration (Fig. 11.2) are generally considered as toxic effects.

Soil pH and Plant Growth

The degree of acidity or alkalinity of soils, as well as their mineral element content, may have marked effects on plant growth. Most plants grow best in soil with a pH (11, Appendix A) of 6 to 7, although some species such as camellias, azaleas, and cranberries thrive only in an acid soil with a pH of 4 to 5.5, and a few species are restricted to alkaline soils of about 7.5 to 8. Plants may be able to survive in soils with an unsuitable pH, but their growth is severely restricted.

If the pH is extremely high or low (over 8 or below 4) there may be direct damage to the plants, but in general the influence of an unfavorable pH is indirect through one of the following factors: (1) If the pH is too low, the physical condition of clay soils becomes poor because of the loss of crumb structure. The separated colloidal clay particles then pack tightly together, and they may also be washed into the subsoil where they precipitate into an impervious layer known as hardpan. (2) The availability of the essential mineral elements is affected by pH, generally because of its influence on the formation of insoluble compounds. Phosphorus becomes less available when the pH drops below 6.5. Calcium and magnesium are also less available in acid soils. Iron, manganese, copper, zinc, and boron become less available when the pH rises above

7. (3) Low pH is unfavorable to most of the bacteria of the nitrogen cycle, resulting in a decrease in available nitrogen. (4) Certain fungus diseases develop only in acid soils, whereas other diseases occur only when the pH rises above a certain minimum. (5) The pH also influences the solubility of toxic substances. At low pH ranges, soluble aluminum and iron compounds become concentrated enough to be toxic. (6) In an acid soil, H^+ ions displace other cations from the soil particles by cation exchange, and these cations may then be lost by leaching.

For agricultural and horticultural purposes the pH of a soil may be increased by the application of lime (calcium hydroxide or calcium carbonate), whereas the pH may be reduced by the use of ammonium sulfate, aluminum sulfate, or powdered sulfur.

The pH of the water that aquatic plants grow in is just as important as is the pH of the soil for land plants. Bacteria and fungi grow well only in limited pH ranges, and when they are cultured in laboratories it is important to adjust the pH to a suitable level.

► ## Questions

1. Explain why chemical analysis of a soil may give an inaccurate measure of its fertility.

2. Wood ashes are sometimes used as fertilizer. Is this a sound practice? Explain your answer.

3. Carbon dioxide produced by the respiration of roots diffuses into the soil. Does this have any relation to the mineral nutrition of plants? Explain.

4. Suppose you have some spiraea plants that show chlorosis. How could you determine the cause of the chlorosis in the shortest possible time?

5. Under what conditions would addition of nitrogen fertilizer to the soil fail to improve plant growth?

6. Installation of drain tiles in a poorly drained field sometimes increases the supply of nitrogen in the soil. Explain.

7. A gardener applied agricultural lime (calcium carbonate) to the soil in his garden and found that his plants grew much better. He ascribed the improved growth to reduction of soil acidity. Can you suggest several other possible reasons?

8. A soil was chemically tested and was found to contain adequate amounts of all the essential elements, yet plants growing in the soil exhibited mineral deficiency symptoms. Can you offer an explanation?

9. Why does the addition of aluminum sulfate, ammonium sulfate, or sulfur to a soil increase its acidity? Which of the three would you expect to change the pH the most slowly and why?

▶ *References*

For Reference

1. Aldrich, D. G. et al., *The Care and Feeding of Garden Plants.* Washington: American Society for Horticultural Science & National Fertilizer Association, 1954.
2. Ferry, James F. and Henry S. Ward, *Fundamentals of Plant Physiology.* New York: The Macmillan Co., 1959, Chapter 6.
3. Gericke, W. F., *The Complete Guide to Soilless Gardening.* Englewood Cliffs, N. J.: Prentice-Hall, 1940.
4. Gilbert, F., *Mineral Nutrition of Plants and Animals.* Norman: University of Oklahoma Press, 1948.
5. Hambidge, Gove, ed., *Hunger Signs in Crops.* Washington: National Fertilizer Association, 1941.

For Reading

6. Anderson, A. J. and E. J. Underwood, Trace element deserts. *Scientific American* 200(1):97–106, January 1959.
7. Burt, J. C., Desert in the Appalachians. *Nature Magazine* 49:486–488, 1956. (The Copper Basin)
8. Cannon, Grant, Nitrogen will feed us. *Atlantic Monthly* 192(3):50–53, September 1953. *Reader's Digest* 63(5):36–38, November 1953.
9. Kamen, Martin D., Discoveries in nitrogen fixation. *Scientific American* 188(3):38–58, March 1953.
10. Larson, J. David, The story of nature's soil. *Nature Magazine* 46:209–212, 1953. (Organic gardening)
11. MacInnes, D. A., pH. *Scientific American* 184(1):40–43, January 1951.
12. McElroy, W. D. and C. P. Swanson, Trace elements. *Scientific American* 188(1):22–25, January 1953.
13. Robertson, R. N., Electrolytes in plant tissue. *Endeavour* 16:193–198, 1957.
14. Scarlott, C. A., Phosphorus: a staff of life. *Science Digest* 33(4):66–69, 1953.
15. Throckmorton, R. I., Organic farming—bunk. *Reader's Digest* 61(4):45–48, October 1952.
16. Trelease, Sam F., Bad earth. *Scientific Monthly* 54:12–28, 1942. (About selenium)
17. Wallace, T., Mineral deficiencies in plants. *Endeavour* 5:58–64, 1946.
18. Wing, Andrew S., Soil pros and cons. *Nature Magazine* 42:135–137, 1949. (Organic gardening)

12. Plant Growth and Development

P<small>LANT AND ANIMAL GROWTH</small> is one of those common, every-day things usually taken for granted, but to biologists growth is one of the most complex, puzzling, and interesting aspects of living organisms. Plant growth involves all the plant activities already discussed as well as many others, and its end products are the highly organized cells, tissues and organs of the plant. Much is known about plant growth, but many problems remain to be clarified and solved by future research. No one really knows just how the single cell of a fertilized egg gives rise to certain numbers of cells of specific kinds, at just the appropriate time and place with only a rare mistake, resulting in the development of a particular kind of plant or animal. One specific problem is presented by development of sieve tubes, companion cells, and other cells of the phloem from cells cut off to one side by the cambium, whereas cells cut off to the other side of this same meristematic tissue always develop into vessel elements and other cells of the xylem. It is relatively easy to describe such differences in cell development, but their causes have been quite elusive. The better understanding of growth that biologists are gradually accumulating is of great practical, as well as theoretical, importance. For example, the solution of the cancer problem depends on better knowledge of growth, and research on both normal and abnormal plant growth, as well as animal growth, is contributing to an understanding of cancer (8).

The Nature of Growth

DEFINITION OF GROWTH

Growth is not easy to define. We usually think of growth as involving an increase in weight, but children may grow taller without gaining weight. The weight of a growing plant may fluctuate up and down as it gains and loses water during the course of a day. Plants may grow rapidly in the dark, but aside from the water in them, the weight of their component substances is constantly decreasing as they grow. Growth also usually involves an increase in size, but a frog embryo may have developed several hundred cells and yet be no larger than the fertilized egg from which it grew. As the turgidity of plant cells increases, plants get somewhat larger without really growing. Perhaps the best indication of growth is an increase in the quantity of protoplasm in an organism, but since this is difficult to measure it does not provide a very practical criterion of growth. Perhaps the best way to define **growth** is an increase in the amount of protoplasm in an organism, usually accompanied by an irreversable increase in size and weight and involving the division, enlargement, and (usually) the differentiation of cells.

GROWTH AND DEVELOPMENT

The differentiation of cells, tissues, and organs in a growing organism, resulting in its characteristic pattern of organization, is referred to as **development** or **morphogenesis**. Some biologists consider development as one aspect of growth; others regard the two as separate things and restrict the term *growth* to purely quantitative increases in size, weight, or amount of protoplasm.

MEASUREMENTS OF GROWTH. In studies of growth, quantitative data are usually desired, so measurements of increase in size, fresh weight, or dry weight are obtained, and in some experiments all three are used. While size and fresh weight of an organism can be measured at intervals, dry weight can be determined only once for any individual since it is killed in the process of drying. Development is generally not subject to quantitative measurements, at least of any simple type, and so is usually described, illustrated, or represented by a system of graphic symbols.

GROWTH RATES. After a seed germinates, the seedling plant grows rather slowly for a while and then enters a period of much more rapid growth that is maintained until the plant approaches maturity, when growth slows down or even ceases. If the height of such a plant is measured at intervals and plotted on a graph, the growth curve has something of an S shape (Fig. 12.1). Such S-shaped growth curves are characteristic of animals as well as plants. Population growth—whether of yeasts or humans—also has the same type of curve. The growth curve may, of course, be modified considerably if a plant is, for example, treated with a growth inhibitor or if growth is inhibited by the lack of some essential environmental factor such as a mineral element. Most plants grow less than an inch a day, but asparagus may grow as much as a foot per day and bamboo sometimes grows two feet in a day.

Plant growth is not steady but varies diurnally and seasonally. Seasonal growth variations are the most striking in trees, shrubs, and other perennials and in biennials. Many trees grow rapidly only during the spring and early summer, the growth of some species being limited to a few weeks during the spring. Sometimes the statement is made that plant growth continues as long as the plant lives, whereas animal growth

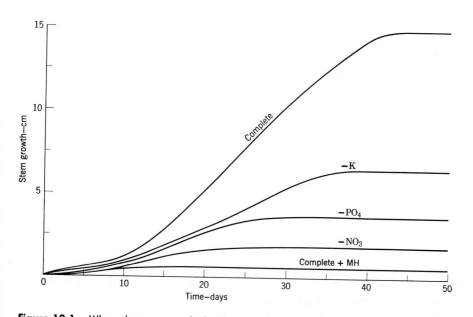

Figure 12.1. When plants are supplied with a complete mineral nutrient solution and otherwise good environmental conditions, the growth curve has the typical shape. Plants supplied with all the essential elements except nitrogen, phosphorus, or potassium showed greatly reduced growth. Plants treated with a growth inhibitor (maleic hydrazide) grew very little, even though they were supplied with all essential elements. (Data of Greulach.)

ceases long before the animal dies of old age. Although this is generally true, it should not be construed to mean that plant growth is continuous without interruptions.

Growth at the Cellular Level

All the structural changes we observe as a plant or animal grows depend on cell division, cell enlargement, and cell differentiation. The time, place, rate, plane, and pattern of these cellular activities determine the nature of the resulting tissues and organs of the organism.

CELL DIVISION

All cells arise from the division of other cells. The billions or trillions of cells in a large plant or animal are all derived from a unicellular fertilized egg if the organism is a product of sexual reproduction. Cell division also occurs in unicellular organisms, but there it serves as a means of reproduction (population growth) rather than as a part of the growth of the individual. In vascular plants cell division is mostly restricted to certain regions—the younger portions of roots and stems and the cambium—although cell division also occurs in such regions as young leaves, fruits, and seeds. Cell divisions contributing to the growth in length of stems are frequently said to be restricted to the meristematic tissue of the buds, but several investigations suggest that a considerable amount of cell division may occur in the parenchyma cells of the younger internodes. In grasses and some other plants, continued cell division may occur at the bases of the stem internodes and the leaves, one consequence being the necessity for periodic mowing of lawns.

The activities of nuclei during cell division (mitosis) have already been described (Chapter 4). Although the sequence of events during cell division has been observed and described in considerable detail, relatively little is known about the physiology of cell division. Some substances such as maleic hydrazide inhibit cell division, and consequently growth, and gibberellin and kinetin increase cell division in plants. A better understanding of how such substances affect cell division will probably eventually help clarify the nature of the physiological processes involved in cell division.

CELL ENLARGEMENT

Continued cell division without any cell enlargement would result in an increase in the number of cells but a progressive decrease in cell size and no increase in the size of the tissue or organism. In the meristematic tissues of plants, however, newly-formed cells generally enlarge to about the size of the parent cell before they in turn divide, and so the plant increases some in size. The greatest increase in size of a growing plant, however, is the result of the very extensive enlargement of the derivatives of the older meristematic cells into parenchyma type cells that are many times the volume of meristematic cells. In stems and roots cell enlargement is usually greater longitudinally than laterally.

The initial event in cell enlargement appears to be an increase in the area of the wall, a process that requires the presence of one of the group of plant hormones known as auxins as well as a supply of food that can be used in the synthesis of cellulose and other wall substances. As the wall increases in size, the turgor pressure decreases, resulting in a decreased diffusion pressure of water in the cell and thus inward diffusion of water. Much of this water enters the vacuoles, and the cell becomes more highly vacuolated as it increases in size. In a fully enlarged cell, most of the volume is occupied by the vacuole, the cytoplasm being restricted to a thin layer adjacent to the walls, although in some cells strands of cytoplasm extend through the vacuole. Despite the great vacuolation during enlargement, there is also an increase in the quantity of protoplasm.

CELL DIFFERENTIATION

Cell division and cell enlargement account for the increase in size of a plant as it grows, but a plant carrying on only these two phases of cellular growth would consist of nothing but meristematic and parenchyma tissues. In some types of plant tissue cultures, growth of this kind may occur over extended periods, but development of plants with all their characteristic cell types, tissues, and organs can not occur without cell differentiation. Cell differentiation involves various modifications of cells such as changes in shape, secondary thickening of the walls, incorporation of such substances as lignin and suberin in the walls, formation of chloroplasts or chromoplasts, death and decomposition of the protoplasm, loss of the end walls of vessel elements, and disintegration of the nuclei of the sieve tube elements.

Much is known about the sequence of microscopic structural changes during cell differentiation, but little is known yet about the factors causing cells to differentiate into certain types at specific times and places in a plant. The information we do have suggests that various chemical growth substances or organizers are concerned, but only a few of these have been identified and we know little about the factors influencing their production and distribution in specific regions of plant tissues. Both the hereditary potentialities of the plant and the local environment of the cell undoubtedly play roles. There is evidence that organizing substances may diffuse from differentiating cells into nearby undifferentiated cells, causing them to differentiate. The problem of cell differentiation is a part of the larger problem of development or morphogenesis and this will be considered later in the chapter.

The Interplay of Factors in Plant Growth

The growth pattern and the resulting structural organization of a plant depends both on its hereditary potentialities and its environment. There should be no argument as to whether heredity or environment is more important, for every process involved in the behavior, growth, and development of a plant or animal depends on both hereditary potentialities (genes) and an environment that permits expression of the potentialities. Heredity limits what an organism *can* do, and environment determines which of these things the organism *will* do. Some hereditary potentialities find expression in almost any environment suitable for survival, but others are expressed only in specific environments. The relation of heredity and environment to plant activities and the behavior, growth, and development of plants may be outlined as follows:

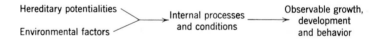

This outline emphasizes an important point: that heredity and environment exert their control over the pattern of behavior, growth, and development through their influence on the many and varied internal life processes and conditions of an organism such as photosynthesis, respiration, protein synthesis, chlorophyll synthesis, digestion, turgor pressure, and mitosis. Although it is relatively easy to observe, measure, and describe the growth and development of a plant with certain hereditary potentialities as it grows in a specific environment, securing even a rough understanding of the internal processes linking these is a difficult problem that generally requires years of research. For example, it has been known since about 1920 that some species of plants (long-day plants) will bloom only when the days are long and the nights are short whereas other species (short-day plants) will bloom only when days are short and nights are long. Plant physiologists still have only a very incomplete understanding, however of the related internal processes and conditions.

Internal Factors Related to Growth and Development

Most of the details of the internal processes and conditions related to growth and development are still quite obscure, but it is probable that essentially all of the physiological processes are concerned in some way or another. In general, these internal factors may be classified under at least three heads. (1) Water, providing adequate turgor pressure and hydration of the protoplasm and cell walls; (2) food, used in respiration and assimilation, along with all the metabolic processes involved in the synthesis, conversion, and use of food and the production of various essential substances from food, as well as the enzymes that activate these processes; and (3) a suitable balance and distribution of **plant growth substances** or **hormones.** Since we have already considered water and food in some detail (Chapters 9 and 10), the present discussion of internal factors is devoted to plant hormones.

Plant Growth Substances

That hormones play important roles in the metabolism and growth of humans and other animals is quite generally known, but many people are not aware of the fact that hormones (14) are also essential in the growth of plants. The term *plant growth substances* includes both the natural plant growth hormones and various synthetic compounds not produced by plants but having hormone-like effects on plant growth. Botanists themselves have become aware of the existence of plant growth substances only during the present century. The **auxins,** the first type of plant growth hormone to be discovered, were definitely established as hormones by the work of F. W. Went in 1928 (9), although somewhat earlier work by other investigators had provided important basic clues (Fig. 12.2). Since the 1920's, plant physiologists have devoted much of their time to the study of plant growth substances and have published thousands of research papers dealing with them, but our knowledge of this aspect of plant growth is still in its infancy.

THE NATURE OF PLANT HORMONES

Hormones are generally considered to be substances produced in small quantities in one part of an organism and transported to other parts of the organism where they exert marked effects on the metabolism and growth of the organism. Unlike animal hormones, plant hormones are not produced in the special ductless glands known as endocrine glands. Both plant and animal hormones act at a very low concentration. For

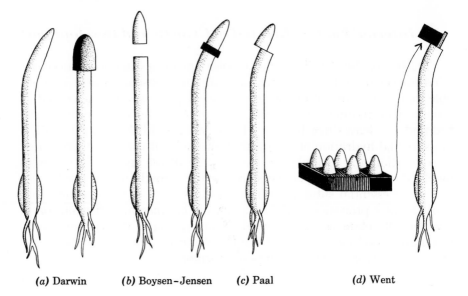

(a) Darwin   (b) Boysen–Jensen   (c) Paal   (d) Went

Figure 12.2. *Avena* (oat) coleoptiles illustrating steps in the development of the avena test and an understanding of the auxins. (a) Charles Darwin (1880) found that coleoptiles did not bend toward the light if the tip was covered with a small light-proof cap. (b) Boysen-Jensen (1910) found that a coleoptile failed to bend toward light if the tip was removed, but that bending occurred if tip was returned to coleoptile, even if a block of gelatin were placed between the two portions. (c) Paal (1918) found that coleoptiles would bend even in complete darkness if cut-off tip were placed to one side of cut coleoptile. (d) Went (1928) placed coleoptile tips on agar and later cut small blocks from the agar and placed them on one side of a cut coleoptile. The bending induced by the agar blocks confirmed the theory that a diffusible hormone produced by the tips caused bending and the experiment provided the basis for Went's avena test for auxin. Modern work on auxins and other plant hormones may be considered to date from Went's work. (Modified from K. V. Thimann, *Amer. Jour. Bot.* **44:**50, 1957.)

example, the optimal concentration of auxin for the growth of roots is commonly about 0.00000001 grams per liter (1000 grams) of water. Any substance effective at such low concentrations is likely to be acting in a catalytic manner, and it is probable that hormones, like vitamins, function principally as coenzymes or as components of coenzymes. Although vitamins and hormones probably play the same general roles they are commonly considered as separate categories as far as animals are concerned, since animals do not make most of their own vitamins and are largely dependent on vitamins present in the foodstuffs they eat. Since green plants synthesize both vitamins and hormones, the two groups of substances are not so readily separated when we are considering plants, and some of the vitamins have all of the properties of plant hormones. Unlike carbohydrates, fats, and proteins, neither vitamins nor hormones constitute a chemically-related group of compounds, both classes of substances being grouped together simply from the standpoint of their physiological effects.

SOME PLANT GROWTH HORMONES

In addition to the auxins, which will be discussed in some detail later, several dozen plant growth hormones have been identified or proposed and many more probably remain to be discovered. Among the established plant growth hormones are **thiamin** (vitamin B_1) and **pyridoxine** (vitamin B_6), both produced by leaves and essential for root growth. The roots of many legumes and some other plants also require **nicotinic acid** as a growth substance. Plant embryos fail to develop if they lack a variety of growth substances including **riboflavin** (vitamin B_2) and **pantothenic acid. Adenine, hypoxanthine,** and perhaps other growth substances are essential for leaf growth. Injured cells of bean fruits and probably other plant organs produce a wound hormone (**traumatin**) that diffuses to nearby cells, inducing cell division that gives rise to scar tissue and heals the wound.

These various growth substances all promote growth in some way or another, but plants also produce a variety of **growth inhibitors,** many of which are still not well understood. In addition, too high concentrations of growth-promoting hormones may inhibit growth. One special group of inhibitors are the **germination inhibitors** (11) present in some seeds, fruits, and other plant organs. Seeds containing germination inhibitors will not germinate even though all environmental factors are favorable. In nature, germination inhibitors are eventually either washed out of the seeds or are destroyed by some condition such as a period of cold weather. From a hormonal standpoint the growth of plants or specific plant tissues is controlled by a delicate balance of a variety of growth-promoting substances at suitable concentrations interacting with a variety of growth-inhibiting substances.

THE GIBBERELLINS

A fungus (*Gibberella fujikuroi*) parasitic on rice causes the infected plants to grow much taller than healthy plants. In 1926 a Japanese scientist discovered that extracts from the fungus promoted plant growth, and by 1938 other Japanese scientists had isolated and identified the growth promoting substance, **gibberellic acid.** However, it was not until 1955 that this growth substance became known in the western world. Since then the very marked promotion of plant growth by the **gibberellins** (gibberellic acid and other compounds with similar effects on plant

Figure 12.3. Dr. S. H. Wittwer of Michigan State University with cabbage plants treated with gibberellic acid. Control plants of the same age are at the left. Cabbage usually develops tall stems and flowers only during the second year of its growth, but gibberellic acid caused these plants to bloom the first year and to grow much taller than ordinary two-year-old plants. (Courtesy of S. H. Wittwer, Michigan State University.)

growth) has created much interest among botanists and horticulturists and hundreds of research papers on the gibberellins (12, 18) have been published. Since gibberellins have now been isolated from beans and other higher plants, it seems likely that the gibberellins are naturally occurring plant hormones.

Plants treated with gibberellins generally grow at least two or three times as tall as untreated plants, and sometimes the growth promotion is much more marked than this (Fig. 12.3). The effect is principally on stem growth, promotion of leaf growth being less marked. Gibberellins have little effect on root growth at concentrations usually used, but higher concentrations inhibit root growth. Some genetic dwarf varieties of corn, peas, and other species grow as high as the tall varieties when supplied with gibberellins. At least several species of plants grow well over a broader temperature range when treated with gibberellins than they do otherwise. One of the more striking effects of the gibberellins is the promotion of flowering, particularly in biennials and long-day plants. Biennials ordinarily do not produce tall stems and flowers until they have been exposed to a period of low temperature, but when treated with gibberellins they develop without the cold treatment. Species that bloom only under long days will bloom even if kept under short days when treated with gibberellins, but gibberellins will not cause short-day plants to bloom if they are kept under long days. Among its other effects, gibberellin overcomes some kinds of seed dormancy and eliminates the light requirement for germination of some seeds such as those of lettuce.

THE FLORIGEN PROBLEM

Many plant hormones have been isolated and identified chemically, but there is one elusive hypothetical plant hormone called **florigen** that botanists have studied extensively for years but have as yet been unable to isolate from plants. Although there may be no such substance as florigen, there is abundant evidence that some sort of stimulus travels from the leaves of plants to the very young buds and causes them to develop into flower buds rather than leaf buds. In some plants the stimulus is produced only when the leaves are exposed to daily light and dark periods of certain lengths. Evidence suggests that the stimulus is a substance rather than some type of energy, but it is possible that the substance may move from the buds to the leaves, although the reverse direction of movement is more likely. "Florigen" from a single leaf of a plant may be sufficient to cause the plant to bloom.

The flowering stimulus can pass from one plant to another through a graft union between the two plants. In one experiment a cocklebur plant caused to bloom by placing it under short days and long nights required by this species was then transferred to long days and short nights and grafted to another plant. This second plant bloomed, even though it had not been exposed to a suitable day and night length. The second plant, in turn, was grafted to a third and so on for seven successive grafts until all the plants bloomed as the result of the stimulus provided by the first plant in the series. Since it seemed rather unlikely that the small quantity of substance supplied by the first plant could last through so many transfers, a virus-like substance that could increase in quantity was suggested. It was impossible, however, to find any such substance in the plants. Despite the various types of evidence for florigen, it must remain hypothetical until it is extracted from plants, purified and identified chemically, and found to induce blooming in plants. Although the gibberellins induce blooming in long day plants and biennials, they can not be identical with florigen since they do not cause short day plants to bloom.

THE AUXINS

Of the various plant hormones known, none has been investigated more thoroughly or has been found to have more basic and diverse effects on plant growth than the first class discovered: the auxins. A number of auxins and a variety of synthetic growth substances with auxin activity are known, but the auxin studied the most and perhaps the most abundant in plants is indole-3-acetic acid, frequently referred to as IAA. The auxins are essential for cell elongation, probably functioning by transferring energy from respiration to the process of cell wall formation. Auxin is also essential for cell division, although it may participate only in the formation of the new cell walls and the relatively small amount of cell enlargement occurring between successive cell divisions. When present in too great quantity, auxins inhibit growth. The concentration suitable for promoting growth varies with the plant organ (Fig. 12.4), and is much lower for roots than for stems.

Auxins are produced the most abundantly by actively growing terminal buds and in other young tissues, as in embryo plants in seeds or in young leaves; but even older leaves produce some auxin. Auxins may diffuse from cell to cell and are also transported through the phloem, but in the phloem they move only from the stem tip toward the roots and never in the reverse direction.

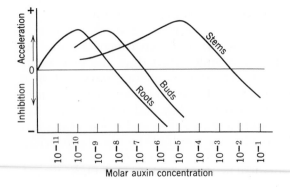

Figure 12.4. A graph showing optimum auxin concentration for growth of different plant organs. Note that a concentration that promotes stem growth may inhibit root growth. (From Leopold and Thimann, *Amer. Jour. Bot.*, **36**:342, 1949.)

Figure 12.5. Successive steps in the Avena coleoptile test. (a) Auxin-producing tip removed. (b) Three-hour interval for depletion of auxin. (c) Second decapitation. (d) Application of agar block containing auxin. (e) Curvature 90 minutes later, resulting from unequal growth. (Redrawn from *Principles of Plant Physiology* by Bonner & Galston through the courtesy of the publisher, W. H. Freeman & Co.)

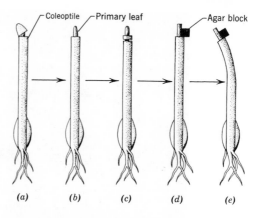

(a) (b) (c) (d) (e)

BIOLOGICAL TESTS FOR AUXINS.   Even the most sensitive chemical tests do not permit the accurate identification and measurement of the small quantities of auxins present in plants, but several much more sensitive biological tests have been devised.   The *Avena* (oat) coleoptile test is the most widely used and is considered as a basic standard.   The **coleoptile** is the cylindrical sheath covering the young leaves of grass seedlings. For the *Avena* test, oat seedlings are allowed to grow in the dark until the coleoptiles are about a centimeter long.   Then, under red light, the coleoptile tips are cut off, the rolled up leaves inside are pulled loose and raised a little above the cut coleoptile tip, and a small block of agar containing the auxin to be measured is placed on the resulting ledge (Fig. 12.5).   Plain agar is used for the controls.   A solution of auxin may be included in the agar before it has gelled, but in testing for auxins in plant tissues the tissue is placed on solidified agar and the auxins diffuse into the agar.   The more auxin contained in a standard sized agar block, the more the side of the coleoptile below the block will grow.   Since the opposite side of the coleoptile is growing little if at all, the coleoptile bends, and the concentration of auxin present can be calculated from the degree of bending of the coleoptile as compared with the bending produced by known auxin concentrations.   As little as a hundred-billionth of a gram of auxin can be measured by the *Avena* test.

Two other auxin tests are suitable for use with solutions containing auxins, but are not so well adapted to measurement of auxins from plant tissues (1).   In the *Avena* straight growth test, 5 mm. long pieces of oat coleoptile are placed in the solutions being tested, the amount of growth in length indicating the quantity of auxins present.   In the slit-pea test (Fig. 12.6), sections of pea stems from seedlings raised in the dark are slit about two-thirds of their length.   The degree of curling of the cut portions of the stems is related to the concentration of auxins present in the surrounding solution.

Figure 12.6. The slit-pea test for auxins and related growth substances. Pieces of pea seedling stems are slit longitudinally about three-fourths their length. When placed in water (lower left) the halves of the stems curve outward, but in auxin solutions they curve inward. The degree of inward curvature is proportional to the auxin concentration. (Courtesy of K. V. Thimann, Harvard University.)

SOME EFFECTS OF AUXINS. Although the fundamental effect of auxins appears to be related principally to cell wall formation and cell enlargement, the auxins have numerous and rather varied observable effects on plant growth. For example, auxin is involved in **apical dominance**, the inhibition of lateral bud growth by terminal buds. If a terminal bud is removed, apical dominance is lost and the lateral buds grow into branches, but if a paste containing an auxin is placed on the stem tip, lateral bud growth is inhibited just as it was by the terminal bud (Fig. 12.7). Normal branching of plants usually occurs only some distance below the terminal bud.

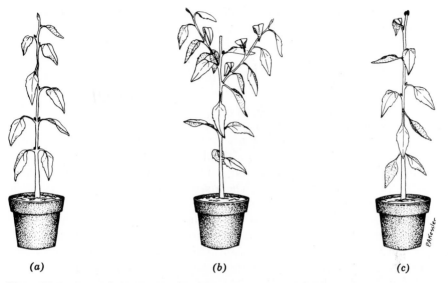

Figure 12.7. Removal of the terminal bud from the usual unbranched sunflower plant (*a*) resulted in loss of apical dominance and the growth of two lateral buds into branches (*b*). When lanolin paste containing auxin was placed on the cut stem end of another debudded plant, lateral bud growth was inhibited (*c*), as in an intact plant.

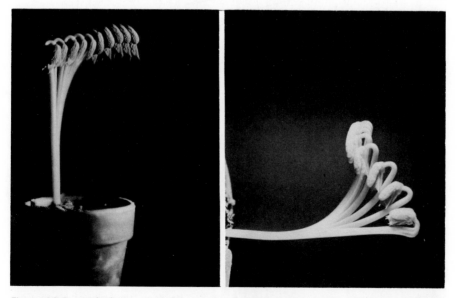

Figure 12.8. Multiple-exposure photographs of the phototropic (*left*) and geotropic (*right*) bending of bean seedlings, the exposures having been made at intervals of 40 and 50 min. respectively. (Reprinted from *College Botany, revised* by Harry J. Fuller and Oswald Tippo, by permission of Holt, Rinehart, & Winston, Inc.)

Auxins are also involved in leaf abscission (10, 13). The abscission of leaves of deciduous plants in the autumn, the abscission of the older leaves of evergreens, and the abscission of leaves during the growing season if they are diseased, extensively destroyed by insects, or subjected to prolonged drought are all results of a reduction in the quantity of auxins reaching the petiole base. This changes the ratio of auxin on the two sides of the petiole base and as a result the leaves abscise. If the blade of a coleus leaf is cut off, the petiole will abscise within a few days, but a dab of lanolin containing an auxin will prevent abscission if applied to the cut end of the petiole. Fruits may also abscise before maturity if they are producing too little auxin. Such premature fruit drop may be prevented by spraying the plants with solutions of auxins or auxin-like synthetic growth substances.

Growing stems exposed to brighter light on one side than another bend toward the brighter light, a response known as **phototropism** (Fig. 12.8). A common but erroneous and teleological explanation of phototropism is that the plants are trying to get more light for photosynthesis. Although this may be a result of the bending, the bending occurs because the light reduces the effective auxin concentration on the more brightly lighted side of the terminal bud and so less auxin reaches the elongating cells on this side of the stem. Since the shaded side of the stem has a higher auxin content it grows faster, the unequal growth resulting in bending as in the *Avena* coleoptile test. The more rapid growth of stems in the dark than in the light is also related to the effects of light on auxin concentration.

If a plant is placed in a horizontal position, its roots will bend and

Figure 12.9. Geotropic response of stems of young tomato plants during a 2-hr. and 15-min. period. The leaves were removed just before the first photograph was taken to make the response clearly evident. Note that the two stems, one back of the other, bent to the same degree during the period. (Courtesy of John G. Haesloop, University of North Carolina.)

Figure 12.10. Cuttings of European silver fir showing adventitious roots formed 6 months after treatment with two concentrations of auxin (*middle* and *right*). The untreated controls have developed callus but no roots. (Courtesy of K. V. Thimann, Harvard University.)

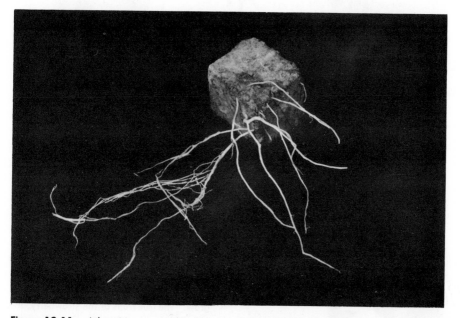

Figure 12.11. Adventitious roots developing on cube of tissue from a potato tuber treated with indoleacetic acid. (Courtesy of the Boyce Thompson Institute for Plant Research, Yonkers, N.Y.)

335

grow downward while its stem will bend until it is again growing vertically (Figs. 12.8, 12.9). This growth movement, known as **geotropism**, also involves unequal auxin distribution. Auxin is more concentrated on the lower sides of both stems and roots oriented horizontally. Whereas this higher auxin concentration promotes growth of the lower sides of the stems, it inhibits growth of the lower sides of the roots, resulting in the two opposite directions of bending. The role of auxins, if any, in other plant tropisms is not known.

The auxins also participate in the formation of adventitious roots, particularly on stem cuttings. The cuttings of some plants such as willow and coleus apparently contain adequate quantities of auxins and root readily when placed in water or moist sand. Cuttings of some species, however, form few or no adventitious roots unless supplied with a suitable concentration of an auxin (Fig. 12.10). Cuttings with leaves

Figure 12.12. Influence of pollination and auxin on development of the strawberry receptacle into the accessory fruit. The strawberry above left was normally pollinated. When pollination was prevented, the receptacle failed to grow into a fruit. The third strawberry developed from an unpollinated flower treated with auxin. At the left is an enlarged view of a strawberry that developed from a flower having only three of its many pistils pollinated, showing localization of the growth-promoting influence. Most of the receptacle failed to grow. The true fruits of the strawberry, the so-called "seeds", that developed from the ovularies of the pollinated pistils are readily visible. (Courtesy of J. P. Nitsch.)

Figure 12.13. Artificial parthenocarpy of holly plants sprayed with 2,4-D when the flowers were just beginning to open. The unpollinated control plant (*left*) failed to develop fruits. (Courtesy of the Boyce Thompson Institute for Plant Research.)

generally root better than those with leaves removed. Auxins can induce root initiation in tissue cultures that would otherwise not root at all (Fig. 12.11).

The development of the ovulary of a flower into a fruit is dependent on the presence of an adequate concentration of auxins. Ordinarily this auxin comes from the developing embryos within the seeds, and so fruits fail to develop on most plants unless the flowers are pollinated. However, if unpollinated flowers are sprayed with an auxin solution, seedless fruits will develop (Figs. 12.12, 12.13). This is known as **artificial parthenocarpy**. **Natural parthenocarpy** occurs in a few kinds of plants such as bananas, seedless grapes, and seedless citrus fruits, adequate supplies of auxin presumably being available from sources other than the usual one.

PRACTICAL APPLICATIONS OF PLANT GROWTH SUBSTANCES

Synthetic auxins and auxin-type plant growth substances have a number of horticultural uses (3, 4, 15), particularly in the rooting of cuttings and in artificial parthenocarpy. Auxins have been especially useful in greenhouse tomato production, and have also been used to prevent preharvest drop of apples and other fruits. Auxins sprayed on pineapple plants bring about blooming and fruit production out of season, although application of auxins to most plants delays rather than promotes blooming. The pineapple industry has profited greatly from the use of plant growth substances that either promote or delay blooming as fruits can now be harvested around the year rather than during a limited period. The packing plants are no longer plagued with a rush season followed by a period of inactivity.

The most widely used plant growth substance is the synthetic compound 2,4-D (2,4-dichlorophenoxyacetic acid). The related compound 2,4,5-T (2,4,5-trichlorophenoxyacetic acid) is also used extensively. These and certain other phenoxy compounds have many of the effects of auxins when used in extremely low concentrations, and since they are considerably less expensive than the auxins, they are used in many of the ways described previously. When used at higher concentrations of around 0.1%, these phenoxy compounds act as **selective herbicides** (3, 4, 15), killing broad-leaved plants but not grasses and certain related plants. Much research has been done on the subject, yet the reasons for this differential effect on the two groups of plants is still not clearly understood. The use of 2,4-D in controlling weeds in lawns, pastures,

Figure 12.14. Leaf modifications caused by treating cotton plants with 2,4-D, compared with a normal cotton leaf (*right*). (Courtesy of Wayne McIlrath and D. R. Ergle, A. & M. College of Texas.)

Figure 12.15. Normal *Kalanchoë* plant (*left*) and *Kalanchoë* treated on stem with lanolin containing parachlorophenoxyacetic acid. The terminal leaves have formed a cup-shaped structure, and the second pair have cup-shaped bases and entire margins. The ortho and meta forms of the chemical have no such effect. All three are similar to 2,4-D, but contain one Cl atom instead of two. Note the plantlets on the margins of the normal leaves (*left*) and at the top of the cup of the treated plant (*right*). (Courtesy of the Boyce Thompson Institute for Plant Research.)

and fields of various grains such as corn, wheat, oats, and rice has been of great practical value. Woody weeds such as poison ivy and Japanese honeysuckle are controlled more effectively by 2,4,5-T than by 2,4-D. Attempts have been made to find a selective herbicide that would kill grasses but not broad-leaved plants, and although several substances of this type have been discovered, they are not as effective as might be desired. Relatively low concentrations of 2,4-D that do not kill broad-leaved plants may, however, cause stem bending and leaf deformations (Fig. 12.14).

Several substances chemically similar to 2,4-D may modify the development of plants, sometimes quite strikingly (Fig. 12.15). Like auxin, 2,4-D and related compounds may induce callus formation (Fig. 12.16).

The gibberellins are now available commercially and may eventually be used in a variety of practical applications. A synthetic plant growth

Figure 12.16. A gall-like callus produced by treating the cut stem end of a *Cleome* plant with a chemical similar to 2,4-D. Photographed 20 days after treatment. Simila callus formation may be induced by auxins and by infection of plants by crown gall bacteria. (Courtesy of the Boyce Thompson Institute for Plant Research.)

substance, **maleic hydrazide**, that inhibits rather than promotes growth has a number of practical uses. Maleic hydrazide causes cessation of cell division in plants (but not in animals and some fungi) and as a result the plants stop growing although they remain alive. Maleic hydrazide is available commercially as MH-30 and MH-40 and has been used extensively to prevent the growth of suckers (branches) on tobacco plants that have been topped and so have lost apical dominance. Maleic hydrazide is also used to prevent sprouting of potatoes and onions in storage, to control the growth of hedges after pruning, and to reduce the labor of mowing plants along highways. Although maleic hydrazide inhibits the growth of lawn grass, it is not extensively used for this purpose since a slight overdose may cause the grass to turn brown. There are other synthetic growth inhibitors with similar practical applications, and auxins have also been used for inhibiting the growth of potatoes, nursery stock, and other plant materials in storage.

Despite the extensive practical applications of plant growth substances the chemical control of plant growth is still in its infancy, and we can expect many more plant growth substances to be discovered and put to use in agriculture and horticulture.

Dormancy

Earlier in this chapter it was noted that there are daily and seasonal variations in the rate of plant growth. Plants or plant parts, particularly seeds and buds, may cease growing and enter into periods of **dormancy**. The striking thing about a dormant bud or seed is that it will not resume growth, even though the environmental factors may be suitable for growth, until the dormancy is broken. The buds of trees and shrubs in temperate regions enter dormancy in the fall and remain dormant through at least the early part of the winter; potato tubers and onion bulbs are dormant for some time after harvesting. Among the species with seeds that are dormant for one to many years are clover, water lotus, cocklebur, pigweed, holly, orchid, vetch, and honey locust. The seeds of many plants such as beans, corn, peas, and radish never become dormant. A seed is not dormant simply because it is not germinating. A dormant seed is one that fails to germinate even though it is living when supplied with water, a suitable temperature, and all other environmental factors essential for germination.

The short days of autumn appear to be the principal environmental factor initiating bud dormancy, but the breaking of dormancy usually occurs only after a period of low temperature. For example, a dormant lilac bush kept over the winter in a warm greenhouse will not start growing, even at the usual time in the spring, but a branch of the plant projecting through a hole in the glass and so exposed to the low winter temperatures will begin to grow as soon as the weather becomes warm enough in the spring. Bud dormancy can also be broken by a variety of chemicals including thiourea and ethylene chlorhydrin, and there is some evidence that the gibberellins may do so, too. Dormant plants are much more resistant to freezing injury than active plants, damage by freezing being the most common in the spring after dormancy is broken. Dormancy keeps buds from opening in brief warm periods during the winter, and so probably has considerable survival value.

Seed dormancy (11) also has survival value, since seeds maturing during the summer or fall will not germinate before at least the following spring if dormant. Dormant weed seeds may remain in the soil for several years before they finally break dormancy and germinate. While the dormancy of some seeds results from the presence of germination inhibitors, in others it results from the fact that the seed coats are impermeable to either water or oxygen or are so hard and resistant that

341

germination can not occur. The latter types of dormancy are generally broken naturally either by the decay of the seed coats or their cracking by freezing and thawing, but can be overcome also by scarifying the seed coats, treating them with strong acid, or simply removing them. Dormancy resulting from germination inhibitors or similar physiological conditions is more comparable with bud dormancy, and is generally broken by periods of low temperature. It can also be broken by treatment with chemicals such as those used on buds.

Plant Morphogenesis

The development of the characteristic tissues and organs of an organism from a single undifferentiated cell or from a group of cells separated from the parent organism is one of the most complex, interesting, and puzzling aspects of life. Growth and development are, of course, the product of the cell division, cell enlargement, and cell differentiation going on in the developing organism. But what is it that determines how many cell divisions will occur in various parts of a leaf primordium and in what planes, or how much the cells will enlarge, thus producing a leaf of a certain characteristic size and shape? What causes the most cell divisions and the greatest cell enlargement in root and stem tips to occur in one direction, thus producing elongated organs, whereas in a developing spherical fruit the cell divisions occur almost equally in all planes? Why do certain cells differentiate into components of xylem and phloem, in a pattern characteristic of the species, whereas nearby cells remain essentially undifferentiated? What causes the first true leaves of a bean plant to be opposite and simple while the subsequently developed leaves are alternate and compound? Why does the spore of a fern develop into a small heart-shaped prothallus and the other unicellular stage in the life cycle, the fertilized egg, develop into a large plant with roots, stems, and leaves (16)? These are just a few examples of the problems that face a student of plant morphogenesis (the origin of form or structure).

The sequence of structural changes, both external and internal, have been observed and described in detail for many specific examples of development. It is obvious that heredity plays an important controlling role in development, since the development of an individual follows the pattern characteristic of the species. Many specific instances of the influence of environment on development have been identified, and it is possible to alter many aspects of development predictably by suitable experimental control of the environment (Chapter 13). Development may also be altered and controlled by the application of various plant growth substances. Yet, with all this information about development,

Figure 12.17. Sterile organ cultures. *Left:* a pollinated tomato flower. *Middle:* a tomato ovulary at the beginning of an experiment. *Right:* after 6 weeks of culture a small tomato fruit has developed from an ovulary. (Courtesy of James Bonner, California Institute of Technology.)

biologists have been able to make only slight progress toward understanding the series of internal processes and conditions linking hereditary potentialities and environmental influences with observable development. It is this aspect of morphogenesis that provides one of the greatest challenges to biologists during the coming years.

The older investigations of development were largely descriptive, and continuing research of this type is still needed, but most of the current work is experimental and it appears that only this type of approach can contribute toward an increased understanding of morphogenesis. The experimental techniques are varied, including manipulation of the environment, use of growth substances and the identification of natural growth substances and organizers, elucidation of metabolic pathways, and appropriate surgical manipulation of the developing tissues. The isolation of cells, tissues, or organs from an individual and their cultivation in sterile cultures (17, Figs. 12.11, 12.17, 14.10) has provided considerable information about development and will undoubtedly provide much more in the future. Tissue cultures provide a somewhat simpler system that is more subject to experimental control than the intact organism. The extensive use of lower plants and animals such as certain algae, hydra, and slime-molds (7, Fig. 6.1, Fig. 6.2) in the study of development is another approach toward securing as simple a system as possible for elucidation of some of the basic problems. Even the vascular plants provide a less complex situation than the higher animals, and we can expect that many of the basic advances in an understanding of morphogenesis will come from work with plants. One experimental advantage of plants over animals is that plants have continuing development from the stem and root tips and in many cases from the cambium, whereas animal development occurs mostly in the embryonic stages. It is for this reason that the study of animal development has been much more closely identified with the science of embryology than has the study of plant development.

Among the aspects of plant morphogenesis are correlations, polarity, symmetry, differentiation, regeneration, and abnormal development (5). We shall be able to consider each of these only briefly.

CORRELATIONS

The influence of one part of an organism on the growth and development of other parts is referred to as **correlation**. Although correlations are basically under hereditary control, in plants they operate through at least two main sets of internal factors: food and hormones. We have already considered several examples of hormonal correlations brought about by auxins: apical dominance, the development of ovularies into fruits following fertilization, and the influence of auxins on root growth.

As an example of a relatively simple type of nutritional correlation, we may take the ratio between the number of leaves and fruits on an apple tree as it influences fruit size. If a tree bears many fruits, the available food is distributed among them and a limited amount reaches each one, but if the same quantity of food is available to a smaller number of fruits each one will grow larger. There are also correlations between fruit development and vegetative growth. For example, tomato plants bearing numerous fruits have reduced vegetative growth, but removal of the fruits results in increased growth.

The ratio between the sizes of the shoots and roots of a plant (the shoot/root ratio) is a correlation controlled by a variety of factors, some of them nutritional. If a plant is supplied with a large quantity of nitrogen in proportion to the carbohydrate produced by the shoot (a low carbohydrate/nitrogen or C/N ratio), a high shoot/root ratio results because the large supply of nitrogen available to the shoots permits the synthesis of much protein and nucleic acid. Consequently, extensive shoot growth occurs. This consumes most of the available carbohydrate and little is translocated to the roots, so root growth is limited by lack of carbohydrate. On the other hand, a high C/N ratio results in a low shoot/root ratio, since the roots use most of the limited supply of nitrogen, leaving relatively little to be translocated to the shoots. However, there is a surplus of unused carbohydrate that is translocated from the shoots to the roots.

Many of the correlations occurring during the growth and development of a plant are more subtle and less well understood than the examples given, but they play essential roles in keeping the pace of growth and development of one part in step with others and so in the production of a characteristic structural pattern.

POLARITY

Most organisms, both plants and animals, have a longitudinal axis that is **polarized,** that is, one end differs from the other. Thus, a fish has a head end and a tail end whereas one end of the axis in vascular plants develops into the roots and the other becomes the shoot. Some filamentous algae have an axial structure without obvious polarity, since one end looks just like the other, but others develop a specialized holdfast cell at the lower end (Fig. 16.2) and so have a polar structure. The spherical *Volvox* colony (Fig. 2.4) is neither axial nor polar and some other lower organisms including coccus bacteria and some unicellular algae lack an obvious axial or polar organization. However, even unicellular organisms may be axial and polar as regards their shape, the location of their cell structures, and the attachment of their flagella (Fig. 2.2, 2.11*d*).

345

Indeed, it appears probable that all cells and organisms have physiological polarity even though they may have no obvious structural polarity. This physiological polarity involves gradients in such factors as electrical potential, pH, rate of respiration, hormone concentration, and osmotic pressure. The translocation of auxins is polar, occurring only in a morphologically downward direction even if a stem is inverted so that the flow is upward in relation to the earth. The translocation of Ca^{++} ions is also polar, occurring only in a morphologically upward direction. There is an electrical potential difference (a difference in voltage) between the two ends of a cell and also between two points along the axis of a plant. Although the possible role of such electrical potential differences in development is little understood, they may play an important part.

That stems have physiological polarity can easily be demonstrated by the fact that stem cuttings develop roots only at the morphologically lower end, whereas the buds at the upper end grow into branches. This occurs even if the pieces of stem are inverted. Transverse polarity is evident in the fleshy roots of the yam. If discs are cut across the root and then sliced in half, roots always develop from the circumference of the half-disc and shoots originate from the cut diameter.

Much work has been done on the development of polarity in the fertilized egg of the brown alga *Fucus* (Fig. 2.7). Soon after fertilization the originally nonpolar egg falls to the bottom of the ocean and within a day it develops a protuberance on its lower side, followed by a cell division at right angles to the protuberance. The lower cell forms the rhizoid that anchors the plant, and the upper rounded cell develops into the main part of the plant. Experiments have shown that the lower light intensity on the under side (rather than gravity as might have been expected) is responsible for the polarization of the egg and the appearance of the protuberance on only the lower side. In the dark, the protuberance may appear on any side. It has also been found that the protuberance will grow toward the positive pole in an electric current, toward a warmer environment, toward a lower pH, toward the centrifugal pole when centrifuged, toward the side to which auxin has been applied, and, in a group of eggs, toward the center of the group. These results suggest some of the internal processes involved in the natural induction of polarity by light and also indicate the types of data needed for a better understanding of other and more complex examples of polarity.

SYMMETRY

One of the striking features of development in most organisms is that it results in a symmetrically organized individual. The symmetry may be radial, as in most stems and roots, in many fruits, in flowers such as those of apple or strawberry, in sunflower flower heads, in the umbrella-shaped sporophores of mushrooms, or in *Volvox*. If a radially symmetrical structure is cut along any radius (i.e., diameter) the resulting halves will be essentially the same. The symmetry generally extends to internal as well as external structures. In a **bilaterally symmetrical** structure, the two sides and also the front and back are similar. Thus, essentially equal halves can be obtained by cutting the structure through the center along either of two, and only two, diameters. The flattened stems of some cacti and the leaves of iris are good examples of this rather rare type of symmetry. **Dorsiventral symmetry** is sometimes considered as bilateral, but differs from true bilateral symmetry in that the front and back sides are different, so that the structure can be cut along only one plane to get similar halves. Most leaves have dorsiventral symmetry, although the leaves of some plants such as elm and beech are unsymmetrical. Many flowers such as those of sweet pea and snapdragon have dorsiventral symmetry. Horizontal stems are sometimes dorsiventral rather than radial, and the branches of several conifers in turn branch only in a horizontal plane, producing a flattened dorsiventral spray.

Symmetry is found, not only in individual organs of plants, but also frequently in the shoot and root systems as a whole. Trees growing in the open where they are subjected to reasonably uniform environmental conditions on all sides show a general radial symmetry, although factors such as shading on one side may prevent this symmetrical development. Nonuniform environments may also modify the natural symmetry of individual organs.

Leaves may appear to be attached to stems in a random pattern, but closer observation reveals that they are symmetrically arranged in a definite pattern characteristic of the species. Some species have opposite leaves, the leaves of one node generally being at a 90° angle from those at the next node. More species have alternate leaves arranged on the stem in a spiral pattern, the steepness of the spiral being a characteristic of the species. In the simplest type of alternate arrangement, the successive leaves are 180° apart around the stem and so every second leaf is directly above another leaf. In going from a leaf to the one directly above it through the intervening leaf one spiral is made around the stem. This situation may be represented by the fraction $\frac{1}{2}$, the numerator representing the number of turns around the stem and the denominator the number of leaves from the starting point. We can describe the **phyllotaxy**, or pattern of leaf arrangement, of such a plant merely with the fraction $\frac{1}{2}$. Another common kind of phyllotaxy is $\frac{1}{3}$, the third leaf being directly above the first one and one spiral turn around the stem being required to reach it. Only a limited number of phyllotaxies are found, the series being $\frac{1}{2}, \frac{1}{3}, \frac{2}{5}, \frac{3}{8}, \frac{5}{13}, \frac{8}{21}, \frac{13}{34}, \frac{21}{55}, \frac{34}{89}$, and so on, although the

347

phyllotaxies from $\frac{8}{21}$ on are found only in cones and other compact structures with modified leaves. It is interesting that any phyllotaxy in the series represents the sum of the numerators over the sum of the denominators of the previous two phyllotaxies.

DIFFERENTIATION

The differentiation of the cells, tissues, and organs of a developing organism constitutes the core of most morphogenetic problems. We have already considered cell differentiation briefly, and the differentiation of tissues and organs involves the differentiation of certain kinds of cells at specific places and times. However, the differentiation of organs cannot be accounted for entirely by cell differentiation. The location and shape of an organ are determined primarily by the pattern of cell division. Thus, cell divisions at precisely spaced points on the stem apex result in outgrowths that are the leaf primordia. Further cell divisions, largely in one plane, result in the formation of a young leaf in its characteristically flat form. Whether the leaf will be entire or lobed, simple or compound, as is characteristic of the species, also depends on the pattern of cell division. The size of the leaf depends largely on how long cell division continues before it stops, and so depends on the number of cells present rather than on their size. This is also generally true of other organs, although the size to which cells enlarge also influences organ size to some degree. Thus, the pattern of cell division determines the phyllotaxy, size, and shape of leaves, whereas the differentiation of certain types of cells at specific places determines the character of its tissues. Protuberances also grow from the stem apex in the axils of the leaf primordia (Fig. 5.1), and through their own characteristic pattern of cell division and differentiation they develop into the axillary buds. In contrast with the stem apex, the root apex is smooth and lacks outgrowths and so does not produce leaves and buds. This basic difference in development is just one of the many morphogenetic problems without a satisfactory solution.

The difference between woody and herbaceous stems is basically a matter of how long cell divisions in the cambium continue. Although some herbaceous annuals have no cambium at all, others have a cambium but it remains active only one year, whereas woody stems have a cambium that remains active year after year. Of course, some plants considered as herbaceous annuals in temperate climates are woody perennials in tropical climates.

The pattern of differentiation may depend on the age of the plant. Thus, the first leaves (the juvenile leaves) of a plant may be quite different in size and shape from the ones developed later. What appears to be an extreme example of this occurs in the English ivy, which may grow for long periods of time as a vine with relatively large lobed leaves and no flowers. When flowering branches finally appear they have smaller, entire leaves and the branches grow out in a rather rigid, shrubby pattern. Cuttings taken from such branches produce bushy plants with entire leaves, although seeds from these plants grow into plants with lobed juvenile leaves. The discovery that gibberellic acid causes flowering branches to produce lobed juvenile leaves provides a clue to some of the internal factors controlling leaf form. Some plants such as the morning glory have a series of leaves at successive nodes with shapes gradually progressing from the juvenile to the adult form.

The age of a plant may influence flower, as well as leaf, development. Thus, in the acorn squash the first flowers are all underdeveloped staminate flowers. Normal staminate flowers develop at the next several nodes, then for some time a mixture of staminate and pistillate flowers appears, followed by a mixture of inhibited staminate flowers and giant pistillate flowers. Finally, only pistillate flowers that produce fruits parthenocarpically are formed. The sequence of development seems fixed, but the length of each stage is influenced by day length and temperature.

The conversion of bud primordia from a vegetative to a reproductive condition is an interesting example of differentiation. As has been pointed out earlier, the controlling factor appears to be a flowering hormone translocated from the leaves, and this is produced by some plants only during certain lengths of day and night. The transformation from a vegetative to a flower bud involves several basic changes in development. (1) The leaves are modified into flower parts (sepals, petals, stamens, and carpels in that order); (2) lateral bud formation is suppressed; (3) the internodes do not elongate; and (4) continued growth of the stem apex ceases. The result is a bud that develops into a flower rather than a leafy branch. One of the striking things about the development of a flower is the switch from the formation of sepals to petals and then to stamens and carpels as development progresses along the minute distance from one modified leaf to the next.

Essentially nothing is known about the complex of internal factors providing such precise and specific control of differentiation, even though it is known that environmental factors such as length of day may determine whether an imperfect flower will be staminate or pistillate. In some flowers, especially those with numerous parts, there may be an intergrading series between petals and stamens (Fig. 5.38), suggesting a gradual change in developmental factors. In some plants, age, as well as environmental factors, influence flower differentiation. Trees that do not bloom until they are several years old are extreme examples.

REGENERATION

The restoration of lost parts by an organism is known as **regeneration.** Plants and certain invertebrate animals such as hydra, planaria, and starfish can regenerate entire organs but regeneration in higher animals is limited to the healing of wounds. The role of the hormone *traumatin* in healing wounds in plants has been mentioned earlier. The restoration of bark that has been scraped from a tree trunk is another example of regeneration in plants. If a portion of a herbaceous stem is cut out so as to interrupt one or more vascular bundles, the bundles may be regenerated by the differentiation of a series of pith cells into what are essentially short, vascular elements. If a stem tip is cut vertically into several segments, each segment will regenerate the missing portions, thus forming several stems in place of the original one.

There are many examples of more extensive regeneration in plants. If a terminal bud is removed, not only do lateral buds begin growing because of the loss of apical dominance, but the uppermost bud often begins growing vertically, assumes dominance, and thus essentially replaces the missing terminal bud. A piece of a stem cut from many kinds of plants will develop adventitious roots at its lower end, thus regenerating an entire plant. It has been found that even a small piece of a stem tip, as short as 0.25 mm., from some plants will grow on a suitable nutrient medium and the resulting stem may form adventitious roots, thus regenerating an entire plant. Pieces cut from the roots or leaves of some species develop adventitious roots and buds, regenerating an entire plant, although the leaves of many species can produce neither roots or buds, or perhaps only roots, and so fall short of complete regeneration. Stems bearing lemon fruits can regenerate roots (Fig. 12.18) but not buds. Cuttings that can regenerate all missing organs are widely used in the vegetative propagation of plants, and all means of vegetative propagation depend on the capacity for regeneration. Regeneration in relation to plant propagation is discussed in Chapter 15.

The fact that applied auxins promote the formation of roots on cuttings of many species that do not otherwise root readily (Fig. 12.10) provides some information about the internal factors involved. Presumably species that root readily contain an adequate supply of auxin. Cuttings from some species, however, will not initiate adventitious roots even when auxin is supplied so there are evidently other factors to be considered.

One of the most striking examples of regeneration is the development of carrot plants from isolated phloem cells detached from carrot root segments growing in sterile culture media. The first cell divisions appear to be random and form an apparently unorganized mass, but after a time xylem begins differentiating inside the cell mass and organ-

Figure 12.18. Development of adventitious roots on lemon cutting with fruit. Treatment with auxins is not necessary to induce rooting, though they increase roots. (Courtesy of L. C. Erickson, University of California.)

ization continues until an embryo plant similar to those developed in seeds appears. If these embryos are transferred to a nutrient medium solidified by the inclusion of agar they develop shoots as well as roots. These young plants can later be transplanted to soil, where they may develop to maturity and produce flowers and seed. However, F. C. Steward of Cornell University, who has conducted these experiments, has been able to secure such complete regeneration only when the usual culture media containing foods, essential minerals, vitamins, and auxin are supplemented by the addition of amino acids and coconut milk (the liquid endosperm of the coconut seed) or liquid endosperm from young corn or buckeye seeds. These young, milky endosperms contain a number of growth substances essential for differentiation and growth of embryo plants, although apparently not for mature plants. When endosperm is not added to the culture medium, the isolated cells may continue to live and grow but they fail to differentiate into organized embryos. Much effort has been devoted to fractionating and analyzing coconut milk, and a number of the growth substances it contains have already been isolated and identified. Experiments such as these not

351

only provide information about growth substances essential for development but they also make it clear that even cells isolated from mature tissues retain the capacity for developing into complete plants provided that all essential growth substances are available.

ABNORMAL DEVELOPMENT

Development usually proceeds in a highly organized manner, resulting in an individual with a structural pattern characteristic of the species. However, the normal course of development is sometimes disrupted, resulting in an abnormal individual. The amazing thing is not that such deviations from normal development occur occasionally, but that they do not occur more frequently. Since there is a considerable range of hereditary variation in most species, and since environment can modify development markedly, it is a little difficult to determine just where the line can be drawn between normal and abnormal development. For example, an etiolated plant that has been growing in the dark differs considerably in structure from a plant of the same species growing in the light, but we would not consider it abnormal. Indeed, its development has been normal for that particular environment. Genetic mutations sometimes result in the development of structures that can be described as abnormal, but they could also be regarded as normal features of a new hereditary strain.

One class of abnormalities is the product of known environmental factors. Thus radiation may cause extremely distorted development (Fig. 13.7), insects, fungi, or other organisms may cause the development of galls (Figs. 14.7–11), or applications of growth substances may cause callus formation (Fig. 12.16) or may greatly modify leaf form (Fig. 12.14) or stem form (Fig. 12.15). Other abnormalities may appear to occur spontaneously, although they are undoubtedly the result of changes in internal processes or conditions brought about by an unusual combination of environmental factors or localized hereditary changes. For example, sepals may occasionally develop into what are essentially foliage leaves, the stem bearing a flower may not stop growing as it normally does, resulting in a flower located around a stem rather than at the end of it, or tendrils may develop into leaf-like structures. Stems and other radially symmetrical structures occasionally become fused and flattened into broad ribbons, an abnormal type of development known as **fasciation**. A better knowledge of the causes of such types of abnormal development can also contribute to an understanding of normal development. Much has already been learned by studies of the growth of calluses in tissue culture, and these unorganized and unsymmetrical masses of tissue can certainly be considered as examples of abnormal growth.

352

► *Questions*

1. Give several possible explanations for the fact that cuttings of some species can be rooted much easier than those of other species.

2. A plant physiologist found that excised tomato roots in tissue culture grew no better when vitamin B_6 (pyridoxine) was added to the culture medium than when it was omitted. Give as many possible explanations as you can.

3. Could the amount of natural auxins moving from a terminal bud downward to the lateral buds be increased experimentally? If so, suggest possible procedures.

5. Name several species of house and garden plants that could be expected to respond to gibberellin treatments by modified development that would be found desirable by the gardener. Name several other species that would probably develop in undesirable ways after gibberellin treatments. Give reasons for all your selections.

5. Can you think of any stems that are not geotropic? If so, can you suggest possible reasons for the lack of the usual geotropic response?

6. Would you expect to find a larger percentage of native plant species with seed dormancy in the lowlands of Panama or in Canada, or would the proportion be about the same both places? Explain your answer. Would you expect any difference in the mechanisms of breaking dormancy in the two regions?

► *References*

For Reference

1. Audus, L. J., *Plant Growth Substances*. Revised Edition. New York: Interscience Publishers, 1959.

2. Galston, A. W., *The Life of The Green Plant*. Englewood Cliffs, N.J.; Prentice-Hall, 1961.

3. Mitchell, J. W. and P. Marth, *Growth Regulators in Field, Garden and Orchard*. Chicago: University of Chicago Press, 1947.

4. Tukey, H. B., ed., *Plant· Regulators in Agriculture*. New York: John Wiley and Sons, 1954.

5. Sinnott, E. W., *Plant Morphogenesis*. New York: McGraw-Hill, 1960.

For Reading

6. Bonner, J. T., The growth of mushrooms. *Scientific American* 194(5):97–106, May 1956.

7. Bonner, J. T., Differentiation in the social amoeba. *Scientific American* 201(6): 152–162, December 1959.

8. Braun, A. C., Plant cancer. *Scientific American* 186(6):66–72, June 1952.

9. Gabriel, M. L. and Seymour Fogel, eds., Great Experiments in Biology. Englewood Cliffs, N. J.: Prentice-Hall, 1955, pp. 141–152. (Auxins)

10. Jacobs, W. P., What makes leaves fall. *Scientific American* 193(5):82–89, November 1955.

11. Koller, Dov, Germination. *Scientific American* 200(4):75–84, April 1959.

12. Lang, Anton, Chemistry of growth in plants. *Natural History* 68:142–151, 1959. (Gibberellins and other growth substances)

13. Muir, R. M. and R. E. Yager, Abscission. *Natural History* 67:498–501, 1958.

14. Salisbury, Frank B., Plant growth substances. *Scientific American* 196(4):125–132, April 1957.

15. Weiss, F. J., Chemical agriculture. *Scientific American* 187(2):15–19, August 1952.

16. Wetmore, Ralph H., Morphogenesis in plants—a new approach. *American Scientist* 47:326–340, 1959.

17. White, Philip R., Plant tissue cultures. *Scientific American* 182(3):48–51, March 1950.

18. Wittwer, S. H. and M. J. Bukovac, The effects of gibberellin on economic crops. *Economic Botany* 12:213–255, 1958.

13. The Physical Environment

T HE HEREDITARY POTENTIALITIES of a plant determine what the plant *can* do, but the environment of the plant determines what the plant actually *does* and to what degree (Chapter 12). The environment of any organism may be separated into two principal sets of factors: the **biological environment**, consisting of all the varied plants and animals that in any way affect the organism, and the **physical environment**, composed of the diverse forms of matter and types of energy surrounding the organism (8). The influence of any natural environment on the behavior and growth of a plant is an intricate complex of many factors acting concurrently, but botanists have been able to isolate and identify the specific effects of many environmental factors by conducting suitable controlled experiments (19).

The influences of environment on plant growth are of great interest and importance in agriculture and horticulture (20), and farmers and gardeners spend much of their time providing their crop plants with an environment as conducive to good growth as knowledge, experience, and practical feasibility permit. Until relatively recently, most of the information on environmental effects on crop plants was rule of thumb, resulting from trial and error, but more and more cultural practices are now being based on sound experimental information about the effects of specific environmental factors on plant growth and development, with resulting increases in yields. However, our knowledge of the influences of environment on plant growth is still quite incomplete, and botanists have devoted much time and effort toward extending this knowledge by devising better and more precise means of controlling the environment of plants experimentally. Many botanical laboratories now have experimental plant growth chambers providing precise control of temperature and light, and there are a few complex installations such as the phytotron at the California Institute of Technology where greenhouse environments can be precisely controlled (5).

The Factors of the Physical Environment

The factors of the physical environment of plants may be classified in various ways. Basically, they may be divided into forms of matter and manifestations of energy. The principal substances important in the environment of a plant are water, salts, acids, bases, organic remains of dead organisms, and several gases, particularly oxygen and carbon dioxide. The most important types of energy are heat, light and other radiation, gravity, the various manifestations of kinetic energy, electricity, and possibly magnetism. The physical factors are often classified as **edaphic** or soil factors and **climatic** factors (2), although this system is not particularly adapted to plants that do not grow in the soil, such as epiphytes, parasites, or aquatic plants. The soil factors include the structure and texture of the soil, mineral salts, acidity, water, and soil aeration. The climatic factors include temperature, light, atmospheric humidity, gaseous composition of the atmosphere (18), air movements, air pressure, and precipitation. Such factors as topography may be important in the environment of a plant, but exert their influence through effects on either the edaphic or local climatic conditions.

The physical environment affects plant growth in at least three ways: it influences both the rate of growth and the pattern of development and also determines where plants with certain hereditary potentialities can survive and grow, thus affecting the geographical distribution of plants. We have already considered some of the effects of water, mineral salts, acidity, soil structure and aeration, and gravity on plant growth. Unfortunately, the scope of this book does not permit additional consideration of these factors or discussion of all the other factors of the physical environment. In the available space we shall consider only two of the more important factors of the physical environment: temperature and radiation.

Influences of Light on Plant Growth

We are using the term *light* to include the visible portion (wavelengths from about 390 to 760 millimicrons) of the electromagnetic radiation spectrum (Fig. 13.5). The influence of radiation of shorter and longer wavelengths on plants will be considered later. We have already mentioned the roles of light in photosynthesis, chlorophyll synthesis, phototropism, and stomatal opening. All of these light-related processes as well as others, such as the influence of light on protoplasmic viscosity, play roles in growth (16, 17). In addition, some of the light absorbed by plants is converted into heat, and the resulting temperature rise influences almost every process going on in the plants. Light affects some processes of certain fungi, including pigment formation, spore discharge, and phototropism, but unlike photosynthetic plants most fungi flourish and reproduce even when kept in total darkness throughout their lives.

PHOTORECEPTOR PIGMENTS

Before light energy can be used in any biological process it must be absorbed by some substance within the organism. Such substances are known as **photoreceptors** (16). All photoreceptors of visible light are colored because of the unequal absorption of the various wavelengths making up white light and so are frequently referred to as **pigments.** Some photoreceptor pigments like the chlorophylls and carotenoids are so abundant that they impart a color to the tissues containing them, but other pigments are so dilute that we can not detect their influence on the color of the tissue. Each pigment has a characteristic **absorption spectrum** in which the peaks of maximum absorption of light energy generally correspond closely with peaks of maximum efficiency of the light-requiring process under various wavelengths of light (the **action spectrum**) (Fig. 10.8). An action spectrum for a process is determined by exposing a series of plants to light of different colors (i.e., different narrow wavelength bands) by the use of either colored filters or a projected spectrum and then measuring the rate of the process under each wavelength band. The relationship of a photoreceptor pigment to a certain photochemical process cannot be considered as definitely established until the absorption spectrum of the pigment is known to correspond with the action spectrum of the process. Among the more important photoreceptor pigments of plants are chlorophyll, protochlorophyll, the carotenoids, flavin compounds such as riboflavin, and phytochrome.

Besides its wavelength composition (**quality**), light has two other

357

aspects that are biologically important: its **intensity** (measured in **foot candles** or other units) and its **duration**.

RED, FAR-RED REACTIONS

We shall devote the remainder of our discussion of light and plant growth to a consideration of three of the plant responses having the peaks of their action spectra in the red region of the spectrum: seed germination, seedling growth, and photoperiodism. Although the three growth responses are quite different, they all have the same action spectrum and so apparently are all related to the same photoreceptor pigment. This pigment (**phytochrome**) has been extracted from plant tissues, although its concentration is too low to impart a color to plants. It exists in two forms, one with an absorption peak in the red (at 660 millimicrons) and the other with its absorption peaks in the far red (at 710 and 730 millimicrons). Red light activates the various growth processes and at the same time converts the pigment to its far-red absorbing form (7, 10). Far-red light reverses the effects of the red light, and also converts the pigment to its red-absorbing form. When both red and far-red light are present simultaneously, as in sunlight or the light from ordinary electric lamps, the promoting effects of the red light predominate.

LIGHT AND SEED GERMINATION

The seeds of many plants will germinate either in light or darkness, but the seeds of a good many other species become sensitized to light after they have imbibed water. The germination of some seeds, including those of primose (*Primula spectablis*), *Phacelia*, and many members of the Lily family, is prevented by light, whereas the germination of other seeds such as those of tomato and Jimson weed is retarded by light. On the other hand, the seeds of many species, including some varieties of tobacco and lettuce, peppergrass (*Lepidium*), *Lobelia*, mullein, and *Primula obconica*, will not germinate unless they have been exposed at least briefly to light after they have imbibed water. Seeds of carrot, some figs, and many grasses are among those that germinate better after exposure to light, but will germinate in darkness. If the light intensity is great enough, the soaked seeds require an exposure to light of only a few seconds.

When soaked seeds of a light-requiring type such as tobacco or lettuce are exposed to red light they will germinate, but if the exposure to red light is followed by exposure to far-red light the seeds do not germinate. A second exposure to red light will again permit germination. These alternating treatments with red and far-red light can be repeated a number of times, the last treatment always being the one that is effective in either promoting or inhibiting germination. The light requirement for the germination of lettuce and some other seeds has been reduced or eliminated by treating the seeds with gibberellins, suggesting that these or similar growth substances may be involved at some point in the internal processes associated with germination.

SEEDLING GROWTH

Plants growing in the dark have a pattern of development very different from that of similar plants growing in the light. For example, bean seedlings growing in the dark lack chlorophyll; they have unusually long and weak hypocotyls with a hook that fails to straighten out, and have leaves that fail to unfold and enlarge. Such a plant is said to be **etiolated.** Less extreme etiolation occurs when the plants are growing in dim light. The absence of chlorophyll results from the lack of either blue or red light that can be absorbed by the protochlorophyll, while the elongated hypocotyl results from the lack of blue light that would be absorbed by yellow pigments, so these effects are not related to the red, far-red pigment system. However, both the straightening of the hypo-cotyl hook and the unfolding and expansion of the leaves are red, far-red reactions. Exposing to red light bean seedlings that have been growing in the dark promotes both hypocotyl hook opening and leaf

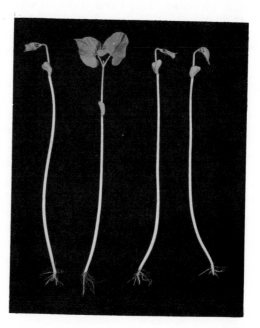

Figure 13.1. Influence of red and far-red light on the growth of bean seedlings. The first of these 10-day-old plants (*left*) grew in complete darkness. The second was exposed to 2 min. of red light, the third to 2 min. of red followed by 5 min. of far red, and the fourth to 5 min. of far red. Otherwise, the plants were kept dark until photographed. Note the effect of red light in promoting leaf expansion and straightening of the hypocotyl hook (plant 2), and the cancellation of this effect by far red (plant 3). (Courtesy of Crops Research Division, U.S. Department of Agriculture, Beltsville, Md.)

expansion, and as in seed germination, the effect can be cancelled by a subsequent exposure to far-red light (Fig. 13.1).

PHOTOPERIODISM

That photoperiodism is a red, far-red response has been learned only in recent years, as is also true of the other red, far-red reactions. **Photoperiodism** (13, 15, 16) is the influence of the *duration* of the daily periods of light and darkness on the growth, development and reproduction of plants and animals. The discovery just after World War I of this previously unsuspected environmental influence on organisms ranks as one of the major biological advances of the present century. Photoperiodism was more or less accidentally discovered during the course of an experiment being conducted for other reasons in the Washington, D. C. area by W. W. Garner and H. A. Allard of the U. S. Department of Agriculture. Maryland Mammoth, a new variety of tobacco, failed to bloom and produce seeds at the usual time but instead continued to elongate. The plants were eventually moved into a greenhouse and finally began to bloom. The investigators became interested in this unusual flowering behavior and turned from their original experiments in an effort to determine the reasons for the delayed flower formation by Maryland Mammoth. After painstakingly eliminating all possible known environmental factors such as temperature and light intensity by a series of experiments, they came to the rather startling conclusion that blooming had been induced by the short days of late autumn. Their conclusion was substantiated when they found that Maryland Mammoth could be induced to bloom even in midsummer if artificially short days were provided by placing the plants in the dark for part of each day.

Before publishing their results, Garner and Allard investigated the influence of day length on the reproductive development of many other species of plants and found that plants could be classified into at least three groups as regards their response to day length: (1) **Short-day** plants that initiate flowers only when the days are below a certain critical length (Fig. 13.2), (2) **long-day** plants that initiate flowers only when the day length is above a certain minimum length (Fig. 13.3), and (3) **day-neutral** plants, that bloom under either long or short days. The report on their research, published in 1920, contained such extensive and convincing evidence for photoperiodism and provided such a surprising explanation of the previously puzzling seasonal blooming of plants that it created a sensation among botanists. Garner and Allard conducted many more experiments on photoperiodism and other botanist soon began research on the subject. Not long after the discovery of photoperiodism in plants it was found that aphids (plant lice) have

Figure 13.2. Chrysanthemum plants of the same age kept under 8 hr. of light and 16 hr. of darkness (*left*) and under 16 hr. of light and 8 hr. of darkness (*right*), illustrating the photoperiodic response of a short day species. (Courtesy of Crops Research Division, U.S. Department of Agriculture, Beltsville, Md.)

a photoperiodically-controlled reproductive cycle. Since then the seasonal breeding of many other invertebrate animals and of birds and other vertebrates, as well as such seasonal responses as changes in fur colors of mammals and possibly bird migrations, have been found to be photoperiodic.

By 1940 the photoperiodic responses of hundreds of species and varieties of plants had been determined, a few of them being listed in Table 13.1. In addition to its influence on blooming, day length was found to influence many other aspects of plant development. For example, long days promote onion bulb development and the vegetative growth of most species of plants, whereas short days favor tuber formation and promote the onset of both dormancy and leaf abscission. In some plants such as *Rudbeckia* and mullein, long days not only initiate blooming but also bring about elongation of the internodes of the stems. Under short days such plants have virtually no internodes and their leaves are all close to the ground in a pattern known as a **rosette.**

Temperature has been found to have a modifying influence on the photoperiodic responses of some species, some plants being day neutral

361

Figure 13.3. Dill plants of the same age kept under 8 hr. of light and 16 hr. of darkness (*left*) and under 16 hr. of light and 8 hr. of darkness (*right*), illustrating the photoperiodic response of a long day species. Note the influence of long days on internode elongation as well as on blooming. (Courtesy of Crops Research Division, U.S. Department of Agriculture, Beltsville, Md.)

at one temperature range and either long or short day at another. Much has also been learned about the influence of alternating light and dark cycles of unusual length on the photoperiodic responses of plants. One of the more important discoveries is that interruption of the long dark period accompanying short days by only a brief period of light will prevent blooming in short day plants (Fig. 13.4), provided that the interruption occurs somewhere near the middle of the dark period. The few minutes to an hour of light required, depending on its intensity, are not enough to make the total light period equal a long day. These results indicate that slow reactions requiring a long dark period for completion are involved in photoperiodism, and that short-day plants are really long-night plants whereas long-day plants should be called short-night plants.

Despite much information like this about the photoperiodic responses of plants under different environmental conditions, and some information about the inheritance of photoperiodic potentialities of plants, little is known yet about the internal processes and conditions associated with the photoperiodic responses. Although photoperiodism has been identified as a red, far-red reaction and evidence suggests that a flowering hormone is involved, the hormone has not been isolated or identified (Chapter 12). Furthermore, little is known about the entire internal sequence of events from the absorption of light (or its absence during the dark period), through the production of the stimulus in the leaves and the transmission of the stimulus to the buds, and its final influence on the pattern of bud development. However, most of the current research on photoperiodism is directed toward obtaining a better understanding of the internal processes and we can expect that they will be gradually clarified.

Our lack of knowledge of the internal mechanisms of photoperiodism has not hampered practical application of the discovery. Soon after Garner and Allard discovered photoperiodism, its possible practical applications became evident, and for many years greenhouse plants have been brought into bloom out of season by either extending or reducing the natural day length. During the fall, winter, and early spring, long days may be provided by extending the day length with ordinary incandescent light bulbs. Less than one foot-candle of light is generally adequate, although the light intensity supplied is usually greater than this. During the summer, short days can be supplied by placing the plants in the dark for part of each day. Florists can now count on having Easter lilies even for an early Easter, poinsettias by Christmas,

TABLE 13.1. **PHOTOPERIODIC CLASSIFICATION OF SELECTED PLANTS AS REGARDS FLOWER INITIATION, WITH APPROXIMATE CRITICAL DAY LENGTH IN HOURS IF KNOWN**

Short-Day Plants		Long-Day Plants		Day-Neutral Plants
Bryophyllum	12	Chrysanthemum frutescens		Bean, string
Chrysanthemum indicum	15	Clover, red	12	Buckwheat
Cocklebur	15	Dill	11	Celery
Cosmos, Klondyke	13	Hibiscus syriacus (Althea)	12	Corn (most)
Goldenrod		Larkspur		Cotton
Orchid		Radish		Cucumber
Poinsettia	12	Rudbeckia hirta	12	Geranium
Ragweed		Ryegrass, Italian	11	Pansy
Rye, winter	12	Sedum	13	Snapdragon
Soybean, Biloxi	14	Spinach	13	Strawberry (everbearing)
Strawberry (most)	10	Sugar beet		Tobacco (most)
Tobacco, Maryland Mammoth	14	Wheat, winter (most)	12	Tomato

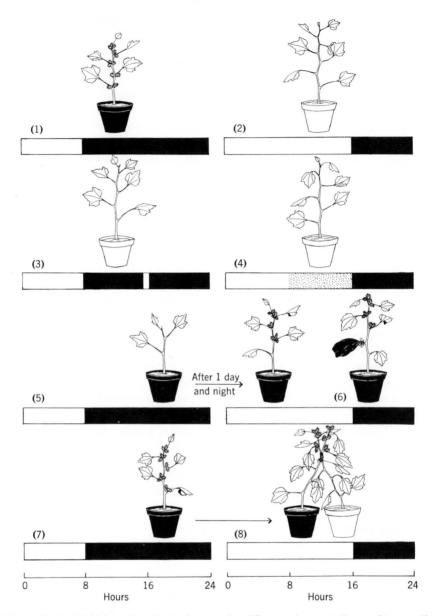

Figure 13.4. Cocklebur (*Xanthium*) plants under different photoperiodic conditions. The white bars indicate light periods, the black bars dark periods, and the shaded area low intensity artificial light. Long nights (1) induce blooming, short nights (2) keep plant vegetative. Interruption of the long dark period by high intensity light (3) prevents flower formation, as does extension of day by low intensity light (4). A young plant induced to bloom by one short day-long night cycle (5) continues reproductive development even though transferred to long days. A plant under long days blooms if only one leaf is subjected to short days and long nights by covering it with a light-proof black bag (6). When a plant induced to flower by long nights (7) is grafted to another plant (8) and kept continuously under long days—short

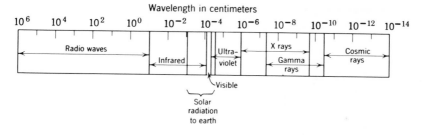

Wavelength in centimeters

Figure 13.5. The spectrum of electromagnetic radiation. For an expanded spectrum of the visible radiations (light) see Fig. 10.8. The wavelength scale here is in centimeters, but for light and the shorter wavelength radiations millimicrons (10^{-7} cm.) and angstrom units (10^{-8} cm.) are the more commonly used units.

and chrysanthemums for supermarket openings even in mid-summer. Controlled day lengths have also been used to bring different varieties of a species into bloom simultaneously, thus permitting them to be crossed for the first time. Photoperiodic control of garden and field crops is less feasible, but floodlights have been used experimentally to prevent the blooming of sugar cane plants. This results in a greater yield of sugar, since none is used in the growth and development of flowers.

Photoperiodism is a factor in the geographic distribution of plant species, since the natural day lengths vary with latitude as well as season. At the equator, the daylight period is about 12 hours throughout the year, but as we go from the equator to the poles the daylight period is progressively longer in summer and shorter in winter. Short day plants could not reproduce in natural arctic environments because the temperature is too low for active growth when the days are short. At or near the equator the daily light period is never long enough for the reproduction of long day plants. Several plant species of wide distribution include varieties with differing photoperiodic requirements, progressively longer critical photoperiods being found from the lower latitudes toward the poles.

Influences of Other Radiation on Plant Growth

The visible wavelengths of radiation that have such varied and important influences on plants occupy only a short segment of the entire spectrum of radiation (Fig. 13.5). Just beyond the visible far-red radiation that plays a role in photoperiodism and other processes there

nights, this second plant blooms as a result of transfer of the photoperiodic stimulus (florigen ?) from the induced plant.

Figure 13.6. Aerial view of a radiation test plot at the Brookhaven National Laboratory. A cobalt-60 gamma radiation source that can be lowered into an underground radiation-proof chamber to permit working with the plants is located at the center of the circle. The controls are in the building at the upper left. Since radiation decreases in intensity inversely with the square of the distance, plants can be exposed to different known intensities of radiation by planting them different distances from the cobalt-60 source. (Courtesy of A. H. Sparrow, Brookhaven National Laboratory.)

is a broad band of invisible **infrared** or heat radiation. Still longer than the infrared waves are the **radio** or electrical waves. Beyond the other end of the visible spectrum (violet) are the short **ultraviolet** waves, and still shorter than these are the **X rays, gamma rays,** and **cosmic rays.**

We have little knowledge of the possible influences of radiation with longer waves than visible light on plants. Infrared radiation increases the temperature of plants but is not known to have any other specific influence. The shorter (high frequency) radio waves have recently been found to have adverse effects on some microorganisms and animals when applied at high intensity, but little is known about their possible effects on plants. These waves are not an important factor in the natural environment. The longer radio waves used in broadcasting apparently have no effects on plants.

Radiation with shorter waves than light does, however, have marked influences on organisms (1, 9, 12). Some of the shorter ultraviolet rays are lethal to microorganisms and injurious to the surface tissues of multicellular plants and animals, but the short-wave ultraviolet radiation from the sun is quite effectively filtered out by the atmosphere. Some plant pigments have absorption peaks in the ultraviolet as well as in the visible spectrum, whereas other plant constituents absorb radiation principally in the ultraviolet region. However, the fact that plants grow well in greenhouses, even though the glass filters out practically all the ultraviolet, indicates that ultraviolet is not essential for plant growth. Like X rays and gamma rays, but to a lesser degree, ultraviolet rays may increase the rate of mutation (Chapter 17). The X rays and gamma rays are not an important part of the natural environment, but are being generated in constantly increasing quantity as a product of human manipulations (Fig. 13.6). In addition to promoting mutations, X rays and gamma rays have marked influences on plant development (Fig. 13.7). Gamma rays are emitted by radioactive atoms, along with fast-moving atomic particles (electrons or beta parti-

Figure 13.7. A tobacco hybrid (*Nicotiana glauca* × *N. langsdorfii*) exposed to gamma radiation from cobalt-60 for 11 weeks (*right*) compared with a control plant (*left*) of the same age. Note the extensive structural malformations caused by the radiation. (Courtesy of A. H. Sparrow, Brookhaven National Laboratory.)

cles, protons, neutrons, deuterons, and alpha particles). Although these particles are not really radiation they are sometimes referred to as such since many of their effects are similar to those of short-wave radiation. Cosmic rays are very penetrating and are universally present on Earth. Aside from the possibility that they may play an important role in natural mutation, their possible influences on organisms is unknown.

Short-wave radiations and high speed atomic particles can ·disrupt molecules, resulting in the production of ions that would otherwise not be formed, and so are frequently referred to as **ionizing radiation** (14). It appears likely that such ionization is the principal means through which radiation brings about abnormal development and mutations.

Influences of Temperature on Plant Growth

Except for purely photochemical reactions, such as the light re-action of photosynthesis, all of the many biochemical processes of plants and all physical processes such as diffusion and water transport are influenced by temperature (11). The rates of both physical and chem-cal processes in plants increase with temperature to the point where it becomes high enough to inactivate enzymes or injure protoplasm, unless some other factor is limiting. Plant growth, however, is gen-erally the most rapid at moderate temperature ranges, most temperate zone plants growing best between 70°F and 80°F. Decreased growth at higher temperatures results from such factors as the more rapid in-crease of respiration than of photosynthesis with a rise in temperature (Chapter 10), and the marked increase in transpiration and the sub-sequent wilting and stomatal closure (Chapter 9). In addition to its influence on the rate of growth, temperature also has some marked effects on the pattern of plant development.

EFFECTS OF TEMPERATURE EXTREMES ON PLANTS

Plants may be killed by either very high or very low temperatures. Most actively growing plants die within a minute or so at 140°F and after only a few minutes at 120°F, presumably because of denaturation of enzymes and other proteins. A few species of blue-green algae and lichens, however, flourish in hot springs at 185°F, and some fungi thrive at 120°F. At the other extreme, some plants from cool climates are severely injured or even killed after a relatively short exposure to tem-peratures of 90°F to 100°F.

Many tropical plants are killed by only a short period of freezing and may even be injured by prolonged cold above the freezing point. Other more hardy species regularly survive severe freezing, some at the lowest temperatures found in nature, provided that they have entered dormancy. Although freezing injury is not completely understood it involves both disruption of the protoplasm by the ice crystals and the desiccation of the cells as water is removed by ice crystal formation.

For many years gardeners have followed the practice of **hardening** young plants of cabbage and other species before transplanting them outside by keeping them at temperatures just above freezing for several days. Such hardened plants can withstand freezing that would kill them had they been transplanted directly from a warm greenhouse. During hardening the protoplasm becomes more resistant to mechanical injury, the permeability of the plasma membranes increases, and there is a marked increase in both protein content and solutes that reduce the freezing point of the water in the cells. Similar changes may occur as a plant enters dormancy.

Not all cold injury results from ice formation. During relatively warm periods in the winter evergreens may have a high rate of transpiration whereas water absorption from the cold or frozen soil is very slow, resulting in desiccation of the tree. Alternate freezing and thawing may lift the root systems of plants out of the soil or may tear and loosen them, and prolonged deep snow may kill low plants by cutting off light and air. Dry or dormant seeds of most species can withstand freezing even though the plants may be quite susceptible to freezing injury.

LOW TEMPERATURE PRECONDITIONING

Relatively low temperatures are effective in breaking both bud dormancy and some kinds of seed dormancy (page 341). Since the effects of the low temperature do not become evident until growth is resumed or germination occurs, this breaking of dormancy is an example of **low-temperature preconditioning** (Fig. 13.8). Similar low-temperature preconditioning is a natural prerequisite for the formation of elongated internodes (**bolting**) and blooming of winter wheat, celery (Fig. 13.9), cabbage, foxglove, and all other **biennials**, that is, plants that bloom the second year after planting and then produce seed and die. Some biennials also require a long photoperiod in addition to the low temperature preconditioning. Before the importance of low-temperature preconditioning was discovered, truck gardeners sometimes had a complete failure of biennial crops such as celery because the plants bolted and bloomed the first year, making them unsuitable for marketing. After it was learned that this resulted from transplanting the young plants outdoors too early, thus subjecting them to low temperature preconditioning, crop failures have been avoided simply by waiting to transplant until all danger of cold weather is past. While the pre-conditioning requires temperatures a few degrees above freezing, it does not require freezing. Low-temperature preconditioning can be applied to seeds soaked in just enough water to permit germination to start but not to continue. This process is called **vernalization**. Vernalization is used mostly with winter wheat in Russia, where the winters are so cold that winter wheat planted in the fall is killed by freezing, and where suitable varieties of spring wheat are not available. Spring wheat varie-ties are annuals rather than biennials and, like annuals, generally do

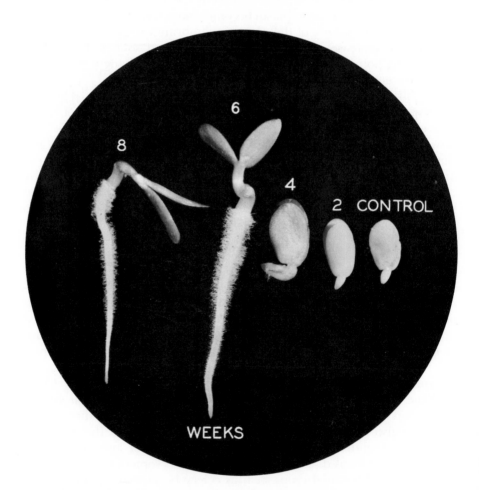

Figure 13.8. Embryos of the European Mountain Ash (*Sorbus aucuparia*) kept for the indicated number of weeks at 1°C before being returned to room temperatures. Note that even 4 weeks of low temperature preconditioning was not enough to break dormancy and permit normal germination. (Courtesy of the Boyce Thompson Institute for Plant Research.)

Figure 13.9. Effect of temperature on bolting and blooming of celery plants of the same age. The plants on the left were exposed to temperatures of 50°F to 60°F; those on the right were exposed to 60°F to 70°F. (Courtesy of H. C. Thompson, Cornell University.)

not require low temperature preconditioning. The term *vernalization* is sometimes extended to include all low-temperature preconditioning and also the high temperature preconditioning of seeds, for example cotton seeds.

THERMOPERIODICITY

The day to night temperature fluctuations have marked effects on the growth of most species of plants (**thermoperiodicity**). Most kinds of plants grow best when the night temperatures are lower than the day temperatures, but a few species such as the African violet flourish best when it is somewhat warmer at night than during the days. Night temperatures are particularly important in their effects on growth; a difference of only a few degrees frequently produces very different growth patterns (Fig. 13.10). The optimal day and night temperatures vary from species to species, and in addition the optima may change as a plant grows older. Tomatoes are particularly sensitive thermoperiodically, the reduced fruiting of tomatoes during hot summer weather resulting from too high night temperatures. Young tomato plants grow best when the

371

Figure 13.10. Effect of night temperature on the growth of *Browallia*. Both plants grew under day temperatures of about 70°F. The plant at the left was kept at 50°F at night, the one at the right at 65°F. Both are the same age. (Courtesy of the Department of Floriculture and Ornamental Horticulture, Cornell University.)

day temperature is about 79°F and the night temperature around 68°F, but mature plants grow and set fruit best at night temperatures of 59°F and no fruit at all develops if the night temperature is over 77°F, even though the plants are blooming. A number of bulbous species such as hyacinth, tulip, and narcissus have quite different temperature requirements at different stages of growth, corresponding with the usual seasonal temperature changes in regions where they flourish.

The thermoperiodic requirements of most species have still not been determined, but it is already obvious that there is a close relationship between the optimal thermoperiods for a species and the prevailing temperature fluctuations during the growing season in regions where the plants either grow naturally or are cultivated successfully. Apparently most species of plants flourish only when both the thermoperiod and photoperiod are optimal for the species, even though the plants may be day neutral as far as reproduction is concerned. A better knowledge of the thermoperiodic and photoperiodic requirements of economic species promises to be of great value in the selection of regions for the cultivation of specific crops and in the control of greenhouse environments (20).

Endogenous Rhythms of Plants

Many aspects of the metabolism, behavior, growth, and development of plants and animals occur in rhythmic cycles or sequence, generally over a period of a day (24 hours), a lunar tidal period ($29\frac{1}{2}$ days), or a year ($365\frac{1}{4}$ days). For example, the rates of cell division and of respiration exhibit daily rhythms whereas such things as dormancy and blooming have an annual rhythmic cycle. Some of these rhythms have been definitely linked to rhythms in factors of the physical environment such as temperature, light intensity, and photoperiod and the natural rhythms can be altered by artificial control of the effective environmental factor. However, other biological rhythms apparently related to rhythmic environmental changes continue even though the organism is placed in a controlled constant environment. These rhythms are referred to as **endogenous rhythms.**

For example, bean leaves are extended in an essentially flat plane during the day but at night the leaflets fold together (the so-called sleep movements). It had once been assumed that this was a direct response to the daily rhythm of light and darkness, but it has been found that the daily leaf movements continue either in continuous light or continuous darkness provided that the plants have had at least a brief initial exposure to light. The time at which this initial exposure to light occurs determines the time of the daily opening and folding of the leaves. Sections of potato tubers show both daily and seasonal rhythms in rate of respiration even when kept in a controlled environment with all known environmental factors constant or nonrhythmic. The brown alga *Dictyota* produces eggs and sperm once a month in phase with the lunar tidal period. The plants in one area may be synchronized with a different phase of the moon than those in another. Among plants such lunar rhythms are mostly restricted to marine algae. Many other endogenous rhythms in both plants and animals have been demonstrated (6, 10).

The biologists investigating endogenous rhythms are of two schools of thought when it comes to explaining them. One group believes the endogenous rhythms are completely internal and are not controlled by any environmental factor, either known or unknown, even though they may be synchronized with rhythmic changes in some environmental factor. The other group believes that endogenous rhythms are controlled by rhythmic changes in environmental factors such as perhaps barometric pressure or cosmic radiation that were really not controlled in the experiments that have been done. The continuing active research on endogenous rhythms will probably solve this problem, and may also identify factors of the physical environmental that have biological influences not now known or even suspected.

▶ Questions

1. In Alaska crop plants such as hay and various garden vegetables generally have unusually rapid and lush growth and produce high yields. What are some possible explanations?

2. Why do northern species of plants frequently fail to survive when transplanted to semitropical or tropical regions? Some others may survive, but fail to reproduce. Give possible reasons.

3. Could a prediction be made as to whether or not a species of crop plant from another country would thrive in a certain region of the United States? If so, what information about the plant and its environment would be needed?

4. Apple trees planted on north-facing slopes of hills are generally less liable to be injured by freezing than those on the south-facing slopes. Explain.

5. Would it be possible to raise bean plants that are green and have relatively short hypocotyls, but still show other symptoms of etiolation, that is, have unopened hypocotyl hooks and unexpanded leaf blades? If so, how could it be done?

6. Does the fact that dogwood trees bloom in the early spring necessarily mean that they are short-day plants? Could they be long-day plants? Explain your answers.

▶ References

For Reference

1. Alexander, Peter, *Atomic Radiation and Life*. Pelican Books edition. Baltimore: Penguin Books, 1957.

2. Daubenmire, R. F., *Plants and Environment*, 2nd ed. New York: John Wiley and Sons, 1959.

3. Ferry, J. F. and H. S. Ward, *Fundamentals of Plant Physiology*. New York: The Macmillan Co., 1959.

4. Galston, A. W., *The Life of the Green Plant*. Englewood Cliffs, N. J.: Prentice-Hall, 1961.

For Reading

5. Bosen, Victor, Phytotron: all-climate greenhouse. *Science Digest* 32(5):13–17, 1952.

6. Brown, Frank A., Jr., The rhythmic nature of plants and animals. *American Scientist* 47:148–168, 1959. Life's mysterious clocks. *Saturday Evening Post*, December 24, 1960, p. 18.

7. Butler, W. L. and R. J. Downs, Light and plant development. *Scientific American* 203(6):56–63, December 1960.

8. Cole, LaMont C., The ecosphere. *Scientific American* 198(4):83–92, April 1958.

9. Hollaender, A. and G. E. Stapleton, Radiation and the cell. *Scientific American* 201(3):94–100, September 1959.

10. Hendricks, S. B., The clocks of life. *Atlantic Monthly* 200(4):111–115, December 1957.

11. Johnson, Frank H., Heat and life. *Scientific American* 191(3):64–68, September 1954.

12. Long, Daniel, Strange plants in an atomic garden. *Science Digest* 42(4):86–93,1957.

13. Naylor, A. W., The control of flowering. *Scientific American* 186(5):49–56, May 1952.

14. Platzman, R. L., What is ionizing radiation? *Scientific American* 201(3):74–84, September 1954.

15. Salisbury, Frank B., The flowering process. *Scientific American* 198(4):109–117, April 1958.

16. Veen, R. van der and G. Meijer, *Light and Plant Growth*. New York: The Macmillan Co., 1959.

17. Wald, George, Light and life. *Scientific American* 201(4):92–108, October 1959.

18. Went, F. W., Air pollution. *Scientific American* 192(5):62–73, May 1955.

19. Went, F. W., The role of environment in plant growth. *American Scientist* 44:378–398, 1956.

20. Went, F. W., Climate and agriculture. *Scientific American* 196(6):82–94, June 1957.

14. The Biological Environment

IN THE LABORATORY at least some kinds of plants and animals can be cultivated in pure culture, completely isolated from all other species of living organisms. But in nature, plants and animals are surrounded by and affected by other organisms of many different species that constitute their **biological environment.** The biological environment of a plant may have effects on its processes, growth and development, and even its reproduction and survival that are quite as important and striking as the effects of the physical environment. The varied interactions among organisms in nature may be classified as **social** and **nutritive** (2). In a social interaction neither organism secures food from the other, whereas in a nutritive interaction one of the organisms does so. We have already considered the diverse plant communities of the earth and their successional development (Chapter 7). The community level of plant organization is a product of the interactions of the varied factors of both the physical and biological environments on the organisms constituting the community. Here our attention is directed more specifically toward the effects of the biological environment on individual plants, but toward the end of this chapter we shall take a look at the relation of such biological interactions to the dynamics of plant and animal communities.

Social Interactions

Although the organisms in some social plant interactions are in physical contact with each other part or all of their lives, perhaps the more important kind of social interactions are those that occur even though the organisms are not in actual physical contact. We shall consider two classes of interactions of the first type (epiphytes and vines) and two of the second type (antibiosis and the effects of organisms on factors of the physical environment).

EPIPHYTES

Plants such as Spanish moss (Fig. 2.32) and many species of orchids that grow perched on another plant but do not secure food from it are called **epiphytes**. Epiphytes are particularly abundant in tropical forests (Fig. 14.1). The epiphytes may benefit by the relationship since they frequently receive more light than they would if growing on the ground. Epiphytes have no contact with the soil and they secure their water directly from rain or from the water vapor of the air and their mineral salts from air-borne dust particles. Epiphytes do not take food or water from the supporting trees; however they may affect the trees in other ways. For example, Spanish moss may become so thick that it shades the leaves of the tree and reduces their photosynthetic productivity. Spanish moss may also be heavy enough, especially after a rain, to break some branches off the tree. Most species of the pineapple family, of which Spanish moss is a member, are epiphytes, the common pineapple being one of the exceptions. Lichens and algae growing on the trunks or branches of trees are also epiphytes.

VINES

Vines may climb on and over other plants, but they differ from epiphytes in that they have roots in the soil. Like epiphytes, vines may benefit from the relationship by securing more light than they would trailing on the ground, and they may also affect the supporting plant by shading its leaves. In addition, some woody vines such as wisteria may coil around the trunk of a tree and constrict the trunk as it grows in diameter. This may result in crushing the phloem and either partial or complete girdling that can injure or even kill the tree (10).

ANTIBIOSIS

Although the use of **antibiotics** from fungi and other microorganisms in the treatment of diseases is now a well-known practice, it is not so

377

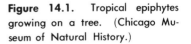

Figure 14.1. Tropical epiphytes growing on a tree. (Chicago Museum of Natural History.)

generally recognized that antibiotics play an important role in biological interactions in nature. Antibiotic substances diffusing from a mold or other plant may inhibit the growth of nearby bacteria and other organisms (Fig. 1.7), thus reducing competition (6, 8). Antibiotics may also protect the organisms producing them against certain parasites. At least some vascular plants such as the black walnut tree and the desert shrub *Encelia* are known to produce antibiotics that inhibit the growth of other plants in their immediate neighborhood (7). Antibiosis may play a more important role in the composition and structure of plant communities than is generally recognized.

INFLUENCES ON THE PHYSICAL ENVIRONMENT

Among the more important social interrelations of plants and animals are those in which one organism affects another by modifying the ordinary factors of its physical environment. The trees in a forest have a marked effect on the physical environment of the other forest plants through shading, temperature reduction, increased atmospheric humidity, absorption of water and mineral salts, and contribution of organic matter to the soil. The restriction of certain animals to specific types of plant communities results, not only from the availability of suitable food supplies, but also from the influence of the plants on the physical environment of the animals. Animals may also be responsible for marked effects on the physical environment of plants. For example, dams built by beavers (not to mention men) may result in the complete alteration of the physical environment of a limited area. Of all organisms, man has perhaps had the greatest influence in altering the natural physical and biological environments, as he has removed forests, cultivated land, and constructed roads and buildings. Such activities are an essential aspect of modern civilization, but they are creating increasing concern. Even the natural communities not directly destroyed may be seriously affected by changes in such things as drainage patterns and water availability, soil erosion and the silting of streams. Man has just begun altering the environment in another way that may have marked effects on life on earth: dispersal of radioisotopes.

Considered from a broad and long-range standpoint, however, no group of organisms has had as marked an influence on the physical environment as photosynthetic plants. Without photosynthesis the atmosphere would be devoid of oxygen and most kinds of organisms would be unable to survive. Some biologists now believe that during the early history of life on earth there were no photosynthetic plants and that the atmosphere was not only devoid of oxygen but also contained high concentrations of carbon dioxide and also of other gases such as hydrogen, ammonia, and methane that would not last long if oxygen were present (Chapter 19). The change from such an atmosphere to our present atmosphere can be credited to the appearance and spread of photosynthetic plants. If it were not for land plants there would be little or no soil since the rate of erosion would generally exceed the rate of soil formation. It is obvious that organisms may have marked effects on the physical environment (25), just as the physical environment has marked effects on organisms.

Nutritive Interactions

In considering nutritive interactions between organisms, we are concerned only with the plants and animals that secure their food from living organisms, not with those that synthesize their food by photosynthesis or chemosynthesis (**autotrophic** organisms), that grow on nonliving organic matter (**saprophytic** bacteria and fungi), or that consume dead plants or animals (**scavengers**).

PHAGOTROPHISM

Ingestion of one organism by another may be referred to as **phagotrophism**. Most phagotrophic organisms are, of course, animals, but the few species of carnivorous plants (Figs. 5.28, 5.29) qualify for inclusion in this category (12). Carnivorous vascular plants, however, contain chlorophyll, and it seems likely that the greater portion of their food is derived from photosynthesis. The organism consumed in a phagotrophic relationship can hardly be said to benefit, but as we shall see later, phagotrophism plays an important role in the scheme of biological checks and balances. The kinds and numbers of herbivorous animals present in a biological community may have a marked influence on the nature of the vegetation. For example, in England hillside pastures grazed by sheep are dominated by bilberry plants and a grass called sheep's fescue, whereas similar ungrazed hillsides are covered with a member of the heath family called ling. Overgrazing in forests may result in the destruction of most of the young trees, and so to the gradual disappearance of the forest as the older trees die or are cut down. Many insects and other animals consume only portions of plants and the effects on the plant may be minor, but at times swarms of insects consume such a large portion of the leaves or other organs of a plant as to interfere seriously with its growth and development (5, 14, 19).

PARASITISM

An organism that lives in or on another organism part or all of its life, securing its food from this host organism but not benefiting the host in any way, is referred to as a **parasite**. Many, but not all parasites are **pathogens**, that is, disease-producing organisms. Even a single species of parasite may be pathogenic in some hosts and not in others. For example, typhoid bacteria cause typhoid fever when they become estab-

Figure 14.2. Destruction of the stem tissues of a cactus plant by parasitic bacteria. (Courtesy of the U.S. Department of Agriculture.)

Figure 14.3. Stages in parasitism by dodder. (a) A dodder seed has germinated near the plant. (b) The stem of the dodder coils around the stem of the plant. (c) Outgrowths of the dodder stem (haustoria) have penetrated the stem of the host plant and the dodder stem has lost its connection with the ground. (d) Several weeks later the dodder has grown luxuriantly and almost covers the host plant. Note the haustoria and flowers of the dodder. (Photos by Ross R. Hutchins, Mississippi State College.)

lished in most people, but typhoid carriers harbor large numbers of the bacteria and still have no symptoms of the disease. Generally the principal damage to the host by the parasite results from destruction of tissue (Fig. 14.2) or the production of toxic substances by the parasites. Other factors may also be involved such as the plugging of the xylem vessels by certain kinds of wilt bacteria and fungi.

The majority of the plants parasitic either on other plants or on animals are bacteria or fungi, but a few species of plants in other groups are completely or partially parasitic. The common mistletoe contains chlorophyll and probably synthesizes much of its own food, but it at least obtains water and mineral salts from the host tree. Another chlorophyll-

Figure 14.4. A hornet killed by a parasitic fungus. Note the fungus hyphae and sporangia growing from the insect. (Photo by Ross E. Hutchins.)

containing seed plant that is probably only a partial parasite is the witchweed, a plant parasitic on the roots of corn and some other grasses (11). Witchweed has only recently been introduced accidentally into the Carolinas from Africa and is causing serious damage to corn. Every effort is being made to control this pest and to prevent its spread, but this is difficult because of the numerous and very small seeds produced by the witchweed. One of the most common and destructive parasitic seed plants is dodder (Fig. 14.3). Although dodder (16) contains small quantities of chlorophyll, it probably obtains most of its food from the host plants. The various species of dodder parasitize numerous plants, including many crop plants.

Several species of seed plants lack chlorophyll entirely and are complete parasites. These include a number of different genera of the broomrape family parasitic on the roots of plants, among them the beechdrops that parasitize beech trees. *Rafflesia*, a genus of Malaysian plants parasitic on grape roots and a member of the Aristolochia family, is one of the most unusual of all seed plants. The vegetative organs grow entirely within the tissues of the host roots and have been reduced and modified until they resemble a fungal mycelium. The only organs visible above the ground are the large, malodorous flowers, that are about a yard in diameter in one species. The white Indian pipe (Fig. 10.1) is frequently given as an example of a saprophytic seed plant,

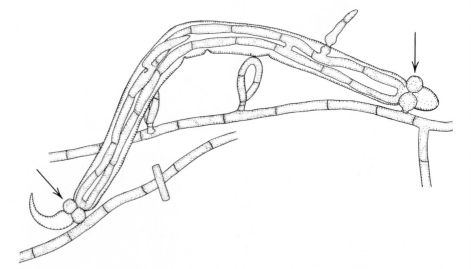

Figure 14.5. A nematode-trapping fungus with a nematode caught in the loops of two adjacent hyphae of the fungus. Note the swollen cells of the loops (arrows) containing the nematode and the fungal hyphae growing inside the nematode. (After a drawing by John N. Couch, University of North Carolina.)

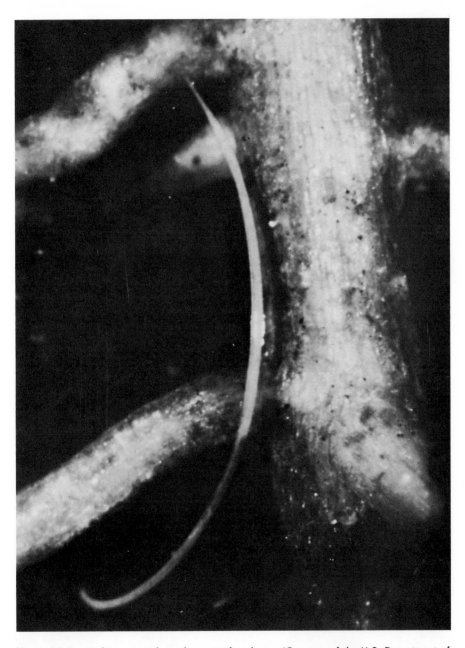

Figure 14.6. A whip nematode on the roots of a plant. (Courtesy of the U.S. Department of Agriculture.)

Figure 14.7. The spiny rose gall on a blackberry plant. (Photo by Ross E. Hutchins.)

but it is apparently parasitic on a fungus, reversing the more usual parasitic relationships between fungi and seed plants.

Bacteria parasitize a wide variety of hosts, including practically all kinds of plants and animals. Fungi are perhaps best known as parasites of vascular plants (1), but they also parasitize animals (Fig. 14.4), algae, and even other fungi. Among the fungi parasitic on humans are those causing ringworm and athlete's foot and a variety of species causing ear infections and pulmonary diseases (4). One group of fungi is parasitic on mosquito larvae and may prove to be valuable in mosquito control. Another group of fungi parasitic on nematode worms has a noose that contracts when a nematode passes through it, thus trapping the nematode (Fig. 14.5) which is then killed and digested by the fungus (21).

When plants are considered as hosts rather than as parasites, we find that almost every species of plant has parasites of one kind or another. It has been reported that the ginkgo tree is one species relatively free of parasites. Types of organisms parasitic on plants include not only other plants such as bacteria, fungi, and vascular parasites, but also nematode worms (Fig. 14.6), scale insects, and other animals (1). Biologists are just beginning to realize how extensively nematode parasites damage plants and reduce crop yields. Whether viruses are parasites depends on whether they are considered to be living organisms

Figure 14.8. A gall caused by a moth on the stem of a goldenrod plant. In the photo on the right, the gall has been cut open, showing the larva of the moth. (Courtesy of Wm. J. Robbins, New York Botanical Garden.)

or not, but at any rate viruses are among the more important causes of plant disease.

Naturally man is distressed when he or his domestic plants or animals are attacked by parasites, but parasitism is just as normal a biological interaction as any other and is an important component of the general system of biological checks and balances.

GALLS. Some parasites of plants, particularly insects, fungi, and bacteria, cause the development of characteristically shaped abnormal

Figure 14.9. Tumors on a *Kalanchoë* leaf caused by crown-gall bacteria. (Photo by J. A. Carlile, courtesy of Armin C. Braun, Rockefeller Institute for Medical Research.)

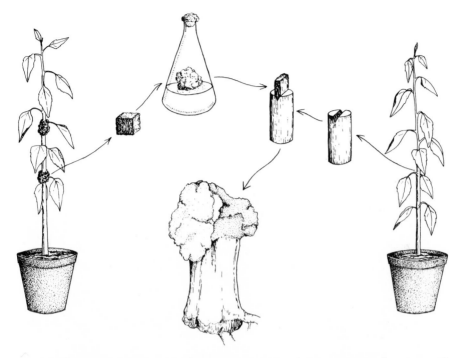

Figure 14.10. A small cube of tissue from a crown gall (*left*) continues growth in tissue culture without added auxin. If a bit of tissue from the tumor culture is grafted to a piece of stem from a normal plant (*right*) and cultured, the tumor tissue not only continues to grow, but also induces tumor growth from the tissue of the stem. (Redrawn from *Principles of Plant Physiology* by Bonner and Galston, with the permission of the publisher, W. H. Freeman & Co.)

structures (**galls**) by the host plants (Figs. 14.7–11). Galls are of diverse sizes and shapes and may be quite complicated in structure, their characteristics being determined by an interaction between the host and parasite species (15, 23). Gall organisms generally parasitize only one species of plant, or at most a few closely related species.

Wasps are probably the most common gall-inducing organisms. They lay their eggs in the tissues of the host plant, and as their larvae develop, the galls develop from the surrounding tissues. The larvae use some of the tissues of the gall as food. Oak trees are particularly susceptable to attack by gall wasps of various species.

Although it appears certain that gall organisms produce growth substances that cause the plant tissues to differentiate into characteristic galls, little is known about the nature or mode of action of most of these growth substances. It is known, however, that the galls caused by the crown-gall bacteria (Fig. 14.9) contain an unusually high concentration of auxin. The bacteria are apparently responsible for the initiation of the auxin production, but once a crown gall is established in a plant it may give rise to bacteria-free galls in other parts of the plant. These bacteria-free galls still have the capacity for synthesizing high auxin concentrations. If part of one of these bacteria-free galls is grafted to healthy plant tissue, it will cause the development of an auxin-producing tumor (Fig. 14.10). In contrast, the apparently similar gall-like growths

Figure 14.11. A cedar apple gall on a cedar tree. Teliospores produced in the gelatinous horns germinate into basidia that produce basidiospores. The basidiospores are carried by wind to apple trees, the alternate host of the rust. (Courtesy of the Crops Research Division, U.S. Department of Agriculture, Beltsville, Md.)

Figure 14.12. After the cedar apple rust fungus has infected apple trees, aeciospores are produced in the aecia on the leaves and fruits of the apple tree. These spores will infect only cedar trees, whereas the basidiospores produced by the cedar stage of the fungus infect only apples and their close relatives. (Courtesy of the Crops Research Division, U.S. Department of Agriculture, Beltsville, Md.)

produced by treating plants with auxins (Fig. 12.19) do not spread and do not have the capacity for producing auxin themselves.

ALTERNATE HOST PARASITES

Some parasites (the **alternate host parasites**) complete certain stages of their life cycle in one host, but can complete other essential stages only in another host species that is generally not closely related to the first host. A well known example of an alternate host parasite is the protozoan that causes malaria and is parasitic on man and a mosquito. The most common alternate host parasites of plants are the rust fungi. Of the many species of rusts, three of the more important are the black stem rust of wheat (with wild barberry bushes as its alternate host), the white pine blister rust (with currant or gooseberry bushes as alternate host), and the cedar apple rust of apple trees and cedar trees (Figs. 14.11, 14.12). The diseases caused by these and other rusts have resulted in serious economic losses, particularly of wheat and white pine.

The black stem rust of wheat is diagrammed and described in Fig. 14.13. For our present discussion this life cycle is less important for its technical details than for emphasizing the fact that certain specific

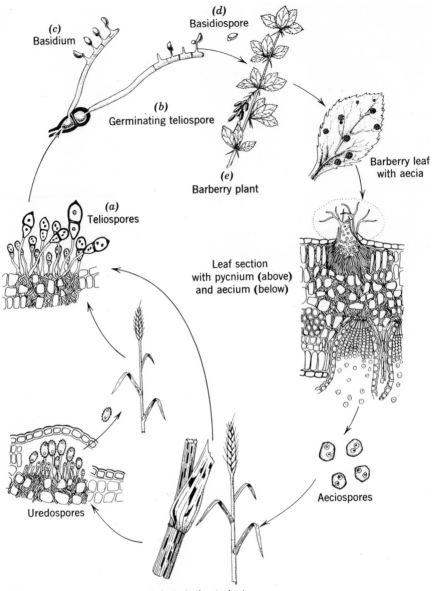

(c)
Basidium

(d)
Basidiospore

(b)
Germinating teliospore

(e)
Barberry plant

Barberry leaf
with aecia

(a)
Teliospores

Leaf section
with pycnium (above)
and aecium (below)

Aeciospores

Uredospores

Infected wheat plant

Figure 14.13. Life cycle of the black stem rust of wheat. The teliospores (a) produced on wheat germinate (b) into basidia (c) that produce basidiospores (d). These basidiospores infect only wild barberry bushes (e). The aeciospores produced on the barberry infect only wheat. The uredospores produced on wheat infect other wheat plants, and so the disease may spread from one wheat plant to another during the growing season. (Redrawn from *Botany* by Sinnott and Wilson, with the permission of the publisher, McGraw-Hill.)

stages of development occur in each of the two hosts and that the full life cycle can be completed only when both host species are present. The diagram also illustrates the complexity of a rust life cycle.

Eradication of the less important host species provides a means of disease control limited to alternate host parasites. Thus, white pine blister rust has been controlled to some degree by eradication of as many wild current and gooseberry plants as possible, wild barberry bushes have been killed to control wheat rust, and cedar trees in the neighborhood of apple orchards have been cut down. This method of control is, however, not always effective against wheat rust, since the rust can spread directly from one wheat plant to another by means of the uredospores (Fig. 14.13), and since in regions with mild winters the uredospores can survive until the next spring and infect the new crop. In cooler climates only the barberry stage can survive the winter. The breeding of rust-resistant varieties of wheat has provided a more effective means of disease control, but even this is not a permanent solution since new strains of rust to which the wheat is not resistant keep arising by mutations and by genetic recombinations occurring during sexual reproduction of the rust.

SYMBIOSIS

The word **symbiosis** is used in at least two different ways: (1) To cover all interactions between two different species (although sometimes limited to interactions involving physical contact), and (2) to include only nutritive interactions beneficial to both organisms. We shall use the term in the second sense, although the term **mutualism** is preferred by some biologists for this type of biological interaction. It is sometimes difficult to determine whether an interaction is parasitism or symbiosis. Lichens (20), the composite plants consisting of algae within the mycelial mass of fungi (Figs. 14.14, 2.20, and 2.21), are frequently cited as examples of symbiosis because the fungus obtains food from the alga and the fungus in turn is said to protect the alga from desiccation and other hazards. However, it appears probable that at least in some lichens the algae gain no benefits and the fungi are simply parasitic on the algae.

Certain species of fungi grow in or on the roots of many species of forests trees, orchids, members of the heath family, and other plants (Fig. 14.15). The rather stubby root-fungus complexes are called **mycorhiza** (13). The fungi obtain food from the roots, and since in many cases, at least, the mycorhiza appear to be important or even essential in the absorption of mineral salts by the plant the relationship is generally regarded as symbiotic. Mycorhiza may also participate in water absorption, and may benefit the plant in other ways. Many common forest mushrooms are the reproductive structures of mycorhizal fungi.

Some plants do not thrive without mycorhiza, but others seem to grow as well without mycorhiza as with them, and in such instances it is possible that the mycorhizal fungi are simply parasites.

The association of nitrogen-fixing bacteria with leguminous plants (Chapter 12) is almost certainly beneficial to both organisms and so should be classed as symbiotic. An unusual habitat of one species of unicellular alga is among the cells of a hydra (a simple relative of the jellyfish), thus producing a green hydra. This composite organism is considered a symbiont by some biologists. The hydra probably obtains food and oxygen from the alga, and the alga obtains carbon dioxide, mobility, and possibly protection from the hydra. Green hydra, unlike the usual kinds, are attracted toward regions of brighter light.

Symbiosis does not necessarily involve continued close contact between the organisms. Thus, the relationship between bees and other pollinating animals and plants is symbiotic. The bees use both the nectar and pollen they collect as food, but the plants are pollinated in the process. Birds and other animals that eat fruits and seeds play an important role in plant dispersal, since at least some of the seeds pass through their digestive tracts without being digested or injured. The relationship between man and the plants and animals he raises for food

Figure 14.14. Section through a portion of a lichen showing the spherical unicellular algae among the hyphae of the fungus.

Figure 14.15. Cross sections of two mycorhizas, hickory on the left and pine on the right. Note the interwoven fungal hyphae around the root tissues. (Redrawn from *Plant Ecology* by W. B. McDougall with the permission of the publishers, Lea & Febiger.)

may be considered as symbiotic, since most domesticated plants and animals could not survive without man's care, having been selected for desirable commercial qualities rather than for characteristics contributing toward survival in nature.

FOOD CHAINS AND ENERGY TRANSFERS

The final dependence of all living things on photosynthetic or chemosynthetic organisms has already been pointed out (Chapter 10). In a forest, grassland, desert, lake, ocean (24), or any other natural community, photosynthetic plants provide the basic food supply and constitute the broad base of the ecological pyramid (Fig. 14.16). At the second level are organisms that secure their food directly from the plants, including herbivorous animals and many different kinds of organisms living on the plants as parasites or symbionts. At the third level are carnivorous animals that use the herbivorous animals and other second-level organisms as food, including the parasites of these second-level organisms. At the fourth and subsequent levels are carnivorous animals that live on other carnivores, and again, parasites. Finally, the saprophytic bacteria and fungi and the scavenger animals live on the remains of dead plants or animals.

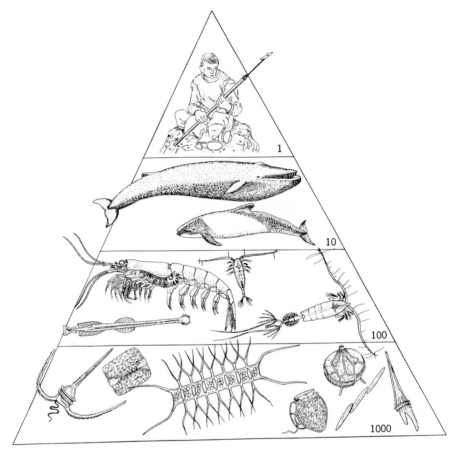

Figure 14.16. This simplified food pyramid of Antarctic life begins with microscopic floating algae (plankton) and ends with man. The energy loss at each step is about 90%. 1000 pounds of plant plankton support 100 pounds of animal plankton, 10 pounds of whale, and 1 pound of man. (Redrawn from the *Scientific American*, January 1958, with the permission of the publishers.)

As food is transferred through the food chain and up through the pyramid, it is reduced in quantity at each successive level, since all organisms use a considerable portion of their food supply in respiration. The energy freed from foods by respiration and expended by each organism is also lost as far as the next level of consumer organisms are concerned, so that at each step up the pyramid a smaller and smaller portion of the energy originally derived from sunlight during photosynthesis is still available. Consequently, the total bulk of organisms at any level in the food pyramid is less than in the next lower level.

In a plant-herbivore-carnivore food chain there is also an increase in size of the animals and a decrease in their numbers as the food pyramid is ascended from one level to the next. Food chains leading from hosts to parasites, however, go in the reverse direction, from a few larger organisms to many smaller ones.

Each biological community has only a limited level of productivity, dependent in the final analysis on the amount of photosynthesis possible in the community, and there is a definite limit to the total bulk of living organisms that can be supported at each level in the food pyramid (3, 24). In a mature and balanced community the actual bulk of organisms at each level is at the possible maximum.

The food pyramid is applicable, in a modified form, to man and his agricultural plants and animals as well as to natural biological communities. Since man is herbivorous as well as carnivorous he may be considered to belong to both the second and third levels of the agricultural food pyramid. None of our domestic animals is strictly carnivorous (although some of our seafood is), so the agricultural food pyramid does not extend beyond the third level, unless we wish to consider human parasites. In accordance with the general principles of food chains and pyramids, any region can support a larger human population if the bulk of the food supply comes directly from the crop plants rather than indirectly through meat, milk, eggs, and other animal products. In many parts of Asia and other regions where there is a pressure of the population on the food supply, the great bulk of the human food consists of rice and other plant products. There humans are living almost entirely at the second food level.

During the past century the rate of increase of the human population of the Earth has greatly accelerated (Fig. 14.17), principally as a result of the prolongation of life by application of the medical sciences. If the present rapid rate of population increase continues for another century or so, world wide starvation may result, since even with the most intensive cultivation of all available land areas, increased use of food from the oceans, and the culture of algae as food sources, it is unlikely that sufficient food can be produced on Earth to support the prospective human population (9, 18, 26, 27). For one thing, it has been noted that any increase in food supply of underdeveloped countries merely results in further population increases. At the very least, our descendents may be forced to secure essentially all of their food directly from plants as people do now in many parts of Asia. As the population continues to increase, more and more land will be taken out of cultivation, just when it is needed most, by the encroachment of cities and highways. Even if it were possible to raise enough food to keep everyone alive at a subsistence level the time will come (within the next century according to several estimates) when there will simply not be enough room on earth

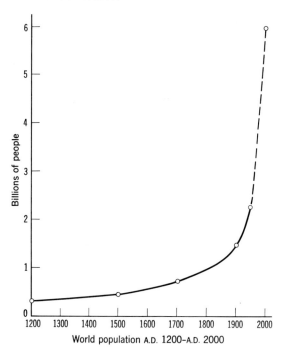

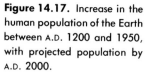

Figure 14.17. Increase in the human population of the Earth between A.D. 1200 and 1950, with projected population by A.D. 2000.

World population A.D. 1200–A.D. 2000

for everyone if the present rate of human population increase continues. Many students of the population problem have come to the conclusion that the only effective and humane solution is a decrease in the birth rate.

Although saprophytic bacteria and fungi and perhaps scavenger animals may be considered to operate somewhat outside the main food pyramid, they play a very important role in the general biological system by consuming dead organisms and converting their constituent substances into simple compounds such as carbon dioxide, ammonia, water, and mineral salts that can be used by green plants and so may again flow through a food chain. Wood-rotting fungi and termites may, for example, be regarded as destructive organisms by man, but in nature they play useful roles.

While the flow of matter through organisms is cyclic, any particular atom moving from the environment into organisms, from one organism to another, and back into the environment many times, the flow of energy through a biological community is a one-way process. Light energy transformed into chemical bond energy during photosynthesis is eventually converted to heat energy that is then dissipated and lost to the community. Some of this heat is a direct product of respiration, and the remainder is produced after the energy in ATP has been utilized in doing useful work in organisms.

BIOLOGICAL CHECKS AND BALANCES

Food chains have another important aspect: they serve as a system of biological checks that, along with other biological interactions, contribute toward the establishment of balanced plant and animal communities. Every species has a much greater reproductive potential than is ever realized in nature, principally because so many individuals are consumed by animals or killed by parasites. Without these checks on its population increase, almost any species might well increase in numbers to epidemic proportions, limited only by the availability of food and a suitable physical environment. In a climax community, however, the checks imposed by the food chain result in a remarkably stable population level for each species in the community, generation after generation.

Disturbed Biological Balances

The biological balance of a plant and animal community is delicate, and may be upset by any substantial change in the physical environment, the partial or complete removal of one or more of the species making up the community, or the addition of species from other regions into the community. Any disturbance of a balanced community results in the initiation of a succession (Chapter 7) that eventually leads to the establishment of a new balanced climax community, although hundreds of years may be required for completion of the succession. The problems of conservation of our biological resources result largely from disturbance of natural biological balances by man.

UPSETTING BIOLOGICAL BALANCES BY
ALTERING THE PHYSICAL ENVIRONMENT

We have already mentioned several ways that man may alter the physical environment, and all of these may result in some degree of disruption of the natural biological balances (22). A specific example may help to emphasize the degree to which man may upset a natural community by a relatively minor disturbance of the physical environment. Previous to 1918, Currituck Sound on the North Carolina coast was a sportsman's paradise. It teemed with fish and served as a winter feeding ground for ducks and geese, both the fish and the birds living on the numerous submerged water plants. In 1918 the sea-level locks of the canal connecting the Sound with the waters around Norfolk, Virginia were removed. This made it possible for the north winds to blow brackish, sewage-laden water into the Sound from the Norfolk

399

area. This brackish water also contained numerous small jellyfish that covered and smothered the water plants of the Sound. As the plants died, soil from the bottom of the Sound that had been held in place by the roots became stirred up and made the water muddy. The mud and sewage cut off much of the light from the few remaining plants, reducing their rate of photosynthesis so greatly that the plants starved. With their food supply gone and the oxygen content of the water reduced, the fish died and the ducks and geese went to other feeding grounds. By the mid-twenties, disruption of the balance of life in the Sound was complete, ruining an investment of over $5,000,000 and the means of livelihood of around 10,000 people in a region that had been a favorite hunting and fishing area for thousands of sportsmen each year. Years of painstaking biological study were required to clarify the series of causes and effects that resulted in the disappearance of the water plants, fish, and game birds. Once the situation was understood the army engineers were persuaded to restore the locks, and by 1943 the water life of the Sound was again flourishing.

Natural geological processes such as erosion, deposition, and the submergence or emergence of land masses, as well as major long range changes in climate may have even more extensive disruptive effects on biological communities than the activities of man. For example, the forest trees occupying the southwestern part of what is now the United States several thousand years ago died when the region became more arid and were replaced by desert vegetation. About 3,000 years ago the area now occupied by Ohio, Indiana, and Illinois became much drier than it had been and as the forests died out they were replaced by extensions of the western grasslands. When the climate once again became more humid, the grasslands in turn gave way to forests, except in isolated areas where the soil factors and topography favored the survival of the grasses. These prairie patches were a striking feature of the natural landscape before most of the region was placed under cultivation.

UPSETTING THE BIOLOGICAL BALANCE BY SUBTRACTION

We shall cite only a few of the many examples of disturbed biological balances resulting from removal of one or more species from a community. In Sumatra a good many years ago tigers were killing rather substantial numbers of people and domestic animals, so a systematic program of tiger extermination was begun. The extermination was so successful that wild pigs, an important source of food for the tigers, became very numerous and consumed most of the young palm trees. As the older trees died the palm tree population declined so greatly that the natives, who relied heavily on the palms for both food and shelter, became impoverished.

Another incident occurred in a London park, where wasps were exterminated because they had become a nuisance to park visitors. Soon the grass in the park began to die. At first there seemed to be no connection between the two events, but investigation by biologists revealed that the two events were related. The wasps had been keeping crane flies under control, and since the crane fly larvae lived on grass roots the increased crane fly population injured the grass seriously.

In our own country many upset balances, perhaps less spectacular than the ones just mentioned but at least as serious, have resulted from the destruction of native organisms. The killing of carnivorous animals such as wolves and foxes has resulted in increased numbers of rabbits, squirrels, and mice and consequent extensive damage to both native and cultivated plants. Destruction of birds and snakes results in an increase in plant-destroying insects. Although most native birds are now protected by law, birds may be poisoned by eating poisoned insects. Widespread use of insecticides may also kill useful insects such as bees and insects parasitic on the insects that attack plants, thus further upsetting the natural balance. This may result in the use of even larger quantities of insecticides to control the insect pests of plants and so the still further reduction in the organisms exerting biological control over the harmful insects.

UPSETTING BIOLOGICAL BALANCES BY ADDITION

In the fifteenth century, Portuguese settlers brought goats to the island of St. Helena, then covered with dense forests. The goats flourished to such an extent that they were soon consuming all the young trees as well as other low growing plants. As the older trees died or were cut down the forests gradually disappeared, the fertile soil eroded into the ocean, and the entire biological balance was destroyed. Similar situations exist in our own country where forests are too heavily grazed, and many people are concerned over the probable eventual results of granting grazing rights in our national forests.

In Jamaica, rats became serious pests when they invaded the island from ships, and so the mongoose was imported from India to destroy the rats. The mongoose did such a thorough job of this that it soon had to turn to poultry, native game birds, and snakes for food. The decrease in the populations of these insectivorous animals in turn resulted in a great increase in insects and extensive destruction of both native and cultivated plants. Within a period of about twenty years both the biological balance and economy of the island were seriously

Figure 14.18. *Above:* typical Australian scene showing extent of spread of the introduced prickly pear cactus. *Below:* this area was formerly as thickly covered with prickly pear cactus

affected by the introduction of a pest and a well-meaning but misdirected attempt at biological control of the pest.

Australia has been particularly unfortunate in having its biological balances upset by the introduction of foreign plants and animals. In 1840 a Dr. Carlyle took some prickly pear cactus plants to Australia and planted them in his yard. Since the environment was favorable and since none of the natural enemies of the cactus had been brought with it, the cactus plants flourished and spread rapidly. By 1916 cactus had overrun some 23,000,000 acres of land, making them unsuitable for cultivation or grazing, and was spreading at the rate of over a million acres a year. Biologists have now been able to bring the cactus under control by introducing an insect that in its larval stage lives in and destroys the cactus (Fig. 14.18). Here, biological control has been effective, as is biological control in general if it is well planned in advance.

Water cress, introduced into Australia from England, has also become a pest and is so dense in even the larger streams that it hinders navigation. In England, water cress flourishes in only the smaller streams, for it is kept under control by its natural enemies. Still another introduced pest in Australia is a species of rabbit that, despite extensive hunting and long fences designed to restrict its extension, has spread over the country in immense numbers, causing extensive damage to crops and native plants. Biological control by the introduction of a parasite causing a serious disease of the rabbits finally seemed to be solving the problem, but the few rabbits immune to the disease are now repopulating the country.

Many of our serious plant and animal pests, including weeds, plant diseases, insects, and undesirable birds such as starlings and English sparrows are introductions from other countries where the natural biological controls keep them from being serious pests. Efforts at biological control are not always successful in their new environment. In Japan one of the most effective enemies of the Japanese beetle is a wasp, but efforts to introduce the wasp into the northeastern United States to control the beetle have failed since the wasp can not survive our cold winters as it can the relatively mild Japanese winters. The Japanese beetle is particularly destructive since it attacks so many species of plants; the adults eat leaves and fruits and the larvae attack the roots of plants.

The problems resulting from disturbed biological balances are undoubtedly among the most important of all practical biological prob-

---

as the one above, but the cactus plants were killed by the parasitic cactus moth introduced as a means of biological control of the cactus. (Courtesy of Biological Section, Department of Public Lands, Brisbane, Australia.)

lems, and are being given much consideration by ecologists as well as by conservationists and agricultural scientists. Our fundamental knowledge of the complex interrelations existing in biological communities is gradually increasing, but it is still far from complete, particularly in regard to specific situations. Unfortunately, much of the knowledge we do have is not applied and man is still disturbing biological balances with serious results.

▶ *Questions*

1. Give as many possible explanations as you can for the fact that many of the low-growing forest plants fail to thrive or survive when transplanted to a lawn. What sort of experiments might be devised to determine which factors are operating in a particular instance?

2. Under what conditions might the killing of plants by insects be either biologically or economically desirable?

3. Suggest some possible measures that might be taken to prevent the spread of witchweed from the Carolinas to other parts of the country and to hold it in check or eliminate it.

4. What would be the effects on the biological balances if all parasites could be eradicated? Could balanced plant and animal communities exist if there were no parasites? Why?

5. How could it be determined whether, in a particular kind of lichen, the alga and fungus are symbiotic or the fungus is simply parasitic upon the alga?

6. Show the connection between these two facts: (*a*) Gases are more soluble in cold water than warm water. (*b*) Eskimos are able to survive in relatively barren polar regions.

▶ *References*

For Reference

1. Dodge, B. O. and H. W. Rickett, *Diseases and Pests of Ornamental Plants.* New York: Ronald Press, 1948.
2. McDougall, W. B., *Plant Ecology*, 2nd ed. Philadelphia; Lea & Febiger, 1931.
3. Odum, Eugene P., *Fundamentals of Ecology*, 2nd ed. Philadelphia; W. B. Saunders Co., 1959.

For Reading

4. Ainsworth, G. C., Fungous diseases of man and animals. *New Biology* 27, 1958.
5. Beck, Stanley D., An insect and a plant. *Scientific American* 198(5):87–94, May 1958. (The corn borer and corn)
6. Bernstein, Joseph, Nature's own chemical warfare. *Natural History* 63:120–127, 1954. (Antibiotics in nature)
7. Bonner, James, Chemical warfare among the plants. *Scientific American* 180(3):48–51, 1949. Chemistry in plant societies. *Natural History* 68:508–513, 1959.
8. Burkholder, Paul R., Cooperation and conflict among primitive organisms. *American Scientist* 40:601–631, 1952.
9. Deevey, Edward S., Jr., The human population. *Scientific American* 203(3):194–204, September 1960.
10. Dobzhansky, T. and João Murca-Pires, Strangler trees. *Scientific American* 190(1):78–80, January 1954.
11. Eleazer, J. M., Witchweed invades America. *Science Digest* 43(6):69–73, June 1958.
12. Grave, E. V., A plant that captures animals under water. *Natural History* 66:74–77, 1957.
13. Harley, J. L., The mycorhiza of forest trees. *Endeavour* 15:43–48, 1956.
14. Holloway, James K., Weed control by insect. *Scientific American* 197(1):56–62, July 1957.
15. Hovanitz, Wm., Insects and plant galls. *Scientific American* 201(5):151–162, November 1959.
16. Hutchins, Ross E., Dodder—a vampire plant. *Natural History* 64:378–381, 1955.
17. Hutchins, Ross E., Ants that grow mushrooms. *Natural History* 65:476–481, 1956. Acacia's an ant palace. *Natural History* 66:496–499, 1957.
18. Huxley, Julian, World population. *Scientific American* 194(3):64–76, March 1956.
19. Kennedy, J. S., Aphids and plant growth. *New Biology* 11:50, 1951.
20. Lamb, I. M., The remarkable lichens. *Natural History* 67:86–93, 1958. Lichens. *Scientific American* 201(4):144–156, October 1959.
21. Maio, J. J., Predatory fungi. *Scientific American* 199(1):67–72, July 1958. (Discusses nematode-trapping fungi)
22. Milne, Louis J. and Margery, The eelgrass catastrophe. *Scientific American* 184(1):52–55, January 1951.
23. Palmer, E. Laurence, Common galls of woody plants. *Nature Magazine* 40:305–312, 1947.
24. Pequegnat, Willis E., Whales, plankton, and man. *Scientific American* 198(1):84–90, January 1958.
25. Redfield, A. C., The biological control of the chemical factors of the environment. *American Scientist* 46:205–221, 1958.
26. Sax, Karl, *Standing Room Only: The Challenge of Overpopulation.* New York: Beacon Press, 1955.
27. Sears, Paul, Where is the population boom taking us? *Science Digest* 48(2):14–20, August 1960.

Section IV. FROM GENERATION TO GENERATION

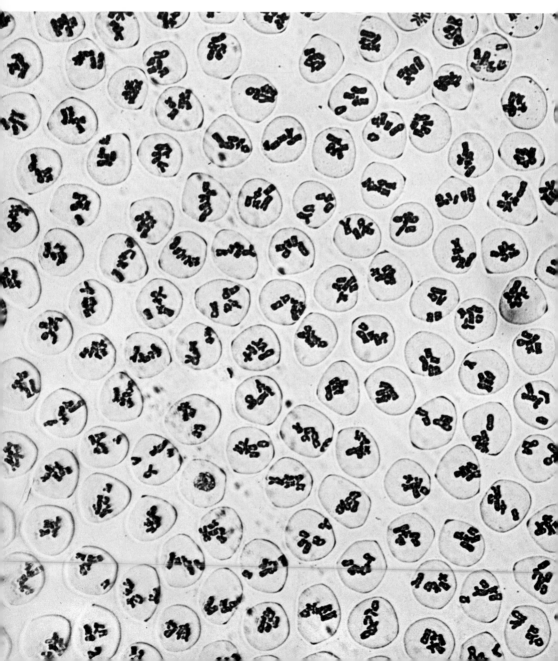

15. Asexual Reproduction

P ERHAPS NO OTHER SINGLE FEATURE distinguishes living organisms from nonliving things better and more completely than the capacity of every species for reproduction. Without it life would continue for only a single generation since every living individual is faced with eventual death, whether after a life of only a few days or thousands of years. Reproduction is also the means of increasing the population of a species, and plants are generally dependent on dispersal of reproductive structures such as seeds and spores for movement from one favorable habitat to another. Reproduction plays at least one other important role: the hereditary variations associated with reproduction have played a major role in the evolution of the numerous and diverse plant and animal species inhabiting the Earth.

In this section we shall focus our attention on the reproductive continuity of plant life from generation to generation, the associated transmission of hereditary potentialities from parent to offspring, and the evolution through the ages of new plant species as a result of changes in these hereditary potentialities.

Sexual and Asexual Reproduction

Basically, reproduction is detachment of a cell or group of cells from the parent and their development into a new individual. If reproduction is **sexual,** one detached cell must unite with another before development of the new individual proceeds. In **asexual** reproduction there is no fusion of cells; the detached cells, tissues or organs develop directly into new individuals. Like most species of animals, the great majority of plant species can reproduce sexually, and we shall consider the sexual reproduction of plants in the following chapter. Unlike most animals, many plants can reproduce asexually as well as sexually, whereas many species of plants that do not have asexual reproduction in nature are propagated asexually by man. Only a few kinds of plants, including the bacteria, blue-green algae, and some fungi, are propagated entirely by asexual reproduction, and it now appears that even these structurally simple organisms may possess some rudiments of sexual reproduction. Several species of vascular plants, mostly cultivated ones, are sterile and do not produce seeds even though they have flowers. Such plants, including cultivated bananas, seedless grapes, seedless citrus fruits, and most sweet potatoes are propagated vegetatively (asexually).

Sexual and asexual reproduction differ greatly in the degree of hereditary variation associated with them. Offspring reproduced sexually rarely have the same assortment of hereditary potentialities (genes) as either parent, and so they differ from the parents in many hereditary traits even though they possess the general characteristics of the species. On the other hand, plants reproduced asexually are really just a detached portion of the parent, and except for rather rare mutations have exactly the same hereditary potentialities as the parent. The descendents of an individual produced asexually, even though they may number in the thousands, may be regarded as extensions of the single individual and are referred to as a **clone.** Thus, since apple trees are propagated vegetatively by grafting, every Winesap apple tree on Earth is really just a part of the original Winesap tree. Winesap apple trees constitute one clone, Delicious apple trees another.

Asexual Reproduction of Nonvascular Plants

The algae, fungi, bacteria, and bryophytes all include species that reproduce asexually by a variety of methods (3). We shall consider some of the more important ones here.

FISSION

Bacteria and unicellular algae and fungi, as well as protozoa in the animal kingdom, generally reproduce by a process known as **fission** (Figs. 15.1, 15.2). Fission is the simplest possible type of reproduction,

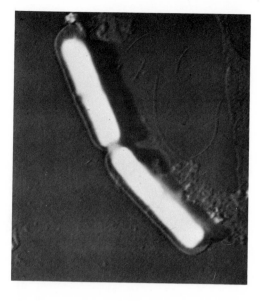

Figure 15.1. Electromicrograph showing a bacterium (*Bacillus subtilis*) undergoing fission. Magnified 10,800 times. (Courtesy of E. R. Squibb & Co.)

consisting merely of cell division, the two cells produced by the division separating instead of remaining attached as do dividing cells in a multicellular plant or animal. Each cell resulting from fission is a new individual, the only growth being the enlargement of the new cells to the size of the parent cell. Since the parent cell now exists only as part of each of the offspring, all individuals produced by fission may be considered to be "orphans." On the other hand, since there is no such thing as old age or death from old age, organisms reproducing by fission may be considered to have a sort of immortality.

Reproduction by fission may be quite rapid. Under good conditions some bacteria divide every 20 minutes. If this rate were maintained for 12 hours, a single cell would have almost 68 billion descendents. However, such rapid increases in population are only theoretically possible, since many individuals die or fail to divide as food and water become exhausted and toxic waste products of metabolism accumulate. Despite this, the actual population increases are frequently very rapid.

BUDDING

Yeasts reproduce by a modified type of fission known as **budding**. In budding the offspring cells are smaller than the parent cell and may remain attached to the parent cell for some time (Fig. 2.13, 15.2). The daughter cells may in turn produce a still smaller cell before becoming separated, thus forming a short chain of cells. Eventually all the cells separate and enlarge to the size of the parent cell. In budding, the

409

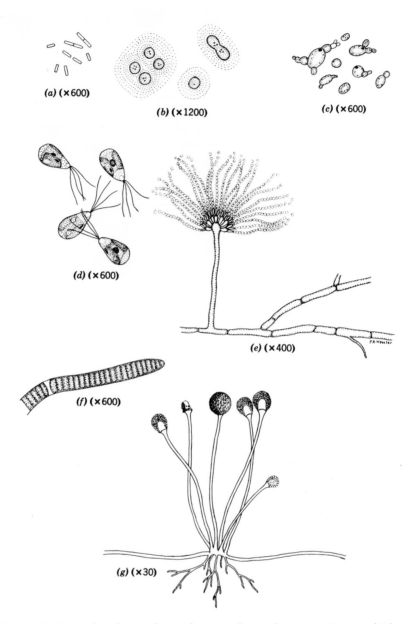

(a) (×600)

(b) (×1200)

(c) (×600)

(d) (×600)

(e) (×400)

(f) (×600)

(g) (×30)

Figure 15.2. Examples of asexual reproduction in lower plants. (*a*) Bacteria dividing by fission. (*b*) Unicellular blue-green algae (*Gleocapsa*) reproducing by fission. Several cells may be held together by the gelatinous sheath for a time. (*c*) Yeast cells budding. (*d*) Zoospores of a green alga (*Ulothrix*). (*e*) Conidia being produced by an *Aspergillus* mold. (*f*) Fragmentation of a blue-green alga (*Oscillatoria*). The clear heterocyst separates the two hormogonia. (*g*) Sporangia and spores of the bread mold, *Rhizopus*.

parent cells thus retain their identity, unlike parent cells reproducing by fission.

SPORULATION

True asexual **spores** are found only among the algae and fungi; the spores of the common bread mold (Fig. 15.2) are a good example. The spores of the bread mold and a good many other fungi are borne within a **sporangium;** other fungi such as some species of *Penicillium* and *Aspergillus* (Fig. 15.2) bear their spores in chains of cells that become detached as they mature. Such spores are called **conidiospores** or simply **conidia.** Aquatic algae and fungi generally produce motile spores (**zoospores**) that swim through the water by means of very slender filaments called **flagella** (Fig. 15.2). The flagella (4) contain fibers that apparently contract in a rhythmical sequence, causing the flagellum to move in a whiplike fashion. Flagellar movement requires energy from respiration, and the energy transfer mechanism may be quite similar to that of muscle contraction. The few kinds of flagella that have been investigated all have eleven contractile fibers, and it is rather interesting that the flagella of plant sperm, protozoa, and other flagellated animal cells, as well as the tails of animal sperm, all seem to have the same number and arrangement of contractile fibers as the flagella of zoospores.

An individual plant usually produces from hundreds to millions of spores, aerial spores generally being produced in greater numbers than zoospores (5, 6). Although most of the zoospores produced by a plant may germinate and grow into a new individual, only a small portion of the aerial spores are generally deposited by air currents in environments suitable for the germination and growth of the spores. Because of the immense numbers of aerial spores produced, however, they provide an effective reproductive mechanism and in view of the small quantity of protoplasm in each spore the failure of most of the spores to germinate is not particularly wasteful. Most spores are single cells, although a few species of fungi have spores composed of two or more cells.

The term *spore* has, unfortunately, been used for several different kinds of plant cells playing various roles in life cycles, including the thick-walled resistant spores that permit survival of some bacteria, algae, and fungi through periods of unfavorable environment such as extreme desiccation or high temperature, and certain cells (**zygospores**) resulting from sexual fusion. The most widespread kind of spores in the plant kingdom are the **meiospores,** which are produced by reduction divisions (Chapter 16) and which are really a stage in the sexual reproduction of plants. The spores of bryophytes and of the ferns and other vascular plants are all meiospores, as are some of the spores produced by algae

411

and fungi. None of these various types of spores are the true asexual spores that have been considered here.

VEGETATIVE PROPAGATION

The term *vegetative propagation* is sometimes used more or less synonymously with *asexual reproduction;* however, we shall use it here to include those types of asexual reproduction involving the detachment of a multicellular mass from the parent plant. **Fragmentation** by multicellular algae or fungi, particularly filamentous types, into two or more individuals may be considered as vegetative propagation. Although fragmentation is frequently accidental, some filamentous blue-green algae have specialized enlarged, thick-walled dead cells (**heterocysts**) at intervals along their filaments (Fig. 15.2) that are associated with fragmentation. The filaments separate at the heterocysts, thus propagating the species. Many fungi, particularly species that grow saprophytically in the soil, spread over large areas through the continued growth of their hyphae and any separation of hyphae from the parent plant results in a new individual, although one that is still a member of the clone. Cultivated mushrooms are generally propagated, not by spores, but by portions of the culture medium containing hyphae of the mushroom, referred to as **spawn**.

Several kinds of nonvascular plants have specialized structures involved in vegetative propagation. For example, liverworts may produce small bud-like structures called **gemmae** within cup-shaped organs (Fig. 15.3). The gemmae eventually break loose from their stalks and may be washed by rains to locations where they may grow into new

Figure 15.3. A liverwort showing gemmae cups and gemmae. The gemmae become detached and may be transported to other places where they may grow into a new plant. (From *Essentials of Plant Biology,* by Frank D. Kern, through the courtesy of the author and with the permission of the publisher, Harper and Brothers.)

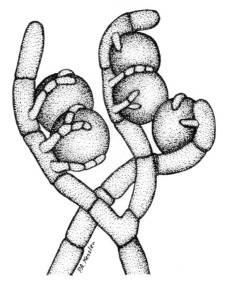

Figure 15.4. Soredia of a lichen, consisting of a few algal cells and fungal hyphae. The soredia become detached from the lichen and serve as a means of propagating the compound organism as a unit.

plants. Lichens produce reproductive bodies known as **soredia** (Fig. 15.4), which consist of a small cluster of both the fungal hyphae and the algal cells that constitute the lichen. This results in the reproduction of the composite "organism" as a unit.

Asexual Reproduction of Vascular Plants

All the various kinds of asexual reproduction found among the vascular plants may be considered as forms of vegetative propagation. Any of the organs of a vascular plant—stems, leaves, roots, and even flowers—may be involved in vegetative propagation. The most convenient way of classifying the types of vegetative propagation found among the vascular plants is on the basis of the organ concerned.

PROPAGATION BY STEMS AND BUDS

Perhaps the most common type of vegetative propagation occurs in plants with horizontal stems growing either above ground (**runners or stolons**) or underground (**rhizomes**). Plants with stolons include the strawberry (Fig. 15.5), the creeping buttercup, Kudzu vines, St. Augustine grass, and hen and chickens (*Saxifraga sarmentosa*). Many different species of plants have rhizomes; among them are most ferns, iris (Fig. 15.5), lilies of the valley, wild morning-glories, cattails, sedges, water hyacinth, blueberries, bananas, and numerous species of grasses. Both

413

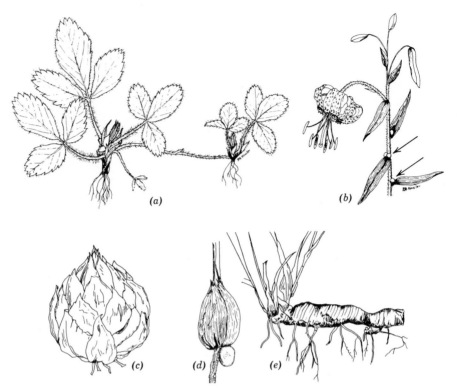

Figure 15.5. Several types of vegetative propagation by stems. (*a*) The runners (stolons) of a strawberry plant. (*b*) The modified axillary buds (bulbils) of the tiger lily. (*c*) A lily bulb. (*d*) A *Freesia* corm. (*e*) An Iris rhizome.

stolons and runners produce aerial shoots and adventitious roots at their nodes, or sometimes at alternate nodes as in the strawberry, and so the plants spread over extensive areas. Many of the dominant grasses of our natural grasslands have rhizomes that undoubtedly contribute to the rapid spread and dominant position of these species in the community. Many of the beach grasses also have stolons or rhizomes. As long as the stolons or rhizomes remain intact, the entire colony is really still only one individual plant, even though it may cover a considerable area and include many spaced and apparently independent shoots. When, however, some of the connecting stolons or rhizomes die or are accidentally severed, we may consider that a new individual has been added to the clone and that vegetative propagation, rather than just the spread of an individual plant, has occurred.

Several plants including the Irish potato and the Jerusalem artichoke are propagated vegetatively by **tubers** (Fig. 15.9), the thickened, fleshy ends of rhizomes. Since the aerial shoots, the roots, and the rhizomes of tuber-bearing plants usually die at the end of the growing season, the isolated tubers may each give rise to a new individual the following season and so serve as a true means of vegetative propagation.

Some plants such as raspberries, dewberries, wild roses, currants, and gooseberries have long slender stems that may droop and touch the ground. When this occurs, adventitious roots develop from one of the nodes near the stem tip and the bud grows into an upright stem (Fig. 15.10). Although this is called **tip layering** it is not basically different from the development of roots and shoots at the node of a stolon. Almost impenetrable thickets of raspberries or dewberries may arise from tip layering.

The submerged water plant, *Elodea*, is propagated vegetatively by the fragmentation of its fragile stems. Fragmentation of the stems of cacti is rather common, the broken-off stem segments falling to the ground and rooting. Stems may also be broken off willow trees growing along stream banks, and if the end of the stem happens to become immersed in the soft mud of the banks, roots will usually develop and the twig may grow into a tree.

Tiger lilies and some other species of lilies produce compact, spherical axillary buds superficially resembling seeds (Fig. 15.5). These buds abscise and fall to the ground, where they may develop into new plants. **Bulbs** (Fig. 15.5), such as those of onions, tulips, and lilies, are essentially large buds and provide a means of vegetative propagation. Bulbs form small branch bulbs that eventually develop to full size and grow into new individuals. Although bulbs are generally underground structures, onions may develop aerial bulbs in addition to their usual underground bulbs. **Corms,** the short, fleshy vertical underground stems of a number of species including gladiolus and crocus, differ from bulbs in that they have more stem tissue and small scale leaves rather than large fleshy leaves (Fig. 15.5). Like bulbs, corms form branches that give rise to young plants.

PROPAGATION BY ROOTS

The horizontal roots of various plants, including the Canada thistle, milkweed, and many other weeds as well as a number of trees and shrubs such as beech, Osage orange, sumach, and elderberry, serve as a means of spread and vegetative propagation much as do stolons and rhizomes. The horizontal roots, however, form adventitious buds whereas the stolons and rhizomes form adventitious roots. Plants may spread over considerable areas with numerous shoots growing from their horizontal roots. When most hardwood trees are cut down, numerous sprouts develop from the stump and roots even though the

Figure 15.6. Sprouts developing from adventitious buds of a sweet potato root. The individual sprouts are separated from the root and planted.

species may not otherwise form adventitious shoots from the roots. The fleshy, clustered roots of plants such as sweet potatoes (Fig. 15.6), dahlias, and peonies also provide a means of vegetative propagation. Sweet potato roots form numerous adventitious buds that grow into new plants. Dahlia and peony roots, however, do not normally produce adventitious buds and so are effective in propagating the plants only when a portion of the stem is attached to the roots.

PROPAGATION BY LEAVES

Leaves are not as common a means of vegetative propagation in nature as are stems or even roots. However, several species of plants propagate vegetatively by means of their leaves. For example, when the tips of the long leaves of the walking fern come in contact with the ground they form adventitious buds and roots that grow into a new plant (Fig. 15.7). This may be considered as tip layering, comparable with the tip layering of stems. The fleshy leaves of the African violet, some species of begonia, and a number of other plants form adventitious buds and roots when removed from the plant and brought in contact with the soil. It is possible that in nature leaves accidentally broken from the plants may come in contact with the soil and give rise to young plants.

The most striking examples of leaf propagation are found in the genus *Kalanchoë* (*Bryophyllum*). In some species of this genus, well-formed tiny plants develop in the notches of the fleshy leaves even while the leaves are attached to the plant (Fig. 12.15). These plantlets abscise from the leaves and fall to the ground, where they take root and continue to grow into mature plants. The plantlets develop under long days, and flowers form only under short days. In some other species of *Kalanchoë*, the plantlets do not appear unless the leaves are removed from the plants.

The very small floating seed plants known as duckweeds commonly propagate vegetatively by the development of new individuals from their leaves. In the autumn small bulblets form on the leaves and sink to the bottom of the water. The following spring these bulblets rise to the surface and develop into mature plants. Duckweeds rarely produce flowers and seeds; some species practically never bloom.

VEGETATIVE PROPAGATION BY FLOWERS

Although flowers are primarily associated with the sexual reproduction of plants, various tissues of flowers may occasionally be involved

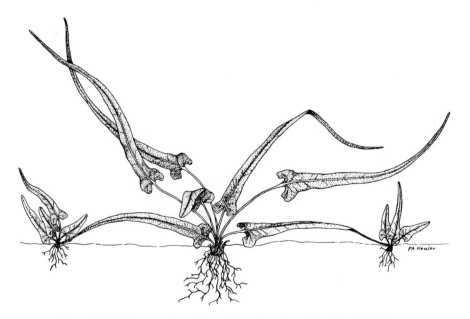

Figure 15.7. Propagation of the walking fern by tip layering of the leaves.

Figure 15.8. Aerial bulbs of an onion that developed on the pedicles of the inflorescence in place of some of the flowers. (Courtesy of J. Arthur Herrick, Kent State University.)

in vegetative propagation. The clustered aerial bulbs of onions (Fig. 15.8) actually arise from flower buds, and the flowers of some grasses may be replaced by vegetative propagules. In some species of plants, among them the dandelion, the eggs develop into embryo plants without fertilization. This is known as **parthenogenesis.** Since no fusion of sex cells is involved, parthenogenesis is really a form of asexual reproduction even though it is a modification of the normal pattern of sexual reproduction. At times embryo plants may arise from cells of the ovule other than an egg cell. The development of such cells into embryos is clearly a case of vegetative propagation. These embryos may occur in the seed along with an ordinary sexually produced embryo or may replace it.

REGENERATION IN RELATION TO VEGETATIVE PROPAGATION

In general, the vegetative propagation of plants is possible only because of the capacity of the propagating tissues or organs for forming either adventitious buds (that include, of course, stems and leaves) or adventitious roots or both. The formation of adventitious buds and roots, particularly in portions of plants lacking them, may be considered as examples of **regeneration.** Thus, when a detached twig developes adventitious roots it is regenerating the only lacking organ of an otherwise complete vegetative plant. The dependence of vegetative propagation on the regeneration of buds and roots is shown most clearly by the differing regenerative capacities of leaves of various species of plants. The leaves of a good many species of plants normally cannot form either adventitious buds or roots, whereas detached leaves of a good many other species readily form adventitious roots but no adventitious buds. Only leaves of the third type that can regenerate both buds and roots can, of course, serve as a means of vegetative propagation. Regeneration is not always associated with vegetative propagation. For example, the growth of sprouts from the stump of a tree is regeneration, but there is no propagation.

The capacity for regeneration and vegetative propagation are widespread throughout the plant kingdom, but only lower animals such as starfish, sponges, and some kinds of jellyfish and worms have great enough regenerative capacities to permit a portion of the animal to develop into a complete new individual and so undergo what is essentially "vegetative" propagation. Although some higher animals such as lobsters and salamanders can regenerate missing legs, most higher animals can regenerate nothing more than limited areas of skin and certain other tissues.

Vegetative Propagation as a Horticultural Practice

The propagation of our cultivated plants, along with the associated efforts to create and maintain desirable varieties, constitutes one of the most important aspects of agriculture and horticulture (1, 2). Most annual and biennial plants, including practically all farm crops and garden plants, are propagated sexually through seeds, but a very large portion of both herbaceous and woody perennials are commonly propagated vegetatively. For example, strawberries are propagated by runners, iris by division of the rhizomes, Irish potatoes by tubers, sweet potatoes by roots, tulips by bulbs, gladioli by corms, and African violets by leaves. Most or our ornamental shrubs are propagated by stem cuttings, and our orchard trees and roses are usually propagated by grafts. All these plants are propagated by seeds only as a means of developing new varieties.

ADVANTAGES OF VEGETATIVE PROPAGATION

The most obvious advantage of vegetative propagation as a horticultural practice is that it makes possible the propagation of plants such as bananas, seedless grapes, and citrus fruits, and the cultivated hydrangea and snowball bush that have lost their capacity for sexual reproduction. Other plants, including some kinds of Bermuda and Zoysia grasses, are propagated vegetatively because they produce only small quantities of seed. Another advantage of vegetative propagation is that some plants including lilies, tulips, and gladioli require several years to reach maturity when propagated by seeds, whereas they mature in a season or two when propagated vegetatively. Perhaps the most important advantage of vegetative propagation, however, is that all offspring propagated vegetatively have exactly the same hereditary potentialities as the parent plant, except in the rare cases of mutations, whereas great hereditary variation generally accompanies sexual reproduction. For example, if a thousand seeds from Winesap apples were planted, there would be only a slight chance of securing even a single tree bearing apples with all the characteristics of the Winesap variety. It might be possible to produce a variety of apples that would come true to form from seeds by means of an extensive breeding program designed to produce a considerable amount of hereditary uniformity (as has been done with beans, peas, wheat and other plants propagated by seeds), but the procedure would be lengthy, time-consuming and highly impractical. Whenever cultivated plants can conveniently and practicably be propagated vegetatively, this means of reproduction is used in preference to seeds because of the ease of maintaining desirable combinations of hereditary traits, even though the vegetative propagation possesses no other advantage. The availability of vegetative propagation for many plants frequently makes plant breeding a simpler procedure than animal breeding.

USE OF NATURAL METHODS OF VEGETATIVE PROPAGATION

Man makes use of all types of natural vegetative propagation already discussed, such as tubers, bulbs, rhizomes, runners, and fleshy roots. Frequently, procedures are employed that increase the effectiveness of the natural method. Thus, a potato tuber simply left in the ground will give rise to only one potato plant, but if the tuber is cut into pieces (Fig. 15.9), each piece will produce a plant providing that it contains a bud (an "eye"). In tulips and other bulbous plants the conical stem can be cut out from the under side of a bulb. Each scale then gives rise to a new bulb at its base, thus increasing the rate of propagation. The scale leaves are frequently removed from lily bulbs and planted

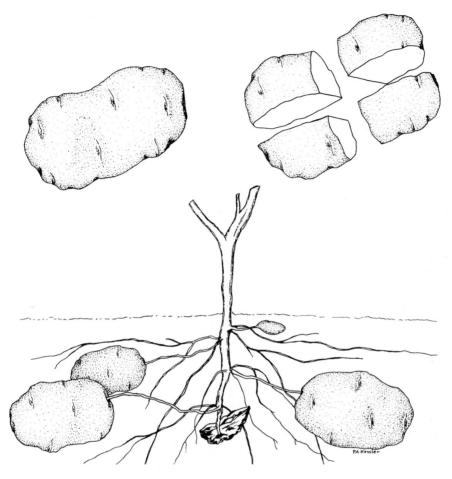

Figure 15.9. A portion of a potato plant showing roots, young tubers, and the piece of tuber from which the plant grew. Above, tubers used in propagating potatoes are cut into pieces, each with a bud, so more plants can be propagated from the tubers.

separately, a method that is really comparable with the leaf propagation of African violets and begonias. In addition to using natural methods of vegetative propagation, man has devised several extensively used methods that rarely, if ever, provide natural means of vegetative propagation. The most important of these artificial methods are **cuttings**, modified types of **layering**, and **grafting**.

PROPAGATION BY CUTTINGS

Although the division of any plant organ—roots, stems or leaves— into pieces for propagation may be considered as cutting, stem cuttings

421

are the type most commonly used (Fig. 12.10). Branches cut from many species of both woody and herbaceous plants will readily develop adventitious roots when placed in water or in a rooting medium such as moist sand or soil. Species that do not root readily can frequently be induced to root by treating the cuttings with dilute solutions of auxins (Fig. 12.10) or dusting the cut ends with powders containing auxins. Most ornamental shrubs, sugar cane, pineapple, and many greenhouse plants including chrysanthemum, coleus and geranium are propagated by stem cuttings.

PROPAGATION BY LAYERING

Layering differs from cutting in that the formation of adventitious roots or buds occurs before, rather than after, separation of the propagule from the parent plant. Some species that can not be propagated successfully by cuttings are readily propagated by layering. In addition to utilizing natural tip layering in propagating plants such as raspberries (Fig. 15.10), man has devised several modified types of layering such as **mound layering** and **air layering** (Fig. 15.11). In mound layering, the bottoms of the lower branches of a plant are covered with soil, and after adventitious roots have developed on the branches the rooted branches are cut off and planted. In air layering, a branch is first cut about half way through and from this cut a longitudinal slit is made about 3 inches upward through the center of the stem. The cut surfaces are then generally dusted with a powder containing auxin-

Figure 15.10. Propagation of a raspberry plant by tip layering.

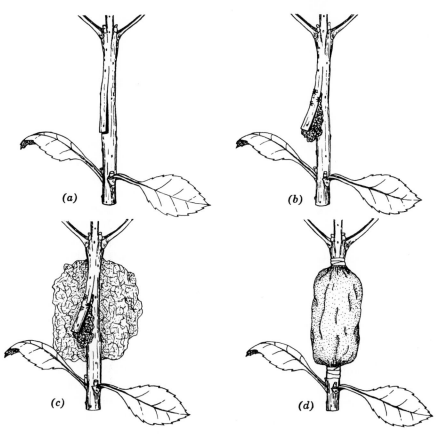

(a)

(b)

(c)

(d)

Figure 15.11. In air layering, a slit is made in the stem (a) and sphagnum moss is inserted under the flap (b) after the cut surfaces have been dusted with a powder containing auxin. The stem is then covered with moist sphagnum moss (c) and moisture-proof plastic (d). After adventitious roots have developed, the stem is cut off and planted. (Modified from *Introduction to Plant Science* by Northen, with the permission of the publishers, The Ronald Press.)

like growth substances. Moist sphagnum moss is then inserted between the cut surfaces and wrapped around the cut region of the branch. Finally, the ball of moss is wrapped with a sheet of polyethylene plastic. The plastic is permeable to oxygen but not to water, and so retains moisture. As in other types of layering, the branch is cut off and planted after adventitious roots have developed.

PROPAGATION BY GRAFTS

Grafting is essentially just another modified method of propagation by cuttings. The cuttings, instead of being rooted, are grafted to another plant of the same species or genus, but generally of a different variety. The cutting is known as the **scion**, and the plant to which it is grafted is known as the **stock**. The stock is generally secured by planting seeds and using the young plants that grow from the seeds or in some species the stocks may be produced by vegetative propagation. The stock provides the root system and the lower portion of the stem of the composite plant produced by grafting, and the scion generally provides the upper part of the main stem and all the branches. However, sometimes a portion of the shoot system of the stock is retained and scions of one or more other species or varieties are grafted to it, producing a plant bearing the flowers and fruits of several different varieties or species. Such composite plants are generally produced only as horticultural curiosities, although an apple or pear tree bearing several different varieties may be useful to a person with a small lot who wishes to produce an assortment of fruits in limited quantities for home consumption.

One of the principal advantages of grafts over cuttings is that a variety or species with a more vigorous, more rapidly growing, and more disease-resistant root system than that of the plant used as the scion may be selected for use as the stock. Thus, apples are usually grafted on wild apple stocks, roses on wild rose stocks, and lilacs on California privet stocks.

In making a graft, the stems of the stock and scion are cut so that they will closely dovetail into each other. A variety of cuts is employed (Fig. 15.12). The stems of the stock and scion need not be of the same diameter at the point of union, but the cambia of the two must be in close contact. After the stock and scion have been fitted together, the graft union is tied with waxed string and covered with wax to prevent drying out and the entrance of bacteria, fungi, or insects. Grafts are generally successful when the two plants used are in the same species or genus and when their rate of growth in diameter from the cambium is about the same. Successful grafts have been made, however, between different genera of the same family, as between pear and quince, tomato and potato, and tomato and tobacco, and a few grafts have been produced between members of different but related families. Grafting may be done either early in the growing season or in the winter while the plants are dormant.

The dwarf, early bearing fruit trees sold by nurseries are products of grafting. Certain kinds of stocks have a dwarfing effect on the scions. Quince stocks cause the dwarfing of pear scions, apricot stocks the dwarfing of peach scions, and certain varieties of apples the dwarfing of apple scions. Apple trees may also be dwarfed by grafting only a short piece of the stem of a dwarfing variety between the scion and a nondwarfing stock.

A modified type of grafting known as **budding** (Fig. 15.12) is used

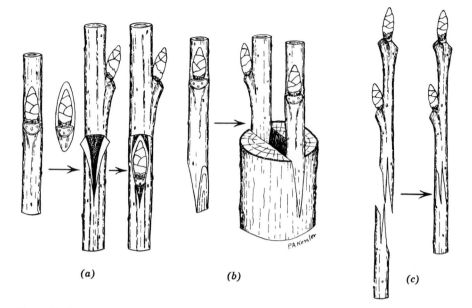

Figure 15.12. Budding and grafting. (a) A bud removed from the tree being propagated is inserted under the bark of the stock. (b) In cleft grafting, small scions are grafted onto a larger stock. (c) In tongue grafting the stock and scion are of the same size and are cut to fit tightly together. In all three procedures the cut surfaces are covered with grafting wax and tied securely together with waxed string.

extensively by nurserymen, budding being used almost exclusively for some species such as pecan. Budding differs from other types of grafting in that a bud rather than a developed branch is used as the scion. In budding a piece of bark containing the bud and at least some of the cambium is cut from the plant being propagated, inserted under a cut made in the bark of the stock, and tied and waxed. Branches growing from the buds of the stock must be cut off until the grafted bud assumes apical dominance and so prevents further development of buds of the stock.

Grafting is employed largely as a means of propagating horticultural plants, but it is sometimes useful as an experimental tool. For example, much information about the transmission of the floral stimulus in photoperiodism has been obtained by grafting photoperiodically induced plants to noninduced plants (page 329), whereas grafts between tobacco and tomato plants have revealed the fact that nicotine is synthesized in the roots of tobacco plants even though it accumulates in the leaves.

Like other methods of vegetative propagation of plants, grafting is an old horticultural practice, and many misconceptions about grafting have become prevalent. Perhaps the most common misconception is that grafting is a means of hybridizing plants, when as a matter of fact hybridization can occur only in the course of sexual reproduction. Except in the rare cases of mutations that may occur in the buds of plants whether they have been grafted or not, the hereditary potentialities of both the stock and scion remain exactly the same as they were before grafting. If it were not for this, grafting would be unsuitable as a means of propagating a certain species and variety of plant. The stock may, of course, influence the scion physiologically as in dwarfing or in the absence of nicotine in the leaves of tobacco scions grafted on tomato stocks.

Some of the misconceptions about grafting as a means of hybridization may have resulted from the fact that occasionally a bud developing at the graft union may be composed partly of cells from the stock and partly of cells from the scion. The resulting branch will then contain tissues derived from both plants. These composite shoots are known as **graft chimeras.** Chimeras may be of varied composition— the scion may contribute the epidermis and the stock the other tissues, or vice versa, or one side of a stem may be composed of stock cells and the other side may be composed of scion cells. Some of the flowers and fruits on a chimeral branch may develop from stock tissue, some from scion tissue, or perhaps from both, resulting in the presence of different kinds of flowers and fruits on the same branch. However, each cell of a chimera still retains exactly the same hereditary potentialities as the stock or scion that it came from.

► ## Questions

1. How would you go about producing a new variety of potato? How would you propagate the new variety?

2. What physiological differences might exist between a species of plant with leaves that can produce both adventitious roots and buds (and so can be used in propagating the plant) and another species with leaves that can develop adventitious roots but no adventitious buds? How might you go about trying to induce adventitious bud formation in leaves that do not naturally produce them? Some kinds of leaves form neither adventitious roots or buds. Would it be a waste of time to try to induce adventitious root and bud formation in these plants?

3. Since vegetative propagation has a number of advantages over propagation of plants by seeds, why are all cultivated plants not propagated vegetatively as a matter of course? What advantages do seeds have as a means of plant propagation?

4. Weed A occurs in large, dense patches that increase in size quite rapidly, but does not readily spread to new localities. Weed B occurs as more isolated plants and readily spreads to new localities at some distance. How is each weed propagated? Give examples of each type of weed.

5. Suppose that when vascular plants first evolved they all lost the capacity for sexual reproduction and reproduced themselves entirely by various methods of vegetative propagation. What effects would this have had on the plant life of the Earth? Would our present day vegetation be different from what it actually is, and if so, how? What influence would this have had on the origin and development of human civilization?

► ## *References*

For Reference

1. Hartmann, H. T. and D. E. Kester, *Plant Propagation: Principles and Practices.* Englewood Cliffs, N. J., Prentice-Hall, 1959.

2. Mahlstede, John P. and E. S. Haber, *Plant Propagation.* New York; John Wiley and Sons, 1957.

3. Robbins, W. W., T. Elliott Weier, and C. Ralph Stocking, *An Introduction to Plant Science.* New York; John Wiley and Sons, 1957, Chapters 17–20.

For Reading

4. Astbury, W. T., Flagella. *Scientific American* 184(1):20–31, January 1951.

5. Brodie, Harold J., Nature's splash guns. *Natural History* 61:403–407, 1952. (Spore discharge)

6. Ingold, C. T., Spore liberation in the higher fungi. *Endeavour* 16:78–83, 1957.

16. Sexual Reproduction

T HAT PLANTS REPRODUCE SEXUALLY was suspected in ancient times, when the practice of hanging clusters of "male flowers" in the date groves assured an abundant crop of fruit. However, the details of the process have been known for only a little over a hundred years.

Most species of plants reproduce sexually. The sexual method had simple beginnings in some of the very early members of the plant kingdom, and became more elaborate through evolutionary changes in many succeeding species. However, the elaboration entailed no changes in the basic nature of the process, but consisted principally of the development of structural refinements to surround the essential action. It is the purpose of the present chapter to trace the story of plant change as shown by the details of the sexual reproductive process in a series of selected species.

Selected Algae

The unicellular, motile green alga, *Chlamydomonas*, is an example of a primitive sexually reproducing form, which, like many others, also reproduces asexually. Asexual reproduction is effected by the division of the protoplast into two or four motile **zoospores** that are released by the breakdown of the parent cell wall. The liberated spores, morphologically like the parent, enlarge to adult size (Fig. 16.1*a,b,c*). Under certain conditions, however, the protoplast reproduces sexually by the division of the parent cell into eight cells resembling the asexual zoospores except for size. These smaller motile cells, called **gametes,** swim free for a time, then unite in pairs. The resultant product may continue to swim freely for a short time, during which two nuclei can be discerned in the cell. Finally it settles down, the two nuclei fuse, and a thick wall is secreted. This fusion product, called the **zygote,** ultimately germinates, releasing four motile zoospore-like cells. We shall call these by the distinctive name **meiospores,** even though they resemble ordinary spores, for a reason that will become clear later on. The meiospores enlarge to become adult *Chlamydomonas* plants like the original one (Fig. 16.1*a,d,e,f,g*). Occasionally, two adult plants may themselves act as gametes; that is, they fuse. The resultant zygote behaves as described previously.

The zygote is of special interest, for it develops not directly into a

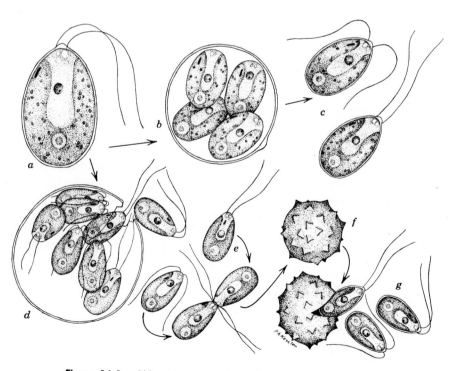

Figure 16.1. *Chlamydomonas.* Asexual and sexual reproduction.

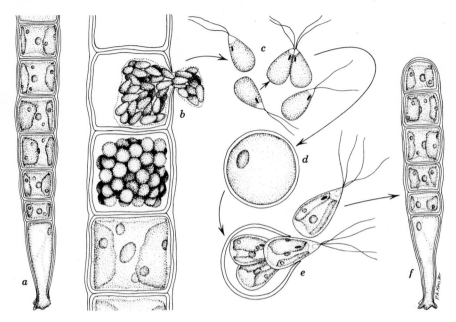

Figure 16.2. *Ulothrix.* Sexual reproduction.

new *Chlamydomonas* plant but, instead, into the four meiospores which, in their turn, become new plants. This is a special phase of the sexual reproductive process in plants to which we shall repeatedly refer. Before we discuss this in detail and comment on its significance, let us consider other algae.

The filamentous alga *Ulothrix* is a multicellular organism with simple structural differentiation (Fig. 16.2a). The filament, consisting of many cells, grows attached to the bottom of a stream by means of a specialized anchoring cell, or **holdfast.** The specialization of this cell is expressed not only in its form and function, but also in the fact that it is regularly without a chloroplast, and it does not contribute to growth or reproduction of the filament. The free-living, self-maintaining organism here is clearly the whole filament, not any single cell. It is therefore not a colony of independent cells, but truly a multicellular plant.

Ulothrix may reproduce asexually by the formation of 4 or 8 zoospores in any cell of the plant, except the basal one (10). Each spore has four anterior flagella. After a period of swimming, the spores settle down and divide transversely, the bottom cell becoming the holdfast. Further divisions in the upper cell give rise to the remainder of the filament.

In some circumstances, a cell of the filament may produce as many as 64 gametes (Fig. 16.2b). The gametes are strikingly similar to the spores, except that they are smaller and have only two flagella (Fig. 16.2c). If two gametes from different filaments meet, they promptly fuse. The resultant zygote develops a hard, thick wall and settles to the bottom of the stream where it may remain for a period of time (Fig. 16.2d). The zygote may be subjected to very low temperature and drying without evident injury. Under favorable conditions it may germinate, yielding 4 meiospores each with 4 flagella (Fig. 16.2e). New filaments arise from these.

In *Ulothrix* we again see the structural similarity of gametes and spores. The zygote is of special interest in view of its capacity to carry the plants over periods unfavorable to growth.

The filamentous alga, *Oedogonium*, in general structure and asexual reproduction resembles *Ulothrix* (Fig. 16.3a). In sexual reproduction, the protoplast of a cell of *Oedogonium* may in its entirety become organized as a single large gamete (**egg**) which remains within the cell (**oogonium**) (Fig. 16.3c). A group of 2 to several short cells (**antheridia**) are produced by division of other cells on the same or a different filament. Antheridia each yield 2 small motile gametes (**sperms**) which escape by the opening of the antheridial wall. The sperms are very similar to the zoospores, but smaller (Fig. 16.3b). One of the sperms gains entrance

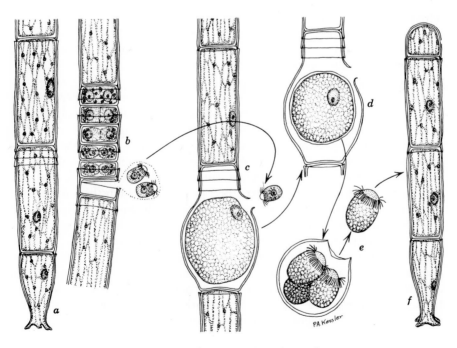

Figure 16.3. *Oedogonium.* Sexual reproduction.

431

into the oogonium through a pore, and fuses with the egg. The resultant zygote (Fig. 16.3d) develops a thick wall, is freed by rupture of the oogonial wall, and falls to the bottom where it remains dormant. Four meiospores, resembling the zoospores, are produced at germination of the zygote and after a period of swimming grow into new filaments (Fig. 16.3e,f).

In comparing the sexual behavior of *Oedogonium* with that of *Ulothrix*, a number of interesting innovations appear, even though the basic pattern is unaltered. First, the fusing gametes of *Oedogonium* are distinguishable, whereas those of *Ulothrix* are not. Morphologically similar gametes are termed **isogametes;** morphologically dissimilar gametes are **heterogametes.** *Oedogonium*, therefore, demonstrates a first step in sexual differentiation in the development of a large nonmotile egg (**megagamete**) and small, motile sperms (**microgametes**). The union of gametes occurs, in *Oedogonium*, within the egg-producing cell, not in the surrounding water as in *Ulothrix*.

The plants we have discussed were selected because they probably reflect the origins and early modifications of sexual reproduction in plants. A fact of special interest in the life cycles is the striking similarity, except in size, of the gametes and zoospores of the same species. In the isogamous species, both gametes resemble the spores; in the heterogamous species, the motile gamete (sperm) bears this resemblance. This fact gives rise to the theory that gametes were derived from spores, and that sexual reproduction probably originated with the fusion of two "small-sized spores." Similarly, the isogamous condition would be considered to have preceded the heterogamous.

If we think about the life cycle of such a plant as *Oedogonium*, we realize that it really consists of two recognizable **phases.** These phases are characterized by their contribution toward completion of the sexual cycle. One of these phases, the free-growing filament, is expressly given over to the production of gametes. The other phase, the zygote, contributes meiospores. These two distinctive structures occurring in the sexual life cycle of *Oedogonium* are not unrelated things, but are recognizable parts of an uninterrupted process in which the protoplasm of the plant temporarily exists in two different forms. For this reason we call these manifestations *phases* of a life cycle. Gametes are produced by a "gamete plant," and meiospores by a "meiospore plant." Translating into more usual botanical terminology, the gamete plant is the **gametophyte,** the meiospore plant is the **meiosporophyte,** which we shorten to **sporophyte.** Thus, in a sexual cycle a **gametophytic phase** is followed by a **sporophytic phase,** and as the countless new generations of *Oedogonium* appear, the regular unvarying alternation of these two phases continues.

Meiosis

Study has revealed that there are differences between the gameto-phytic phase and sporophytic phase more fundamental than external appearance. You will recall from Chapter 4 that, among other things, a species of plant is characterized by the number of chromosomes in its cells. Chromosome counts of both the sporophytic and gametophytic phases have been made for many species of plants. Typically, with but few exceptions, the sporophytic number is twice the gametophytic or, expressed symbolically, the sporophytic is **2n** or **diploid** (double) and the gametophytic **n** or **haploid** (single). In many species the chromo-somes making up the gametophytic complement are distinguishable, so that a definite assortment or set of chromosomes can be recognized. Thus the expression $2n$ is to be taken to indicate not merely twice the n number, but *two complete sets*. That is to say, each type (size, shape) is represented by a *pair*.

The gametophyte produces its gametes by ordinary mitoses, that is, by equational nuclear divisions. Therefore, the gametes will contain the n number of chromosomes. Sometimes the basic n number of chromosomes is called the **gametic number**. When, as a result of gametic fusion, the zygote is formed, it obviously will receive an n set from each gamete, and will therefore be $2n$. Since the meiospores produced by the zygote directly yield filaments with n chromosomes, the reduction of chromosome number from $2n$ to n obviously occurs at meiospore forma-tion. This is indeed the case, and of the two divisions required to pro-duce four meiospores, the first accomplishes the reduction. This operation is performed in an interesting manner (Fig. 16.4). Thus, when the chromosomes of the zygote assume the metaphase position on the spindle, the members of each pair become closely associated phys-ically. The physical association of members of a pair is spoken of as the pairing or **synapsis** of **homologous** chromosomes, and suggests that the members of a pair are highly compatible and are mutually attractive because of a qualitative similarity. When the spindle becomes organ-ized, the fibers attach to the members of the several pairs. During the ensuing anaphase, members of the several pairs separate and move to opposite poles (4). Thus, at telophase, each of the two daughter nuclei receive one complete n set. Two haploid cells are thus derived from a diploid cell (Fig. 16.4a–e). The nuclear division that effects this reduction from $2n$ to n is quite properly called a **reductional division**. In general performance it clearly resembles mitosis, except that whole chromosomes, members of pairs, are separated, rather than chromatids of a single chromosome.

Reductional division can, of course, occur only in cells with pairs of chromosomes ($2n$), whereas mitosis or equational nuclear division may

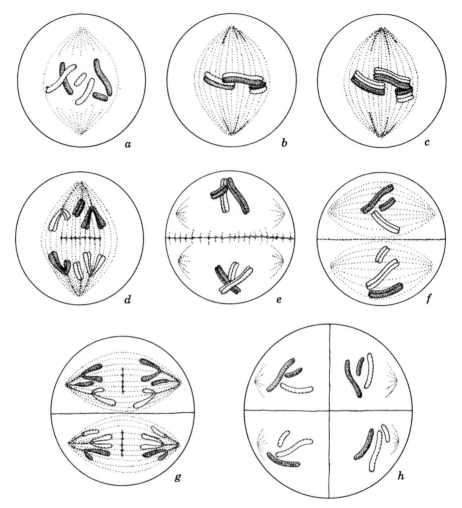

Figure 16.4. Diagrammatic representation of the meiotic divisions of a meiospore parent cell with three pairs of chromosomes. One set of three is shaded; one is unshaded. *a.* Late prophase of the first or reductional division. *b, c.* Metaphase. Note that each chromosome appears as two chromatids in c. *d.* Anaphase. *e.* Telophase of the reductional division and beginning of the second or equational division. *f.* Metaphase. *g.* Anaphase. Chromatids are separating. *h.* Meiosis complete with formation of four meiospores.

occur in cells with either *n* or *2n* chromosomes. As previously stated haploid meiospores are regularly produced in groups of four. Thus a further division of each of the haploid cells resulting from the reductional division of the diploid cell occurs. This division is of the equational or mitotic type (Fig. 16.4*f–h*). The diploid cell that undergoes the successive reductional and equational divisions yielding the four haploid meiospores is a **meiospore parent cell.** The combination of reductional and equational divisions is called **meiosis** (to make smaller), or the **meiotic divisions.** Because meiospores are produced by the special method described, it is necessary to distinguish them from the asexual spores produced directly by the haploid plant, hence the name *meio*spore.

Since homologous chromosomes are separated at the reductional division of meiosis, it follows that the chromosome of any one pair contributed to the zygote by the sperm will be separated from its homologue contributed by the egg. However, since the arrangement of the pairs at metaphase of the first division (reductional division) is random, the haploid set of each daughter cell will have various assortments of sperm-contributed and egg-contributed chromosomes. The significance of this fact will be fully dealt with in Chapter 17.

A Moss

We shall now attempt to apply our analysis of the sexual reproductive method to the bryophytes, a group judged to be more advanced in evolution than the algae. Of the two main divisions of the bryophytes, liverworts, and mosses, the better known mosses serve our purpose.

A consideration of the moss may well start with its conspicuous phase, the green "leafy" plant. At the apex of a moss axis, surrounded by the terminal leaves, is a cluster of slender, multicellular, delicately proportioned, vase-shaped female reproductive structures, the **archegonia** (Fig. 16.5*a,c*). In the enlarged basal portion of each is a large cell, the megagamete. On the same or another moss axis, the **antheridia** (the male reproductive organs) occur in the form of a group of club-shaped sacs, along with some hair-like filaments (Fig. 16.5*b,d*). The antheridia contain microgametes (Fig. 16.5*e*). The leafy moss plant will thus be recognized as the gametophyte, bearing multicellular sex organs, the egg-producing archegonia and the sperm-producing antheridia. All of these structures are, typically, haploid.

The microgametes, released from the antheridium through a rupture at the tip, are rapidly dispersed over the surfaces of the plants by splashing rain drops, or they may swim through the thin film of water usually covering the plant surfaces (Fig. 16.5*d*). A microgamete swims down the slender neck canal of the archegonium and fuses with the megagamete (Fig. 16.5*e*). The product of the fusion is the diploid zygote, the first cell of the sporophytic phase. From this cell, through rapid cell divisions, a simple embryo-like structure is produced with a tapering

435

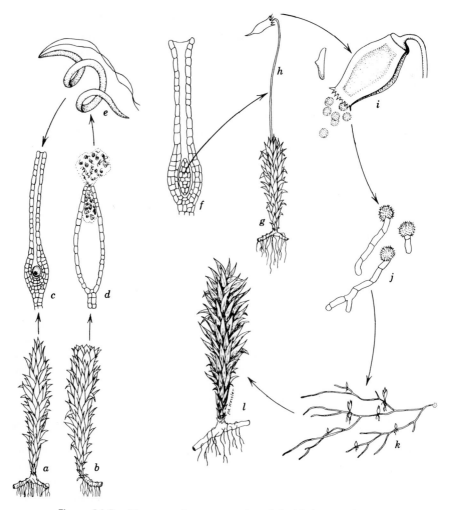

Figure 16.5. Diagrammatic representation of the life history of a moss.

absorbing **foot** deeply buried in the tissue of the gametophyte (Fig. 16.5*f*). Food is absorbed mainly from the green gametophyte, growth of the embryo occurs, and a slender **stalk**, surmounted by an enlarging **capsule**, is produced (Fig. 16.5*h*). The foot, stalk, and capsule constitute the sporophyte. During growth, the sporophyte is green with chlorophyll and thus is at least partly self-sustaining. At maturity, however, the chlorophyll is lost and the whole structure becomes brown. The capsule, along with its stalk, is a multicellular structure and contains many diploid meiospore parent cells. The structural complexity of the moss sporophyte has been brought about by a period of vegetative growth of the zygote.

Meiosis, occurring in the meiospore parent cells of the capsule, produces a large number of meiospores (Fig. 16.5*i*). These are produced in fours, as meiospores always are, by meiosis. Meiospore formation marks the beginning of the haploid phase. The capsule is a specialized meiospore case called a **sporangium**. The meiospores are released from the capsule when the air is dry and are scattered by air currents. Germination of a meiospore on the moist soil yields a green, branched filament of cells. Specialized nongreen branches of this filament (**rhizoids**) penetrate the soil and anchor it firmly, and some of the green branches grow vertically and become the "leafy" moss axis bearing the antheridia and archegonia (Fig. 16.5*j,k,l*).

Certain features of the moss deserve special mention. The entire organization of the plant, in both gametophyte and sporophyte, seems pointed toward a terrestrial mode of life. Note especially that the meiospores are produced in great numbers from elevated structures, and that they are air dispersed. Only a relatively small proportion of the total meiospores produced ever germinate. The sporophyte, although attached to the gametophyte, contains some chlorophyll and so has a limited measure of nutritional independence. It probably secures most of its food from the gametophyte, which has considerable photosynthetic tissue in its leaf-like outgrowths. Although these features are judged to be land-plant characteristics, complete release from aquatic habitats has not been achieved. The moss has no vascular tissue nor specialized absorbing structures, and thus is, therefore, essentially restricted to wet habitats. The wetness of plant surfaces is also very important in the reproductive cycle, for the union of gametes depends on the motility of the microgamete.

The evolutionary position of the bryophytes is difficult to assess, for factual evidence in the form of fossil remains is scanty. However, both the structural features and the life cycles of bryophytes represent a condition intermediate between those of the green algae and the vascular plants. It seems probable that the bryophytes are derived from algal forms, probably some which had developed independent multicellular sporophytes. The modern species of moss have probably undergone a reduction of the sporophyte to a relationship dependent on the gametophyte. The filamentous early stage of the moss gametophyte is quite alga-like. Bryophytes are believed to occupy a kind of evolutionary dead end. Although the tracheophytes are a higher group in the evolutionary scale, the most generally accepted view at present is that they were derived directly from an algal ancestor, probably one of the green algae, rather than from a bryophyte.

Tracheophytes: A Fern

The acquisition of vascular tissue by the tracheophytes represents a significant step toward the development of a terrestrial mode of life, for it permits water absorption from the deeper layers of the soil by specialized absorbing roots and the rapid conduction of water through the plant. The great group of plants that have acquired this advantage have come to be ecologically more diverse and wider spread than those that have not. A small segment of the vascular plants, including the ferns, lycopods, and horsetails, however, have retained a feature (to be

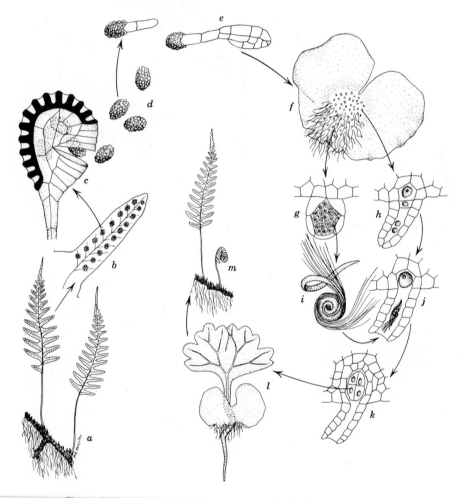

Figure 16.6. Diagrammatic representation of the life history of a fern.

Figure 16.7 *Polypodium.* Lower surface of leaflet showing clusters (sori) of sporangia. (Copyright, General Biological Supply House, Inc., Chicago.)

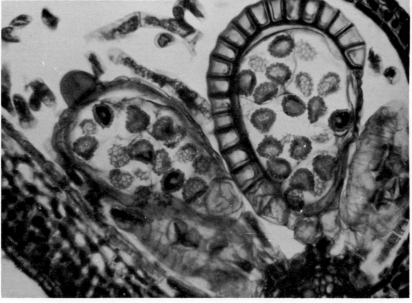

Figure 16.8. *Pteris.* Photomicrograph of sporangium and meiospores. (Photograph courtesy of Carolina Biological Supply Co.)

439

described later) that binds them closely to their aquatic ancestors, although in other respects they have evolved an effective land habit.

The plant body of a fern (7, 8), as we encounter it in nature, consists of a vascular axis bearing highly differentiated leaves and roots

Figure 16.9. Discharged meiospores from a sporophyll of the fern, *Osmunda.* (Courtesy of Carolina Biological Supply Co.)

Figure 16.10. Fern prothalli. (Copyright, General Biological Supply House, Inc., Chicago.)

(Fig. 16.6a). The internal organization of all these parts bears a striking resemblance to the corresponding structures in the seed plant. The fern leaves, sometimes called fronds, bear on their under surfaces a very large number of **sporangia,** variously grouped, each producing numerous meiospores (Figs. 16.6b, 16.7). The fern plant, therefore, is a sporophyte. The spore-bearing leaves are **sporophylls.** The sporangia are minute, multicellular, stalked sacs (Figs. 16.6c, 16.8). A special ring of thick-walled cells called the **annulus** causes the sporangium to break open, under dry conditions, in such a way that the contained meiospores are thrown free and carried off by air currents (Figs. 16.6c,d, 16.9). In the familiar species of fern, as in the mosses and in the algae discussed, all the meiospores are similar in appearance. This condition is called **homospory,** and the species are described as **homosporous.** A few species of highly-specialized ferns of aquatic habitats produce meiospores of two sorts and are thus **heterosporous.**

A meiospore germinates on suitable moist soil, producing a short filament of green cells, the young gametophyte (Fig. 16.6e). Some of the filament cells develop slender protuberances, called **rhizoids,** which penetrate the soil surface and provide anchorage. The terminal cells of the filament undergo repeated divisions yielding a thin flat sheet of cells that finally, by differential growth, attains a heart shape (Figs. 16.6f, 16.10). This structure, called a **prothallus,** commonly less than 1 cm. wide and closely appressed to the moist soil, is the mature gametophyte. On its underside it develops multicellular antheridia and archegonia (Fig. 16.6g,h). The motile microgametes are released from the antheridia through a terminal pore and swim free in the film of water (Fig. 16.11). Meanwhile, the disorganization of cells within the neck of the archegonium creates a passage through which several microgametes swim (Fig. 16.6i,j). A single microgamete enters the megagamete, fuses with the nucleus, and thus initiates the sporophytic stage.

The zygote, or fertilized egg, gives rise to a simple embryo that grows

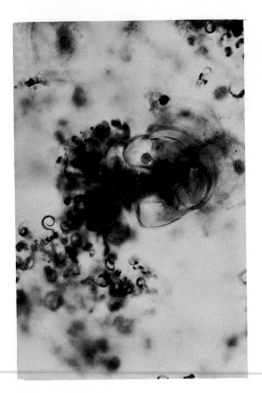

Figure 16.11. Swimming microgametes of fern in the vicinity of a receptive archegonium. (Photograph courtesy Carolina Biological Supply Co.)

into a young sporophyte, consisting of foot, root, stem, and leaf (Fig. 16.6*k,l,m*). When the sporophyte has become well established, the gametophyte withers and disappears. The sporophyte of some fern species produces an erect stem that may attain a height of up to 30 to 40 ft., as in the tree ferns of the tropics (Fig. 2.27). The stems of most ferns, however, are relatively short, and many are subterranean.

The conspicuous phase of the fern life cycle is the sporophyte, which is perennial and conspicuous, whereas the gametophyte is ephemeral and relatively inconspicuous. Both phases contain chlorophyll and so are autotrophic. The fern may properly be judged a terrestrial plant by virtue of its vascular axis and air-dispersed meiospores. However, as in the moss, the motile microgamete is the primitive ancestral feature that reflects the fern's ancient aquatic origins.

Tracheophytes: A Gymnosperm

The gymnosperms (naked seed) are a relatively small (about 700 species) but botanically and economically very important group. As representative of the gymnosperms, we shall select the familiar pine.

In general structure of the vegetative plant body, the pine is similar to that of the flowering plant described in Chapter 5. It will be re-called that the secondary xylem is composed principally of pitted tracheids rather than vessels and fibers. The pine tree is the sporophytic phase of the life cycle. In contrast with most ferns, pine produces two kinds of meiospores, **microspores** and **megaspores**. The pine, therefore, is heterosporous. The microspores are formed in **microsporangia** borne in pairs on **microsporophylls,** and these are arranged spirally in a cone structure, the **microsporangiate cone,** which is commonly referred to as the male cone (Fig. 6.12*a,b,c*). **Megasporangiate** or female **cones,** borne upon the tips of the other branches of the same tree, consist of **megasporophylls** bearing **megasporangia** and **megaspores** (Fig. 16.12*i,j,k,l*).

The microspores arise by meiosis from diploid microspore parent cells (Fig. 16.12*c,d*). While still in the microsporangia, the haploid nucleus of each meiospore undergoes two successive mitotic divisions, giving two **prothallial cells** and an **antheridial cell** (Fig. 16.12*e*). The antheridial cell now divides to form a **tube cell** and a **generative cell** (Fig. 16.12*f*); meanwhile the prothallial cells are degenerating. These divisions of the microspore constitute the beginning of germination of the meiospore, that is, the four-celled structure produced is a young **microgametophyte.** These two-winged microgametophytes are the **pollen.**

The megasporophylls of the female cone are relatively thick scales spirally arranged upon the cone axis, each in the axil of a small and inconspicuous **bract** (Fig. 16.12*i,j*). Two ovules are borne upon the

443

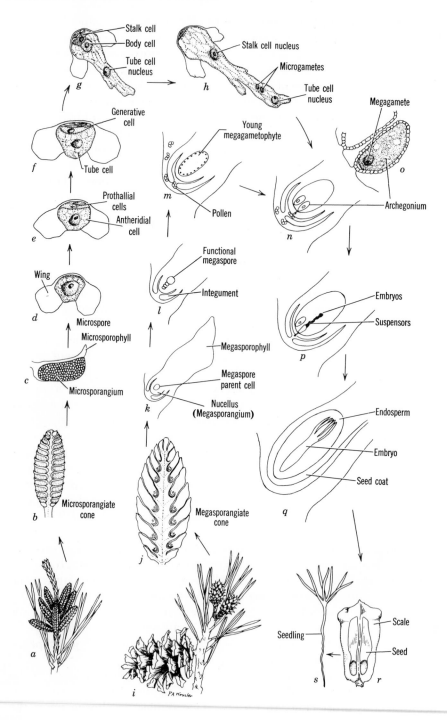

upper surface of each cone scale (megasporophyll). An ovule consists of a massive **nucellus**, or **megasporangium**, with a single integument (Fig. 16.12*k*). The **micropyle** of the ovule is directed inward toward the cone axis. A megaspore parent cell develops early in the nucellus (Fig. 16.12*k*) and undergoes meiosis, giving a row of four megaspores (Fig. 16.12*l*). Three of the megaspores disintegrate and the remaining functional megaspore germinates, producing a bulky megagametophyte lying deeply buried in the nucellus (Fig. 16.12*m*). Two or three archegonia develop at the micropylar end of the megagametophyte and each of these contains a single megagamete (Fig. 16.12*n*).

The pollen grains are shed by rupture of the microsporangium and may be carried many miles by strong wind. Some of the pollen grains fall among the open scales of the young female cone and come to rest near the micropyle of the ovule (Fig. 16.12*m*). The pollen grains are drawn into the micropyle by the evaporation of a sticky fluid exuded from the micropyle; thus they come in contact with the nucellus where they continue to grow, producing a **pollen tube**. This tube grows through the nucellus toward the archegonia (Fig. 16.12*g,n*). As the pollen tube grows, the generative cell divides to give a **stalk cell** and a **body cell** and the nucleus of the tube cell moves forward to the advancing tip. The body cell then divides, forming two microgametes (Fig. 16.12*h*).

The union of micro- and megagametes (fertilization) occurs about one year after pollination. The zygote undergoes a series of free nuclear divisions, followed by wall formation, creating four tiers of cells, each of which gives rise to an embryo (Fig. 16.12*p*). Three of the embryos finally abort and the remaining one is forced by growth of the **suspensor cells** deep into the megagametophyte, which has been transformed into **endosperm** by the deposit of reserve food in the cells. The completely

Figure 16.12. Diagrammatic representation of life cycle of pine. *a.* Branchlet with cluster of microsporangiate cones. *b.* Microsporangiate cone in longitudinal section. *c.* Microsporophyll with microsporangium in longitudinal section. *d.* Winged microspore. *e.* Young microgametophyte showing two prothallial cells and antheridial cell. *f.* Same, showing prothallial cells degenerating and tube and generative cells (from antheridial cell). *g.* Tube cell has become young pollen tube; stalk and body cells were derived from generative cell. *h.* Mature microgametophyte with two microgametes derived from body cell. *i.* Branchlet with young megasporangiate cones and old cone from former season. *j.* Megasporangiate cone in longitudinal section. *k.* Megasporophyll with ovule in longitudinal section showing ovule consisting of megasporangium and integument. *l.* Ovule in longitudinal section, three megaspores degenerating. *m.* Young, free-nuclear gametophyte developed from functional megaspore; pollen at micropyle in stage shown in *f. n.* Archegonia organized, pollen tube penetrating nucellus. *o.* Detail of archegonium. *p.* Suspensors and proembryos penetrating deep into gametophyte. *q.* Mature embryo surrounded by food-laden megagametophyte (endosperm). *r.* Ripe cone scale with two mature winged seeds. *s.* Seedling.

developed embryo (sporophyte) consists of a **hypocotyl,** an **epicotyl,** and several **cotyledons** (Fig. 16.12*q*). The internal development described is accompanied by changes in the integument which converts it into a hard seed coat, and general growth of the female cone whose scales close up and become woody (Fig. 16.12*r*).

The ripe pine cone opens by a reflexing of the scales, and then the winged seeds fall out and are dispersed by the wind.

Certain features of the life cycle of the pine should be emphasized and comparisons made with corresponding features of the common fern we have studied. Pine is heterosporous, producing its micro- and megaspores upon micro- and megasporophylls borne in separate cones. Appropriately, micro- and megagametophytes result from the germination of the two kinds of meiospores, and these are much reduced in size and complexity and are dependent on the sporophyte. The microgametes are not motile, but are carried to the archegonium by growth of the pollen tube. Thus the pine is not dependent on the presence of an external film of water for the movement of the microgamete. The embryo is relatively highly developed, encased in a copious food reserve (the endosperm), and well protected by the seed coat. In this situation, the embryo may remain dormant for a period of time. Many of these features foreshadow conditions to be found in the life cycle of angiosperms, yet are believed to be derivable from and are associated with more primitive features shown by the ancient fern type.

Tracheophytes: An Angiosperm

The organization of the flower (3), the specialized reproductive structure of the flowering plant, or angiosperm, was described in Chapter 5. In this chapter we shall deal with important details of the sexual reproductive process omitted in that chapter. It may be helpful to review flower structure at this point.

The tree, shrub, or herb bearing flowers is the sporophytic phase of the life cycle of angiosperms. The micro- and megasporophylls (stamens and carpels, respectively) are borne upon the torus of the flower, along with the associated corolla and calyx. The flower is essentially a cone of sporophylls, somewhat like the cones of pine, except that, typically, both micro- and megasporophylls are in the same cone (Fig. 16.13*a*).

The anther (microsporangia) of a stamen in a young flower bud, as seen in cross sectional view, consists usually of two or four chambers that contain a mass of large cells, the microspore parent cells (Fig. 16.13*c*). Each microspore parent cell by meiosis produces four microspores (Fig. 16.13*e*). The microspore nucleus divides and the daughter nuclei become incorporated into two cells of unequal size by the formation of separating membranes. The larger is called the **tube cell**, the smaller, the **generative cell**. This division is accompanied by thickening of the microspore wall and concomitant formation of ridges, spines, or grooves on the surface. The division of the microspore and its wall modification have transformed it into a young microgametophyte or pollen grain. At this time, in most flowering plants, the walls between adjacent chambers break down, thus creating two **pollen sacs**. The pollen sacs open by pores or splits as the flower matures, freeing the pollen (Fig. 16.13*f*).

During organization of the pollen, as described, other events are taking place in the pistil. Within the ovulary of a young developing pistil, one or more small protuberances arise on a **placenta**, commonly where carpel margins meet. The protuberance is a hemispheric mass of cells, the megasporangium, or nucellus, in which a single large megaspore parent cell develops (Fig. 16.13*h*). After a slight elongation at the base, the megasporangium becomes almost completely enveloped by one or two collars of cells originating at the base. The enveloping layers are the **integuments**. The small opening left at the rim of the integuments is the **micropyle**. Differential growth at the base usually begins at this time so that the micropyle becomes turned toward the placenta.

By meiosis the megaspore parent cell produces a linear series of four **megaspores**. Usually, the three megaspores nearer the micropyle disintegrate, leaving the basal one functional (Fig. 16.13*i*). The functional megaspore enlarges rapidly, its nucleus undergoes three successive divisions yielding eight nuclei, and the cytoplasm develops a large central vacuole (Fig. 16.13*j,k,l*). Four of the eight nuclei are situated at each end. One nucleus from each group of four moves to the approximate center and each of the remaining six becomes incorporated into a cell by the formation of separating membranes. Thus three cells stand near the micropyle and three at the basal end. This structure, consisting of six cells and two free nuclei and contained within the much extended megaspore wall, is the mature megagametophyte, or **embryo sac** (Fig. 16.13*m*). In most flowering plants the enlargement associated with formation of the embryo sac results in the destruction of tissue of the megasporangium, so that the megaspore wall (embryo sac wall) comes to lie against the integument. The entire structure, consisting of embryo sac plus integuments, constitutes a mature **ovule**.

The position of the cells and nuclei of the embryo sac carries special significance, for their behavior and the role they play in subsequent events is characteristic. The two free nuclei that migrate to the center of the sac are called **polar nuclei**. The three cells farthest from the micropyle are the **antipodal cells**. One of the three cells near the micropyle is the **megagamete**, or egg, and the remaining two are called **synergids**

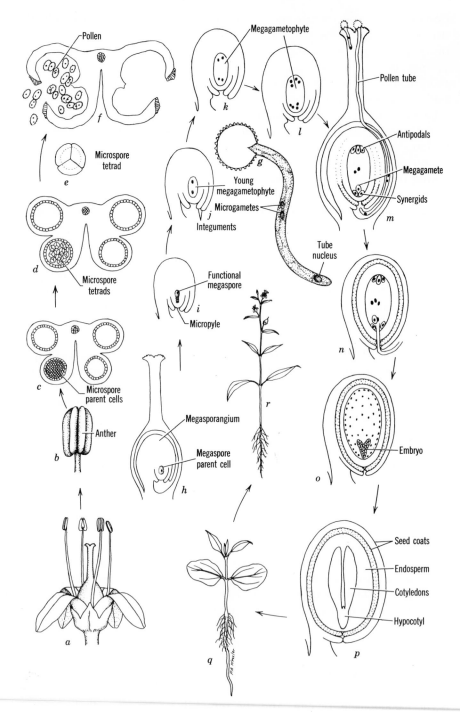

(Fig. 16.13*m*). The antipodal cells and synergids are apparently functionless in embryo production, for they take no part in subsequent development and commonly soon disintegrate.

The type of embryo sac development described is one of the commonest, but among the angiosperms much variation in detail is observed from species to species, and ten or more distinct types have been described. These types differ with respect to such features as the number of megaspores participating in embryo sac formation and the number and arrangement of cells in the mature structure.

Now let us turn our attention again to the pollen grains in the open pollen sacs of the anther. By one means or another, as we shall discuss later in this chapter, pollen grains are transferred to the stigma of the same or another flower where they become firmly fixed by contact with a viscid stigmatic secretion. The transfer of pollen from anther to stigma is called **pollination**. Under the stimulating influence of the stigmatic fluid, the pollen grain germinates and sends downward through the stigma and style a slender pollen tube. As the tube emerges from the pollen grain and grows forward, the tube nucleus usually assumes a position just behind the advancing tip. Shortly, the generative cell moves into the pollen tube where it divides to produce two microgametes, or sperms (Fig. 16.3*g,m*). The pollen tube is the mature microgametophyte. The tip of the pollen tube enters the micropyle of the ovule, penetrates the wall of the embryo sac, and discharges the tube nucleus and two sperms into the embryo sac. The tube nucleus probably functions, as its name implies, as the nucleus for the growing pollen tube and after discharge into the embryo sac it disintegrates. One of the sperms moves deep into the sac and takes part in a **triple fusion** that involves also the two polar nuclei. The product of the triple fusion is called the **primary endosperm nucleus**. The remaining sperm fuses with the egg (2, 6). The fusion of sperm and egg constitutes fertilization (Fig. 16.13*n*). The fertilized egg is the zygote, the first cell of the embryo, and thus the beginning of the new sporophytic phase. It is usually at this time that the synergids and antipodals disintegrate.

Figure 16.13. Diagrammatic representation of the life cycle of a flowering plant. *a.* The flower. *b.* Anther of stamen. *c.* Anther in cross section showing chambers and microspore parent cells. *d.* Same, tetrads of microspores have been formed by meiosis. *e.* Microspore tetrad. *f.* Cross section of dehiscing anther with escaping pollen. *g.* Pollen tube with microgametes. *h.* Young ovule with megaspore parent cell. *i.* Four megaspores in nucellus, three disintegrating. *j.* 2-nucleate megagametophyte. *k.* 4-nucleate stage of megagametophyte. *l.* 8-nucleate stage. *m.* Longitudinal section of pistil showing mature megagametophyte and pollen tubes. *n.* Discharge of microgametes into embryo sac. *o.* Young embryo in free-nuclear endosperm. *p.* Mature seed with embryo, endosperm, and seed coats. *q.* Seedling. *r.* Mature flowering plant.

From this point on, events move rapidly and culminate in the development of a seed. The fertilized egg, lying close to the micropyle, undergoes several cell divisions to yield a row of cells extending a little way into the embryo sac. The terminal cell of the row now divides transversely and longitudinally, producing a spherical cluster of eight cells. This group of cells will contribute the major portion of the embryo, whereas the lower part of the row serves as a suspensor and through continued growth pushes the developing embryo more deeply into the embryo sac.

Meanwhile successive divisions of the primary endosperm nucleus produce a large number of free **endosperm nuclei** which congregate around the developing embryo and along the walls of the embryo sac (Fig. 16.13o). The endosperm nuclei gradually become incorporated into cells by the formation of separating membranes, and the cells so formed (the endosperm) grow rapidly and accumulate food in the form of starch, protein, or oil. The accumulated food comes, of course, from the parent plant. In some seeds the embryo soon reaches the limit of its growth, and is enveloped by a large mass of **endosperm** (Fig. 16.13p). This condition obtains in such seeds as those of castor bean and corn. In other species such as pea and bean, the developing embryo continues to grow until all of the endosperm is absorbed and its food substance is transferred to the cotyledons, which become very fleshy.

The one or two integuments, meanwhile, have undergone modification of the outer cell layer and now are the seed coats. The modification may take many forms. For example, in the bean the outer coat is heavily cutinized and rather tough, in the peanut it is thin, brown and papery. In cotton, some of the cells of the outer integument extend outward like fine hairs, producing the long cotton fibers. In some species, such as trumpet vine, the seed coat develops membranous, wing-like extensions, or as in milkweed, feathery tufts of hairs (Fig. 5.43) which assist in dispersal by wind currents.

In the bean and many other seeds the micropyle may still be visible as a small depressed dot just above the **hilum** or scar where the seed was attached to its stalk. In seeds with outer coats of low permeability, much of the imbibition of water, which initiates germination, takes place through the hilum.

Pollination

Something more should be said about pollination. It is a fascinating subject which brings into view some of the most interesting aspects of plant form and behavior. The germination of pollen upon the stigma, the production of sperm, and the subsequent fertilization of the egg are indispensable to the usual development of viable seed. Pollination also plays an important role in the natural development of the fruit. Each seed produced involves the action of a separate pollen grain. A tomato with a hundred seeds had at least a hundred pollen tubes that reached one hundred ovules, all at about the same time.

Air currents and insects are the principal agents for pollen transfer. Plants pollinated by air currents often have small and inconspicuous flowers borne well exposed on the plant. Frequently the corolla is much reduced in size, or lacking. Such plants produce a great abundance of buoyant pollen and have large feather-like stigmas. Many of these plants are among the early spring blooming species. Corn, the common grasses, oaks, hickories, elms, and ragweed are examples of wind-pollinated species. Hay fever sufferers are especially aware of the wind-borne pollen of certain species.

Insect-pollinated species usually produce conspicuous and brightly colored or nectar-bearing flowers with sticky pollen. The transference of pollen by the insects is, of course, incidental to the insects' search for food. Pollen adheres to the body and legs of insects chiefly of the bee order (Hymenoptera), although some moths and butterflies (Lepidoptera) are effective pollen carriers. Elaborate flower modifications are known that seem designed to assure pollen collection by insect visitors. In such flowers the positions of stigma, stamens, and nectaries are such that insects in search of nectar cannot avoid collecting and distributing pollen.

Based on the source of the pollen, two types of pollination may be recognized. **Self-pollination** is the transfer of pollen from anther to stigma of the same flower or of another flower on the same plant. **Cross-pollination** occurs when pollen is carried to the stigma on another plant of the same or related species. Many species are regularly self-pollinated. This is usually brought about by pollination before the flower opens fully, or by growth of the receptive stigma among the ripe stamens. Self-pollination may occur by either insects or air currents, but these agents, as a rule, are more significant in effecting cross-pollination. Cross-pollination is probably more general than self-pollination. In many instances, it has been shown that plants of greater vigor and productivity result from cross-pollination than from self-pollination.

Many species possess structural and functional modifications that tend to prevent or reduce the possibility of self-pollination (5). For example, liberation of pollen in some flowers occurs at a time when the stigma of the same flower is nonreceptive. Although this tends to favor cross-pollination, it does not preclude self-pollination involving other flowers on the same plant. In some species a condition of **self-sterility** is encountered, in which the plant's pollen is ineffective upon its own stigmas. Insect-pollinated species, however, possess the most complex mechanisms for ensuring cross pollination. In sage, a plant of the mint family, a bee may light upon the lip of the corolla and push into the flower for nectar, and in doing so cause the stamens to trip forward and dust his back with pollen. When the insect subsequently visits another, older flower in which the stigma has grown receptive, his pollen-laden back brushes against the stigma, transferring the pollen (Fig. 16.14). Several species produce, on different plants, flowers of two types in which the relative positions of stigma and anthers are reversed, so that the part of the insect's body bearing pollen picked up in one flower will deliver it to the stigma of the second flower (Fig. 16.15).

Knowledge of the pollination characteristics of some cultivated plants may be of great importance to orchardists. For example, although many apple varieties are **self-fertile** and set fruit when self-pollinated, they often do better when other varieties are available as a pollen source. Some varieties are quite self-sterile and do not set fruit unless they are cross-pollinated. Thus commercial orchards are often planted so as to provide compatible cross-pollinating varieties whose periods of flowering coincide. Some varieties of cherry require cross-pollination. Peaches, on the other hand, are all self-fertile.

The pollen of seed plants (and the spores of lower forms) are interesting objects for study. In size, shape, patterns of surface sculpture, and in other features, they present a great variety. Many of them are objects of great beauty in the intricacies of their design, and for very many species and larger categories they are distinctive. The outer walls are commonly quite resistant and thus they readily become fossilized in sedimentary formations. Wind-dispersed pollen becomes widely distributed and much of it falls into bogs and swamps where it accumulates over long periods of time. Microscopic examination of such situations frequently yields information about the kinds of plants that grew in or near ancient sites. This history of forest migrations and the dating of coal deposits have been worked out by pollen and spore analyses.

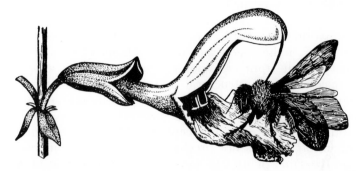

Figure 16.14. Stigma of sage flower contacting pollen-laden back of bee. (After Kerner, Natural History of Plants.)

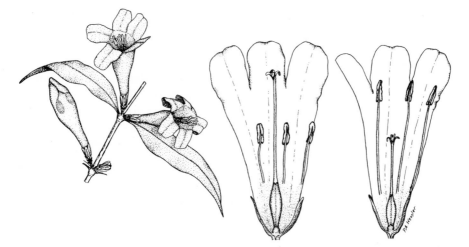

Figure 16.15. *Gelsemium.* Dimorphism of the flower assuring cross pollination by insects.

The petroleum industry is using such data on an increasing scale in the exploration for oil. The study of pollen and spores, called **palynology,** is an important division of botany.

Comparison of Flowering Plants and Gymnosperms

Comparison of a flowering plant and a gymnosperm, as represented by pine, should now be made with respect to certain features of their life cycles. They are similar, of course, in that both are heterosporous, the mature microgametophyte of both consists of a pollen tube, and both produce a seed that consists of an embryo plant, protective seed coats, and a food reserve. They are different, however, in important ways. The gymnospermous ovules are borne exposed on open, flat megasporophylls, whereas those of angiosperms are typically enclosed within an **ovulary** that develops into a true fruit (Chapter 5). The gametophytic phases of the flowering plant are somewhat simpler. The angiospermous microgametophyte consists of a single cell (the pollen tube and its nucleus) containing two sperms, and the megagametophyte (embryo sac) consists usually of only six cells and two free nuclei contained within the megaspore wall. Archegonia are not present in the megagametophyte of angiosperms. However, it may be interesting to interpret the embryo sac as a single, much reduced archegonium in which the synergids may be regarded as the remains of a more extensive archegonial wall and the antipodals as vestiges of a bulkier gametophyte. The endosperm of pine is the food-enriched tis-

453

sue of the megagametophyte, whereas the endosperm of the flowering plant is the product of the special triple fusion of one sperm with two polar nuclei.

Seed plants are distributed in nature by the dispersal of young sporophytes (embryos). In the lower forms of plants (ferns, and the lower tracheophytes, bryophytes, and thallophytes) the dispersal structures are spores or meiospores, the gametophytes of these forms being capable of independent existence apart from the sporophyte. With various modifications of seeds and fruits, seed plants may effectively utilize a variety of agents for dispersal.

The seed, with its well-advanced embryo, efficient protective seed coat, and food supply is, perhaps, chiefly responsible for the great success of the seed plants. The seed confers on the species tremendous survival potential through improved chances for successful establishment.

Summary for Sexual Reproduction in Plants

A number of interesting and important themes may be discerned in a comparative study of sexual reproduction in plants, from the most primitive to the most advanced. One of the most striking is a progressive reduction in the comparative size and complexity of the gametophytic phase as it progresses from the thallophytes to the higher tracheophytes. From a condition of structural dominance and independence in the sexually reproducing algae, the gametophyte becomes a dependent, microscopic structure of simple organization in the angiosperms. Concomitantly, the sporophytic phase becomes progressively larger and more complex and ultimately the dominant, independent phase.

Other general trends involve evolutionary changes in the form and behavior of various structures. Thus, motile isogametes are succeeded by nonmotile heterogametes; motile isospores are succeeded by nonmotile heterospores. It must be remembered however, that these evolutionary changes do not in any way alter the biological significance of any structure, within its own cycle. Although homologous structures may change in appearance in the course of evolutionary development, their basic functions and their position in the sexual cycle remain unchanged. Thus we may state this generalization:

$$\text{sporophyte }(2n) \rightarrow \text{meiospore }(n) \rightarrow \text{gametophyte }(n) \begin{array}{c} \nearrow \text{gamete }(n) \searrow \\ \searrow \text{gamete }(n) \nearrow \end{array} \text{sporophyte }(2n)$$

and observe that there occurs in a sexual life cycle a regular alternation of sporophytic and gametophytic phases.

► ## *Questions*

1. Sometimes eggs develop into embryos without fertilization, a process known as *parthenogenesis*. Is this sexual reproduction? Explain your answer.

2. Which of the following are essential for sexual reproduction: male and female individuals, eggs and sperm, gametes, fertilization, pollination, meiosis? Explain your answers.

3. Willow trees that bear staminate flowers are sometimes referred to as male trees whereas those bearing pistillate flowers are called female trees. Are these suitable designations? Why?

4. In heterosporous clubmosses, germination of the megaspore often occurs before it leaves the megasporangium, the megagametophyte still being confined within the megaspore wall. The embryo resulting from fertilization becomes embedded in a bulky megagametophyte that accumulates food reserves. Is this structure a seed? Why?

5. The part of the pistil referred to as the *ovulary* in this textbook is frequently called the *ovary*. Many botanists regard the latter term as inappropriate. Why? What reproductive structures of plants are true ovaries? Angiosperms do not have true ovaries, but if they did where would you expect to find them?

6. The statement is sometimes made that flowers have colored petals in order to attract insects. Evaluate this statement and draft a more satisfactory one if you consider it unacceptable. How could you determine whether the colors of flowers play a role in attracting insects or not?

7. Eggs of chickens are sometimes jokingly referred to as "hen fruit." Is a bird egg actually comparable with a fruit to any reasonable degree at all, either from the standpoint of similar basic structure (homology) or of similar function (anaolgy)? Would a bird egg be more nearly homologous with or analogous to a seed rather than a fruit? Would your answer be different for an infertile egg and a fertile egg containing an embryo? Explain all your answers.

8. Compare the life cycle of a vertebrate animal with the summary life cycle of plants on page 454, noting points of similarity and difference. What further evolutionary changes in angiosperms would result in a life cycle comparable with that of animals?

9. Yucca flowers can be pollinated only by the pronuba moth, the female depositing eggs in the ovulary at the time she stuffs pollen into the hollow style. The moth larvae consume some but not all of the developing seeds as food. The two species are thus quite interdependent on one another for reproduction. Discuss some of the problems involved in the origin of such a symbiotic relationship by evolution, and the possible types of interrelations between the ancestors of the yucca and the moth.

► ## *References*

For Reference

1. Sinnott, E. W. and Katherine S. Wilson, *Botany: Principles and Problems.* New York: McGraw-Hill, 1955, Chapter 17–25.

For Reading

2. Allen, R. D., The moment of fertilization. *Scientific American* 201(1):124–134, July 1959.
3. Heslop-Harrison, John, The sexuality of flowers. *New Biology* 23, 1957.
4. Longwell, A. and M. Mata, The distribution of cellular matter during meiosis. *Endeavour* 19:100–107, 1960.
5. Mather, K., Mating discrimination in plants. *Endeavor* 2:17–21, 1943.
6. Monroy, Alberto, Fertilization of the egg. *Scientific American* 183(6):46–49, December 1956.
7. Peattie, D. C., In quest of fern seed. *Atlantic Monthly* 185(6):35–37, June 1950.
8. Spencer, Hugh, The double life of the fern. *Nature Magazine* 45:40–43, 1952.
9. Wollman, E. F. and F. Jacob, Sexuality in bacteria. *Scientific American* 195(1):109–118, July 1956.
10. Zahl, P. A., The evolution of sex. *Scientific American* 180(4):52–55, April 1949.

17. Heredity

IN CHAPTER 12 we pointed out that the hereditary potentialities of an organism, interacting with the various factors of the environment, determine the nature and course of the processes and conditions within the organism, and that these in turn dictate the pattern of
behavior, growth, and development. We have already considered some
of the influences of environment on plants, and now that we have described the reproductive processes of plants we are in a position to
discuss the nature and mode of action of hereditary potentialities, their
transmission from generation to generation, and their role in hereditary
variation.

Although in this, as in other considerations of inheritance, hereditary
variations will receive the greater part of our attention, hereditary
stability is more universal and of at least equal importance in the biological world. Pea plants may differ from one another in height, flower
color, seed color, and many other hereditary traits, but they all have
in common a multitude of traits that set them apart as a distinct species
of plants and that have been transmitted unchanged through countless
generations. The fossil record reveals that many species of plants and
animals have remained essentially unchanged through millions of years,
a fact that is sometimes neglected as we center our attention on the

evolution of new species through the natural selection of hereditary variations. Such hereditary stability generation after generation is even more remarkable than hereditary variation, especially when we consider the complex and delicate nature of living substance and the narrow protoplasmic bridge—commonly only a unicellular spore or zygote—that links one generation with another.

The Development of Our Concepts of Inheritance

EARLY IDEAS ABOUT HEREDITY

For centuries man has apparently recognized that plants and animals beget their own kind and that offspring may differ from parents in many details, yet even these basic and obvious concepts have not always been universally accepted. During ancient and medieval times people commonly believed that one kind of living organism could give rise to another (e.g. that geese developed from goose barnacles) and that worms, molds, and other lower forms of life arose spontaneously from slime and decaying matter. It was not until about 1650 that experiments discrediting such beliefs in spontaneous generation were first conducted, and until Pasteur's experiments in 1864 there was still much controversy as to whether microorganisms arose by spontaneous generation (Chapter 19).

Even in those instances where organisms were recognized as being produced by parents of their own kind, the transmission of hereditary traits and hereditary variation remained a complete mystery for centuries. One barrier to any understanding of heredity was an almost complete lack of knowledge of sexual reproduction. It was not until 1676 that Nehemiah Grew suggested the true role of ovules and pollen, and it was in 1694 that Rudolph Camerarius first presented conclusive evidence that plants reproduced sexually. In 1761 Joseph Koelreuter announced his discovery of fertilization in plants and during the next several years he engaged in extensive hybridization of plants. Animal sperm were first described by Lazzaro Spallanzani early in the eighteenth century, but it was 1845 before Kolliker demonstrated that sperm and eggs are cellular products and thus their roles in reproduction began to be clarified. During the preceding 15 years, Robert Brown had discovered nuclei, and several biologists observed cell division and described some of the stages in mitosis, but it was 1890 before the nature and significance of mitosis was reasonably well understood. Fundamental discoveries such as these that were basic to an understanding of heredity were being made, and yet extensive practical breeding of plants and animals was being carried on, even though it was haphazard because there was no understanding of how traits were inherited. The general conclusion was that offspring tended to be intermediate between their parents. John Goss did observe the segregation of traits in peas in 1822, and in 1823 Andrew Knight reported dominance and recessiveness as well as segregation in peas. However, neither they nor other investigators detected any regular patterns or numerical ratios in their data, and hereditary variation remained essentially a mystery.

THE WORK OF GREGOR MENDEL

In 1866 Gregor Mendel, an Austrian monk who had done careful and extensive experiments on inheritance in peas, published his *Experiments in Plant Hybridization* (25), a report now recognized as being one of the most important of all contributions to biology and providing the foundation of modern **genetics**, the science of heredity.

Mendel's principal experiments were conducted on seven pairs of sharply defined hereditary traits of peas (Table 17.1). For each pair of traits he found that when he cross-pollinated or hybridized a plant having one of a pair of traits with a plant having the other trait of the pair, all the offspring were exactly like one of the two parents as regards the trait, rather than intermediate. Thus, when a plant bearing smooth-seeds was crossed with a plant bearing wrinkled seeds, all the offspring (the F_1 generation) produced smooth seeds. This was true whether the smooth-seeded parent provided the pollen or received it. Mendel concluded that the trait for smooth seeds was **dominant** over the **recessive** trait for wrinkled seeds. The dominant and recessive traits discovered by Mendel in his other six experiments are listed in Table 17.1.

Mendel's next step was to cross the hybrid F_1 plants with each other. Several hundred to several thousand offspring (the F_2 generation) were

TABLE 17.1. DATA OF MENDEL ON RATIOS OF DOMINANTS AND RECESSIVES IN THE SECOND GENERATION (F_2) PEA PLANTS FOLLOWING SINGLE FACTOR CROSSES

Experiment	Dominant Character	Recessive Character	Number of Plants	Ratio of Dominants to Recessives
1	Smooth seeds	Wrinkled seeds	7324	2.96:1
2	Yellow seeds	Green seeds	8023	3.01:1
3	Red flowers	White flowers	929	3.15:1
4	Inflated pods	Constricted pods	1181	2.95:1
5	Green pods	Yellow pods	580	2.82:1
6	Axial flowers	Terminal flowers	858	3.14:1
7	Tall stems	Dwarf stems	1064	2.84:1

secured in each of the seven experiments. In the experiment with round and wrinkled seeds, 7324 F_2 plants were obtained, and Mendel found that although 5475 of them produced smooth seeds as did both their parents, the other 1849 plants produced wrinkled seeds, a ratio of 2.96:1. In each of the other six experiments, the ratio of plants having the dominant characteristic to those having the recessive characteristic was essentially the same, all being about 3:1 (Table 17.1).

Mendel also conducted experiments in which he followed the inheritance of two pairs of contrasting traits at the same time (14). For example, when he crossed pure tall, smooth-seeded plants with another pure parent that was dwarf and had wrinkled seeds all the F_1 offspring were tall and had smooth seeds. When he then crossed the F_1 plants and secured an F_2 generation, he found that approximately $\frac{9}{16}$ of the F_2 plants were tall and had smooth seeds, $\frac{3}{16}$ were tall and had wrinkled seeds, $\frac{3}{16}$ were dwarf and had smooth seeds, and $\frac{1}{16}$ were dwarf with wrinkled seeds. In all the **dihybrids** (involving two pairs of factors) that Mendel studied, he found that the dominant traits always appeared in the F_1 generation, and that in the F_2 generation all four possible combinations of traits always appeared in approximately a 9:3:3:1 ratio, the $\frac{9}{16}$ group having two dominant traits, the $\frac{3}{16}$ groups one dominant each, and the $\frac{1}{16}$ group no dominant traits. The 9:3:3:1 ratio is actually the product of two 3:1 ratios:

$$
\begin{array}{r}
3:1 \\
\times\, 3:1 \\
\hline
9:3:3:1
\end{array}
$$

Mendel's great contribution to an understanding of heredity was his recognition of the fact that inherited traits are transmitted as unit factors that occur in pairs; that one member of the pair may be dominant over the other; that the factors of a pair are segregated or separated in the formation of the gametes (although Mendel thought in terms of pollen and ovules rather than gametes), each gamete receiving only one of the pair; that different pairs of factors may assort independently into all possible combinations, and then combine at random during fertilization; and that dominants paired with recessives segregate with purity (i.e., neither factor was modified by their association). This concept of hereditary factors as units that could be dealt with statistically was a marked advance over the previous vague ideas about a general hereditary complex that somehow blended and produced offspring intermediate between the parents. Although some previous investigators had evidence for unit factors, dominance, and segregation, they failed to formulate a satisfactory general theory of heredity because, unlike Mendel, they did not have enough quantitative data to provide meaningful ratios from which conclusions could be drawn.

Mendel's theorems were based principally on the nature of the off-spring of two like hybrids, that is, the F_2 generations. His basic assumption was that all pure progeny are produced by the union of pure and like gametes. His data showed that hybrids bred with like hybrids produce some pure progeny, that there are as many kinds of pure progeny as there are possible pure combinations of the unit factors being considered (2^n, where n is the number of pairs of unit factors), and that there are equal numbers of each kind of pure progeny. From these data and his basic assumption, Mendel concluded that hybrids produce pure gametes, that the number of different pure gametes is $2n$, that there is a pure gamete for each possible combination of pure characters, and that there are equal numbers of the different kinds of pure gametes. These conclusions would have been impossible without the ratios derived from the large numbers of F_2 progeny.

Mendel was fortunate in that all the traits he selected for study showed dominance, that they all assorted independently, that they all interacted to produce $9:3:3:1$ F_2 ratios, and that he was working with plants that are usually self-pollinated, thus facilitating the production of the original pure parental strains (the P_1 plants). If he had happened to select traits that showed incomplete dominance, or were linked or interacted to produce other ratios, he might well have become confused. Yet it was not all luck, and Mendel must receive great credit for selecting specific traits for study, for designing suitable experiments, and for using enough plants to provide significant ratios that he could analyze and use in formulating hypotheses and drawing conclusions.

FROM 1866 to 1900

Mendel's excellent work might have been expected to create a sensation among biologists, but actually it was almost completely ignored. Apparently, few outstanding biologists even read the paper, although Mendel distributed copies quite widely to biologists and breeders, and those who did read it missed its significance. Thus biology in general still lacked any real understanding of inheritance. One reason for the neglect of Mendel's work was that, at the time, most biolgists were greatly concerned with Charles Darwin's work on evolution. Another reason may have been that most biological work was still descriptive, and biologists who did read Mendel's paper may not have been prepared to appreciate his analytical approach.

Furthermore, Mendel's hereditary unit factors were purely hypothetical and neither Mendel or any other biologist was aware of the nature and significance of mitosis, meiosis, chromosomes, and genes and their relation to heredity. Between 1875 and 1890 the work of many biologists gradually clarified the nature of mitosis and meiosis and the behavior of chromosomes during these two types of nuclear division as well as during fertilization of eggs by sperm. This newly accumulated understanding of the cellular basis of heredity set the stage for a real appreciation of Mendel's work, and in 1900 three botanists—Hugo DeVries of Holland, Carl Correns of Germany, and Erich von Tschermak of Austria—working independently established the basic principles of heredity in plants, only to discover that Mendel had anticipated them by 34 years. The triple announcement of the rediscovery and verification of Mendel's work created great interest among biologists, and only a few failed to realize its importance in establishing the basic principles of inheritance. The science of genetics was now on a firm footing that made possible its rapid development during the twentieth century. Within a few years after the rediscovery of Mendel's principles of inheritance, they were found to apply to animals as well as plants. The relationship between chromosomes and heredity was discovered, and Mendel's unit factors were identified as **genes** located in the chromosomes.

The Cellular Basis of Heredity

It has already been pointed out that during mitosis (Chapter 4) each chromosome is duplicated and that consequently each of the resulting cells has the same number and kinds of chromosomes as the parent cell, whereas during meiosis (Chapter 14) the chromosomes are reduced from the $2n$ or diploid number of the spore parent cell (and other cells of the sporophyte) to the n or haploid number of the meiospores (and so of the gametophytes and gametes). Since both meiosis and fertilization play critical roles in the recombination of genes during sexual reproduction, we shall consider their genetic aspects briefly.

MEIOSIS AND HEREDITY

Each diploid cell contains two complete sets of chromosomes, one contributed by the egg and one by the sperm that gave rise to the zygote from which the plant developed. Any particular chromosome in one set has a homologous mate in the second set, comparable with it in gene content as well as in size and shape. Since only homologous chromosomes pair at synapsis, each meiospore receives, not only one complete set of chromosomes, but also one complete set of genes. However, since it is just a matter of chance as to which chromosome of a homologous pair happens to be on one side of the equator or another at the metaphase of reductional division, the set of chromosomes in any particular meiospore can consist of any possible combination of the chromosomes

462

of the two original sets (Mendel's principle of independent assortment). It is this shuffling of the two sets of chromosomes during reduction division that makes possible the extensive recombination of genes during sexual reproduction.

FERTILIZATION AND HEREDITY

Any individual produces a considerable variety of meiospores (and thus gametophytes and gametes) according to the assortment of chromosomes and genes the meiospores contain; thus the assortment in any particular gamete is just a matter of chance. Since it is also a matter of chance as to which sperm will fertilize any particular egg, fertilization provides the second point in any sexual life cycle where hereditary variations arise. Once a sperm has fertilized an egg and thus produced a zygote, the hereditary potentialities of the individual are established.

Hereditary Variation through Recombinations

We can now explain some of Mendel's results by centering our attention on the one of the seven pairs of chromosomes present in the cells of pea plants that contains the genes affecting the height of the plants. Since we are concerned with only one pair of factors or genes, we shall be dealing with a **monohybrid** difference.

A MONOHYBRID WITH DOMINANCE

One of the two parent generations (P_1) used by Mendel was pure for tallness; that is, each of the two chromosomes of the pair contained a gene for tallness that we can represent by a capital T, the gene content of the plant then being TT. Since the other P_1 parent was pure for dwarfness, we can represent its gene content by tt, the small letters being used for the recessive trait. As a result of meiosis, each meiospore, gametophyte, and gamete of the tall plants contained one gene for tallness, represented by a single T, and each gamete of the dwarf plants contained one gene for dwarfness, represented by a single t. Thus, any gamete from a tall plant fertilizing any gamete from a dwarf plant would produce a zygote, and subsequently a hybrid plant, with a gene content represented by Tt. Since tallness is dominant over dwarfness, all the first generation plants (F_1) resulting from crossing of the pure P_1 plants are tall, like the TT parent. However, even though they have the same visible traits as the tall parent (i.e., the same **phenotype**) they differ in their gene content (**genotype**), having one dominant and one recessive gene (Tt) rather than two dominant genes (TT) as did the tall parent.

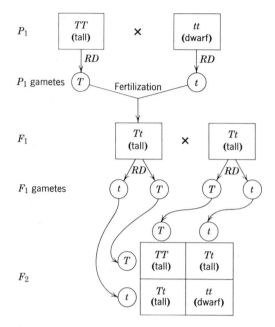

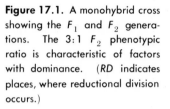

Figure 17.1. A monohybrid cross showing the F_1 and F_2 generations. The 3:1 F_2 phenotypic ratio is characteristic of factors with dominance. (*RD* indicates places, where reductional division occurs.)

When both genes of the pair are identical, as either *TT* or *tt*, the individual is said to be **homozygous**, whereas if the genes of a pair (the **alleles**) differ from each other (*Tt*) the individual is said to be **heterozygous**. Thus, although both the tall P_1 plants and the tall F_1 plants belong to the tall phenotype, they have different genotypes; the P_1 plants are homozygous tall (*TT*) and the F_1 plants are heterozygous tall (*Tt*).

When reduction division occurs in the F_1 plants, half of the spores receive a gene for tallness and the other half the gene for dwarfness. Consequently, half of the eggs and half of the sperm carry gene *T*, and the other half carry gene *t*. In a large number of fertilizations, it is equally probable that either kind of sperm will fertilize either kind of egg. Thus we can expect all four possible types of fertilizations (*T* sperm × *T* egg, *T* sperm × *t* egg, *t sperm* × *T* egg, and *t* sperm × *t* egg) to occur with essentially the same frequency. As a result we have an F_2 generation consisting of $\frac{1}{4}$ homozygous tall plants, $\frac{2}{4}$ heterozygous tall plants, and $\frac{1}{4}$ homozygous dwarf plants (Fig. 17.1). The genotype ratio is 1:2:1, but the phenotype ratio based only on appearance is 3 tall:1 dwarf, the ratio discovered by Mendel.

MONOHYBRID BACKCROSSES AND TEST CROSSES

If an F_1 plant (*Tt*) were crossed with its recessive parent (*tt*) or another dwarf plant, half of the offspring would be expected to be tall and the other half dwarf (Fig. 17.2). In such a **backcross** both the genotype and phenotype ratios are 1:1. If a geneticist wants to know whether a tall plant is homozygous or heterozygous, he can make a similar cross with a dwarf plant, known as a **test cross**. If the test cross offspring are about half tall plants and about half dwarf plants, it it evident that the genotype of the tall parent is Tt, for a plant with the genotype TT would have all tall offspring. Even if there are only a few test cross offspring and only one or two are dwarf, it is evident that the tall parent is heterozygous. On the other hand, if there are only a few offspring and all are tall, we can not conclude that the tall parent has a TT genotype, since there is a chance that although the plant has a Tt geno-type, none of the gametes carrying the recessive t gene happened to participate in the formation of a zygote. Only after a rather large number of offspring, all of them tall, have been secured can one be reasonably certain that the tall parent was homozygous (TT). Genet-icists can observe phenotypes but not genotypes, yet they are able to deduce the genotype of an individual by observing its phenotype and the phenotypes of its offspring. Thus, it is evident that a dwarf pea plant has the genotype tt, since if only one of the genes were the dom-inant T the plant would be tall. Although we know that a tall plant has at least one dominant gene, we can determine whether the second gene is T or t only if we know the phenotypes of its offspring or perhaps if we know the genotypes of its parents.

A MONOHYBRID WITH INCOMPLETE DOMINANCE

Mendel worked only with factors or genes that show dominance and recessiveness, but there are some alleles that exhibit **incomplete dom-**

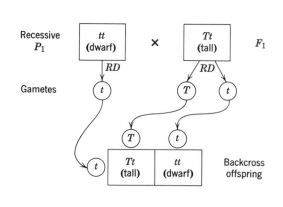

Figure 17.2. A backcross of an F_1 plant with the recessive P_1 plant. The 1:1 phenotypic ratio is characteristic of monohybrid backcrosses. In a test cross, a plant showing the dominant trait but of unknown genotype (wheth-er TT or Tt) is similarly crossed with a P_1 recessive. If the ratio is about 1:1, it is evident that the tall plant tested had the genotype Tt. If all of many test cross off-spring are tall, the plant tested is concluded to have the genotype TT.

465

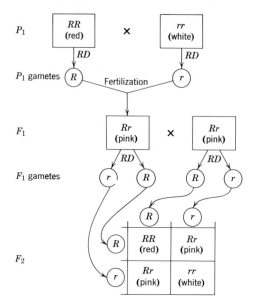

Figure 17.3. A monohybrid cross with incomplete dominance. Although the procedures and genotypic ratios are the same as if the trait exhibited dominance, the F_2 phenotypic ratio is 1:2:1 rather than 3:1 as in dominant traits. While red is incompletely dominant over white in some plants śuch as snapdragons, it is dominant over white in peas, as Mendel discovered.

inance, the heterozygous genotype producing a phenotype intermediate between the two homozygous ones. In snapdragons, for example, the genotype RR provides the potentiality for red flowers, the genotype rr for white flowers, and the genotype Rr for pink flowers (Fig. 17.3). All the F_1 plants are pink, a phenotype different from that of either parent, and the phenotype ratio in the F_2 generation is 1:2:1, the same as the genotype ratio.

A DIHYBRID

Mendel's experiments involving the simultaneous consideration of two sets of hereditary traits (**dihybrids**) provided important information not available from monohybrids. If a pure (homozygous) tall, red flowering pea plant ($TTRR$) is crossed with a pure dwarf, white-flowering pea plant ($ttrr$), all the F_1 offspring will be heterozygous tall, red flowering ($TtRr$). Since the genes for height are on a different pair of chromosomes from the genes for flower color, the genes assort independently and the F_1 plants can produce four types of gametes: TR, Tr, tR, and tr. We now know that this independent assortment discovered by Mendel results from the fact that during the metaphase of the reductional division of meiosis, a particular chromosome of a homologous pair may be on one side just as readily as on the other, the position of the paired chromosomes being a matter of chance. If in a particular reductional division the chromosome containing gene T and the chromosome containing gene R happen to be toward the same side, the chromosomes containing genes t and r will be on the opposite side, and one resulting cell will receive TR and the other tr. There is an equal chance, however, that T and r might be on one side in another cell undergoing meiosis, and t and R might be on the other side, the result being cells containing tR and Tr. Since one lineup is as likely as the other, in a large number of reductional divisions we can expect essentially equal numbers of the four types of meiospores (TR, Tr, tR, and tr) and thus gametes to result.

The four types of eggs and four types of sperm produced by the F_1 generation can unite in sixteen possible combinations (Fig. 17.4), with any one of them just as likely to occur. There are, however, only nine different combinations (different genotypes) and four different phenotypes, as shown by the following tabulation of the F_2 genotypes and phenotypes from Fig. 17.4:

Genotypes	Phenotypes
$\frac{1}{16}$ $TTRR$	
$\frac{2}{16}$ $TtRR$	
$\frac{2}{16}$ $TTRr$	$\frac{9}{16}$ tall, red
$\frac{4}{16}$ $TtRr$	
$\frac{1}{16}$ $TTrr$	
$\frac{2}{16}$ $Ttrr$	$\frac{3}{16}$ tall, white
$\frac{1}{16}$ $ttRR$	
$\frac{2}{16}$ $ttRr$	$\frac{3}{16}$ dwarf, red
$\frac{1}{16}$ $ttrr$	$\frac{1}{16}$ dwarf, white

Here we have the 9:3:3:1 phenotypic ratio observed by Mendel and found by many other investigators when they were studying any two pairs of genes that showed dominance and were located on different pairs of chromosomes. Genes may, however, show incomplete dominance or may interact with one another in a variety of other ways, so dihybrid F_2 phenotypic ratios other than the common 9:3:3:1 ratio are frequently encountered by geneticists.

An important result of the preceding dihybrid cross was the production of two new combinations of hereditary traits that did not exist in either the P_1 or F_1 generations: tall, white-flowering plants and dwarf red-flowering plants. These might be considered as new varieties of peas. Plant and animal breeders make extensive use of such recombinations of hereditary potentialities in the development of new and im-

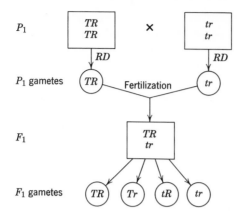

P_1

P_1 gametes — Fertilization

F_1

F_1 gametes

Figure 17.4. A dihybrid cross with two traits being followed simultaneously. The F_1 plants can produce four genetically different kinds of gametes and the gametes can unite in sixteen possible combinations, as shown in the F_2 checkerboard.

F_2

	TR	Tr	tR	tr
TR	TR TR	Tr TR	tR TR	tr TR
Tr	TR Tr	Tr Tr	tR Tr	tr Tr
tR	TR tR	Tr tR	tR tR	tr tR
tr	TR tr	Tr tr	tR tr	tr tr

proved varieties. Thus, a high-yielding disease-resistant variety of wheat may be produced by crossing a high-yielding but susceptible variety with a variety that is disease-resistant but has low yields.

CONTINUOUS VARIATIONS

So far we have considered only **discontinuous** hereditary variations. Pea plants are either tall or dwarf and the seeds are either green or yellow, with no intergrading heights or colors between these extremes. Although heterozygous snapdragons (Rr) have pink flowers, there is still no series of shades between pink and red or pink and white. Many hereditary variations such as height in humans or in some plants, the length of ears of corn, the color of wheat grains, some flower colors, and the size and weight of fruits of tomatoes, squashes, and many other plants are, however, **continuous** variations with a graded series of phenotypes connecting the two extremes.

Mendel studied only discontinuous variations, and this is probably another reason for his success in establishing the basic principles of heredity. Many of the earlier students of heredity had centered their attention on continuous variations and were unable to discover any logical explanation for them. We now know, however, that continuous variations, like the discontinuous ones, are influenced by genes assorting and recombining on the basis of Mendelian principles. The difference is that continuous variations are controlled by two or more pairs of genes which influence the same hereditary trait. As an example we shall consider the simplest possible type of such **multiple gene** heredity, where two pairs of genes (Aa and Bb) located on different pairs of chromosomes influence fruit weight. We shall assume that the genes of the A set have the same influence as the genes of the B set, although this may not always be the case. Each dominant gene (A, B) increases fruit weight by $\frac{1}{4}$ pound whereas the recessive genes (a, b) do not add to the basic fruit weight of 1 pound. Thus, a plant with the genotype $aabb$ will have 1-lb. fruits and a plant of the genotype $AABB$ will bear 2-lb fruits (1 lb. $+ 4 \times \frac{1}{4}$lb.). An F_1 plant ($AaBb$), or any other plant with two dominant genes ($AAbb$ or $aaBB$) will have fruits weighing $1\frac{1}{2}$ lb. (1 lb. $+ 2 \times \frac{1}{4}$lb.). Similarly, plants having any three dominant genes will bear $1\frac{3}{4}$ lb. fruits whereas those plants with only one dominant gene will produce $1\frac{1}{4}$ lb. fruits. There will, then, be a graded series of phenotypes of fruit weight from 2 lb. at one extreme, through $1\frac{3}{4}$, $1\frac{1}{2}$, and $1\frac{1}{4}$ lb., to 1 lb. at the other extreme.

If a plant of the genotype $AABB$ is crossed with a plant of the genotype $aabb$, the F_1 plants will have the genotype $AbBb$ and will bear $1\frac{1}{2}$-pound fruits. Up to this point it would be impossible to determine whether fruit weight was a case of monohybrid incomplete dominance (as in snapdragon flower color) or multiple gene heredity. But when the F_2 generation (Fig. 17.5) is analyzed, we find a 1:4:6:4:1 phenotype ratio in order of increasing fruit weight so we know that two pairs of independently assorting genes are involved. Although this ratio differs from the 9:3:3:1 phenotype ratio in the dihybrid previously considered because of a different kind of gene interaction, the assortment of genes during reduction division, the gene recombinations during fertilization, and the F_2 genetype ratios are just the same as in any dihybrid cross involving independent assortment.

One point worth noting is that $\frac{5}{16}$ of the F_2 plants bear fruits heavier than those of the F_1 parents, whereas another $\frac{5}{16}$ have lighter fruits than the parents. Even in natural populations it is quite common for offspring to be more extreme in continuous variations than either parent, since heterozygosity is quite prevalent in nature.

Another thing that should be stressed again is that genes are only hereditary potentialities and are expressed as phenotypic traits only when the environment is suitable for their expression. A plant with

469

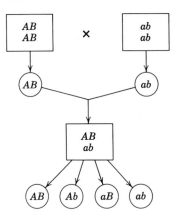

Figure 17.5. Multiple gene heredity involving two alleles (gene pairs). The mechanics of this cross and the F_2 genotypic ratios are the same as in a dihybrid cross, but the F_2 phenotypic ratios of the two crosses are quite different.

	(AB)	(Ab)	(aB)	(ab)
(AB)	AB AB	Ab AB	aB AB	ab AB
(Ab)	AB Ab	Ab Ab	aB Ab	ab Ab
(aB)	AB aB	Ab aB	aB aB	ab aB
(ab)	AB ab	Ab ab	aB ab	ab ab

the potentiality for developing 2-lb. fruits ($AABB$) might produce fruits weighing a pound or even less in an environment unsuitable for optimal growth—for example if some of the essential mineral elements were deficient, if there was a lack of sufficient food or water, or if the plants had been treated with a growth inhibitor such as maleic hydrazide. Phenotypes are a product of the interaction of heredity and environment, and geneticists must always be on the alert to make certain that the phenotypic expression of the hereditary potentialities is not being limited by an unfavorable environment. Of course, plants with an *aabb* genotype can not produce fruits weighing more than 1 lb. regardless of how favorable the environment is, although supplying an internal factor that can not be synthesized by the *aabb* genotype might make possible the development of heavier fruits. The influence of gibberellic acid in causing genetic dwarf plants to grow as tall as those that carry genes for tallness is an example of this sort of thing, the gene for tallness apparently providing the potentiality for synthesis of gibberellin or a similar growth hormone.

If the 1:4:6:4:1 ratio of F_2 phenotypes is plotted on a graph against fruit weight, an inverted V-shaped distribution curve results. If a continuous variation is influenced by three pairs of genes instead of two, the F_2 phenotype ratio will approximate 1:6:15:20:15:6:1 and the distribution curve will assume more of a bell shape. When still larger numbers of genes are involved, the curve becomes a typical bell-shaped normal distribution curve. In any natural population of plants or animals, continuous hereditary variations that have a normal frequency distribution, such as human height and intelligence or the weight of bean seeds, are controlled by multiple gene heredity involving a substantial number of gene pairs.

GENE LINKAGE

Mendel studied only traits that assorted independently in his dihybrid crosses, and so far we have considered only this type of dihybrid. We now know that independent assortment occurs only when the two pairs of genes being considered in a dihybrid cross are located on two different chromosome pairs. Each chromosome, however, contains many genes, and the genes of any particular chromosome are said to be linked with one another, forming a linkage group. Linked genes do not assort independently at reduction division. For example, in tomatoes the genes for height (T and t) are located in the same chromosome as the genes for smooth (S) or hairy (s) stems. If a homozygous tall smooth plant ($\underline{TS}\,\underline{TS}$) is crossed with a dwarf hairy plant ($\underline{ts}\,\underline{ts}$) all the F_1 plants will be tall and smooth just as if the genes were not linked. (The bars under the genes for height and hairs indicate that they are linked.) Since we are dealing with only one pair of chromosomes rather than two, as in previous crosses involving two traits, we can expect the F_1 plants to produce only $\underline{TS}$ and $\underline{ts}$ gametes rather than the four types (TS, Ts, tS, ts) that would result from independent assortment if the two pairs of genes were in separate chromosome pairs. We are dealing essentially with a monohybrid situation and so would expect an F_2 phenotype ratio of 3 tall smooth to 1 dwarf hairy, or a backcross ratio of 1 tall smooth to 1 dwarf hairy.

CROSSING OVER

The results of an actual backcross experiment with tomatoes are given in Table 17.2. Although the backcross ratio was close to the 1:1 ratio expected in complete linkage and far from the 1:1:1:1 ratio that would result if the genes assorted independently, the few backcross plants that were tall hairy and dwarf smooth introduce a complication. The only explanation for these two rather unexpected phenotypes is that in the

471

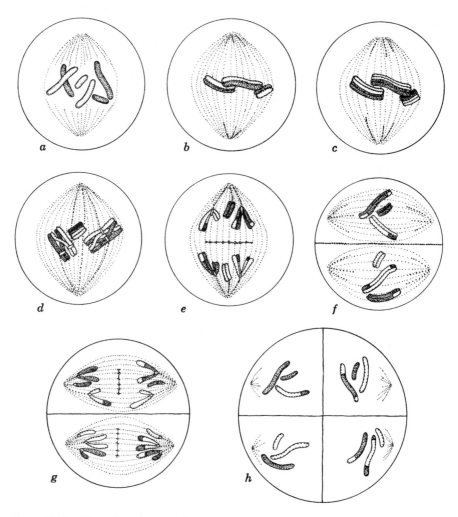

Figure 17.6. The meiotic divisions of a spore parent cell similar to those shown in Fig. 16.4, but with crossing over occurring in two of the three pairs of chromosomes. In *d*, two chromatids of the pair of chromosomes at the left are crossing over and exchanging parts. The other two of the four chromatids remain intact. In the chromosome pair at the right of drawing *d*, two chromatids are crossing over at two points (a double crossover). No crossover is occurring in the short pair of chromosomes. As a result of the crossovers all four spores produced (*h*) are genetically different. The spore at the upper left contains a chromosome resulting from the single crossover, the spore at the upper right a chromosome from the double crossover, the spore at the lower right a chromosome from each crossover. No crossover chromosomes are present in the spore at the lower left. Other combinations of the chromosomes would, of course, have been possible.

TABLE 17.2. RESULTS OF A BACKCROSS OF AN F_1 TOMATO PLANT (TS ts) WITH THE RECESSIVE (ts ts) P_1 PARENT COMPARED WITH EXPECTED RESULTS IF THE GENES WERE EITHER COMPLETELY LINKED OR INDEPENDENTLY ASSORTING

Phenotypes	Genotypes	Number of Backcross Plants	Per Cent of Backcross Plants	Per Cent Expected If the Genes Were	
				Completely Linked	Independently Assorted
Tall smooth	TS ts	96	48.5	50.0	25.0
Dwarf hairy	ts ts	95	48.0	50.0	25.0
Tall hairy	Ts ts	4	2.0	0.0	25.0
Dwarf smooth	tS ts	3	1.5	0.0	25.0
Totals		198	100.0	100.0	100.0

production of a small percentage of the spores (and so thus the gametes), the genes changed linkages. The explanation of linkage changes such as this has been found in chromosomal **crossing over** within a homologous pair. During synapsis, two of the four chromatids frequently twist around one another (Fig. 17.6) and they may then break apart at the twist and exchange parts. When this exchange of parts occurs between chromatids from each of the two chromosomes of the pair, some of the old gene linkages are broken and new linkages are established. Thus, if a crossover occurred between the tomato chromosomes we have been considering at some point between the genes for height and hairs, one of the crossover chromatids would contain the genes T and s whereas the other one would now contain genes t and S, forming the new linkages Ts and tS. The data in Table 17.2 indicate that 3.5% of the F_1 gametes contained chromosomes resulting from crossovers.

CHROMOSOME MAPS

Since crossovers can occur at almost any point along a chromosome, the farther apart two genes are in a chromosome, the greater the chance that crossing over will occur between them. A third pair of genes present in the tomato chromosome pair we have been considering, influences fruit shape, the dominant gene O resulting in oblate (slightly flattened spherical) fruits and the gene o resulting in pear-shaped fruits when homozygous. The per cent of crossovers between T and O is 17.4, indicating that T and O are much farther apart in the chromosome than are T and S. The per cent of crossover between S and O is 13.9. On the basis of this information we know, not only the relative distances between the three genes, but also that they must occur in the

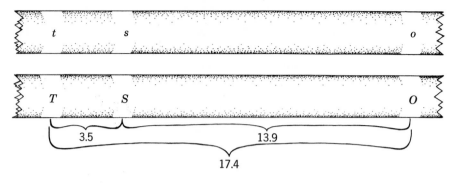

Figure 17.7. Portions of two homologous chromosomes of a tomato plant with the location of three pairs of genes mapped. The production of chromosome maps such as this, or of more complete maps, is possible when the percentage of crossing over among at least three pairs of genes is known. The figures given are actually crossover percentages, but they also indicate the relative distances between genes in the chromosomes.

chromosome in the order T, S, and O (Fig. 17.7). We have thus made a beginning toward mapping the location of the genes of the chromosome.

Geneticists have made rather extensive maps of all of the chromosomes of a few plants and animals, particularly corn and the Drosophila fruit fly. Chromosome mapping is a striking example of the extensive information about genes that geneticists have been able to assemble by the analysis of phenotypic ratios.

CROSSES INVOLVING MORE THAN TWO GENE PAIRS

In a monohybrid cross there are two genetic types of F_1 gametes that can unite in four possible combinations, resulting in three different genotypes and, if dominance is involved, two different phenotypes in the F_2 generation. In dihybrid crosses there are four types of gametes, sixteen possible combinations, nine different F_2 genotypes, and four different phenotypes (if dominance is present in both pairs of genes). If a trihybrid cross were made, the types of gametes would increase to eight, the possible combinations (i.e., the number of squares in the F_2 checkerboard) would be sixty-four, the number of different F_2 genotypes would be twenty-seven, and the number of different phenotypes in the F_2 generation (with dominance in all three pairs) would be eight. Similar data of crosses involving more than three gene pairs is given in Table 17.3, which makes it clear that the hereditary variability associated with gene recombinations increases rapidly as additional gene pairs are considered. Furthermore, the increases occur in a simple mathematical pattern. If we let g represent the number of heterozygous gene pairs being considered, then 2^g is the number of types of F_1 gametes (and also the number of F_2 phenotypes if dominance is found in all gene pairs), whereas $(2^g)^2$ represents the number of possible gamete combinations (fertilizations) and so the number of squares in the F_2 checkerboard, and 3^g is the number of different F_2 genotypes.

The number of pairs of independently assorting genes (g) is limited by the number of chromosome pairs in a species, or in other words the n chromosome number. Thus, in a species where $2n = 16$ and $n = 8$, g can not be larger than 8. The data in the table do not include the added variability resulting from crossovers, and column two represents the number of different F_2 phenotypes only when all gene pairs exhibit dominance. The number of F_2 phenotypes would be quite different, and impossible to determine by any simple formula, if some of the gene pairs showed incomplete dominance, were concerned in multiple gene heredity, or interacted in any of the various possible ways other than simple dominance.

VARIATION BY RECOMBINATION IN NATURAL POPULATIONS

In nature, most plants and animals have a rather high degree of heterozygosity, and will probably have at least one pair of heterozygous genes on each chromosome pair, so the data in Table 17.3 also repre-

TABLE 17.3. POSSIBLE HEREDITARY VARIATION IN F_2 GENERATIONS
WHEN VARIOUS NUMBERS (g) OF HETEROZYGOUS,
INDEPENDENTLY ASSORTING GENE PAIRS WITH DOMINANCE ARE CONSIDERED

Number of Heterozygous Loci (Gene Pairs) that Assort Independently	Number of Different F_1 Gametes (Also Number of Different F_2 Phenotypes)	Number of Possible Combinations (Fertilizations of F_1 Gametes) (Also Number of Checkerboard Squares)	Number of Different F_2 Genotypes
1	2	4	3
2	4	16	9
3	8	64	27
4	16	256	81
5	32	1,024	243
6	64	4,096	729
7	128	16,384	2,187
8	256	65,536	6,561
9	512	262,144	19,683
10	1,024	1,048,576	59,049
17	131,072	17 billion	70 million
23	8,388,608	70 trillion	94 billion
g	2^g	$(2^g)^2$	3^g

sent the minimum amount of hereditary variation that may be expected within a species. Since apple trees have 17 chromosome pairs ($2n = 34$), there would be at least 131,072 phenotypes possible when apple trees were sexually propagated. Even this large number does not include the additional variability resulting from crossing over, incomplete dominance, and other kinds of gene interactions. The important point here is not the exact amount of variation possible, but the fact that an immense amount of hereditary variation can occur in a natural population simply as a result of gene recombinations during sexual reproduction. It should now be obvious why we can not expect to get Winesap apple trees by planting seeds from Winesap apples.

Among cultivated varieties of plants propagated by seeds the story is quite different, since these plants generally have been bred and selected for a high degree of pureness or homozygosity, particularly as regards the traits important commercially and characteristic of the variety. Consequently, as long as the pure lines are kept from crossing with other varieties, there is little hereditary variation, and one individual of a variety has essentially the same phenotype as another. Cultivated ornamental flowers are, however, frequently less homozygous and so more variable than garden vegetables or farm crops. The extensive use of hybrids of corn and other crops will be considered later.

Despite the great hereditary variation within most species of plants, each species has many hereditary traits that ordinarily do not vary from one individual to another and are presumably essentially homozygous throughout the species. Thus, all common garden beans (*Phaseolus vulgaris*) regardless of varietal differences have the same type of fleshy cotyledons, lack endosperm in their seeds, have one pair of simple, opposite cordate leaves whereas the remaining leaves are alternate and compound, lack a cambium, and have flowers of a characteristic shape. Such hereditary traits that are generally the same in one member of a species as another are the ones used by taxonomists in describing and identifying members of the species and in distinguishing the species from related ones. Some hereditary traits are even more fundamental and widespread, occurring throughout a family or even a larger taxonomic group such as a class. Thus, all members of the legume family have pods rather than berries, achenes, or other kinds of fruits, and all tracheophytes have vascular tissue—a hereditary potentiality not present among the fungi, for example.

Hereditary Variation Through Mutations

Hereditary variation may result, not only through the recombination of genes, but also from mutations or changes in genes or chromosomes. **Gene mutations** result from alteration in the chemical structure of a gene; **chromosome mutations** (or chromosomal changes) may result from either changes in chromosome structure or altered chromosome numbers.

GENE MUTATIONS

Mutations, or chemical changes, of genes may occur in any living cell of a plant or animal at any time. Although mutations may occur rather frequently, the great majority of new genes resulting from mutation probably are never expressed phenotypically. There are several reasons for this. For one thing, only one gene of the pair in a diploid cell ordinarily mutates and the mutant gene is usually recessive. Even if a cell containing the mutant gene has many cell descendents the recessive mutant trait will not be expressed in the individual in which it occurred or in any asexually produced offspring. The mutation will be present only in those cells derived from the cell where it occurred, and the mutant gene can be transmitted to offspring sexually only if the gametes happen to be among these cells. Even then it may be several generations before the mutation is expressed phenotypically, since the recessive mutation must be present in both the egg and the sperm. At least one other factor may prevent expression of the mutant gene, at least in adult individuals. Some mutations are **lethal**, that is, they result in such marked changes in essential metabolic processes that the individual does not survive beyond an early stage of development. In haploid individuals, such as the gametophytes of bryophytes, algae, and fungi, recessive mutations may be expressed immediately, since there is only one set of chromosomes. Consequently an individual receiving the recessive could not also have the corresponding dominant.

Even in a diploid individual a dominant mutation may appear phenotypically in first generation offspring, or in the individual in which the mutation occurred, providing that the trait affected is expressed in the cells containing the mutant gene. Thus, a mutation from purple to white flowers would be expressed immediately if present in the cells of a petal (Fig. 17.8), but not if present only in leaf cells. When a dominant mutation occurs in a very young bud, some or all of the cells in the branch developing from the bud will contain the mutation and the branch may have an obviously different phenotype from the rest of the plant. Such **bud mutations** or **bud sports** have occasionally given rise to new varieties of commercial value, such as the navel orange and the Golden Delicious apple.

Some mutations may be desirable economically or advantageous to the individual, but most mutations result in phenotypes less adapted for survival than the parent phenotypes. Even when not lethal, muta-

Figure 17.8. A mutation in snapdragon induced by 14 weeks of gamma irradiation from radioactive cobalt. This plant has purple petals, but the flowers derived from the cell where the mutation occurred have white petals. (Courtesy of Arnold H. Sparrow, Brookhaven National Laboratory.)

tions may result in rather marked changes in structure or metabolism that can handicap the individual, or they may result in some type of sterility, that is, the inability to reproduce sexually. Of course, in plants that can reproduce asexually, the latter would not necessarily prevent transmission of the mutation to offspring.

Since mutations apparently occur at random, the question arises as to why most mutant traits are less desirable than the previously existing hereditary potentialities. The answer seems to be that the gene pool of any species has been subjected to millions of years of natural selection, and so any phenotypes not well adapted to the environment have failed to survive or at least to produce offspring and thus propagate the undesirable traits. Selection has, then, resulted in a complex of generally desirable hereditary potentialities and any change in these is likely to be for the worse. The undesirable mutations will, in turn, be subject to elimination by natural selection. Whereas dominant genes with negative survival value may be eliminated quite promptly, undesirable recessive genes may be transmitted through many generations in the heterozygous condition and some of the poorly adapted phenotypes may appear in each generation. However, the natural selection of these will tend to keep the frequency of the undesirable gene in the population at a relatively low level.

Man has found some mutations in plants to be desirable commercially, even though they may have no survival value to the plant or have negative survival value. Thus, a mutation resulting in seedless fruits might make a plant unable to survive in nature, but man could propagate the plant vegetatively. A few of the desirable mutations that man has selected for propagation include pure red sweet pea flowers (as contrasted with the previous purple-red), the large, undulating petals of Spencer sweet peas, and the nectarines (smooth-skinned peaches). Nectarines originated as a bud mutation on a peach tree.

The rate of mutation is greatly increased by mustard gas and a few other chemicals and by the various kinds of ionizing radiations including X rays, gamma rays, and alpha and beta particle radiation (5, 10). Since radioactive isotopes have become available biologists have subjected many plants and animals to irradiation, both to learn more about the nature of mutations and the effects of radiation and in the hope that a few desirable mutations might result. New high-yielding strains of *Penicillium* and several new varieties of ornamental flowers have resulted from such artificially induced mutations, and extensive work is being done with peanuts and other crop plants (21). Biologists are greatly concerned, however, about the probable large increase in mutations in man as well as in plants and animals as a result of radioactive fallout as well as over the direct harmful effects of the radiation on individuals. Since mutations induced by chemicals or radiation ap-

479

parently do not differ in character from those that occur naturally, we can expect most of the induced mutations to be undesirable.

ALTERED CHROMOSOME STRUCTURE

Chromosomes may, from time to time, undergo structural changes that result in changes in hereditary potentialities. For example, a portion of a chromosome may break off, and if it lacks a centromere (kinetochore) it will not be included in either of the two nuclei. The result of such a **deletion** is the loss of a group of genes. Another chromosomal change is the attachment of a detached portion of a chromosome to a chromosome of another homologous pair (**translocation**). Also, a part of a chromosome may break off from either end and then become re-attached to the rest of the chromosome by what was formerly the free end (**inversion**) or a central portion of a chromosome may become inverted (Fig. 17.9). If the order of genes in a chromosome was *ABCDEFGHIJ*, a terminal inversion might result in a new gene sequence *CBADEFGHIJ* whereas a central inversion might result in *ABCGFEDHIJ*, the inverted portions being underlined. Although inversions and translocations do not result in a change in the gene content of the cell, they do result in new hereditary potentialities since the action of a gene is modified by the adjacent genes (**position effect**). For example, gene *C* may provide a different hereditary potentiality when it is next to gene *G* than when it was adjacent to *D*. Chromosome breaks and alterations, like gene mutations, are induced by ionizing radiations (5, 10).

ALTERED CHROMOSOME NUMBER

The cells of animals and sporophytes usually contain the diploid ($2n$) number of chromosomes, but occasionally individuals may have only the haploid (n) number. Haploid sporophytes may originate in several different ways, principally by the development of an unfertilized egg into an individual (**parthenogenesis**). Haploids may be sterile, or more rarely the life cycle may proceed without either reduction division or fertilization. Dandelions have such a parthenogenetic life cycle, except that both the sporophytic and gametophytic generations are diploid. Since parthenogenesis is essentially a type of asexual reproduction, the hereditary variation associated with sexual reproduction is lacking, but as we have seen, mutations can be expected to express themselves more frequently in haploids than in diploids. Of course, recessive genes present in haploids will all be expressed phenotypically, provided that the environment is suitable, and haploids will

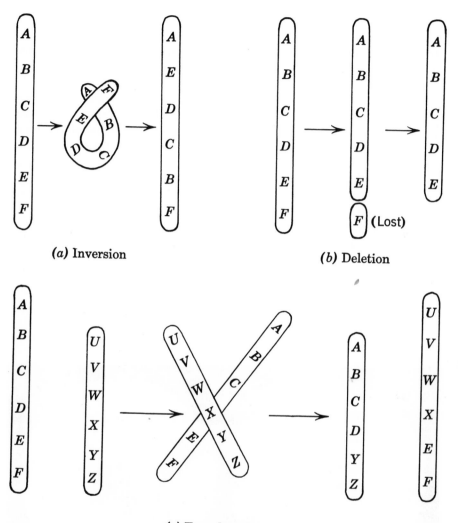

(a) Inversion

(b) Deletion

(c) Translocation

Figure 17.9. Three different types of chromosome changes. (a) The chromosome at the left twists on itself and where the ends cross they break off and exchange positions, resulting in an *inversion*. (b) A portion of this chromosome has broken off. Lacking a centromere, it is not incorporated in the newly formed nucleus and so a *deletion* occurs. (c) Two nonhomologous chromosomes exchange parts, resulting in a *translocation*.

be likely to have fewer dominant genes in multiple gene series controlling continuous variations than will a diploid.

More common than haploid sporophytes are **polyploids** which contain more than two sets of chromosomes per cell (Fig. 17.10). Tetraploids (4n) are perhaps the most common polyploids, but there are also triploids (3n), hexaploids (6n), octaploids (8n), and even higher polyploids. Polyploidy is much more common among plants than among animals. It may come from failure of reduction division or by mitotic division of a nucleus without subsequent cell division. The latter can be caused to occur with greater than natural frequency by treating plants with the alkaloid drug **colchicine**, and plant breeders have produced many valuable polyploids in this way. Polyploids are generally larger and more vigorous than diploids and have larger flowers (Fig. 17.11) and heavier fruits, principally because of the increase in the number of genes involved in multiple gene heredity.

Many cultivated plants differ from their wild relatives in being polyploids rather than diploids. For example, wild strawberries are 2n, whereas different cultivated varieties are 4n, 6n, 8n, 10n, and even 16n. Three species of wheat (4) have 14 (2n), 28 (4n), and 42 (6n) chromosomes; different chrysanthemums have 18, 36, 54, 72, and 90 chromosomes. Cultivated tetraploids include varieties of primrose, petunia, cosmos, zinnia, lily, marigold, apple, blackberry, watermelon, and cantaloupe (11). Some varieties of apple, pear, hyacinth, and tulip

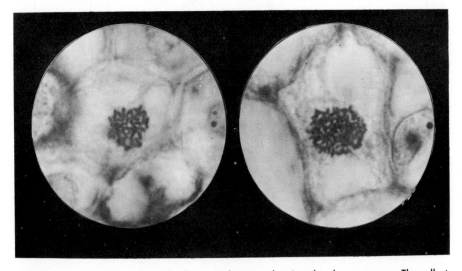

Figure 17.10. Cells from the pith of two apple trees, showing the chromosomes. The cell at the left is from a diploid tree and has 34 chromosomes. The cell at the right is from a tetraploid tree and has 68 chromosomes. The larger cell size at the right is generally characteristic of tetraploids. (Courtesy of the U.S. Department of Agriculture.)

Figure 17.11. The flowers of a diploid (left) and a tetraploid (right) snapdragon. Larger structures and more vigorous growth usually characterize tetraploids as compared with diploids. The tetraploid plant was produced by use of colchicine. (Courtesy of the W. Atlee Burpee Seed Co.)

are among the cultivated triploids. Although all are sterile, they can be propagated vegetatively.

Plant Breeding

The application of genetics to the breeding of better and more productive varieties of cultivated plants and domesticated animals has, up to now, been of incalculable value to man and has contributed greatly to the ability of agriculture to provide adequate supplies of food for the ever-increasing human population of the Earth. Applied agricultural research really has only two basic goals: the production of improved varieties and the provision of the best possible environment for them.

Plant and animal breeding were practiced long before Mendel discovered the basic principles of inheritance, but the procedures were time consuming, rather haphazard, and frequently not too effective. Since most of our species of crop plants were already cultivated by man during the earliest days of recorded history, it seems likely that even prehistoric man engaged in the selection of desirable variations, if not in plant breeding. With the development of genetics during the present century, plant and animal breeding has been placed on a firm scientific basis, and breeders no longer have to work in the dark. Luther Burbank was perhaps the last of the productive plant breeders who worked without the benefit of basic genetic information about his plants, and he almost certainly would have been even more productive if he had used the available genetic information.

Plant and animal breeding is essentially an exercise in accelerated and controlled evolution. First, plant breeders deliberately increase hereditary variation by hybridization (Fig. 17.12), the production of polyploidy through the use of colchicine (Fig. 17.11), the stimulation of mutation by radiation treatments, and the use of other techniques (11, 21, 28, 30, 31). Second, the breeders select the most desirable phenotypes and genotypes obtained in these ways for propagation. Occasionally, they may be fortunate enough to find a desirable natural hybrid or mutant. When plant breeders are dealing with plants that

Figure 17.12. Burpee's Red and Gold hybrid marigold (lower center) was produced by crossing an African marigold plant (upper left) with a Dwarf French marigold plant (upper right). The African marigold is a diploid ($2n = 24$), the French marigold a tetraploid ($4n = 48$), and the hybrid is a sterile triploid ($3n = 3b$). In contrast with the usual situation, the diploid has larger flower heads than the polyploids. (Courtesy of the W. Atlee Burpee Seed Co.)

can be propagated vegetatively on a practical basis, they have a distinct advantage over animal breeders, since even sterile hybrids or mutants can be propagated and since it is not necessary to develop a pure (homozygous) strain that will breed true to form.

The improved varieties produced by plant breeders are too numerous to mention in detail, but every important farm crop, garden vegetable, orchard fruit, and ornamental species includes numerous varieties developed by scientific plant breeding (7, 28, 31). In general, the hereditary traits plant breeders strive to incorporate in their creations include vigor, high yields, desirable quality, and disease resistance. In recent years considerable interest has developed in the breeding of improved varieties of forest trees, particularly rapidly growing varieties, for use in making paper pulp. The breeding of rust resistant varieties of wheat (23) may be cited as just one example of the immense importance of plant breeding to man. If no rust resistant varieties had been developed it is quite likely that today there would be a serious shortage of wheat, rather than the surplus the government purchases each year. But the wheat rust fungus, like other plants, mutates and hybridizes and new types of the rust fungus that attack wheat resistant to previous types continue to appear. Consequently, new varieties of wheat resistant to the mutant rust must be bred. Similar genetic contests between plant breeders and mutating parasites are in progress with other species, too.

HYBRID CORN

In 1932 the average yield of corn in the United States was 26 bushels per acre and in 1957 the average yield was 45 bushels per acre. Although improved cultural practices may have contributed some to this great increase in productivity, the increase was largely the result of one of the more important products of scientific plant breeding: hybrid corn (8, 22). The first substantial planting of hybrid corn by farmers was in 1933 and its use has increased until now almost 95% of the corn crop is hybrid corn. The average yields are far below those possible under the best environmental conditions. In Illinois, the average yield is about 64 bushels per acre, in the state of Washington it is about 80 bushels per acre, but yields of over 100 bushels per acre are not uncommon. Despite the great increase in productivity resulting from the use of hybrid corn, the total production of corn is only slightly more than in 1932 (Table 17.4). The important point is that hybrid corn has made possible an increase in total production and also an increase in quality with the expenditure of much less labor and the release of some 38 million acres of farm land for other uses. At present there is a surplus of corn in this country, but it is quite likely that before the

TABLE 17.4. INFLUENCE OF THE INTRODUCTION OF HYBRID CORN (BEGINNING in 1933) ON THE YIELD OF CORN IN THE UNITED STATES.

Year	Millions of Acres of Corn	Billions of Bushels of Corn	Average Yield, Bushels per Acre
1932	113	2.9	26
1946	90	3.3	37
1957	75	3.4	45

end of this century the increasing population will need all the food farmers can raise (Chapter 14).

Unlike plants such as peas that are commonly self-pollinated, the wind-pollinated corn can not easily be inbred and so pure breeding lines are difficult to establish and maintain. Furthermore, pure (homozygous) strains of corn are generally low in vigor and yield and small in size, at least partly as the result of numerous undesirable homozygous recessive traits. When, however, two pure lines are crossed, the hybrids are large vigorous plants with long, uniform ears and high

Figure 17.13. Hybrid corn plants (center) with the two parent strains on either side. Hybrid vigor is shown, not only by the larger size of the hybrid plants, but also by the larger and more numerous ears of the hybrids. (Courtesy of Donald F. Jones, Connecticut Agricultural Experiment Station.)

yields (Fig. 17.13). Since they are an F_1 generation, the plants are also uniform both phenotypically and genotypically. The **hybrid vigor** found in corn has also been observed in many other species of plants and animals, particularly in those that are naturally cross fertilized and so are extensively heterozygous. Hybrid vigor is probably the result of a variety of different gene interactions and is rather complicated and difficult to explain satisfactorily (30), but it may result in part from the fact that most of the less desirable traits seem to be recessives. For example, pure line A may synthesize only small quantities of growth substance x because of genotype $xxYY$, whereas pure line B may synthesize only small amounts of growth substance Y because of genotype $XXyy$, so growth is restricted in the two pure lines for different reasons. The hybrid ($XxYy$) will be able to synthesize adequate quantities of both growth substances and so will be larger than either parent.

The first hybrid corn was produced in 1907 by the American botanist G. H. Shull, who developed several essentially homozygous parent (P_1) lines by self pollination of corn plants and then crossed two different P_1 lines to obtain a F_1 hybrid generation. The hybrid plants were uniform phenotypically (as would be expected in an F_1 generation), exhibited great hybrid vigor, and were large and high yielding. However, the F_1 population was always small because the P_1 plants produced only a few small ears and consequently a limited supply of seeds containing F_1 embryos. Although the F_1 plants were high yielding, the grain they produced could not be sold to farmers for use as seed corn since it represented an extremely heterogeneous F_2 generation. For these reasons hybrid corn could not be made available to farmers for general use.

The problem of producing an adequate supply of hybrid seed corn for farmers was finally solved by the development of **double cross hybrids,** but it was 1933 before double cross hybrid seed corn became available to farmers. To produce double cross hybrids, four P_1 strains are required (Fig. 17.14). Strain I is then crossed with strain II, producing an F_1 hybrid that can be designated as (I × II). Similarly, strains III and IV are crossed to produce hybrid (III × IV). Then (I × II) plants are crossed with (III × IV) plants. The grains produced by this cross contain the double cross hybrid embryos, and it is these grains that are sold to farmers for planting.

Hybrid seed corn is expensive because of the extensive labor required to produce first the pure lines and then the hybrids, but farmers have found that the high yields of hybrid corn make it much more profitable to raise than the open pollinated varieties they previously used. Many different pure inbred P_1 lines have been produced, and from them many different kinds of hybrids adapted to different regions of the country have been developed.

487

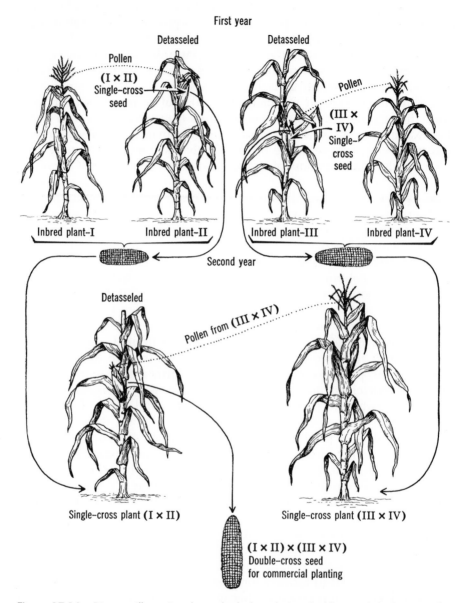

Figure 17.14. Diagram illustrating the method of producing double cross hybrid corn. The first year parent strain I is crossed with parent II, producing grains containing (I × II) embryo plants on the detasseled parents. Similarly, parent strains III and IV are crossed. The second year the single cross hybrid plants (I × II) and (III × IV) are crossed, the resulting grain being the hybrid seed corn sold to farmers for planting.

The production of hybrid corn has been facilitated by the development of two different methods of controlling the formation of functional pollen, thus eliminating the task of detasseling the female parent plants. One method is genetic, the genes for male sterility being included in the genotype of one of the strains being crossed. The other method is biochemical: treatment of the plants with maleic hydrazide inhibits the development of mature stamens without inhibiting pistil development.

The great success of hybrid corn has resulted in the use of similar hybridizing techniques with many other crop plants and domestic animals, generally with marked increases in yield and quality. Hybrids of many species such as tobacco, tomato, cotton, chickens, turkeys, hogs, and cattle are now available or in the process of development.

The Nature of Genes and Gene Action

Although genetic research during the first half of the present century produced a very large amount of information about gene recombinations, gene interactions, mutations, and other aspects of heredity, and although plant and animal breeders made extensive and effective use of this information in the development of new and improved varieties, very little was known about the chemical structure of genes and chromosomes or about the nature of gene action until after World War II. Just how hereditary potentialities, as for red flowers or tallness, influenced the internal processes of a plant and resulted in the development of a tall, red-flowering phenotype remained essentially a mystery. The Swiss biochemist, Friedrich Miescher, discovered the presence of deoxyribonucleic acid (DNA) as well as proteins in nuclei, back in 1869, but the structure of DNA was not clarified until recent years, and it was not until some time after Miescher's discovery that biologists recognized the role of chromosomes in heredity.

DNA AND GENES

As it became evident that genes (17) are located in the chromosomes and that the chromosomes are composed mostly, if not entirely, of nucleoproteins (combinations of DNA and proteins, Chapter 3), the nucleoproteins became recognized as the carriers of hereditary potentialities. Since immense numbers of different proteins were known to exist, and since it was believed that all DNA was essentially identical, the proteins were for a long time considered to be the component carrying genetic information. It is now known, however, that although all DNA has the same general structural pattern, one molecule of DNA may differ from another in the sequence in which its structural units occur, and evidence from a variety of sources supports the theory that DNA is the carrier of the coded genetic information.

DNA molecules are presumably long helical double chains of units (**nucleotides**) composed of deoxyribose phosphate sugar linked to one of four different organic bases (Chapter 3, Figs. 3.8 and 3.9). Two of the organic bases (**adenine** and **guanine**) are **purines**, with a double ring structure, and the other two (**thymine** and **cytosine**) are **pyrimidines**, with a single ring structure. The rings of both contain nitrogen as well as carbon atoms. Thus, four different nucleotides are involved in DNA structure. For simplicity, we may simply designate them as A, G, T, and C. For a time it was thought that in DNA from any source the nucleotides were always arranged in the sequence $ACGT$, this same four unit sequence being repeated time and time again for the length of the DNA molecule. If this were the case DNA could not possibly be the component of the nucleoproteins carrying coded information. We now know, however, that the nucleotides are not linked together in a uniform sequence, but rather can be linked in any possible sequence, thus providing the variation essential if DNA is serving as a genetic code. Evidence of various types indicates that the coded information of the nucleoproteins is actually carried by the DNA rather than by the proteins.

The bonds linking the two coils of a DNA molecule together are between the organic bases of the two coils. Because of their molecular structures, adenine can bond only with thymine and cytosine only with guanine. The result is that the code units are really A-T, T-A, C-G, and G-C. Since a molecule of DNA contains about 10,000 to 20,000 nucleotides and since the code units can occur in any order, an almost unlimited number of different arrangements of bases is possible in DNA molecules, each different arrangement presumably providing different coded genetic information (15). Thus, even if only a short chain is considered, AT-CG-CG-AT differs from both CG-AT-GC-AT and GC-TA-GC-CG and other possible combinations. A change in only a single unit may cause a change in the information carried. By analogy, the word *last* differs from *lost* by only one letter, but they provide much different information. Also, *lost*, *lots*, and *slot* all contain the same four letters but their three arrangements convey quite different meanings, whereas the combinations *tlos* and *otls* convey no meaning at all. A gene might be thought to correspond with one DNA molecule, but no one knows yet what the correspondence between the two is and it may be that each DNA molecule functions as several to many genes, since as few as 3000 units seem to be ample for a gene.

CHROMOSOME STRUCTURE

We now turn our attention to the possible ways DNA and proteins may be organized into chromosomes. At first it was thought that DNA molecules might be joined end to end, forming a long continuous helix, but calculations showed that to account for the quantity of DNA in a chromosome the chromosome would have to be 10,000 times longer and only $\frac{1}{100}$ as thick as it actually is. Several theories of chromosome structure that overcome this and other objections have been proposed, one of the more satisfactory ones being that of Ernst Freese (29). He proposed that the DNA molecules are oriented across a chromosome in a zigzag fashion, the end of one helix of the DNA molecule being attached to a protein molecule on one side and the end of the other helix to a protein molecule on the other side (Fig. 17.15). Thus one end of each helix is free. The protein molecules on either side of the chromosome are linked together longitudinally, perhaps by calcium bridges. The result is a ladder-like structure, the protein forming the uprights and the DNA the zigzag rungs.

Freese proposes that the increased visibility of chromosomes during the prophase of mitosis and meiosis results from the coming together of the two protein chains, resulting in a hollow cylinder, and the contraction of the protein chains at their bonds. However, the formation of the two chromatids presumably occurs while the chromosome is still in its ladder-like shape.

CHROMOSOME DUPLICATION

As a chromosome begins duplicating itself, one DNA molecule after another begins to uncoil from the free end of the double helix and the bonds between the organic bases are progressively broken (Fig. 17.16). Once the bond between thymine and adenine, for example, is broken, the thymine can link with another adenine molecule and the adenine can link with another thymine (9). Presumably, prefabricated sugar-phosphate-base units are present, and as one after another of the bonds holding the double coils of DNA breaks and the coils unwind, a new coil forms against each of the old ones. The formation of the new coil involves bonding together of the sugars through their phosphate groups as well as the bonding of the bases of the new and old coils. The important point is that since thymine will bond only with adenine and cytosine only with guanine, each new coil will be an exact duplicate of the old coil it is replacing, and thus each of the chromatids will contain the same sequence of bases and thus the same genetic information as the chromosome giving rise to it. As the new DNA coils form, they become attached to new protein chains. The result is that half of each

491

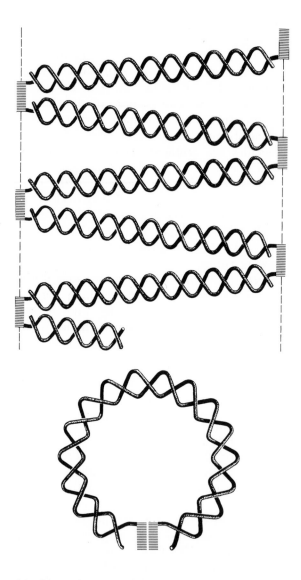

Figure 17.15. Model of a small portion of a chromosome suggested by Ernst Freese. The molecules of DNA are arranged diagonally between two protein columns extending lengthwise of the chromosome and possibly held together by calcium bonds (shown as dotted lines). One chain of each DNA molecule is attached to the left-hand protein column, the other to the right-hand column, one end of each DNA coil being free. As a chromosome duplicates itself in two chromatids, the DNA molecules uncoil from the free ends, one after the other in a zipper-like action, and a new coil is assembled against each of the old coils from nucleotides (sugar-phosphate-base units). Since adenine unites only with thymine and cytosine only with guanine, each newly assembled coil is an exact duplicate of the coil it is replacing. Also, each newly formed DNA coil becomes attached to a new protein column. The result is that each of the two chromatids is composed half of DNA and protein present in the parent chromosome and half of newly synthesized DNA and protein. The ladder-like structure of the chromosome exists in nondividing cells, but as cell division begins, the two protein columns contract and come to lie side by side, forming a shortened, hollow cylinder that is readily visible under the microscope. In the lower drawing the cylindrical form of a chromatid is shown in end view, in contrast with the top view of the ladder-like form. Although this model of a chromosome is theoretical, it appears to be workable and generally in accord with known facts. (From the *Scientific American*, June 1958, with the permission of the publishers.)

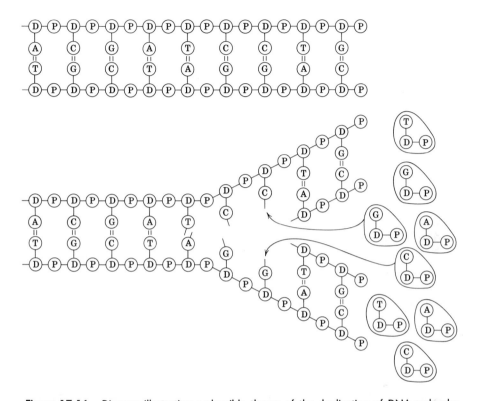

Figure 17.16. Diagram illustrating a plausible theory of the duplication of DNA molecules that accounts for the fact that each of the two resulting molecules has precisely the same sequence of nucleotides as the parent molecule. Above: a small portion of one end of a DNA molecule. The double coiled structure is not shown to make the diagram as simple as possible. Below: the same molecule in the process of duplication. It is progressively unzippering from the right end by the breaking of the hydrogen bonds between the organic bases (A-T and C-G). The first four bonds are broken and the fifth is just breaking. Each base is now free to bond with the base of a nucleotide from the pool shown at the extreme right. Since C can bond only with G and T only with G, each side of the molecule makes an exact replica of the other side from which it has just separated. Two new nucleotides are already in place on each side and the arrows indicate the third pair to be added. The unzippering and subsequent incorporation of new nucleotides continue until the entire original molecule has been replaced by two identical molecules. Note that each of the two molecules has one coil or chain from the parent molecule, the other coil being composed of newly assembled nucleotides. It is possible that the bases may first be incorporated into the molecule followed by the deoxyribose phosphate rather than being incorporated as preassembled nucleotides. D — deoxyribose, P — phosphate, A — adenine, C — cytosine, G — guanine, T — thymine.

chromatid is composed of protein and DNA from the parent chromosome and the other half is composed of newly formed DNA and protein. Two identical DNA-protein ladders (chromatids) now exist in place of one. Although these concepts of chromosome structure and duplication are still theoretical, they seem to be in accord with known facts.

GENE ACTION

For some time it had been suspected that genes exerted their influence on the course of the internal processes of an organism at least partially by controlling the synthesis of enzymes, and that the kinds of enzymes present determined what processes could occur. There was, however, no satisfactory experimental evidence for this until the American geneticists, G. W. Beadle and E. L. Tatum (6), demonstrated numerous examples of specific gene-enzyme relations in the red bread mold (*Neurospora*). Their work, done around 1945, won them the Nobel Prize.

To give only one example, *Neurospora* generally can synthesize the essential amino acid **tryptophane** from **indole** and **serine**, the latter being another amino acid. The reaction is catalyzed by the enzyme **tryptophane synthetase**. Since most *Neurospora* plants can synthesize tryptophane, it is not necessary to supply this amino acid in the culture medium. Beadle and Tatum produced a mutant *Neurospora*, however, that would not grow well without an external supply of tryptophane, and found that the mutation had resulted in the inability of the fungus to produce the enzyme tryptophane synthetase. Crosses between the mutants and plants able to synthesize tryptophane resulted in the expected ratios of the two phenotypes among the offspring. Both indole and serine are, in the final analysis, synthesized from sugars and ammonia, and Beadle and Tatum found at least six other mutants unable to make tryptophane, not because they lacked tryptophane synthetase but because they could not produce one of the enzymes essential for the various steps in the synthesis of either indole or serine. Many other examples of specific gene-enzyme relations have now been found in *Neurospora* and other plants and animals (19).

INFORMATION TRANSFER FROM GENES TO ENZYMES

The problem still remained as to how a gene could influence the synthesis of a specific enzyme. Although the problem is still not solved, an attractive theory of gene action has been made possible by the discovery of the probable role of the microsome RNA and transfer RNA in protein synthesis (Chapter 10, page 288). Since apparently the DNA of the chromosomes determines the kinds of RNA produced, and since the RNA in turn controls the kinds of protein produced, we have a plausible explanation of how each organism synthesizes just certain kinds of protein as dictated by its hereditary potentialities (the DNA). Since enzymes are proteins, the kinds of enzymes present in an organism are determined by the genetic codes of DNA transmitted through RNA. In turn, the kinds of enzymes determine what biochemical processes can occur and thus what the phenotype of the organism will be. For example, a plant may be a genetic dwarf because it lacks an enzyme necessary for the synthesis of a growth substance such as gibberellic acid, or it may be an albino because it lacks an enzyme necessary for chlorophyll synthesis. It must not be forgotten, however, that heredity only determines what an organism can do and that environment plays an important role in what it actually does. Thus, a plant may have all the necessary genes (and so all the necessary enzymes) for tallness and chlorophyll and yet it may be dwarf and chlorotic because of a lack of nitrogen or some other essential environmental factors.

Present-day concepts of chromosome and gene structure and of the nature of gene action are still theoretical, but, for the first time they provide us with a reasonably detailed and satisfactory picture of the nature of hereditary potentialities and the way they exert their control over the internal processes of an organism, and so in turn over the growth, development, and behavior of the organism (16). We can expect continuing investigation to provide an increasingly detailed, accurate, and exciting picture of this fundamental aspect of life.

► ## *Questions*

1. When a plant breeder crossed a white-fruited summer squash with a yellow-fruited variety, all 89 offspring were found to bear white fruits. When these 89 plants were crossed with one another, 76% of the offspring had white fruits and 24% had yellow fruits. What can you conclude about dominance and the number of gene pairs involved? Give the genotypes of the P_1, F_1, and F_2 plants.

2. A white-fruited squash plant is crossed with a yellow-fruited plant, and of 56 offspring 26 had yellow fruits and 30 had white fruits. What was the genotype of the white-fruited parent plant?

3. If you were operating a seed company and offered red, white, and pink snapdragon seeds for sale, how would you produce the seed to put in each of the three kinds of packets? What would you tell a customer who had purchased some pink snapdragon seed from you two years ago and complained that the seed she saved from the pink-flowering plants the first year gave red and white flowering plants as well as pink ones?

495

4. A squash plant with white, disc-shaped fruits is crossed with a plant having yellow, spherical fruits. All the F_1 offspring have white, disc-shaped fruits. When one of the offspring was then crossed with a plant having yellow spherical fruits, their progeny were as follows: 25 white sphere, 25 yellow disc, 26 white disc, 24 yellow sphere. What traits are dominant? Are the two pairs of genes linked or not? Give the genotypes of all plants mentioned and outline the crosses made. If two F_1 plants were crossed, what portion of the offspring would have white fruits? Spherical fruits? White-spherical fruits? If you wanted to establish a new variety with white-spherical fruits, how could you determine which of the F_2 plants having this phenotype were homozygous, and thus were suitable parents for the new variety? If you had 800 seeds secured by self-pollinating an F_1 plant, how many could you expect to grow into plants with the desired homozygous white sphere genotype?

5. If, when the foregoing 800 seeds were planted, one grew into a plant bearing green spherical fruits, what would you expect might have happened? When this plant was self-pollinated, three-fourths of the offspring had green spherical fruits. When crossed with either white or yellow fruited plants, half of the offspring had green fruits. What information do these crosses provide about the green trait?

6. A plant breeder wishes to eliminate an undesirable hereditary trait from an otherwise superior variety of plant he has developed. How would he proceed? Would the difficulty of his task be influenced by whether the trait was dominant or recessive? Explain.

7. Can morphological hereditary traits, such as plant height or smoothness of seeds, be explained on the basis of gene-enzyme sequences as can the biochemical traits of *Neurospora?* On the basis of what you have learned in this and previous chapters can you suggest possible biochemical mechanisms involved in any morphological traits?

► # *References*

For Reference

1. Bonner, David M., *Heredity*. Englewood Cliffs, N.J.: Prentice-Hall, 1961.
2. Sinnott, E. W., L. C. Dunn, and T. Dobzhansky, *Principles of Genetics*, Rev. Ed. New York: McGraw-Hill, 1958.
3. Winchester, A. M., *Genetics*, 2nd ed. Boston: Houghton-Mifflin Co., 1958.

For Reading

4. Anonymous, Baring wheat's genetic secrets. *Agricultural Research* 4(11):7–10, May 1956.
5. Auerbach, C., The genetic effects of radiation: the production of mutation. *New Biology* 20:30–52, 1956.

6. Beadle, George W., The genes of men and molds. *Scientific American* 179(3):30–39, September 1948. Genes and chemical reactions in *Neurospora. Science* 129:1715–1719, 1959.

7. Biddulph, Susan, Sugar beet: science-created crop. *Science Digest* 45(3):77–78, March 1959.

8. Crabb, A. R., *The Hybrid Corn Makers: Prophets of Plenty.* New Brunswick: Rutgers University Press, 1948.

9. Crick, F. H. C., The structure of the hereditary material. *Scientific American* 191(4): 54–61, October 1954.

10. Crow, J. F., Ionizing radiation and evolution. *Scientific American* 201(3):138–160, September 1959.

11. Darrow, G. M., Polyploidy in fruit improvement. *Scientific Monthly* 70:211–219, 1950.

12. Dobzhansky, T., The genetic basis of evolution. *Scientific American* 182(1):32–41, January 1950.

13. Dobzhansky, T., Genetics. *Scientific American* 183(3):55–61, September 1950.

14. Gabriel, M. L. and Seymour Fogel, *Great Experiments in Biology.* Englewood Cliffs, N. J.: Prentice-Hall, 1955 (pp. 225–279).

15. Gamow, George, Information transfer in the living cell. *Scientific American* 193(4): 70–78, October 1955.

16. Gay, Helen, Nuclear control of the cell. *Scientific American* 202(1):126–136, January 1960.

17. Horowitz, N. H., The gene. *Scientific American* 195(4):78–90, October 1956.

18. Hotchkiss, R. D. and Esther Weiss, Transformed bacteria. *Scientific American* 195(5):48–53, November 1956.

19. Ingram, V. M., How do genes act? *Scientific American* 198(1):68–74, January 1958.

20. Knight, C. A. and Dean Frasier, The mutation of viruses. *Scientific American* 193(1):74–78, July 1955.

21. Manchester, Harland, The new age of "atomic crops." *Reader's Digest* 73(5):135–140, November 1958.

22. Mangelsdorf, Paul C., Hybrid Corn. *Scientific American* 185(2):39–47, August 1951.

23. Mangelsdorf, Paul C., Wheat. *Scientific American* 189(1)50–59, July 1953.

24. Mangelsdorf, Paul C., Ancestor of corn. *Science* 128:1313–1320, 1958.

25. Mendel, Gregor, *Experiments in Plant Hybridization, 1865,* Cambridge: Harvard University Press, 1941. Also in reference 2.

26. Mudd, Stuart, The staphylococcus problem. *Scientific American* 200(1):41–75, January 1959.

27. Sonneborn, T. M., Partner of the genes. *Scientific American* 183(5):30–39, November 1950. (Cytoplasmic inheritance)

28. Taylor, F. J., Wizard of the vegetable patch. *Reader's Digest* 65(1):132–135, July 1954.

29. Taylor, J. Herbert, The duplication of chromosomes. *Scientific American* 198(6): 36–42, June 1958.

30. Whaley, W. Gordon, The gifts of hybridity. *Scientific Monthly* 70:10–18, 1950.

31. Williams, W. and A. G. Brown, Breeding new varieties of fruit trees. *Endeavour* 19:147–155, 1960.

18. History of the Plant Kingdom

AT ONE TIME MOST BIOLOGISTS subscribed to the belief that the species of plants and animals now living had existed without change since the beginning of life on Earth, and that each species was independently created. However, during the past two centuries, discoveries resulting from careful observation of and experimentation with living organisms have made it increasingly clear that most of the species now living have existed for a relatively short time, that many species formerly living are now extinct, and that through change one species has given rise to others. The history of the Plant Kingdom, therefore is the history of change. That is to say, our modern flora and fauna are the products of organic evolution from ancestral species. Presumably all plants and perhaps all living things (12) can be traced back to a single common ancestor, the first relatively simple unicellular organism. Although this view is supported by the fundamental biochemical, physiological, and cellular similiarities among all living organisms, some biologists believe that life may have originated at several different times and places and that thus not all organisms would actually be related in the true sense.

Our present day flora is certainly not the end of change. If we could look two billion years into the future, we might find that further evolu-

498

tion had resulted in changes as great as those accomplished in the past two billion years, assuming that life would still be present on Earth. However, despite the changes that have occurred in the evolution of plants, throughout the Plant Kingdom there runs a profound core of conservatism, both structural and physiological.

Fossils

The record of plant evolution is the accumulation of ancient plant remains (**fossils**) in the sediments and sedimentary rocks of the Earth's crust (1, 3). Most plant remains were deposited in swamp or bog areas where they grew; some were carried by streams to the site of deposition in the sediments of river deltas or lakes. Plant remains may be fossilized only if local conditions prevent their decay. Quick coverage by water, sediments, or ash excludes oxygen and thus preserves the plant tissues for subsequent formation of fossils. Plants that grew in swamps, bogs, or on pond margins and near the sea, were the most likely to be fossilized, whereas plants of inland arid regions were less likely to be preserved.

In general, soft-bodied plants would have had less chance of preservation than those with much woody tissue. Algae, fungi, mosses, and delicate herbs are scarce in the fossil record, even though their ancient habitats were of the proper sort. The more delicate structures were liable to breakage or extreme distortion under the conditions of fossiliza-

Figure 18.1. *Neuropteris,* A Carboniferous seed fern. (Chicago Natural History Museum.)

tion, and thus they may escape recognition. As a result of conditions at the time of and following the deposition of plant remains, fossils may occur in a number of forms. One of the most common is an **impression** formed when a plant part, such as a leaf, falls upon wet sand or clay. Sediments press the leaf into the soft substratum and an impression is made. The impression remains after the leaf disintegrates and the sediments, under pressure, consolidate to hard rock (Fig. 18.1). In some circumstances, the embedded plant may become chemically altered to leave only its carbon residue. Such fossils are known as **compressions** (Fig. 18.2). In these, the cellular structure of the part is not

Figure 18.2. *Annularia,* A Carboniferous horsetail. (Chicago Natural History Museum.)

Figure 18.3. A petrifaction of a giant lycopod stem from the Carboniferous period. (Copyright, General Biological Supply House, Inc., Chicago.)

preserved. Compressions are common in strata, associated with coal beds. Another type of fossil is produced by the infiltration of the tissues with minerals from the water and sediments surrounding the buried plant part. The process may be so complete that the cell walls are literally changed to stone. Fossils of this type are **petrifactions** (Fig. 18.3). When they are cut into thin sections and examined under a microscope, much of the fine structural detail may be seen. In the Petrified Forest in Arizona and other places in the west, there are large petrified trunks of ancient trees, now exposed on the surface.

FOSSILS AND EARTH HISTORY

To reconstruct a wholly satisfying picture of the progress of the Plant Kingdom only from the fossil record is impossible. It can hardly be doubted that the earliest representatives of the Plant Kingdom were simple and delicate in structure. Yet tangible proof of this in the form of fossil remains is scanty, for these are the very forms that largely would have escaped fossilization. Much of the evidence upon which we build the early part of our story of plant evolution, therefore, is derived from other kinds of plant study.

Although the fossil record is obviously incomplete, the sequence of deposition and the relative ages of the fossils are fairly accurately known. Sedimentation occurred in great cycles of time, leaving strata of rock. The fossil plant species dominating the various strata are for the most part quite different from the plants of today, and from each other. Thus the fossil record does not present a series of gradually changing forms. Instead, the record is punctuated by many gaps.

The earth is very old. Geologists have estimated its age to be more than 2 billion and perhaps as much as 4 billion years. The earliest known rocks, about 2 billion or more years old, were formed of molten materials and contain no fossils of plants or animals. The first indirect evidence of the existence of living organisms occurs in certain sedimentary rocks and limestones of an age between 2 and $1\frac{1}{2}$ billion years. The limestones are believed to have been formed by lime-secreting algae, although no fossils of the organisms have been found. In the geologic time scale (Table 18.1), this early period of the earth's history is designated the **Archeozoic** era.

In most of the **Proterozoic** era (from $1\frac{1}{2}$ billion to 600 million years ago) only indirect evidence of organic existence occurs, in the form of lime, graphite, and iron deposits. The living organisms may be supposed to have been simple algae and bacteria, for certain modern species of these forms are associated with similar peculiar deposits of these substances at the present time. The first undisputed fossil plants are found in strata about 600 million years old. These are simple algal types. During this period, the Animal Kingdom was represented by simple worms and crustaceans.

The Cambrian and Ordovician periods of the Early **Paleozoic** era (from 600 million to 381 million years ago) furnish scanty plant remains, but enough is known about them to make it clear that the algae were already well established. Forms representing some of the modern groups of algae were in existence at that time. The Animal Kingdom was represented by higher invertebrates, corals, starfish, and early vertebrates.

The origin of land plants is doubtless to be sought among the algae. No fossils are known that are clearly transitional. It may be supposed that green algae with features that prevented loss of water and death by desiccation became established on land and then developed anchorage and an erect habit. By Silurian and early Devonian periods of the Middle Paleozoic (381 million to 309 million years ago), there appeared a group of small leafless and rootless forms which in their simplicity are alga-like, but whose creeping stems and slender erect branches contain the simplest of vascular tissue. The erect leafless branches were photosynthetic and bore typical stomata. These plants, called the psilophytes (Psilophyta), are the first true land plants in the fossil

TABLE 18.1. GEOLOGIC TIME SCALE

Eras	Periods	Millions of Years from Present	Major Developments in Plant Life as Shown by Fossil Record
Cenozoic	Quarter-nary	Present to 2	Extinction of may trees through climatic changes. Increase in herbaceous flora.
	late Tertiary early	2 to 60	Dwindling of forests; climatic segregation of floras. Rise of herbaceous plants.
			Development of many modern angiospermous families. Rise and world-wide extension of modern forests.
Mesozoic	Cretaceous	60 to 125	Angiosperms gradually become dominant, some modern angiospermous types represented. Gymnosperms decline.
	Jurassic	125 to 185	Earliest known angiosperms. Cycads and conifers dominant; primitive gymnosperms disappear.
	Triassic		Increase of cycads, ginkgo, and conifers. Disappearance of seed ferns.
Paleozoic	Permian	185 to 309	Waning of arborescent clubmosses and horsetails. Early cycads and conifers.
	Carbonif-erous		Extensive coal-forming forests of giant clubmosses, horsetails, and seed ferns. Primitive gymnosperms.
	Devonian	309 to 381	Early vascular plants: psilophytes, primitive club-mosses, horsetails, and ferns. Early forests of arbo-rescent clubmosses.
	Silurian		Algae dominant. First direct evidence of land plants.
	Ordovician	381 to 600	Marine algae dominant. Possibly first land plants.
	Cambrian		Some modern algal groups established.
Proterozoic	600 to 1500		Bacteria and simple algae.
Archeozoic	1500 to 4000		No fossils known; possibly unicellular algae.

Adapted from Eames

record (Fig. 18.4). It is probable that these early land plants repre-sented the sporophytic phase of the life cycle. The transition from the gametophyte-dominant algae to the sporophyte-dominant vascular plant is a vast one to cover and probably involved the evolution of an extensive series of intermediate forms unknown in the fossil record.

Figure 18.4. Glass model of *Rhynia*, one of the earliest tracheophytes, from the Devonian. (Chicago Natural History Museum.)

The early psilophytes evidently did not remain on earth very long, for they disappear from the fossil record before the end of the Devonian period. However, two modern genera of plants, *Psilotum* and *Tmesipteris*, are believed to be descendants of the ancient psilophytes. A recently discovered fossil, *Baragwanathia*, of the Silurian period, poses a problem in that it antedates the psilophytes but strongly resembles the lycopods, a group generally considered more advanced than the psilophytes.

The Devonian was a period of mild and equable climate, a time for rapid plant development. The first representatives of the modern lycopods (Lycophyta) and horsetails (Sphenophyta) appeared. The lycopods were especially vigorous, for they attained heights of twenty feet or more and formed extensive forests. In late Devonian, early ferns (Pterophyta) occurred that were probably the forerunners of our modern ferns. Lungfishes, scorpions, sharks, and early amphibians represented the Animal Kingdom.

Great coal-forming forests characterized the Carboniferous period of the Late Paleozoic (309 million to 185 million years ago (10, 13). Strata of rock in association with coal seams yield abundant fossils of ferns, tree-size lycopods and horsetails, pteridosperms (seed-bearing but fern-like), and primitive gymnosperms (Fig. 18.5). Increasing and widespread aridity and in some places extensive glaciation characterized the succeeding Permian period. During the Permian period many Carboniferous forms dwindled and became extinct. Fossils of primitive reptiles, insects, and early terrestrial vertebrates represent the animals of the time.

The **Mesozoic** era (185 million to 60 million years ago) witnessed

Figure 18.5. Reconstruction of a Carboniferous landscape, showing arborescent clubmosses (1, 2, 3, 4), horsetails (5, 6), ferns (7, 8, 9), seed ferns (10, 11), gymnosperms (12). (Chicago Natural History Museum.)

significant changes in the vegetation. During the early portion, under somewhat arid and warm conditions, most of the giant lycopods and horsetails disappeared, along with the seed ferns. The remaining club mosses, horsetails, and ferns were small species similar to those of the present. Higher types of gymnosperms, such as conifers, cycads, and *Ginkgo* (4) arose and rapidly became the dominant plants. The first angiosperms appeared in Middle Mesozoic under fluctuating climatic conditions, developed rapidly, and by the close of the era had become very abundant as the gymnosperms gradually lost ground (7). Many modern types of flowering plants are represented in the Late Mesozoic flora. Fig, oak, holly, magnolia, sassafras, willows, maples, and many others occurred in the forests. During the Mesozoic era, the giant reptiles appeared and disappeared, specialized insects were numerous, and primitive mammals appeared for the first time.

The Early Tertiary period of the **Cenozoic** era (60 million years ago) was a time of humid, warm climate which supported a rich and widespread flora, with woody angiosperms dominant. During the Late Tertiary the flora became restricted in distribution and segregated into climatic types, as general cooling occurred and climatic zones became established. The redwoods and some associated species disappeared from the inland areas made dry by mountain building. At the close of the Tertiary several species disappeared as a result of the increasing aridity in western North America. Extensive glaciation occured in the Pleistocene (2 million years ago to the present) in the northern hemisphere, profoundly affecting the distribution of many modern plant species (8). Modern herbaceous angiosperms arose and evolved rapidly during this time. Their short life cycle had considerable survival value under conditions of progressive cooling. Developments in the Animal Kingdom during the Early Tertiary include the rise of modern birds and higher mammals, and in the Late Tertiary the appearance of primitive man.

The Theme of Evolution

Obviously the fossil record fails to provide the complete story of plant evolution. Gaps of considerable magnitude, unbridged by transitional forms between the old and the new, occur at many levels in the fossil record. However, studies in the fields of morphology, physiology, and genetics have provided the unifying theme of the story and given some insight into the mechanisms involved.

Morphological study of plants supports the concept of relationship among plant species. Similarities in form and structure indicate relationship. In general, the greater the resemblances, the closer the relationship, and close relationship suggests common ancestry. Thus, two closely related species such as the white oak and the post oak had a common ancestor in the rather recent past, geologically speaking, whereas more distantly related species such as the white oak and the sugar maple would have common ancestors only in the more remote past. Structural and behavioral patterns persisting in a long series may be assumed to identify a line of evolutionary development from an ancestral type. Thus the vascular tissue is remarkably uniform in composition, basic arrangement, and function throughout the tracheophytes, despite the differences in the various types of steles. The basic uniform structural pattern in flowers and the individual role in reproduction played by the several parts persists through a host of modifications. The invariable repetition of the same theme in the sexual reproductive cycles of plants, involving gametes, gametic fusion, meiospore formation, the alternation of phases, and all the rest, suggests that differences in some of the details of execution are only secondary modifications. Thus, sexually reproducing plants have a deep-lying relationship, and these organisms may have evolved one from another in a sequence revealed by their secondary modifications. This is to say that, in spite of the evident versatility or changeability of living things, they are essentially conservative and resistant to fundamental change.

Physiological studies also aid in the understanding of plant relationships. One of the most conspicuous is the similarity of pigmentation in the members of various series. This matter has received much attention in systematic studies among the algae. Although the algae are all chlorophyll bearing, there are at least ten different kinds of chlorophyll whose presence or absence individually or in combination characterize certain of the phyla (Chapter 2). Auxiliary pigments, such as phycophaein and fucoxanthin, are also employed in the evaluation of relationship. Similarly, special aspects of chemical composition may be used in studies of this kind. Similarities or differences in the nature of such constituents as proteins, volatile oils, resins, and alkaloids, may provide valuable data on relationships.

The study of the **genetic behavior** of plants in both natural and artificial circumstances offers evidence in support of the concept of plant relationships and evolution by orderly cumulative change in living organisms. The fact of interfertility of certain plant species indicates a basic compatibility of the hereditary material of the species, just as infertility generally suggests a fundamental incompatibility, and thus a remoteness of relationship. Whether such compatibilities are expressed in terms of viable offspring produced or in terms of chromosome pairing at meiosis makes little difference, since the fact of crossing creates the new genetic complexes upon which the selective action of environment may play.

From such selections come the new populations with still newer genetic complexes.

Geneticists frequently record the spontaneous appearance of new types (mutants) of plants among old familiar parent stock. Such changes may be the result of gene mutations, chromosome alterations such as fragmentation and deletion, or aberrant chromosome behavior. Mutations have been artificially induced by various experimental techniques, involving radiation (5) and chemical treatment. Such mutations, representing relatively permanent changes in the hereditary material, may be passed on to subsequent generations and thus enter the evolutionary stream. Mutations may entail conspicuous changes in form or they may be expressed as relatively inconspicuous physiological changes which alter some aspect of a plant's metabolism. Man has created many new varieties of crop plants by hybridization and selection of mutant stocks. The difficult problem of the taxonomist in recognition and delimitation of poorly defined species may reflect a natural plasticity, that is, proclivity for change, or a compatibility with other species.

ORIGIN OF SPECIES

The concept of organic evolution has been in the minds of men at least since the time of the early Greek philosophers, and since then many biologists have sought an explanation of the mechanisms by which organisms change. Our modern understanding of evolution (still incomplete) stems largely from the work and writings of Charles Darwin (1809–1882). In 1859 he proposed a theory of evolution based on three main points (6).

1. A population of organisms is capable of producing many more offspring than its site can possibly support.

2. All offspring cannot survive under the conditions of limited space and shortage of materials necessary to support them, and thus they compete with each other. Only a small proportion of the total offspring survive the competition, and these are adapted to their particular environment; the unfit perish.

3. Not all individuals of a species are alike. The successful competitors possess highly favorable variations that give them an advantage in the same environment over the unsuccessful ones with less favorable variations. The favorable variations are transmitted to succeeding generations, further variations arise, followed by competition and selection of the best adapted, and so on, generation after generation. In this way, according to Darwin, many new species of organisms come into being, each more favorably adapted to its environment than its predecessor. In the process many ill-adapted individuals disappear.

A population of a species frequently shows many variant forms. Some of these are direct **environmental variations** induced solely by environmental factors acting on the body tissues of the plant. For example, if a plant is grown in the shade, its height and size of its leaves might be different than if the plant were grown in full sunlight. Such variations are not heritable, for they are not controlled by the hereditary substance of the reproductive cells. Selection, acting on such variations, is not, of course, significant in evolution. On the other hand, some variants in the population will transmit their special feature to a succeeding generation irrespective of environmental factors. Such inherited variations are **genetic variations** and they are important in the evolution of the species.

Biologists are familiar with the fact that species are often distinguishable one from another on the basis of features that have no imaginable survival value, that is, they are **nonadaptive characters**. Such characters are, of course, genetically controlled and heritable. However, they are not accounted for in natural selection as Darwin conceived it. It is possible, of course, that such species possess **adaptive characters** of other kinds.

It was Darwin's view that evolutionary changes were accomplished as a result of an infinite number of small, more or less continuous and cumulative variations. Some critics of the Darwinian theory have held that small variations commonly within the range of normal variability of the species are insignificant in bringing about major changes, and that only large variations could be significant in natural selection. Both large and small variations do occur in species populations. Some of the latter are of such magnitude as to constitute new types, or new species.

The emphasis on the importance of large variations as a means to species formation came chiefly from the work of the Dutch botanist, Hugo de Vries (1848–1935). Among plants of certain species of evening primrose he observed the spontaneous appearance of individuals sufficiently different to be regarded as distinct species. Changes of such magnitude de Vries called **mutations**, and he regarded them as the basic units of evolution on which natural selection may act.

With the theories of Darwin and de Vries as bases, modern workers in the fields of cytology and genetics have striven to relate the observed facts of evolution to the physical basis of reproduction in an effort to establish the causes and mechanisms of evolution. All of the facts of evolution are not yet explained and are unlikely to be until much more is known about the nature of the hereditary material. Meanwhile, certain general statements may be made to summarize the current views on evolutionary mechanisms.

The chief hereditary materials are the genes and these largely control the structure and metabolism of the organism. The genes are mutable and the chromosomes in which they reside are subject to physical alteration and aberrant behavior. Such mutations bring about changes of various magnitudes in structure and metabolism. Very large gene mutations or excessive derangement of the chromosome complement may give rise to a fatal imbalance between organism and environment, or the variants may be better adapted to an environment than the parent form, and in a stable environment may supersede the parent form. Changes in environment change the adaptive value of variations (11). Plants with new gene combinations resulting from hybridization and polyploid forms would, of course, be similarly selected on the basis of their adaptive characters. Many additional secondary factors, such as geographic and ecologic isolation, time of flowering, adaptation to pollinating agents, and so forth, have important influences on the origin of new species.

► ## Questions

1. Give as many possible explanations as you can for the large gaps in the fossil record.

2. Mutations appear in fungi more frequently than in vascular plants. Suggest several possible explanations.

3. What factors may contribute to the extinction of a species? Are the higher plants necessarily better fitted for survival than the lower plants?

4. Are evolutionary changes haphazard, or do they appear to occur in certain directions? Give reasons for your answer.

5. Our cultivated crop plants are quite different from their wild ancestors. Plant breeders have developed many new varieties of plants during the past fifty years, and have even produced some plants so different from their ancestors that they may be regarded as new species or genera. Are these examples of evolution or not? Explain your answer.

6. Evolution appears to have been particularly rapid in eras of marked climatic or geological changes. Explain why.

7. Cacti and other desert plants have many structural features that are quite different from those of mesophytic plants and that undoubtedly contribute to their ability to survive in the dry desert environment. How can the evolutionary development of these adaptations be explained? Could apple trees adapt themselves to a desert environment? Explain your answer.

► *References*

For Reference

1. Arnold, C. A., *An Introduction to Paleobotany.* New York: McGraw-Hill, 1947.
2. Moody, P. A., *Introduction to Evolution.* New York: Harper & Brothers, 1953.

For Reading

3. Andrews, H. N., *Ancient Plants and the World They Lived In.* Ithaca, N.Y.: Comstock Publishing Co., 1947.
4. Bastin, E. W., The ginkgo: strange survivor. *Nature Magazine* 43:410, 1950.
5. Crow, J. F., Ionizing radiation and evolution. *Scientific American* 201(3):138–160, September 1959.
6. Darwin, Charles, *The Origin of Species.* New York: New American Library, 1958. (A reprint of the second edition.)
7. Eiseley, Loren, How flowers changed the world. *Science Digest* 45(2):70–75, February 1959.
8. Gamow, George, Origin of the ice. *Scientific American* 179(4):40–45, 1948.
9. Huxley, Julian, *Evolution in Action,* New York: New American Library, 1957.
10. Janssen, R. E., The beginnings of coal. *Scientific American* 179(1):46–51, 1948.
11. Kettlewell, H. B. D., Darwin's missing evidence. *Scientific American* 200(3):48–53, March 1959.
12. Laurence, W. L., Seaweed—man's common ancestor? *Science Digest* 43(4):6–8, April 1958.
13. Lessing, L. P., Coal. *Scientific American* 193(1):58–67, July 1955.
14. Libby, W. F., Radiocarbon dating. *Endeavour* 13:5–16, 1954.
15. Ryan, F. J., Evolution observed, *Scientific American* 189(4):78–83, October 1953.
16. Simpson, G. G., *The Meaning of Evolution.* New York: New American Library, 1951.
17. Simpson, G. G., *Life of the Past.* New Haven: Yale University Press, 1953.

19. Origin of Life

ANY CONSIDERATION of the evolution of the many species of plants and animals inhabiting the Earth leads eventually to an even more difficult and more puzzling problem: the origin of life on the Earth. Even before the time of modern science, man generally assumed that life had not always existed on Earth, and the scientific information now available suggests that life has been present on Earth only about half of the four billion years of the Earth's existence. Before the development of the theory of evolution only two explanations of the origin of life had been suggested: that each species of plant and animal was created supernaturally during a limited period of time in the distant past, or that living things could and did arise spontaneously at almost any time from nonliving things. The supernatural basis of the first proposal automatically excluded it from scientific investigation. The second hypothesis (**spontaneous generation**) was subject to experimental study, but no valid experiments were conducted until late in the seventeenth century.

With the acceptance of the theory of evolution, the problem of the origin of life was in a way simplified—it was now necessary to account for the origin of only the most primitive form or forms of life rather than the variety of complex plants and animals populating the Earth. However, the origin of even the simplest living organisms from a lifeless world presented such a formidable and apparently insoluble problem that for many years biologists simply ignored it in despair. Not until the second quarter of the present century was a theory of the origin of life proposed that was scientifically plausible. Among the hypotheses that never received serious consideration was the proposal that living things from some other planet had colonized the Earth. Aside from the extremely slight probability that this could actually have occurred, the hypothesis was unattractive because it only transferred the problem of the origin of life to some unknown site distant in space as well as in time.

Spontaneous Generation

At least from the days of ancient Greece to the time of Louis Pasteur, scholars as well as the uneducated accepted the doctrine of spontaneous generation in one form or another. The appearance of maggots in meat, molds in fruits, fungi on wood, or a variety of aquatic plants and animals in a newly formed and apparently lifeless pool of water all seemed explainable to the people of the ancient and medieval civilizations only on the basis that living organisms had arisen from nonliving things or perhaps from totally different forms of life, and these concepts persisted well into the Renaissance. An old herbal illustrated the falling leaves of a tree becoming birds and fish, and goose barnacles were commonly supposed to give rise to geese. The idea that horsehairs falling into watering troughs gave rise to worms and snakes persisted among farmers even into the twentieth century. As late as the seventeenth century both scientists and laymen generally believed that slime and decaying substances turned into worms, maggots, or molds, and that parasites such as worms and fungi were the products rather than the cause of disease.

The first scientist to conduct a known experiment on spontaneous generation was the Italian, Francesco Redi (8). About 1650, Redi, having noticed flies hovering over meat that later became wormy, decided to find out if there were any connection between flies and the maggots in the meat. In four jars he placed a dead snake, two dead fish, and some veal, and covered the jars tightly. The same things were placed in four other jars, but these jars were left open. In due time the animals and veal in the open jars became infested with maggots, while those in the covered jars decayed but contained no maggots. "Thus," Redi concluded, "the flesh of dead animals can not engender worms unless the eggs of the living be deposited therein." Redi, however, still continued to believe that other organisms such as intestinal worms and gall flies were generated spontaneously. Gradually, as other experiments similar to Redi's were conducted and as information on the life cycles of plants and animals was assembled, scientists came to accept the fact that worms and other visible organisms did not arise spontaneously.

At about the time that Redi was conducting his experiments, however, the microscope was just coming into use as a biological tool, revealing an entirely new world of microscopic plants and animals. These microorganisms, many scientists believed, arose spontaneously even though larger organisms did not. About 1780, John Needham, an English priest, used Redi's techniques to determine whether microorganisms would be generated spontaneously in meat broth and hay infusions, and found abundant organisms in both the sealed and open containers. Lazzaro Spallanzani, an Italian scientist contemporary with Needham, questioned Needham's conclusion that the microorganisms were generated spontaneously and repeated the experiments, modifying them by boiling the contents of the flasks to kill any organisms present before sealing (10). No organisms appeared in the flasks boiled after sealing, and Spallanzani considered he had shown that even microorganisms do not arise by spontaneous generation. Other scientists repeated his experiments with similar results, but some scientists still believed in spontaneous generation, insisting that some factor present in the air and destroyed by heating the flasks was essential for life.

The controversy was not finally settled until in 1864 Louis Pasteur proved beyond doubt that heat did not destroy any vital factor in the air of the flasks, by using flasks with long necks bent in an S-shape (7). This permitted outside air to enter the flasks after boiling but prevented microorganisms from falling into the sterilized flasks. In other experiments Pasteur showed that yeasts were the cause, not a result, of alcoholic fermentation and that bacteria were the cause and not a product of souring milk.

Omne Vivum ex Vivo

Pasteur's work finally discredited the theory of spontaneous generation, and for the first time biologists reached general agreement that all living things arise only by reproduction from living ancestors. *Omne vivum ex vivo*—all life from life—became the biological password. Spontaneous generation, the only theory of the origin of life subject to experimental investigation, had been thoroughly tested and found wanting. Now biologists were left with no theory of the origin of life at all and with what seemed like no possibility of propounding even a plausible hypothesis. After all, there were only two possibilities other than spontaneous generation: the implausible transfer of life to the Earth from another planet and the supernatural creation of life excluded by definition from scientific investigation.

Spontaneous Generation Revived

The first breech in this impasse was made by a Russian bio-chemist, A. I. Oparin, in a book he published in 1936 (6). Oparin suggested that although life can not arise by spontaneous generation under present environmental conditions, life could have been generated spontaneously under the conditions existing on the lifeless Earth some two billion years ago. Oparin's hypotheses about the conditions existing at that time and about the possible physical and chemical processes that could have resulted in the initial generation of life have been modi-fied and extended by other scientists into a reasonably plausible theory, supported in part by experimental evidence (1, 2, 12).

THE PRE-ARCHEOZOIC WORLD

The theory holds that before life appeared on Earth, the land was a wasteland of bare rocks, since any soil formed would rapidly erode away with no plant cover to hold it. The temperature was probably higher than at present and more of the ultra-violet radiation of the sun prob-ably reached the Earth. The atmosphere contained no oxygen and little or no carbon dioxide or nitrogen, but instead was composed mostly of hydrogen, ammonia (NH_3), methane (CH_4), and water vapor. All the oxygen of the earth was chemically bound in the water and rocks. Had free oxygen been present the hydrogen, ammonia, and methane could not have continued to exist, as they would have been oxidized to other compounds. It was in this environment that Oparin suggested life could arise spontaneously, an environment that could exist only because there was no life present. Once life began and flourished it gradually changed the physical environment to something like its present state (5), and with this change all possibility of the further spontaneous generation of life disappeared.

NONBIOLOGICAL ORGANIC SYNTHESES

Without proteins, carbohydrates, fats, nucleic acids, and the many other organic compounds composing organisms, life as we know it could not exist. All these organic compounds are now produced naturally

515

only by living organisms, in the final analysis from the carbohydrate produced by autotrophic organisms. No natural organic compounds arise independently of living things. What, then, was the source of the organic compounds used in the creation of the first living things? Oparin suggested that amino acids and the other organic compounds characteristic of living things might have been synthesized nonbiologically from the hydrogen, ammonia, methane, and water vapor of the pre-archeozoic atmosphere, the necessary energy having been supplied by electrical discharges or ultra-violet radiation. This hypothesis has received some experimental support from the work of S. L. Miller and others in the years following World War II, several of the amino acids common in organisms having been synthesized by a continuous electrical discharge through a mixture of the various gases (1, 2, 12).

The synthesis of amino acids, sugars, fatty acids, and the other relatively simple compounds basic to life is, of course, not enough for the assembly of the first living organism. These basic units must have been reworked and linked together into the much larger and more complicated molecules such as proteins and nucleic acids that are essential constituents of even the simplest organisms. Nonbiological synthesis of these large complex molecules seems quite improbable, but no longer impossible. Their synthesis would doubtless have been extremely slow and the product meager, but it is not impossible that over long periods of time, considerable quantities of all the compounds essential for the assembly of a living organism might accumulate. Today such accumulation of organic compounds would be impossible since they would be oxidized or used by microorganisms as food even if conditions were suitable for their formation. However, in the absence of life and free oxygen it is conceivable that as the rains of millions of years washed more and more organic compounds into the oceans and inland lakes and pools, increasingly concentrated organic broths resulted. Particularly in the smaller bodies of water, evaporation could result in especially high concentrations of organic solutes. Even though it would be expected that some of the organic molecules would break down by a reversal of the synthetic reactions, gradually increasing quantities of the compounds essential for life could have occurred.

In recent years, Sidney W. Fox, of Florida State University (3), and others have accomplished nonbiological syntheses, not only of amino acids, but also of peptides made by polymerizing these amino acids, thus providing support for the theory that proteins and other large and complex molecules characteristic of organisms and essential in their structure could arise nonbiologically. Furthermore, in certain solutions, aggregation of these peptides into microscopic spherules suggestive of cells occurs, though of course these spherules lack the structural and biochemical complexity of cells.

THE PROBLEM OF ORGANIZATION

Even if the waters of the Earth now contained all the compounds essential for life—mineral salts as well as organic compounds and water—they would still have been only a nutritious broth with no living thing to use it as food. What was still lacking was the organization of the various components into the complex structural pattern characteristic of even the simplest organism. This organization is accomplished by every living organism as it assimilates food, but it is difficult to visualize spontaneous organization of such great complexity occurring in the absence of any living organism. Biochemists believe, however, that although such nonbiological assimilation would not be very probable, it would not be impossible, and they point out that given sufficient time any possible event not only can occur but is almost certain to occur. The time available was presumably no problem, and could have been on the order of millions of years. Viewed from this standpoint, and assuming that the hypotheses are valid, the origin of life—however improbable—was something that not only could occur but eventually and inevitably would occur under the conditions existing at that time.

Presumably, one of the first steps in the organization of the first living thing would have been the aggregation of nucleoproteins into units similar to viruses or genes, but unlike them independent of living cells for assimilation and duplication. This would seem to demand the presence of enzymes and some sort of anaerobic respiratory pathway if nothing more. For a structural unit unquestionably classifiable as a living cell, the formation of a limiting, differentially permeable membrane would be an additional requirement. It appears probable that the organization of the first living cells would be more likely in isolated tidal basins than in the open oceans, because of the higher concentration of the essential solutes and the absence of buffeting by large waves that might disrupt the rather fragile developing organisms. Furthermore, it is possible that colloidal clay sediments in such basins might serve as a mold or matrix against which the structural components of the developing organism could be assembled in an orderly manner.

Life might have originated in only one locality, but it is likely that the series of events leading to life may have occurred at several or many places over the Earth. If this were the case, the sequence of events and the resulting organisms might be expected to be similar, although not necessarily identical, in each of the localities.

THE FIRST LIVING ORGANISMS

The first living cells may, then, have been somewhat similar to bacteria, absorbing the unorganized organic compounds surrounding them and using these substances as food. Since there was no free oxygen, the respiration of the cells would necessarily be anaerobic. As these first cells multiplied and flourished, they would have initiated changes in their environment that would eventually make possible the survival of new and important hereditary potentialities in their descendents and make impossible the further spontaneous generation of life. For one thing, it is likely that as the living cells increased in number, they utilized the surrounding organic compounds as foods much faster than they were produced by nonbiological syntheses, resulting in a depletion of the food supply. For another thing, carbon dioxide was probably added to the waters and the air as the cells carried on respiration, thus setting the stage for the next major step in the evolution of life. The mutation rate was probably very high, in view of the intense ionizing ultra-violet radiation from the sun and probably the presence of more radioactive substances than exist today, even though as carbon dioxide accumulated in the atmosphere it probably absorbed a considerable amount of radiation from the sun.

THE BEGINNING OF PHOTOSYNTHESIS

Among the mutations that occurred, undoubtedly the most important for the future of life on Earth were those that made possible the production of light-absorbing pigments and enzymes essential for photosynthesis. With carbon dioxide now available, the environment provided all the factors essential for photosynthesis by organisms that had evolved the necessary hereditary potentialities. Had photosynthesis not appeared, it is quite likely that the incipient life of the earth would have been doomed to extinction since the food supply was undoubtedly being consumed faster than it was being produced by nonbiological synthesis.

Photosynthesis not only provided a new and much more rapid and efficient method of producing organic compounds, but it also initiated a series of extremely important changes in the environment through the release of free oxygen into the waters and atmosphere of the Earth. Most of the hydrogen, ammonia, and methane were oxidized to other substances, removing from the atmosphere the compounds essential for the nonbiological synthesis of organic compounds. Compounds already synthesized were now also subject to destructive oxidation. As a layer of ozone (O_3) accumulated high in the atmosphere, most of the lethal ultra-violet radiation from the sun was filtered out, making life possible on land as well as in the water (which filters out most of the lethal wavelengths), but removing one source of energy for nonbiological organic syntheses. Once the remnants of the nonbiologically synthesized organic compounds were gone, life became dependent forever on photosynthesis (and to a very limited extent on chemosynthesis) for its nourishment and continued existence. The oxygen added to the atmosphere by photosynthesis had at least one other important implication for life on earth, making possible the evolution of aerobic respiration.

THE BEGINNING OF AEROBIC RESPIRATION

Next to the mutations that made photosynthesis possible, perhaps the most important ones that occurred during the early history of life on Earth were the mutations resulting in the capacity for aerobic respiration. Because of the small quantity of energy released from foods respired anaerobically, an anaerobic photosynthetic organism would probably utilize most of the food it synthesized in its own respiration. Such photosynthetic organisms could accumulate little food and could support only a limited number of heterotrophic plants and animals. It seems quite unlikely that the great mass and variety of living organisms inhabiting the Earth could ever have evolved had it not been for the appearance of aerobic respiration. Certainly animals, with their high energy requirements, would have had great difficulty in surviving and thriving if they were limited to anaerobic respiration. It is possible that the primitive photosynthetic organisms may have derived all or most of their ATP from photosynthesis rather than from respiration.

Despite the numerous evolutionary developments that have resulted in the complex and varied assemblage of living things inhabiting the earth, no mutations have been more important for the survival of life on earth than those giving rise to photosynthesis and aerobic respiration during the early days of life on Earth.

This account of the origin and early evolution of life is, of course, hypothetical and to a large extent nothing much more than speculation. However, it does present a picture in accord with known scientific facts and principles and is supported by what little experimental evidence there is. It is likely that as our scientific knowledge increases, a more detailed and accurate picture of the way the first life originated can be drawn.

Is There Life on Other Planets?

We may engage in one more bit of speculation: Has life originated and evolved on other planets (4, 9, 13)? This is, of course, a question no one can answer at present, but information assembled by astronomers indicates that of the planets in our solar system only Mars and Venus, outside the Earth, have environments that could even possibly support life and that on these planets the conditions are certainly not suitable for life as we know it (4, 9, 11). The atmosphere of Venus contains about 500 times as much carbon dioxide as the air on Earth, whereas the oxygen and water vapor content are less than 5% that of the Earth's atmosphere. Furthermore, the surface temperature of Venus may frequently be as high as 200°C or even 300°C. The temperature on Mars may be somewhat more favorable to life, but may vary from as low as −100°C at night to 30°C during the day. The atmosphere of Mars is mostly nitrogen, with 0.3% carbon dioxide, no oxygen, and very little water. Mars is so dry that no lakes, streams, or oceans exist, and only simple anaerobic and xerophytic organisms would appear to be possible on Mars at the most. Astronomers, have, however, recently obtained spectrographic evidence of organic compounds on Mars (9).

Although the Earth seems to be the only planet in our solar system suitable for the flourishing of life, astronomers estimate that there may be at least 100,000 planets of other stars in our galaxy with environments quite as suitable for the origin and survival of life as that of the Earth, whereas the universe as a whole may contain some 10 trillion planets suitable for the origin and survival of living organisms. If these estimates are correct, it is almost certain that life has arisen on many planets other than our own. Perhaps on some of these life is now originating, as it did on Earth two billion years ago; on others, life may have evolved to a more advanced stage than on Earth. Although space travel may before too long permit man to investigate the biology of Mars and Venus, it now seems likely that we shall never have the opportunity of confirming our suspicions that life exists on numerous planets of distant stars. To biologists this will not be frustrating, for there are still innumerable unanswered questions about the plants and animals of the Earth waiting for clarification by further research.

► ## Questions

1. Could chemosynthetic bacteria have evolved before photosynthetic plants? Explain your answer.

2. Plants require oxygen for chlorophyll synthesis, yet presumably there was no oxygen in the atmosphere before photosynthesis began. Does this make untenable the hypotheses in regard to the origin of the first photosynthetic plants? Can you suggest an hypothesis that might explain the first synthesis of chlorophyll in an atmosphere devoid of oxygen?

3. We have suggested that if photosynthetic organisms had not appeared on Earth, the previously existing forms of life might have died of starvation as they increased in number. If this had occurred, how probable is it that the entire process of origin of life might have occurred again?

4. Which of the sun's planets appear to have environments favorable for the existence of life? On the basis of the information available, what would you consider to be the most likely stage of the evolution of life on those planets where it may exist?

5. Is it possible that life on some other planet might consist of rather highly developed plants but no animals? Of rather highly developed animals but no plants? Could life on another planet be so different from that on Earth that the terms "plant" and "animal" would be quite unsuitable?

► *References*

For Reading and Reference

1. Adler, Irving, *How Life Began*. Mentor Books Edition, New York: New American Library, 1959.
2. Evans, E. A., Jr., How life began. *Saturday Evening Post*, November 26, 1960, p. 24.
3. Fox, S. W., How did life begin? *Science* 132:200–208, 1960.
4. Huang, Su-Shu, Life outside the solar system. *Scientific American* 202(4):55–63, April 1960.
5. Landsberg, H. E., The origin of the atmosphere. *Scientific American* 189(2):82–86, August 1953.
6. Oparin, A. I., *Origin of Life*, Academic Press 1936, 1957. Dover Books edition, New York: Dover Publications, 1953.
7. Pasteur, Louis, Memoir on the organized corpuscles which exist in the atmosphere. Examination of the doctrine of spontaneous generation, 1862, in M. L. Gabriel and S. Fogel, *Great Experiments in Biology*, pp. 110–118.
8. Redi, F., Experiments on the generation of insects, 1688, in M. L. Gabriel and S. Fogel, *Great Experiments in Biology*, pp. 187–189.
9. Sinton, W. M., Further evidence of vegetation on Mars. *Science* 130:1234–1237, 1959.
10. Spallanzani, L., Experiments on the generation of plants and animals, 1785, in M. L. Gabriel and S. Fogel, *Great Experiments in Biology*, pp. 189–193.
11. Vaucouleurs, Gérard de, Mars. *Scientific American* 188(5):65–73, May 1953. (Includes a discussion of possibility of life on Mars.)
12. Wald, George, The origin of life. *Scientific American* 191(2):44–53, August 1954.
13. Webster, Gary, Is there life on other worlds? *Natural History* 65:526–531, 1957.

Appendix:

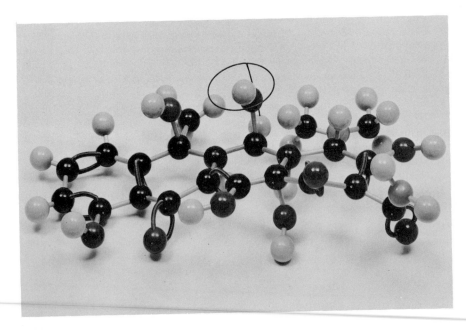

Some Basic Chemistry
for Botany Students

Atoms and Elements

Although the word *atom* has been in everyday use since the advent of the atomic bomb, it is perhaps not generally recognized that all matter is composed of atoms. Atoms are extremely small particles, far too minute to be made visible even by an electron microscope. One gram of iron contains about 10,900,000,000,000,000,000,000,000 (or almost 11 billion billion) atoms of iron. An **atom** may be defined as the smallest part of a chemical element that can participate in a chemical reaction. There are about 100 different chemical elements, among them such common substances as hydrogen, oxygen, nitrogen, carbon, iron, copper, sulfur, and lead. Elements can not be decomposed chemically into other substances, and each element has atoms that differ from those of all other elements. Atoms have a rather wide range of sizes and weights, the lightest being the hydrogen atom and the heaviest naturally occurring atom being uranium, which is 239 times as heavy as the hydrogen atom. The chemical elements of greatest biological interest and importance are listed in Table *A*.1.

As a matter of convenience, each chemical element has been assigned a symbol that generally consists of the first letter or two of its English

TABLE A.1. CHEMICAL ELEMENTS OF BOTANICAL IMPORTANCE, WITH CHEMICAL SYMBOLS AND SOME COMMON IONS OF EACH ELEMENT

Element	Atomic Weight	Symbol	Bonds	Ions
Boron	10.8	B	3	BO_3^{---}
Calcium	40.1	Ca	2	Ca^{++}
Carbon	12.0	C	2, 4	CO_3^{--}
Copper	63.5	Cu	1, 2	Cu^{++}
Chlorine	35.5	Cl	1	Cl^-
Hydrogen	1.0	H	1	H^+, H_3O^+, OH^-
Iron	55.9	Fe	2, 3	Fe^{++}, Fe^{+++}
Magnesium	24.3	Mg	2	Mg^{++}
Manganese	54.9	Mn	2–7	Mn^{++}
Molybdenum	96.0	Mo	3, 4, 6	MoO_4^{--}
Nitrogen	14.0	N	3, 5	NO_3^-, NH_4^+
Oxygen	16.0	O	2	OH^-
Phosphorus	31.0	P	3, 5	$H_2PO_4^-$
Potassium	39.0	K	1	K^+
Sodium	23.0	Na	1	Na^+
Sulfur	32.1	S	2	SO_4^{--}
Zinc	65.4	Zn	2	Zn^{++}

Notes: All cations (positively charged ions) listed except H^+ or ions containing hydrogen (H_3O^+, NH_4^+) are those of metallic elements. Oxygen is a constituent of all the anions (negatively charged ions) listed except CL^-, as well as of the OH^- ion listed after oxygen. Any anion in the table can combine with any cation, the number of charges corresponding with the combining proportions. Thus, potassium chloride would be KCl, potassium sulfate K_2SO_4, and potassium borate K_3BO_3; calcium chloride would be $CaCl_2$. The numbers of bonds each atom can form with other atoms is also given. The atomic weight of each element is given to the nearest tenth.

name, for example H for hydrogen, C for carbon, O for oxygen, P for phosphorus, and Ca for calcium. Some symbols, however, are derived from the Latin names of the elements as in Na for sodium, Fe for iron, K for potassium, Au for gold, and Cu for copper. These symbols are used in writing the equations for chemical reactions and are also used at times in text material in place of the names of elements. You will find it useful to know the symbols of the elements listed in Table A.1.

ATOMIC STRUCTURE

At one time atoms were considered to be indivisible particles, the term *atom* having been derived from a Greek word meaning "uncut" or "indivisible." However, chemists have known since the turn of the century that atoms are composed of still smaller particles. About a dozen different kinds of particles make up atoms, but of these only three

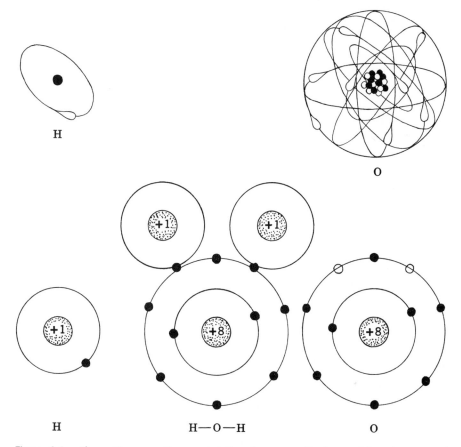

Figure A.1. Above: Diagrammatic representation of an atom of hydrogen (H) and an atom of oxygen (O). The nucleus of the hydrogen atom consists of a single proton, and a single electron occupies the first electron shell. The nucleus of the oxygen atom consists of 8 protons (black) and 8 neutrons (white), with 8 electrons (2 in the first shell and 6 in the second). The diagrams are not to scale. If they were, the electrons of the first shell would be about 30 ft. from the nucleus and the protons and neutrons would be about 1837 times as large as the electrons. Below: An atom of hydrogen (left), an atom of oxygen (right), and a molecule of water (H—O—H) represented even more diagrammatically than above. In the molecule of water, the hydrogen electrons occupy the two unfilled electron sites of the oxygen atom, these electrons being shared by the H and O atoms in covalent bonds. One of every 10 million H_2O molecules is dissociated into an H^+ ion (a proton) and an OH^- ion. In turn, the H^+ ion becomes associated with another water molecule forming a hydronium (H_3O^+) ion. A molecule of water vapor has the formula H_2O as shown, but in liquid water two or more H_2O molecules cluster together into larger molecules which may be represented as $(H_2O)_2$, $(H_2O)_3$, and so on, or in general $(H_2O)_n$. In ice and snow, the water molecules are bound together into crystals.

need be considered here: **electrons, protons,** and **neutrons.** Electrons carry a unit negative electrical charge, protons a unit positive electrical charge, and neutrons are electrically neutral. A proton weighs only 17×10^{-25} gram; a neutron is just slightly heavier. Electrons are much lighter, 1837 electrons weighing as much as one proton.

The protons and neutrons of an atom are arranged rather compactly in the center of the atom and make up the **atomic nucleus** (Fig. $A.1$). The nucleus of an ordinary hydrogen atom consists only of a single proton, but the nuclei of all other kinds of atoms include both protons and neutrons. The electrons of an atom are at relatively great distances from the nucleus, and are arranged in shells or zones. If a nucleus were the size of a pea the nearest electrons would be about 60 ft. away. The largest atoms have 7 shells of electrons, but practically all the elements of biological importance have relatively small atoms with all their electrons in four or less shells. The innermost shell can hold only 2 electrons, whereas the second shell can hold up to 8 and the third up to 18 electrons. The electrons are constantly revolving around the nucleus.

All atoms of a certain element have the same number of electrons and protons. Hydrogen atoms have 1 electron and 1 proton, oxygen atoms have 8 electrons and 8 protons (Fig. $A.1$), carbon atoms have 6 electrons and 6 protons, and calcium atoms have 20 electrons and 20 protons. The distinct and characteristic properties of each element depend on the number of electrons and protons in the atoms of the element. Since the number of electrons in an atom is always equal to the number of protons, atoms are electrically neutral. An atom may thus be defined as an extremely small electrically neutral particle with a nucleus and one or more electrons outside its nucleus.

ISOTOPES

Although all the atoms of a certain element have the same number of protons and electrons, some atoms of an element may have more neutrons in their nuclei than do others. For example, most hydrogen atoms have only a single proton in their nucleus, but some have 1 proton and 1 neutron and still others have 1 proton and 2 neutrons. Most carbon atoms have 6 protons and 6 neutrons in their nuclei, but some have 6 protons and 8 neutrons. The usual number of particles in oxygen nuclei is 8 protons and 8 neutrons, but a few oxygen atoms have 8 protons and 10 neutrons. The different varieties of atoms of any element are called **isotopes,** a particular isotope being composed of atoms that are uniform in neutron content and weight as well as in number of protons and electrons. The different isotopes of an element are identified by superscript numbers, the number being the total of the protons and neutrons in the nucleus of each atom. Thus, we can represent the various isotopes mentioned above as follows: H^1, H^2 (called **deuterium**), H^3 (called **tritium**), C^{12}, C^{14}, O^{16}, and O^{18}.

Most atoms (e.g. those of H^1, H^2, C^{12}, O^{16}, and O^{18}) have a stable structure, but the atoms of some isotopes are unstable and disintegrate into stable atoms of other elements by emission of particles or radiant energy. These are called **radioactive isotopes** (or **radioisotopes**). Among the particles emitted by radioactive atoms are **alpha particles** (a group of 2 neutrons and 2 protons, or a helium nucleus), **beta particles** (rapidly moving electrons), protons, and neutrons. **Gamma rays** (shortwave radiation similar to X rays) are emitted by some radioactive substances. Each kind of radioisotope emits only certain kinds of particles or radiation. For example, radioactive C^{14} emits only beta particles from its atomic nuclei. Since a neutron may be considered as being composed of a proton plus an electron, loss of the beta particle (electron) reduces the number of neutrons in the nucleus from 8 to 7 and increases the number of protons from 6 to 7. Thus, C^{14} is transformed into N^{14}, the common stable isotope of nitrogen. Such a transformation of one element into another is referred to as **radioactive decay**.

Each radioisotope has a characteristic rate of decay, measured in terms of **half life**. The half life of an isotope is the length of time required for half of its atoms to decay. C^{14} decays very slowly, having a half life of about 5000 years, whereas radioactive C^{11} has a half life of only 20 minutes. P^{32} has a half life of about 14 days and S^{35} a half life of about 87 days. Radioisotopes also differ from one another in the kinds of particles and waves emitted and the energy with which they are emitted, and thus in the penetrating power of the emissions. For example, H^3 (tritium) emits only weak beta particles that travel only a fraction of a millimeter, whereas radium 226 emits high-energy alpha particles and gamma rays that travel long distances through the air and penetrate thick layers of metals.

Radioisotopes are of biological interest from two main points of view. 1. Their emissions may have harmful effects on organisms, causing disruption of metabolic processes, mutations, and abnormal growth and development. 2. Radioisotopes are used as tracers in various kinds of biological research and have made possible many important discoveries. For example, the intermediate steps in photosynthesis have been worked out by the identification of the radioactive substances present in plants supplied with $C^{14}O_2$. Also, much has been learned about the absorption and translocation of mineral elements in plants by the use of such radioactive isotopes as P^{32}, S^{35}, Ca^{45}, and Fe^{59}. To be useful as a tracer, an isotope must have a half life of at least several days. Unfortunately, the radioisotopes of nitrogen and oxygen have such short half lives that they are not suitable for tracer use.

BONDING OF ATOMS

The atoms of most elements are capable of uniting or forming bonds with other atoms of the same element or with atoms of other elements. Each element has one or more characteristic bonding capacities, depending on the number of electrons in the outer shell. If the outer shell contains all the electrons it can hold, the atom has no bonding capacity

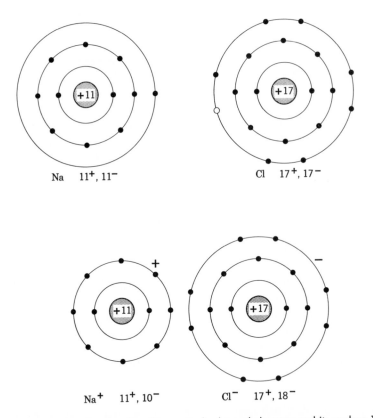

Figure A.2. An atom of sodium has 11 negatively charged electrons and its nucleus 11 positively charged protons, whereas a chlorine atom has 17 protons and 17 electrons. Like other kinds of atoms, both are thus electrically neutral. When an atom of sodium comes in contact with an atom of chlorine, the single electron in the other shell of the sodium atom occupies the vacant electron site in the outer shell of the chlorine atom, forming an ion of sodium (Na^+) and an ion of chlorine (Cl^-). The Na^+ ion has 11 protons and 10 electrons, or a new positive of charge of 1; the Cl^- ion has 17 protons and 18 electrons, or a new negative charge of 1. The oppositely charged ions attract one another and may be considered to constitute a molecule of sodium chloride (Na^+Cl^-, or less accurately NaCl). The bonds between ions such as these are electrovalent. Note that the Na^+ ion is smaller than the Na atom.

Figure A.3. Diagram of a small portion of a crystal of sodium chloride, or common salt. The regular alternation of Na^+ ions (small black spheres) and Cl^- ions (large white spheres) in a cubical pattern is responsible for the cubical shape of sodium chloride crystals. When salt is dissolved in water, the ions separate from one another and become dispersed among the molecules of water as individual Na^+ and Cl^- ions.

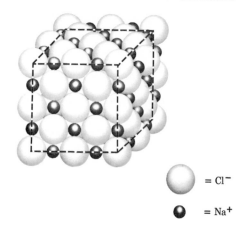

○ = Cl^-

● = Na^+

and is chemically inert, never combining with other atoms. In this group of elements are the gases helium, neon, argon, and krypton. If the outer shell contains all the electrons it can hold except one, the element has a bonding capacity (or **valence**) of 1. A deficit of 2 electrons in the outer shell gives a bonding capacity of 2 and so on. A single element may have more than one bonding capacity. Nitrogen, for example, may be 3 or 5 whereas carbon may be 2 although it is usually 4. Hydrogen is 1 and oxygen is 2. Thus, a carbon atom may be bonded with 2 oxygen atoms (CO_2) or with 4 hydrogen atoms (CH_4).

There are two principal types of bonds between atoms: **electrovalent bonds** and **covalent bonds**. In an electrovalent bond, one or more electrons are transferred from one element to another (Fig. *A*.2). Since the atoms donating electrons now contain more protons than electrons they have a net positive charge, whereas the atoms accepting the electrons have an excess of electrons over protons and thus have a net negative charge. These charged atoms are known as **ions** and have properties quite different from those of the uncharged atoms. Thus, when the metal sodium (Na) reacts with chlorine (Cl) gas, the single electron in the outer shell of a sodium atom moves into the single empty electron space in the outer shell of a chlorine atom, resulting in the formation of sodium (Na^+) and chlorine (Cl^-) ions. Since oppositely charged particles attract one another, the Na^+ and Cl^- ions pair off as units of sodium chloride, or common salt:

$$Na + Cl \longrightarrow Na^+Cl^-$$

Sodium chloride has, of course, quite different properties from either the soft and very reactive sodium metal or the greenish, poisonous chlorine

529

gas. A crystal of sodium chloride is composed of Na^+ and Cl^- ions arranged in a regular cubical pattern (Fig. *A*.3) which is responsible for the cubical structure of the crystal. When salt is dissolved in water the ions separate from one another and move about freely through the water.

In a covalent bond the atoms share electrons with each other rather than giving or receiving electrons as in an electrovalent bond. Thus, when a carbon atom becomes bonded to two oxygen atoms it shares two electrons with each of the oxygen atoms (Fig. *A*.4). Unlike electrovalent bonds, covalent bonds do not result in the formation of ions. However, there are intermediate conditions between strictly covalent and strictly electrovalent bonds and some covalent bonds can break and form ions, particularly when a substance is dissolved in water. Many substances that ordinarily do not dissociate into ions may be ionized by shortwave radiation (such as X rays, ultra-violet rays, gamma rays) or by particles emitted from radioisotopes.

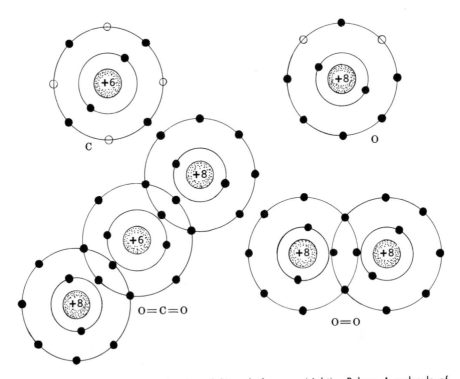

Figure A.4. Above: An atom of carbon (left) and of oxygen (right). Below: A molecule of carbon dioxide (left, O=C=O or CO_2) and a molecule of oxygen (right, O=O or O_2), showing the shared electrons of the covalent bonds. In nature, oxygen exists almost entirely as O_2 molecules (or O_3 molecules) rather than O atoms.

Molecules and Compounds

The particle formed by the bonding or union of two or more atoms is called a **molecule.** The atoms of many elements may unite with one another forming molecules. Thus, hydrogen gas consists of molecules of two hydrogen atoms each (H_2) while oxygen molecules consist of two atoms of oxygen held together by a covalent bond (O_2). When three atoms of oxygen are bonded into a molecule, the result is ozone (O_3), a gas with properties different from those of O_2.

When atoms of two or more different elements are bonded together into a molecule the result is a **chemical compound.** A molecule is the smallest particle of a chemical compound, just as an atom is the smallest particle of a chemical element, although as has been noted a molecule may be dissociated into ions. It must be stressed that the properties of any chemical compound are very different from those of its constituent elements. The difference between the properties of sodium, chlorine, and sodium chloride has already been mentioned. As just one more example, water (H_2O) has very different properties from those of hydrogen or oxygen, the elements which compose it. Although there are only a hundred or so chemical elements, these may combine into many thousands of different chemical compounds.

The **formula** of a chemical compound consists of the symbols of the chemical elements composing it along with an indication of the number of each kind of atom present in the molecule. The simplest type of chemical formula (**empirical formula**) merely lists the numbers of each atom or ion present in the molecule as subscript figures, no subscript being used if only one atom is present. Thus, the formula of H_2O for water shows that a molecule of water is composed of two atoms of hydrogen and one atom of oxygen. The formula for table sugar (sucrose) is $C_{12}H_{22}O_{11}$ and it tells us that each molecule of sugar contains 12 atoms of carbon, 22 of hydrogen, and 11 of oxygen. The formula of a substance with electrovalent bonds such as sodium chloride should really be written Na^+Cl^- to indicate that it is composed of ions, but for convenience the charges are frequently omitted and so we would write NaCl.

Another kind of formula, used particularly for organic compounds, is the **structural formula.** This is essentially a two-dimensional sketch of the molecule, showing the way the atoms are bonded to each other. Frequently the bonds are shown as lines connecting the symbols, or as dots representing the shared electrons as for covalent bonds. For example, the structural formula of carbon dioxide might be written O=C=O or O::C::O and water would be H—O—H or H:O:H. The empirical formula of acetic acid is $C_2H_4O_2$, but this provides little information about its chemical nature. Its structural formula is much more illuminating:

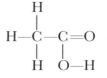

For one thing, no other substance has this structural formula, whereas there are other compounds with the formula $C_2H_4O_2$.

At times it is convenient and desirable to use **semistructural formulae.** The semistructural formula for acetic acid is CH_3COOH. This gives us the essential information about the structure of the compound, including the fact that it is an organic acid as indicated by the presence of a carboxyl (—COOH) group, and also it is simpler to write than the complete structural formula.

Sometimes, in biology in particular, compounds with extremely large and complex molecules are represented by a kind of shorthand using key letters in the name of the compound rather than chemical symbols. Thus, adenosine tri-phosphate is commonly written ATP and di-phospho-pyridine-nucleotide is written DPN. Although such shorthand symbols may be used in chemical equations, we should remember that the letters in them do not represent chemical elements. Another shorthand device commonly used is the representation of the phosphate radical (—H_2PO_3) merely as — Ⓟ.

Electrolytes and Nonelectrolytes

Substances with electrovalent bonds or partially electrovalent bonds are classed as **electrolytes** because their ions carry an electric current through the water in which they are dissolved. The positively charged ions (**cations**) move to the negative electrode (**cathode**) where they pick up electrons and are converted into uncharged atoms; the negatively charged ions (**anions**) migrate to the positively charged electrode (**anode**) where they give up electrons and also become uncharged atoms. Thus, when an electric current is passed through melted sodium chloride, metallic sodium is deposited on the cathode as the Na^+ ions migrate to it and are discharged; the Cl^- ions are converted to chlorine gas at the anode. Electrolytes are mostly salts, acids, or bases.

Nonelectrolytes are substances that are not ionized when dissolved in water. A solution of a nonelectrolyte does not conduct an electric current. Among the nonelectrolytes are gases such as oxygen and hydrogen and most organic compounds, although some organic compounds such as the organic acids are electrolytes.

Acids, Bases, and Salts

Acids may be defined as substances that contribute hydrogen ions (H^+) when in solution. Since a H^+ ion is nothing but a proton (the H atom consisting of a single electron and a single proton), acids are sometimes defined as proton donors. However, H^+ ions almost immediately combine with water molecules forming **hydronium** (H_3O^+) ions, and it is these hydronium ions that give acids their characteristic properties. It is proper to speak of hydronium ions when dealing with acids, but for simplicity we shall follow the usual biological custom of speaking in terms of hydrogen ions. A **base** is a substance that contributes **hydroxyl** ions (OH^-) to a solution. When an acid and a base are present in the same solution they react with each other, forming a salt and water:

hydrochloric acid	potassium hydroxide		potassium chloride	water
HCl	$+$ KOH	$\longrightarrow$	KCl	$+$ HOH

sulfuric acid	sodium hydroxide		sodium sulfate	water
H_2SO_4	$+$ $2NaOH$	$\longrightarrow$	Na_2SO_4	$+2HOH$

In such reactions the acid and base **neutralize** each other, and most of the H^+ and OH^- ions are removed by joining with one another and forming water molecules. Only one out of every 10 million water molecules is ionized, so few H^+ or OH^- ions remain in the solution.

Organic and Inorganic Compounds

Chemical compounds may be classed as **organic** and **inorganic.** Frequently organic compounds are defined as those that contain carbon, all others being designated as inorganic. However, we shall use a somewhat more restrictive definition that limits organic compounds to those that contain both carbon and hydrogen (frequently along with oxygen and other elements). This definition excludes such carbon compounds as carbon dioxide (CO_2), carbon monoxide (CO), calcium carbonate $(CaCO_3)$ and sodium cyanide $(NaCN)$ that are really not organic compounds in the stricter sense of the term. Organic compounds were so named because it was thought that they could be synthesized only by living organisms. Although chemists are now able to synthesize some organic compounds from inorganic compounds in the laboratory, it is still true that organic compounds (in the more limited sense) found in nature at the present time have all been synthesized by plants or animals.

533

Because carbon atoms can bond with one another into rings and long chains, organic compounds may have larger and more complex molecules than inorganic compounds do. There are many more different kinds of organic compounds than there are inorganic compounds. For example, there are probably many million different kinds of proteins alone. Organic compounds include the hydrocarbons (compounds composed only of carbon and hydrogen) of petroleum and natural gas, the carbohydrates, fats, and proteins that constitute the bulk of the dry weight of plant and animal tissues, and thousands of other compounds that are made by plants and animals and which play important roles in their structure and processes (see Chapter 3). The principal inorganic compounds of biological interest are water, acids, bases, salts, and several gases such as carbon dioxide and oxygen.

ISOMERS

Two or more compounds may contain exactly the same numbers and kinds of atoms and yet be different substances with different properties because of a difference in the arrangement of the atoms in the molecules. Such substances are known as **isomers.** Isomers are more common among organic than inorganic compounds. For example, there are many different sugars with the formula $C_6H_{12}O_6$. As a group they are referred to as hexoses or six-carbon sugars. To show the differences in the various hexoses it is necessary to give their structural formulae, as in the following examples:

HC=O	O=CH	HC=O	H HCOH
HCOH	HOCH	HCOH	C=O
HOCH	HCOH	HOCH	HOCH
HOCH	HOCH	HOCH	HCOH
HCOH	HOCH	HCOH	HCOH
HCOH	HOCH	HCOH	HCOH
H	H	H	H
d-glucose	l-glucose	d-galactose	d-fructose

The bonds between carbon atoms are indicated by lines, and the double bonds between carbon and oxygen atoms by double lines, but bond lines are not shown between the carbon atoms and the H and OH attached to them (although they exist, of course). Note that each C atom has four bonds, each O atom two (as C=O or C—O—H), and each H atom one. The mere difference in arrangement of the —H and —OH on the carbons results in compounds with different properties, as in the first three sugars given. Fructose further differs from the other three in that its C=O group is not on the end carbon. The two isomers of glucose are mirror images of one another. Such isomers are known as **stereoisomers** or **optical isomers** and twist a beam of polarized light in different directions when it is passed through a solution of each. The d-glucose twists the light toward the right (dextro) and l-glucose to the left (levulo). Only the d-isomers of the various sugars ordinarily occur in nature.

Atomic and Molecular Weights

The **atomic weight** of an element is its weight relative to that of the common isotope of oxygen, which has been set at 16. For example, the atomic weight of hydrogen is 1.008 and that of carbon is 12.011. The atomic weights, to the nearest tenth, of elements of biological interest are given in Table $A.1$. Each atomic weight unit represents $\dfrac{1}{6.02 \times 10^{23}}$ gram, so the actual weight of an atom of any element can be calculated by multiplying its atomic weight by this very small number. Another unit, the **gram atomic weight**, is of much greater practical importance and utility. The gram atomic weight of an element is its atomic weight expressed in grams. Thus, one gram atomic weight of oxygen is 16 grams and a gram atomic weight of hydrogen 1.008 grams. A gram atomic weight of any element contains the same number of atoms as a gram atomic weight of any other element.

The **molecular weight** of a compound is the sum of the atomic weights of the elements composing the compound. For example, the molecular weight of water (H_2O) is $2 \times 1.008 + 16 = 18.016$. The molecular weight of a hexose sugar would be calculated as follows:

Element	Number of Atoms		Atomic Weight		Total
Carbon	6	×	12.011	=	72.066
Hydrogen	12	×	1.008	=	12.096
Oxygen	6	×	16.000	=	96.000
Molecular weight				=	180.162

The **gram molecular weight** (or **mol**) of any compound is its molecular weight in grams. Thus a gram molecular weight of a hexose sugar is 180.162 grams, whereas a gram molecular weight of water is 18.016 grams. A mol of one substance contains the same number of molecules as a mol of any other substance. MW is a commonly used abbreviation for *molecular weight*.

Chemical Reactions

Chemical elements and compounds can react with one another in various ways, the products of the reactions being other substances. The following main types of chemical reactions can be identified: exchange, synthesis, decomposition, and rearrangement.

In **exchange reactions** one or more atoms of a molecule trade places with one or more atoms of another, forming two other compounds. The reactions between acids and bases given on page 533 are exchange reactions. Here is another:

$$\underset{\text{water}}{HOH} + \underset{\text{ammonium chloride}}{NH_4Cl} \longrightarrow \underset{\text{ammonium hydroxide}}{NH_4OH} + \underset{\text{hydrochloric acid}}{HCl}$$

In **synthetic reactions** two or more molecules may combine and form a single larger molecule, with or without other products:

$$\underset{\text{carbon dioxide}}{CO_2} + \underset{\text{water}}{H_2O} \longrightarrow \underset{\text{carbonic acid}}{H_2CO_3}$$

$$\underset{\text{glucose phosphate}}{C_6H_{11}O_6 \cdot H_2PO_3} + \underset{\text{fructose}}{C_6H_{12}O_6} \longrightarrow \underset{\text{sucrose}}{C_{12}H_{22}O_{11}} + \underset{\text{phosphoric acid}}{H_3PO_4}$$

Decomposition reactions involve the breaking down of a molecule into two or more smaller molecules, and may be the reverse of the comparable synthetic reactions:

$$\underset{\text{carbonic acid}}{H_2CO_3} \longrightarrow \underset{\text{carbon dioxide}}{CO_2} + \underset{\text{water}}{H_2O}$$

$$\underset{\text{sucrose}}{C_{12}H_{22}O_{11}} + \underset{\text{water}}{H_2O} \longrightarrow \underset{\text{glucose}}{C_6H_{12}O_6} + \underset{\text{fructose}}{C_6H_{12}O_6}$$

A decomposition in which water reacts with the substance being decomposed is known as **hydrolysis**. All digestive reactions are hydrolytic, for example the digestion of sucrose as outlined in the second foregoing reaction.

In **rearrangement reactions**, one isomer is converted to another by an internal rearrangement of atoms:

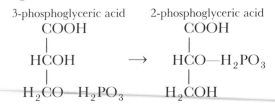

The numbers in the names of these two compounds indicate which carbon holds the phosphate group ($-H_2PO_3$).

BALANCING EQUATIONS

Equations must always be **balanced**, that is, there must be the same number of each kind of atom on one side of the arrow as on the other. In the sample reactions given all the equations are balanced, as can be seen by counting the number of each kind of atom on each side of the equations. It so happened that in all the reactions given only one molecule of each substance is used or produced per molecule of the other substances in the reaction. However, in some reactions two or more molecules of one substance may react with only one molecule of another:

sulfuric acid   potassium hydroxide   water   potassium sulfate

$$H_2SO_4 \ + \quad 2KOH \quad \rightarrow 2HOH + \quad K_2SO_4$$

This equation would not be balanced if only one molecule of KOH and one of HOH were included. The reason is that the sulfate ion (SO_4^{--}) has a negative charge of 2, or an excess of 2 electrons, and so combines with two cations such as H^+ or K^+ having a single charge or with one cation such as Ca^{++} with a double charge. The reaction of sulfuric acid with calcium hydroxide would be balanced as follows:

sulfuric acid   calcium hydroxide   water   calcium sulfate

$$H_2SO_4 \ + \quad Ca(OH)_2 \quad \rightarrow 2HOH + \quad CaSO_4$$

The common ions present in plants are listed in Table $A.1$, and by observing the charges on each ion we should be able to determine its proper combining proportions with other ions of opposite charge and so balance equations in which the ions appear.

If an equation is balanced, the sum of the molecular weights on the left will equal the sum of the molecular weights on the right. For example:

$$H_2CO_3 \rightarrow H_2O + CO_2$$
$$62 \quad = \quad 18 \ + \ 44$$

This is, of course, just a way of saying that matter is neither created or destroyed during a chemical reaction, but is just converted into other substances.

ENERGY TRANSFERS IN CHEMICAL REACTIONS

Every chemical reaction involves energy transfer. Some reactions require an outside source of energy such as heat, light, or electricity to make them go on, and the energy supplied is incorporated in the chemical bonds of one of the substances formed by the reaction. If these bonds are broken in a subsequent reaction, the energy is released, frequently as heat but sometimes as light, electricity, or other kinds of energy. Thus, during chemical reactions energy may either be incorporated in chemical bonds or released from chemical bonds. Or, the chemical bond energy of one of the reacting substances may be transferred to chemical bond energy of one of the products of the reaction. In any event, energy is neither created or destroyed during a chemical reaction.

In synthetic reactions, an outside energy source is generally required to drive the reaction, the energy being incorporated in the molecules of the substance being synthesized. Thus, in photosynthesis, light energy is used to synthesize sugar from carbon dioxide and water and the energy is incorporated in the sugar molecules:

$$\underset{\text{water}}{6H_2O} + \underset{\text{carbon dioxide}}{6CO_2} \xrightarrow[\text{energy}]{\text{673 Cal. light}} \underset{\substack{\text{sugar}\\ \text{673 Cal.}}}{C_6H_{12}O_6} + \underset{\text{oxygen}}{6O_2}$$

The 673 kilogram calories (or 673,000 gram calories) of light energy are sufficient to make one mole (180 grams) of sugar. If a mole of sugar is oxidized by burning or by respiration, 673 kilogram calories are released:

$$\underset{\text{sugar}}{C_6H_{12}O_6} + \underset{\text{oxygen}}{6O_2} \longrightarrow \underset{\text{carbon dioxide}}{6CO_2} + \underset{\text{water}}{6H_2O} + \text{673 Cal. energy}$$

If the sugar is burned, the energy appears as heat and light (the flame). In respiration some of the energy is converted to heat, but most of it is incorporated in the chemical bonds of a substance (adenosinetriphosphate, ATP) that easily decomposes and its bond energy then may be used in useful work in the plant or animal.

When oxygen unites with a substance, the process is called **oxidation** and the substance becomes oxidized. Energy is released in oxidation processes. A substance can also be oxidized by the loss of hydrogen. Basically, a substance is oxidized and releases energy whenever it loses electrons, but from a standpoint of elementary biology it is more convenient to think of oxidation as the gain of oxygen or the loss of hydrogen from a substance accompanied by a release of chemical bond energy. The opposite process to oxidation is **reduction**. Reduction involves an increase in chemical bond energy, and occurs when a substance either loses oxygen or gains hydrogen as well as when there is a gain of electrons otherwise. In any reaction where oxidation occurs, there is also reduction and vice versa, since an electron gained by one atom is lost by another. However, we usually think of photosynthesis as essentially a reduction process, since the carbon is converted from a highly oxidized state (CO_2) to a rather highly reduced state $(C_6H_{12}O_6)$ with much greater bond energy. Similarly, respiration is referred to as an oxidation process, since the carbon is oxidized from sugar to carbon dioxide with the release of energy from the sugar bonds.

Catalysts and Enzymes

Many chemical reactions, particularly exchange reactions between substances with electrovalent bonds, take place spontaneously at ordinary room temperatures. Many other reactions, however, particularly between substances with covalent bonds (that are stronger and not so easily broken), proceed very slowly if at all under ordinary conditions. Even if the reaction is energy-releasing, the reacting molecules must be raised to a certain energy level by heating, application of high pressures, or other means before the reaction will proceed. Thus, wood must be raised to a certain temperature (its kindling point) before it will burn. Once the activation energy level is reached, the process will continue. The situation may be compared with an automobile going up a steep mountain. Much energy is required to reach the crest (the activation energy level), but once the downgrade is reached the automobile does not require further energy expenditure by its motor.

A catalyst is a substance that changes the rate of a chemical reaction without undergoing any permanent chemical change, that is, the catalyst is still present when the reaction is completed. Catalysts speed up reactions by reducing the activation energy level (Fig. A.5). In the automobile analogy, a comparable situation would be a deep cut through the mountain, thus permitting a car with little power to pass through the mountain, whereas it might not be able to climb the steep grade over the mountain. The presence of a suitable catalyst may permit a reaction to proceed at room temperature, whereas without the catalyst a high temperature might be required. Probably the commonest method of catalyst action is that in which the catalyst forms a temporary compound with one of the reacting substances, this compound having a lower activation energy level than the substance itself. Thus, the reaction $A + B = AB$ may be very slow because of a high activation energy level. However, A may react readily with a catalyst (C), forming a compound AC with a lower activation energy level. Then the following reaction proceeds rapidly at ordinary temperatures:

$$AC + B \longrightarrow AB + C$$

Enzymes are organic catalysts produced by plants and animals. Most of the biochemical reactions of organisms can proceed only if catalyzed

539

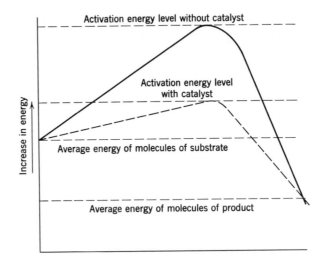

Activation energy level without catalyst

Activation energy level
with catalyst

Increase in energy

Average energy of molecules of substrate

Average energy of molecules of product

Figure A.5. Diagram illustrating an energy-releasing chemical reaction, the product molecules having a lower energy level than the molecules of the substance from which it is formed (the *substrate*). Without a catalyst (solid line), the reacting molecules must reach a high activation energy level. Only a few of the molecules have sufficient energy to get over the activation energy hump, so the reaction proceeds very slowly. However, by supplying heat or perhaps another outside energy source, many molecules are raised to a high enough energy level to clear the hump. The presence of a catalyst (broken line) reduces the activation energy level and so the process proceeds much more rapidly, and at a lower temperature, than when no catalyst is present.

by enzymes, so the enzymes produced by any particular organism determine just what reactions can go on in the organism. Enzymes are highly specific catalysts, each enzyme acting on only one type of chemical bond. Enzymes are proteins, although some enzymes are functional only when associated with a nonprotein **coenzyme**.

Solutions

A solution is a homogenous mixture of the molecules, ions, or atoms of two or more different substances. The dissolving medium is called the **solvent** and the substance dispersed through it is the **solute**. Here, we are concerned principally of liquid solvents, and of these, water is the most important biologically. However, some biological substances are insoluble in water but soluble in oils (liquid fats). The substances dissolved in water may be gases such as oxygen or carbon dioxide, solids such as sugar or salts, or liquids such as alcohol. Most chemical reactions that occur in plants or animals will proceed only when the substances are in solution, and indeed most substances present in cells are in solution (or are dispersed in water as clusters of molecules rather than as individual molecules as in a true solution).

When sugar is dissolved in water, the molecules making up a crystal separate from one another and become evenly dispersed through the water as individual molecules. This, of course, explains why the sugar is no longer visible after it is dissolved. When salt is dissolved in water, the Na^+ and Cl^- ions of the crystals separate from one another and become evenly dispersed through the water. Thus, in a sugar solution the dispersed particles are molecules whereas in a salt solution they are ions. Some solutes, acetic acid for example, are present in solution as a mixture of molecules and ions: CH_3COOH molecules and CH_3COO^- and H^+ ions. Some substances have molecules or ions that absorb some wavelengths of light more than others and so impart a characteristic color to the solution.

EXPRESSING THE CONCENTRATION OF SOLUTIONS

The concentration of a solution may be expressed in a number of different units. A **percentage solution** is based on the percentage that the solvent constitutes of the solution. Thus, a 5% solution of sugar by **weight** could be made by dissolving 5 grams of sugar in 95 grams (or ml.) of water, the total weight of the solution being 100 grams. A 15% solution of alcohol by **volume** could be made by dissolving 5 ml. alcohol in 85 ml. of water. Weight percentage solutions are used for dry solutes; liquid solutes are usually made up as percentage by volume.

Molar solutions are extensively used in scientific work. A 1-molar solution can be made by dissolving a gram molecular weight of the solute in enough water to make a liter of solution. The advantage of molar solutions is that a 1-molar solution of any substance contains just as many molecules as a 1-molar solution of any other substance, though of course there are more dispersed particles if the solute is ionized (like salt) than if the molecules are intact (like sugar).

Normal solutions are used principally for acids and bases. A 1-normal solution of an acid contains a gram equivalent weight (1.008 grams) of replaceable or ionizable hydrogen per liter of solution. Thus, a 1 normal ($1N$) solution of an acid such as HCl that has only one replaceable H per molecule would also be a 1 molar ($1M$) solution. Acetic acid (CH_3COOH) also contains only 1 replaceable or ionizable H atom per molecule, even though there are 3 other H atoms in each molecule. However, a $1N$ solution of an acid such as H_2SO_4 that has 2 replaceable H atoms per molecule would be 0.5M, whereas a 1N solution of H$_3$PO$_4$ would be 0.33M. A 1N solution of a base contains a gram equivalent weight of OH (17.008 grams) per liter of solution. Thus, a 1N solution of NaOH or KOH would also be 1M, whereas a 1N solution of Ca(OH)$_2$ would be 0.5M. The advantage of using normality is that solutions of the same normality all have the same degree of total acidity or total alkalinity. Thus, 10 ml. of 1N HCl would just neutralize 10 ml. of 1N Ca(OH)$_2$ or any other 1N base.

pH OR HYDROGEN ION CONCENTRATION

However, total acidity or alkalinity of a solution is generally of less biological interest than the concentration of hydrogen (H$^+$) or hydroxyl (OH$^-$) ions in the solution. The unit commonly used for expressing the **hydrogen ion concentration** of a solution is **pH**, which is defined as the negative of the logarithm of the hydrogen ion concentration in terms of normality (Fig. A.6). Thus, if a solution has a H$^+$ ion concentration of 0.00001N or 10^{-5}N, its pH is 5, and a solution with a hydrogen ion concentration of 10^{-7} has a pH of 7. Since pH values are logarithms, each whole pH value is ten times more acid than the next higher value. Thus, pH 3 is ten times as acid as pH 4, one hundred times as acid as pH 5 and one thousand times as acid as pH 6. In a pH value such as 4.2, the 2 is the mantissa of the logarithm and should not be read as two-tenths. It is impossible to average pH values by adding

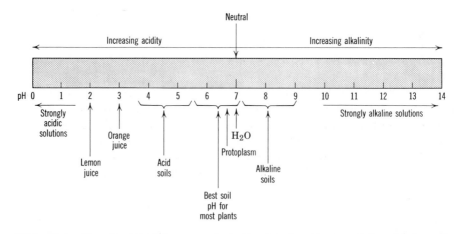

Figure A.6. The pH scale, with some typical pH values for plant materials and soils. pH units are actually negative logarithms of hydronium ion concentration, so each unit value represents ten times less concentration (lower acidity) than the unit below it on the scale.

them together and dividing by the number of values added, since when logarithms are added they are actually being multiplied.

It would not be necessary to use pH values if all acids were ionized to the same degree, but they are not. For example, the pH of a $0.1N$ solution of each of the following acids at 25°C is as follows: hydrochloric 1.1, sulfuric 1.2, citric 2.2, acetic 2.9, and boric 5.2. The strength of an acid depends not on its total acidity (concentration of molecules) but on the concentration of H^+ ions. Although all the acids listed have the same total acidity, it is apparent that hydrochloric is a strong acid and boric a very weak one as shown by its high pH (i.e., a low H^+ ion concentration). A strong base in solution is highly ionized and thus has a high pH, a high OH^- ion concentration, and a low H^+ ion concentration.

As the H^+ ion concentration of a solution increases, the OH^- ion concentration decreases in proportion, and the product of the two always equals a constant value, 10^{-14}; thus pH is a measure of OH^- ion concentration as well as H^+ ion concentration. At pH 6 the H^+ ion concentration is $10^{-6}N$ and the OH^- ion concentration $10^{-8}N$, whereas at pH 7 both ions have a concentration of $10^{-7}N$. Thus, a solution of pH 7 is neutral, any solution below pH 7 is acid (having more H^+ ions than OH^- ions), and any solution over pH 7 is alkaline or basic (having more OH^- ions than H^+ ions). However, even a very strong acid of say pH 1 contains some OH^- ions ($10^{-13}N$) and a strong base of pH 14 has a few H^+ ions ($10^{-14}N$). Pure water has a pH of 7, which is equivalent to saying that one of every 10 million water molecules is dissociated into H^+ and OH^- ions.

BUFFER SYSTEMS

If an acid is added to water, the pH decreases rapidly; if a base is added to water, the pH continues to rise as more is added. However, a solution may be buffered against marked and rapid changes in pH resulting from the addition of acids or bases. The most common type of **buffer system** consists of a weak acid plus one of its salts, for example acetic, phosphoric, or carbonic acids. If a strong acid such as hydrochloric is added to a solution buffered by acetic acid and sodium acetate, the following reaction keeps the pH from dropping markedly:

$$H^+Cl^- + CH_3CO^-Na^+ \longrightarrow CH_3COOH + Na^+Cl^-$$

Many of the hydrogen ions are thus incorporated into acetic acid molecules, relatively few of which are ionized, rather than remaining as highly ionized HCl molecules. If a strong base such as KOH is added to the buffered solution, the following reaction prevents a marked rise in pH by limiting the number of OH^- ions:

$$K^+OH^- + CH_3COOH \rightarrow CH_3COO^-K^+ + HOH$$

Many of the added OH^- ions thus become incorporated in very slightly ionized water molecules. Of course, if too many H^+ or OH^- ions are added to a buffered solution one of the components of the system (either the acetic acid or the sodium acetate in the example used) will be entirely consumed and then the pH will begin changing rapidly.

Index